KV-422-206

FREIGHT FORWARDERS

003549

AUSTRALIA
The Law Book Company Ltd.
Sydney : Melbourne : Brisbane

CANADA AND U.S.A.
The Carswell Company Ltd.
Agincourt, Ontario

INDIA
N. M. Tripathi Private Ltd.
Bombay

ISRAEL
Steimatzky's Agency Ltd.
Jerusalem : Tel Aviv : Haifa

NEW ZEALAND
Sweet & Maxwell (N.Z.) Ltd.
Wellington

PAKISTAN
Pakistan Law House
Karachi

FREIGHT FORWARDERS

BY

D. J. HILL, LL.M., PH.D., ASSOC. INST.T.,
Professor of Commercial Law, University of Nairobi
Advocate of the High Court of Kenya

LONDON
STEVENS & SONS
1972

First published in 1972 by
Stevens & Sons Limited
of 11 New Fetter Lane
London — Law Publishers
and printed in Great Britain
by The Eastern Press Ltd.
of London and Reading

SBN 420 42490 3

©
D. J. Hill
1972

PREFACE

THE field of transportation is one of ever increasing complexity in the modern world, particularly with the advent of containerisation. Much of the commercial activity in this field has for long been channelled through a wide range of intermediaries of whom singularly little has been written. In an attempt to fill this gap this book has been written.

Wherever possible I have tried to place the law within its commercial framework rather than to squeeze trade practice into a legal framework in which it is often ill at ease. The common law countries of the Commonwealth have been treated as one single jurisdiction on the grounds that the forwarding trade is no respecter of jurisdiction and no real pattern of relationships can be otherwise established. American law and practice has been referred to where relevant, although no attempt has been made to deal with it in depth as it is the subject of a book in itself, owing to the vast amount of statute law and cases on the subject.

To a limited degree reference has been made to Continental civil law although again it is impossible to do justice in a limited space. Discussion has therefore been restricted to the important questions of status and secured rights over goods for non-payment. The question of status is of importance in relation to the freight forwarder owing to the concept of the contract of commission in civil law systems. Similarly under the civil law, complex systems of rights of preference and retention exist which find no exact parallel at common law.

In writing this book it has been necessary to bring together many diffuse threads of law and practice from many countries. I would therefore like to express my profound gratitude to the forwarders, lawyers and trade associations throughout the world without whose assistance this book would not have been possible. In particular I would like to thank the following for the painstaking assistance they have given me in my work:

Professor Gordon Borrie, University of Birmingham.

Lord Chorley, London School of Economics.

Brian Kelleher, Alltransport Ltd.

E. J. Cohn, Lincoln's Inn.

F. W. Redman, Director General, Institute of Freight Forwarders Ltd.

C. W. G. Wilson, National Surface Forwarder Division, Institute of Freight Forwarders Ltd.

Desmond Leeper, Lep Transport Ltd.

J. M. Fetherston, Thomas Meadows & Co. Ltd.

J. Gatford, Thomas Meadows (Insurance) Ltd.

J. A. Dow, Traffic Officer, National Freight Federation (N.F.C.) Ltd.

H. T. Parkin, formerly of Lep Transport.

Alan Donald, Ernest A. Notcutt & Co. Ltd., Incorporated Insurance Brokers.

Geoffrey Hall, Editor, *Lloyd's Law Reports*.

My thanks are also due to the following in other common law countries:

Gerald Ullman, Counsel to New York Foreign Freight Forwarders and Brokers Association Inc.

Canadian International Freight Forwarders Association Inc., Montreal.

Dominion Chartered Customs House Brokers Association, Ottawa.

Australian Road Transport Federation.

J. Robson, Robson Transport Ltd., Wellington, New Zealand.

N. Maugham, Thomas Cook & Son South Africa (Pty.) Ltd., Cape Town.

Lep Transport (N.S.W.) Pty. Ltd.

Thomas Meadows & Co. (Aust.) Pty. Ltd.

On the Continent I would particularly like to thank the following for their assistance:

R. H. Rutten, Secretary, FENEX, Amsterdam.

Dr. Erich Krein, Bundesverband Spedition under Lagerei e.v., Bonn.

Dr. Andre Hennebicq, Legal Counsellor, Unidroit, Rome.

Professor Jan Ramberg, University of Stockholm.

Fédération des Expéditeurs de Belgique, Antwerp.

Federazione Nazionale Spedizionieri, Rome.

Dr. Kapin, Zentralverband der Spediteure, Vienna.

Dr. Zdenko Kocian, Transjug, Yugoslavia.

Fédération Française des Commissionnaires, Paris.

Schweizerischer Spediteur-Verband, Bern.

W. Zeilbeck, Director, F.I.A.T.A., Zurich.

Finally I would particularly like to thank Dr. Clive Schmitthoff for recommending freight forwarding to me as a subject for research.

As a footnote I would add that I have endeavoured to incorporate available materials in this rapidly developing subject to date. However two books have been drawn to my attention at the time of going to press which are worthy of note—Rodière, *Traité général de droit maritime*, Volume 3, Dalloz, Paris, 1970, and Giles, *Uniform Commercial Law*, Sijthoff, Leyden, 1970.

D. J. HILL.

Nairobi,
November, 1971.

CONTENTS

PART III

THE OBLIGATIONS OF A FORWARDER

PART IV

DOCUMENTS OF TITLE AND PAYMENT

PART V

THE FORWARDER IN RELATION TO ASSOCIATED COMMERCIAL TRANSACTIONS

APPENDIX

CASES

FORWARDING CONDITIONS

* These Conditions are common to Freightliners Ltd., British Railways Board and National Carriers Ltd. with certain additions (see §§ 611–614). References to the Conditions of any of these organisations have been included here for convenience.

PRINCIPAL CONVENTIONS AND AGREEMENTS

CONVENTIONS

AGREEMENTS

COMMERCIAL CODES

CIVIL CODES

ABBREVIATIONS

A.D.S.P.	Allgemeine Deutsche Spediteur-bedingungen, 1971
A.Ö.S.P.	Allgemeine Österreichische Spediteur-bedingungen 1947
B.R.S. Conditions	British Road Services Ltd. Conditions of Carriage, 1969
C.G. (Belgium)	Conditions Generales des Expediteurs de Belgique 1969
C.G. (France)	Conditions Generales de la Fédération Française des Commissionaires etc., 1967
C.G. (Italy)	Condizioni Generali Practicate dagli Spedizionieri Italiani, 1958
C.G. (Swiss)	Conditions Generales de l'Association Suisse de Maisons d'Expedition, 1967
C.I.M.	International Convention for the Carriage of Goods by Rail, 1961
C.M.R.	Convention for the International Carriage of Goods by Road, Geneva, 1956
D.F.C.	Dutch Forwarding Conditions, 1956
F.B.L.	F.I.A.T.A. Combined Transport Bill of Lading, 1971
F.I.A.T.A.	International Federation of Forwarding Agents Associations, Zurich
N.F.C.	Northern Forwarding Conditions (Scandinavia) 1959
N.Y.F.F.	New York Foreign Freight Forwarders and Brokers Association Inc. Terms and Conditions, 1970
R.H.A. Conditions 1961	Road Haulage Association Ltd. Conditions of Carriage, 1961 (U.K.)
R.H.A. Conditions 1967	Road Haulage Association Ltd. Conditions of Carriage, 1967 (U.K.)
S.T.C.	Standard Trading Conditions of the Institute of Freight Forwarders Ltd. 1970
T.C.M.	Draft Convention for the Combined Transport of Goods, Rome-Tokyo, 1970
UNIDROIT	International Institute for the Unification of Private Law, Rome
Y.F.C.	Yugoslav Forwarding Conditions 1970

PART I

INTRODUCTION

PART 1

INTRODUCTION

CHAPTER 1

INTRODUCTION

1 THE development of transportation in the Western world has been tied up to a considerable extent with the growth of commerce and industry in general. Without the means of transport to move commodities from their place of origin to that of consumption, the great trading nations of the world could not have developed. Transportation has been essential not only across the oceans of the world but also along the rivers, canals and highways, which serve the manufacturing centres situated away from the coastal areas. This pattern of communication was given a considerable impetus in the nineteenth century with the growth of the railways, although with the development of the motor car there has again been a shift of emphasis back to the roads as a method of communication. In the twentieth century, the airplane has offered an even faster means of transport from one end of the world to the other, and has accentuated the ever-decreasing size of the world.

As a corollary, the need to match supply and demand, that is to bring producer and consumer together, has produced a pattern of intermediaries whose sole purpose is to fulfil this function.[1] In the commodity markets, the broker has existed for many centuries, and similarly in the marine market, the shipbroker has gradually developed to fulfil a demand there. With the growth of alternative methods of transport and an ever-increasing number of specialised products, the shipping and forwarding agent has developed to fulfil a requirement as an indispensable intermediary between shipper and carrier in the twentieth century. Although he operates under different names in different countries, "freight forwarder" in the U.S.A., "Spediteur" in Germany, "commissionnaire de transport" in France, and similar variants in other countries, his functions are basically similar in most parts of the world.

In England, his two-part name has resulted from the fact that during the last century, there were two categories of operators. Firstly, those in the trade who were indigenous owed their origins to the shipping industry, being sometimes also ship's agents, etc. The other category was composed of those who began as the London offices of continental forwarding agents. The two functions of shipping and forwarding are therefore indivisible parts of the same operation; therefore to simplify the terminology used the term "forwarder" will be used throughout the study.

---

[1] Much of the general information in this chapter has been obtained with the assistance of Alltransport, Lep Transport, Thomas Meadows and the Institute of Freight Forwarders.

[3]

2   The forwarder is an intermediary between either the consignor or consignee of goods and the transport carriers, wharfingers, customs authorities and other third parties with whom the seller or buyer of goods would otherwise have to negotiate himself. The multiplicity of functions that he performs renders a clear understanding of what he does very essential, and to achieve this it is necessary to trace his historical origins in the principal trading nations of the world.

3 Historical origins

The origin of the forwarder cannot be traced to one particular source. Unlike many other categories of commercial intermediary, whose development has followed a regular pattern, the forwarder can trace his roots to divers sources which owe their particular method of growth to local economic factors. Two principal criteria have been common to their development though. First, the need to service ocean-going ships both in respect of cargo and stores, and the problem of moving goods across the wide continental land mass. Secondly, the basic problem of transporting goods while possessing no means of transportation.

4   From the thirteenth century onwards, the "Frachter"—the intermediary who acted both as a carrier and freight forwarder—gradually developed in Western Europe as an essential intermediary between the many bankers and merchants situated in the principal cities of Italy, Germany and France. He controlled and organised reliable wagon trains, and handled such other matters as customs dues and levies, issued bills of lading and arranged collection of moneys due from consignees. Eventually with the coming of the railways system which rapidly brought tremendous impetus to international trade, the forwarder showed himself invaluable in handling the problems of transportation across national boundaries. Again with the advent of the aeroplane, and the need for cargo co-ordination in air-freight operations, the forwarder proved himself equal to the task.[2]

In the field of maritime transportation, we find in 1775 the ship's husband being described as "a class of agents so called, whose chief Employment in Capital Sea-port Towns, particularly in the Port of London, is, to purchase the Ship's stores for the voyage; to procure cargoes or Freight; to settle the Terms and obtain Policies of Insurance. to receive the Amount of the Freight both at home and Abroad";[3] Similarly the shipbroker is described as being "employed in buying and selling Ship's and Cargoes, either by private Contract or by public Sale."[4]

5   To understand the pattern of development though it is instructive to trace the growth of these transportation intermediaries in seaboard

---

[2] See A. Murr, *Export/Import Traffic Management and Forwarding*, 2nd ed., Maryland, p. 1.
[3] Wyndham Beaves, *Lex Mercatoria Rediviva*, 1775, p. 49.
[4] *Ibid.*, at p. 482.

cities.[5] In the City of London as commercial men expanded their trade in foreign lands, they found the need to employ someone to assemble their goods and to arrange shipping and insurance for them. In many cases, as trade developed through the coffee houses, it was the landlord to whom they turned as a trusted acquaintance. An early form of forwarding which developed in this manner was that of parcels and letters to foreign countries prior to the growth of efficient and cheap postal facilities in the United Kingdom.[6] From such obscure origins the various categories of agents relating both to transportation and international trade gradually developed. During the nineteenth century firms and companies sprang up covering a few or many of these functions, some eventually specialising in broking or forwarding, others expanding to cover all aspects of the trade. Some, such as Lep Transport, Schenkers and General Transport, were direct offshoots of continental companies. Others, such as Thomas Meadows and Wingate & Johnston, were originally ship's agents whose forwarding business gradually predominated. Finally, a few like Thomas Cook's developed their forwarding work as an adjunct to their passenger agency business.

6 Functions

Although the main function of the forwarder is to ensure that goods are transported, his function varies in different countries, and on the Continent of Europe, his sphere of action is rather wider than in England which, being an island, lacks any land frontiers or adjacent countries to which access is possible by land transport. As in England, agents either began as ship's agents and expanded into the forwarding business or vice versa. On the other hand though, specialists in the various stages of transportation also developed. The stevedore, wharfinger, ship-broker and customs broker became recognised specialist fields of operation, as did the forwarding business, although such specialisation did not preclude the growth of large multiple organisations which perform two or more of these functions.

7 Groupage

Owing to the fact that continental shipping companies have been prepared to pay commission to forwarders, unlike their English counterparts, the development of forwarding has received a much stronger impetus in Europe. In the United Kingdom only exclusive sales agents or loading brokers are permitted to receive commission for their services. This has resulted through stronger competition on the Continent for goods traffic, and the forwarder's entrenched position in rail transit through groupage services. For reasons best known to themselves the British railway companies attempted to carry out their own groupage,

[5] Unfortunately, information as to the history of the British forwarding trade is very sparse in contrast to the shipping industry, which is very well documented.
[6] See Kenneth Rowse, *The Forwarding Agents*, Philatelic Specialists Society, Toronto, Canada, 1966.

and were opposed to the forwarder carrying out this function. As a result the English agent has not in the past offered a groupage service in respect of inland rail transit.[7] Hence, although with the advent of the liner train the pendulum is swinging in the opposite direction, the highly organised continental groupage system with its own goods depots has no parallel in this country. Thus, with the exception of services to the Continent, the forwarder generally gets no sea freight commission in this country and must therefore charge his client a freight commission instead.

With regard to both the questions of rail groupage and sea freight commission, most other countries, including notably the United States, have followed the continental practice. However, as a result of their virtual exclusion from internal rail freight business in this country, with the rapid development of carriage of goods by air since 1945, the forwarder has expanded into this field of activity, and has played a considerable part in the growth of this new medium. Moreover, as there were no historical antecedents to hamper his participation, the forwarder was able to obtain a freight commission from the beginning.[8]

In the field of groupage the continental forwarders are in a very favourable position. This enables them to quote highly competitive through rates and reduces the time of transit. They are particularly of use for liner services, that is, regular scheduled services, as opposed to irregular tramping services, as they bring traffic which would be difficult to cater for unless the forwarder consolidated the shipments. In this they have the support of the European railway companies, who offer special freight train services from frontier to frontier, with special rebates for carload shipments. Thus, although steamship companies may appoint loading brokers or exclusive sales agents in continental ports for particular areas, they would find it difficult to dispense with the assistance of a general forwarder in obtaining business.

8   Europe

In name and organisation the forwarder differs to some extent. In Germany for instance, he is known as a Spediteur, and as such plays a very important part in handling freight shipments, both internally and for international trade. The railways leave all small freight consigning to him, and the larger forwarders have their own terminal installations. In France on the other hand, the forwarder is known as a commissionnaire de transport, of which there are several categories, and with whom the railway companies both co-operate and compete in parcels traffic. To a greater degree co-operation has replaced competition owing to the impact of competition from road transport. In Belgium, where he is designated a commissionnaire-expéditeur, the set-up is rather similar,

---

[7] *Crouch* v. *L.N.W.R.* (1854) 14 C.B. 255—this case gives an interesting account of parcels forwarding in the mid-nineteenth century.
[8] *Per* correspondence with Thomas Meadows & Co. Ltd.

although not as well organised as an indispensable ancillary to transportation as in Germany. Similarly in other European countries, under the designation of spediteur or a variant thereof, the forwarder fulfils an important function as an intermediary between shipper and carrier.

9 United States

In the New World, the shipping and commission merchants grew up combining the functions of both merchant and broker in import and export transactions, and were sometimes shipowners too. Also at the beginning of the nineteenth century, the shipbroker made his appearance to bring together merchant and shipowner. With the growth of the canals, roads and railways, the forwarding merchants also developed as the forerunners of the domestic freight forwarders and express companies in the U.S.A. At the same time they acted as commission houses in respect of the prime commodities. Also in the earlier days of the railroads in the U.S.A., a special type of forwarder developed to handle through shipments over two or more connecting lines, until eventually the former took this over themselves. [9]

As a result of the vast size of the country, freight forwarding developed in two directions. First, domestic freight forwarding originated in the first years of this century, reputedly when a New York broker arranged to consolidate a quantity of small import consignments into a carload lot for shipment to Chicago. As a result the freight forwarder today offers a comprehensive freight service for small consignments domestically, making his profits from the difference between leasing complete cars at a cheap rate, and offering parcels traffic at a rate slightly cheaper than the rate offered by the carrier himself for shipping small consignments. In other words, by consolidating shipments, the forwarder has developed as an important intermediary in transportation, and often without owning any transportation himself, apart from local delivery services, has become an indirect carrier himself.

10   In international or foreign forwarding, the term forwarding has a rather different meaning from that in the domestic trade, where it merely covers the consolidation of small shipments to obtain the benefit of reduced freight rates for carload lots. The foreign freight forwarder fulfils a multiple function as shipbroker, export carloader and as an indirect carrier in some cases. He takes charge of goods ensuring that they reach their destination through a network of overseas offices or correspondents, acting largely for inland manufacturers exporting their products to foreign countries. As Kaufman J. explained in *New York Freight Forwarders* v. *F.M.C.*,[10]

> " Most American exporters use the services of ocean freight forwarders who, in essence, act as export departments for their shipper clients. An exporter who ships goods abroad customarily consigns

[9] A. Murr, *Export/Import Traffic Management and Forwarding*, 2nd ed., Maryland, p. 6.
[10] [1965] A.M.C. 605 at p. 606. See G. Ullman, *Ocean Freight Forwarder, the Exporter and the Law*, Cornell, 1967.

the merchandise to a forwarder who then makes all arrangements for dispatch to a foreign port. Thus, the forwarder will secure cargo space with a steamship company, give advice on governmental licensing requirements, proper port of exit and letter of credit intricacies, and arrange to have the cargo reach seaboard in time to meet the designated vessel. The forwarder also prepares required shipping documents, including the dock receipt, delivery order, bill of lading, export declaration and the consular invoice required on shipments to certain countries. Often the forwarder performs so-called accessorial services, such as arranging insurance either under his own policy or the exporter's open maritime policy.[11] He may provide for local trucking of less than carload parcels to the pier and occasionally he will store partial shipments. To reimburse himself for the cost of arranging these accessorial services the forwarder charges the shipper a fee greater than his actual disembursement. Most forwarders receive their revenues from two sources. They are paid by shippers for the various forwarding services performed and on many shipments forwarders receive, in addition, brokerage payments from ocean carriers."

The foreign freight forwarder therefore fulfils both the functions of the English forwarder and those of the loading broker, both functions being treated as part of the same operation. In this country however a clear distinction is drawn between them.[12]

11   Non-industrial countries

The forwarding business is one that is largely dependent, at least internationally, on a prosperous manufacturing economy. Where there is largely a primary producing country there is either a total absence of them or else, as in the case of Canada, the numbers are relatively few, most of the import/export procedures being carried out by customs house brokers. A similar situation exists in South America, where industrial activity is in its infancy. To take Argentina, which is probably the most developed South American republic, there are no forwarders, and no organisation exists resembling the vast range of activities embraced by a forwarder, such as in England, Europe and the U.S.A. Some foreign forwarders have local agents, mostly established in Buenos Aires, but their activities are mainly concerned in canvassing importers for business to be channelled through their principals abroad. These representatives do not carry out any activities as forwarders in regard to exports, but in certain instances may execute limited formalities for goods handled by their principals concurrently with local customs house brokers who handle much of the business.[13]

12   New Zealand

In New Zealand, where there is a similar preponderance of primary

[11] See *Aquascutum* v. *The American Champion* [1970] 1 Lloyd's Rep. 448, for a description of trans-Atlantic forwarding practice.
[12] See *Heskell* v. *Continental Express Ltd.* at § 48.
[13] *Per* Argentina Consulate.

products, there is no clear-cut division between carrier and customs agent. All carriers and customs agents act as forwarders, this being regarded as a necessary adjunct to service their clients, although a carrier does not necessarily operate as a customs agent, nor vice versa, though in fact the businesses are often combined; one section bringing business to the other. Customs clearance was originally a service supplied by carriers merely to obtain cartage, but since 1939 a separate organisation has been set up to cope with the increasing complexity of customs agents' work. Even so the latter still offer a complete service including customs clearance, forwarding and delivery, and arranging cartage if they are not carriers themselves.[14]

13 Australia

In Australia, on the other hand, there is a clear distinction between a customs agent and a forwarder, the latter phrase not being common. A customs agent merely controls the clearance and delivery of goods to a client in Australia, and generally has no substantial overseas representation if any. Forwarders, of which there are probably four of any size, specialise in the routing of traffic from a foreign point of origin to a delivery point in Australia, and offer a composite service including customs clearance. There is however a large number of domestic forwarders within the country, who as in the U.S.A. offer rail, road or air consolidations or a combination thereof, which are used by a large number of manufacturers. No international forwarder however consolidates for domestic operations.[15]

14 India

In India a slightly different breakdown of functions occurs. In Europe and North America the forwarder often performs a dual function of customs broker as well as freight agent. In India however there is a distinction between freight brokers who do not normally act as forwarders, and customs house agents who usually fulfil the function of a freight forwarder too. The former merely finds suitable steamers for exporters, and books the required space, for which the steamship company pays him a commission. Also with regard to rail transit, car loading companies exist who load and unload shipments as this is not usually undertaken by the railway administration, except for a small parcels service. Air cargo movement, internally, at least, is still in its infancy, and the forwarder is therefore not very developed in this area of activity. Reliance is still mainly placed upon the railway system, which some years ago introduced a quick transit service, which has speeded forwarding to and from the main commercial centres.[16]

15 South Africa

In South Africa, the forwarder is known as a clearing and forwarding

---

[14] *Per* correspondence with New Zealand Society of Customs Agents Inc.
[15] *Per* correspondence with Lep Transport (N.S.W.) Pty. Ltd.
[16] *Per* correspondence with Federation of Custom House Agents Association in India.

agent, and almost invariably acts as a customs agent. Generally they only operate road haulage services as an ancillary to their other operations. They often act also as steamship agents and as shipbrokers and charterers, and in a number of cases as warehousemen with bonded stores.[17]

16 Eastern Europe

Socialist countries have a rather different type of organisation. It is usual for one sole forwarding organisation to exist for the whole country, with branch offices in different centres, Masped in Hungary, and Cechofracht in Czechoslovakia for example. In Yugoslavia, on the other hand, a more flexible type of socialism has produced a series of "community organisations" since 1951. There are twelve to fifteen independent forwarding trade organisations which compete freely to do business with the varying manufacturing enterprises, though there exists in the framework of the Federal Chamber of Economy in Belgrade a special body composed of representatives of all existing forwarding trade organisations in Yugoslavia, to promote the interests of the profession as a whole and to keep in touch with other sectors of the economy.[18]

17 United Kingdom

Finally, in England, the services of the forwarder are used by the majority of consignors or consignees. A few larger shippers and manufacturers have their own export department, and often carry out their own forwarding operations. Most exporters however do not have a sufficient volume of work to warrant maintaining a shipping depot, but depend on the forwarder to perform these functions for him. Moreover the average exporter is not only situated at a distance from the main ports inland, but is also unfamiliar with the details of export procedure. As a result the forwarder has become an indispensable link in the foreign trade of the country.

18   The procedure adopted is as follows. Prior to a shipment, the forwarder will advise the shipper as to the best port to use taking into consideration the inland freight rates to the port, sailing dates, port congestion and any special needs of the product in question. He will also check and arrange for export and import licences, and ensure that the requirements of a letter of credit are complied with. After the preliminaries are complete, the forwarder will arrange shipment to the port in question, and book cargo space on a vessel. Next the requisite documentation including an ocean bill of lading will be prepared and the goods cleared with the customs authorities. A consular invoice will then be made out together with a complete set of documents to conform with the letter of credit. The movement of the goods will be co-ordinated with the loading schedule of the vessel, and separate cargo lots will be

[17] *Per* correspondence with Thomas Cook & Sons (South Africa) Ltd.
[18] *Per* correspondence with Transjug, Yugoslavia.

consolidated into one shipment, or in the case of small shipments will be consolidated on one bill of lading to obtain lower freight charges. Finally, various ancillary services may be performed, such as arranging marine insurance cover, export packing, warehousing and storage, where such are required. The forwarder will usually also make payment of the ocean freight on behalf of the shipper and assemble and deliver the documents required by a letter of credit to a bank or as instructed by the shipper.

Among the other services performed by forwarders on occasion are negotiations on behalf of their clients for more favourable freight rates to improve the competitive position of the goods in question. In addition, to obtain a more favourable rate structure, forwarders arrange for their clients to execute exclusive service contracts with the steamer Conferences, where a dual rate structure is in effect.[19]

As the forwarder is, to a large extent, involved in transit in the international field he must therefore be in a position to deal with the handling and reception of goods in a foreign country. Likewise, he will require services in the principal commercial centres of the world where he is concerned with importing goods. Forwarders in this country may either maintain branches or associate or subsidiary companies in foreign countries where they have large volume of trade, or may themselves be branches of foreign forwarding organisations. If a forwarder does not have such a network of branches, or in those places not covered by it, a close liaison with their foreign counterparts will be maintained, who, often on a reciprocal basis, will act as correspondent agents on behalf of the home agent in receiving and clearing incoming shipments. They may also be themselves branches of large transportation organisations, or may run a separate road haulage company as a subsidiary to their freight forwarding operations. The extent of such carrier operations will depend on the size of the company from an extensive vehicle fleet, in the case of the larger companies, down to a modest number of delivery vehicles in the case of the smaller ones. It can therefore be seen that a multiplicity of functions is regularly performed within the same group, which will often, if large enough, include a separate insurance brokerage company.[20]

19 Rail transportation

Some of the larger forwarders may also act as rail freight agents on behalf of British Rail and foreign railway companies in obtaining freight for international carriage. In such a case they will also act as the agent of their client at the same time as representing the railway company, thus fulfilling a double function. Such representation does not cover the solicitation of internal shipments, at least as far as this country is concerned, but with the development of the liner train system, the activities of the forwarder may extend into this field too.

[19] See Chapter 15.
[20] See Chapter 17.

20   Air transportation

The most recent extension of the forwarder's activities is into the
field of air transportation. Owing to the prohibitive cost of airfreight,
the cargo side of air transport did not initially develop to anything like
the extent of the passenger traffic. Since the last war, however, through
the activities of the airfreight agent, the volume of freight carried by the
aviation companies has increased manifold. It is through his experience
in shipping goods by other methods and the fact that he is admirably
suited to advise on special lightweight packing and other methods of
obtaining cheaper airfreight tariffs, that has developed this side of the
forwarder's business. It is in this field and that of the rapidly developing
container traffic that the forwarder will probably find new ways of
expanding his business as an intermediary in transportation. Furthermore, with the modern development of a multiplicity of different
methods of transport, two or more of them often being involved in any
particular transit operation, the forwarder's role in commercial relations is one that, far from declining, is likely to develop very considerably with the intensifying of competition in the field of export among the
developing nations.

PART II
THE LEGAL STATUS OF THE FREIGHT FORWARDER

CHAPTER 2

THE FORWARDER DISTINGUISHED FROM
OTHER INTERMEDIARIES

1. INTRODUCTION

21 Definition of freight forwarder

Having discussed the historical development of the forwarder and allied trades in the previous chapter, the interlinking development of their operations becomes apparent. As a result, although it is necessary from a legal viewpoint to differentiate between them to establish their correct status, it is not easy to establish an accurate definition of the forwarder owing to the difficulty of determining the exact scope of his activities. Rowlatt J.[1] in *Jones* v. *European & General Express Company Ltd.* expressed the view that " all he does is act as agent for the owner of the goods," that is not as a carrier. Goddard L.J. expressed himself in equally vague language that a forwarder is someone who is:

" willing to forward goods for you . . . to the uttermost ends of the earth. They do not undertake to carry you, and they are not undertaking to do it either themselves or by their agent. They are simply undertaking to get somebody to do the work, and as long as they exercise reasonable care in choosing the person to do the work they have performed their contract." [2]

Elsewhere in discussing the forwarder, the courts have been equally reticent in proffering any definition of him.[3] Generally, they have considered it sufficient to distinguish his activities from those of other categories of agent and failed to pursue the matter further. Textbook writers have been equally reluctant to define the forwarder's elusive qualities, and it is perhaps necessary to construct one by adapting the statutory definition in the United States Interstate Commerce Act of a domestic freight forwarder, in a slightly amended form so as to cover international freight forwarding also.

---

[1] (1920) 4 Ll.L.Rep. 127.
[2] *C. A. Pisani & Co.* v. *Brown, Jenkinson & Co. Ltd.* (1939) 64 Ll.L.Rep. 340 at p. 342.
[3] However, an early dictum in the U.S. courts describes the position of the forwarder before the Interstate Commerce Act was enacted, and which can be considered as descriptive of the British position today. " A forwarder is one who, for a compensation, takes charge of goods intrusted or directed to him and forwards them; that is, puts them on their way to their place of destination by the ordinary and usual means of conveyance, or according to the instruction he receives. . . . His compensation is limited to his care and trouble and the charges paid by him, in receiving, keeping, and duly forwarding; and when he has placed the goods in the course of transit by the proper conveyance, his duty is at an end. His occupation is further distinguished from that of the carrier by the circumstances that he has no interest in, and receives no part of, the compensation that is paid for the carriage and due delivery of the goods ": *Place* v. *Union Express Co.*, 2 Hilt. (N.Y.) 19.

22   Accordingly the term freight forwarder can be defined as,
" any person which holds itself out to the general public to . . . provide and arrange transportation of property, for compensation,
and which may assemble and consolidate shipments of such
property, and performs or provides for the performance of break-
bulk and distributing operations with respect to such consolidated
shipments and assumes responsibility for the transportation of such
property from point of receipt to point of destination and utilises
for the whole or any part of the transportation of such shipments,
the services of a carrier or carriers, by sea, land or air, or any
combination thereof."

It can therefore be seen that the essential elements in this definition
are the forwarding and/or consolidation of shipments and the subsequent carriage by one or more of the various methods of transportation
commonly in use. In other words the forwarder does not generally offer
to carry himself, he merely offers to act as a professional intermediary
between the consignor or consignee of goods and the carrier, though
this does not preclude him from effecting part of the transit personally.
It is therefore necessary to consider how the forwarder differs from a
carrier and at what point it is possible to draw a line between their
respective functions. Any generalisation would give an unsatisfactory
result when applied to any particular set of circumstances, so that it is
necessary to consider in turn the three methods by which a forwarder
can consign goods.

2. The Carrier by Land

(i) *United Kingdom*

23 The methods of transport by land, at present in use, are motor transport
by road or alternatively by rail or else by a combination of both methods.
A forwarder must therefore use carriers by these methods to forward
goods for a client, but may, in addition, use any road transport which
he himself possesses. Where a forwarder only engages to use independent carriers, whether by road or rail, and does not intend to effect any
part of the transit himself, the distinction between forwarding and carriage is quite clear.

On the other hand, if a forwarder intends to effect part of the transit
himself, his exact status may be in doubt and where a forwarder actually
agrees to carry goods himself, he may be liable as a carrier even if he
does not in fact effect the transit himself, but employs a carrier to do so
instead. For example, in *Claridge, Holt & Co. Ltd.* v. *King & Ramsay*,[4] a
forwarder sued his client for freight and other charges in respect of an
export shipment which he had handled for him, part of which was
destroyed in transit. The court held that as the plaintiffs had pretended
to own a ship, which they did not, they could not claim that they were
merely acting as forwarders and therefore not liable for the loss. They

----
[4] (1920) 3 Ll.L.Rep. 197.

were liable themselves as carriers as they had entered into their own contract of carriage with the defendant, and as there were no exemption clauses in it limiting their liability, they had no defence in respect of the loss.

24 Local delivery services

Similarly, where a forwarder carries out the local delivery or collection of goods for shipment by the principal carrier he will be liable as a carrier for that part of the carriage which he actually executes himself. This factor was specifically recognised by those responsible for drafting the Standard Trading Conditions of the Institute of Freight Forwarders. Although basically it is intended to be a forwarding contract it does not exclude the possibility that the forwarder may in fact operate as a carrier himself, but merely provides that he does not contract as a common carrier.[5]

25 Forwarder and carrier

Again it is not uncommon for intermediaries in transportation to hold themselves out as forwarders and carriers, without specifying which function they are performing at any one time or for any one transaction. For instance, in *Hellaby* v. *Weaver* [6] the defendants were forwarders who collected and forwarded goods by rail, either collecting all freight charges or only those for carriage to the railway station. With regard to the shipment in dispute, as they had in fact collected the total charge they were held to be liable as common carriers, not merely as forwarders, when the goods were lost on the road. Unfortunately, the report of this case is very short, so that it fails to enlarge upon the situation where a forwarder does not collect the total charge for carriage. The presumption is that in such a case the courts would treat the defendant as a mere forwarder, at least in respect of the on-carriage by rail.[7]

26 Common carrier

A further question that arises in this respect is whether the liability of a forwarder when acting as a carrier will be that of a common carrier or of a private carrier. The distinction is of basic importance, because the common carrier, like the common innkeeper[8] has long been subject to a much higher duty of care than the private carrier at common law. His liability will in all cases be strict, that is, he will be liable for all loss or damage howsoever caused, irrespective of whether he is at fault or not, unless it results from one of the four excepted perils; act of God, act of the Queen's enemies, inherent vice of the goods and the consignor's own fault.

---

[5] See § 30, Cl. 1, S.T.C. *Cf.* Art. 11 (6), D.F.C.; Arts. 1 and 18, N.F.C.; Art. 1, N.Y.F.F.; Arts. 1–4, C.G. (Belgium); Art. 1, C.G. (Switzerland); Art. 2, A.D.S.P.
[6] (1851) 17 L.T.(o.s.) 271.
[7] See § 28.
[8] As to the position at common law of the common innkeeper see Paton, *Bailment*, pp. 199 *et seq.*—the position is to some extent altered by subsequent legislation—*cf.* the Hotel Proprietors Act 1956.

Even in respect of these four exceptions though, the common carrier will not be completely free from liability unless he can prove that the loss or damage did not result from his own negligence or that of his servants.[9] In other words, his liability in these cases is merely reduced to that of a private carrier. Furthermore, the common carrier is not in any case free to pick and choose which shipments he will or will not carry. He is bound to accept all goods which are of a category in respect of which he exercises his common calling, provided they are for carriage over a route for which he offers common carriage, he has space on his vehicles, and freight is paid in advance, unless otherwise agreed. He cannot unilaterally exempt himself from this strict liability, although by using contractual trading conditions he can otherwise limit his liability, in respect of which he retains his freedom of contract.[10] If however, he fails to do so, his liability will remain as at common law.

27   Private carrier

Although the common carrier is subject to strict liability the private carrier is merely an ordinary bailee, that is, he is entrusted with the goods of another. The essential elements of bailment are that the bailee receives the delivery or transfer of possession of personal property, and also a specific mandate either requiring the property to be returned in the same condition to the bailor as in the case of a contract of deposit, or else to be dealt with in a particular fashion as in the case of the contract of carriage. The duty of the bailee of goods is that of reasonable care, the extent of which will differ according to the particular purpose for which the bailment has been granted.[11] The private carrier will therefore only be liable for his own negligence, and that of his servants, in respect of any loss or damage which occurs during transit. However, the burden will be on him to prove that such loss or damage was not due to his negligence.[12]

28   The forwarder as a carrier

It can therefore be seen that the extent of a forwarder's liability

---

[9] Kahn-Freund, *Law of Inland Transport*, 4th ed., pp. 199 *et seq.* These are incorporated contractually into Cl. 5, B.R.S. Conditions, in an expanded form. The same provision is made in Cl. 11, R.H.A. Conditions 1967, except that here it is not incumbent upon the carrier to prove that he used all reasonable care and foresight in the carriage of the goods to avoid liability in respect of the " excepted perils." *Cf.* the confused criticism unfavourably comparing R.H.A. Conditions 1967 with B.R.S. Conditions in the *Financial Times*, April 3, 1967, which failed to realise that the requirement of reasonable care only relates to the " excepted perils," but not to any other provisions in B.R.S. Conditions.

[10] *i.e.* the former Standard Terms and Conditions of British Railways which applied until 1962 when the railways ceased to be a common carrier. These however had statutory authority under the Railway Act 1921. As to common carriage generally see E. Beale, *Law of Bailments*, pp. 372 *et seq.* N.B. Whereas by Cl. 2, R.H.A. Conditions 1967, and Transport Act 1962, s. 43, respectively, road hauliers and British Rail are not common carriers, B.R.S. Conditions leaves the question open—see *Hunt & Winterbotham (West of England) Ltd.* v. *B.R.S. (Parcels) Ltd.* [1962] 1 Q.B. 617.

[11] For a classification of the various types of bailment see Beale, *op. cit.*, pp. 49–50.

[12] See *Hunt & Winterbotham (West of England) Ltd.* v. *B.R.S. (Parcels) Ltd.* [1962] 1 Q.B. 617. N.B. After or before transit has ended or commenced, the carrier's liability will be that of a warehouseman.

will differ considerably depending on whether he is classed as a common or private carrier for any transit that he actually effects himself on behalf of a client, either instead of or in addition to, employing an independent carrier for the purpose. Which category does the forwarder therefore fall in? In *Hellaby* v. *Weaver*, the defendant forwarders were held to be common carriers,[13] but at the present day, although there is no direct authority, the fact that forwarders invariably reserve the right to accept or reject shipments rather than hold themselves out to accept any goods offered to them for collection or delivery by their own transport, points to the conclusion that they normally function in the capacity of a private carrier rather than a common one. This premise is supported by two Australian decisions,[14] involving clearing agents, where the courts held that the latter were not common carriers when moving inward shipments, and were therefore not liable for any loss or damage in the absence of negligence on their part.

29   It appears however that whether a forwarder will have a common calling will depend upon the method of his operations. The question was discussed in *Date & Cocke* v. *G. W. Sheldon & Co. (London) Ltd.*[15] where the defendant forwarder also operated as a carrier as an ancillary to his main forwarding business, which amounted to about 20 per cent. of his total business. In an action for the loss of goods through the driver leaving the van unattended, the court was able to decide the case on the basis of the driver's negligence, thus making the defendants liable irrespective of whether they were common carriers or not. Notwithstanding, Bailhache J. made the following comments:

"The defendants have not satisfied me from any instance they have given that they were not exercising the business of common carriers, so far as they were carrying goods about London. It is not necessary that they should carry from one particular destination to another, and the inclination of my opinion is that these defendants were at that time exercising the function and carrying on the business of common carriers, at any rate in regard to that part of

---

13 *Supra* at § 25.
14 *O'Neill* v. *McCormack & Co.* (1913) 15 W.A.L.R. 33, and *Hyland* v. *Mullaly & Byrne Pty. Ltd.* [1923] V.L.R. 193; similarly in *N.Z.E.C.* v. *Pemberton* (1915) 17 G.L.R. 524, and *Wilson* v. *N.Z.E.C.* [1923] N.Z.L.R. 201; *contra*: *N.Z.E.C.* v. *Minahan* [1916] N.Z.L.R. 816, where the N.Z.E.C. who were engaged to dispatch certain goods, and did so by sea, charging against the client the sea freight as a disembursement, were held liable as common carriers and not as a mere forwarder; *cf. Hellaby* v. *Weaver, supra.*

Cf. Hunter v. *Borst* (1856) U.C.Q.B. 141, 210 where the court avoided the issue of whether a forwarder was a common carrier or not by saying that he was not acting as a forwarder at all, but as a warehouseman and wharfinger. He was therefore only bound to deal with the goods as such, so that he was not absolutely liable for them. Merely because a party is not described in a declaration as a wharfinger or forwarder, but without denying either character, cannot make him liable as a forwarder, in the face of the actual evidence.

However, in *Harris* v. *McPherson* (1842) 6 O.S. 366, it was stated that " In this province, the persons commonly designated as forwarding merchants are those who receive goods in their own warehouses to be forwarded in their own vessels on their own account, and therefore common carriers. . . ." *Per* Jones J.
15 (1921) 7 Ll.L.Rep. 53.

the business which was not connected with their business as forwarding agents."[16]

Such short haul business to and from the docks is a common feature
of forwarding business, irrespective of whether a forwarder handles any
other aspects of the transit or not, and it should be noted that in the
above case the court was prepared to treat the forwarder as a common
carrier even though only in respect of a relatively small part of his
business ancillary to the main forwarding business.

30   Standard trading conditions

However, present-day trading methods subject to printed trading
conditions tend to make the question more academic than real, although
the rare case where trading conditions are either not used or are invalid
in a particular transaction can prove the exception to the rule.

Where British forwarders are members of the Institute of Freight
Forwarders, they will normally trade under the Standard Trading
Conditions of the Institute, in which Clause 1 specifically provides that
the forwarder does not contract as a common carrier, so that in practice
the problem will not arise with regard to members of the Institute,
which numbers all the larger companies and many of the smaller ones
too, except where in a particular contract Standard Trading Conditions
have not been incorporated through lack of notice to a client of the
terms thereof.[17]

31   Forwarding and successive carriage

Next it is necessary to consider the position of a carrier who accepts
responsibility for the onward transmission of goods, in respect of which
he is the initial carrier. Such a situation is of common occurrence,
particularly in respect of shipments which have to be delivered to an
inland point beyond the port of arrival in the case of carriage by sea.
The legal status of the initial carrier in such circumstances will depend
upon the exact nature of the contractual relationship entered into by
him with the shipper. If, for example, the initial carrier issues a through
bill of lading,[18] that is a bill covering the whole transit, he will be liable
as a carrier under the terms of the bill for all sections of the carriage
whether loss occurs when the goods are in his charge or not. On the
other hand, where a document is issued that does not constitute a
through bill of lading covering the whole transit, the initial carrier will
only be liable as a carrier for the loss of a shipment while it is in his
own hands.

Where therefore loss or damage occurs whilst the shipment is in the
hands of successive carriers his liability will only be that of a forwarder,
that is, as a mere agent and not that of a carrier. For instance, in *Cliffe* v.

16 *Ibid.* at p. 54.
17 See *McCutcheon* v. *David MacBrayne Ltd.* [1964] 1 W.L.R. 125; [1965] J.B.L. 53.
18 See Chapter 13.

Hull & Netherlands S.S. Co. Ltd.[19] a bill of lading was issued by a shipowner in respect of a shipment from Rotterdam to Hull, with a further proviso that it was "to be forwarded from Hull ... to Manchester." However in considering the question of liability for loss occurring during the land transit to Manchester, the court refused to treat the document as a through bill of lading, and held that the carriers were only acting as forwarders with regard to the transit from Hull to Manchester. Whether the courts will treat a document as a through bill of lading or as a contract of initial carriage plus a contract to forward by a further carrier will depend upon the construction of the document in question, so that the result in each case will depend upon its particular facts.

32   The problem of successive carriage was formerly of importance in rail transit until 1947, with through carriage by several companies, but with the nationalisation of the railways in that year, the question has become purely academic, now that only one rail carrier exists.[20] As regards internal road haulage, where a carrier contracts under R.H.A. Conditions 1961, provision is made in the contract qualifying the initial carrier's position so as to place him in the position of a mere forwarder " as agent for the consignor or consignee for the further carriage of such goods " by another carrier where goods are consigned to points beyond the carrier's usual delivery area.[21] Clause 10 further provides that the carrier's liability ceases when the shipment is held available for collection by or delivery to the on-carrier.[22] Furthermore, the on-carriage will be subject to the contractual terms of the on-carrier, if any exist. This provision is similar in effect to that in Standard Trading Conditions,[23] which similarly incorporate any further limitations of liability which any contract of carriage may contain which is entered into by the forwarder with a carrier on behalf of his client.[24]

33   However it must be noted that whereas R.H.A. Conditions 1961 specifically make the carrier the shipper's agent in effecting any contract

---

[19] (1921) 6 Ll.L.Rep. 136. See also *Moore* v. *Harris* (1876) 1 App.Cas. 318—the bill of lading stated that goods were to be " be delivered from the ship's deck, where the ship's responsibility shall cease, at ... Montreal ... unto the G.T. Ry. Co. and by them to be forwarded " by rail. The Privy Council held that although not liable for damage to the goods after delivery to the G.T. Ry. the carrier was bound to enter into a contract with the latter for their on-carriage. When the carrier has entered into a contract with an on-carrier and delivered the goods to him, his liability will come to an end.— *Armour Johnston Ltd.* v. *Shaw, Savill & Albion Co. Ltd.* [1917] G.L.R. 95. *Cf.* T.C.M. Convention discussed in Chapter 12.

[20] As regards international carriage, this is governed by C.I.M.

[21] Cl. 10, R.H.A. Conditions 1961.

[22] Cl. 10 only appears to cover genuine on-carriage beyond the carrier's delivery area. It would not apply to sub-contracting by a carrier either within his own area of operation instead of carrying himself, nor presumably if he employs a local carrier on a casual basis to effect deliveries from the former's reception depot at a destination point if he also effects such deliveries with his own transport too.

[23] Cl. 3, Standard Trading Conditions. *Cf.* Art. 1 (2) (3), D.F.C.; Art. 6, N.F.C.; Art. 2, N.Y.F.F.; Arts. 9 and 34, C.G. (Belgium); Art. 19, Y.F.C.; Art. 6, C.G. (France); Art. 1, C.G. (Switzerland).

[24] This provision is only intended to further restrict the shipper's rights, not to extend them.

with another carrier, Standard Trading Conditions do not necessarily place the forwarder in the position of an agent when effecting a contract of carriage for his client, being quite ambiguous on this point. The forwarder may therefore be placed in the position of an intermediate principal as in the case of *Lee Cooper Ltd.* v. *C. H. Jeakins & Sons Ltd.*,[25] though this will depend upon the particular circumstances in question.

These provisions have been deleted from R.H.A. Conditions 1967, presumably on the grounds that if all hauliers sub-contract under the terms of R.H.A. Conditions of Sub-Contracting 1967,[26] as recommended by the Association, both carrier and sub-contractor will have mutually satisfactory rights and liabilities. Instead of the provision in the former Clause 10, the carrier contracts as agent on behalf of the sub-contractor, so as to give him the protection otherwise lacking in a *Learoyd* v. *Pope*[26a] type of situation, that is, where a sub-contractor is sued directly by the shipper and is unable to rely upon any limitation of liability in the principal contract of carriage not being privy to it.[27]

34 International conventions

Finally, the forwarder may find himself in the position of a carrier under C.M.R. in relation to the international carriage of goods by road to the Continent. Similarly, under the proposed T.C.M. Convention the forwarder may undertake the obligations of a Combined Transport Operator (C.T.O.), irrespective of whether he actually carries the goods himself or not. Both these questions are dealt with at length in later chapters.

35 (ii) *Australia*

Turning to other jurisdictions, in certain of the Commonwealth countries, it appears that the forwarder may operate both as a direct carrier himself, using his own transport, or else as an indirect carrier, using other carriers to effect transit for him, in addition to performing the usual functions of a mere forwarder. To distinguish the various functions is not always easy, but a clear analysis of the position is essential to ascertain the forwarder's precise liability.

In Australia, the domestic freight forwarder, who specialises in forwarding goods across inter-state boundaries from one part of the federation to another by road or rail or a combination of both, may often perform the complete operation himself. He will collect a shipment from the consignor, consolidate small loads and consign to a deconsolidation point and deliver them to the consignee. For this purpose most forwarders both operate their own vehicles and use the services of owner/drivers as sub-contractors both for inter-state hauls and local delivery and collection services.

Dependent on the method of operation in use, the relationship

[25] See Chapter 11.
[26] See Appendix.   [26a] See § 279, *post.*
[27] Cl. 3 (3), R.H.A. Conditions 1967. See Chapter 11.

THE CARRIER BY LAND

created between the parties may be that of client, forwarder and carrier, or else that of client, carrier and sub-carrier.[28] Although commercially the operator may refer to himself as a freight forwarder, if the Standard Conditions of Contract of the Forwarders Division, Australian Road Transport Federation are used, these refer to him as a carrier, and to the various transport agencies used to move the goods as sub-contractors.[29] Conversely, even where the operator trades as a carrier, and is liable as one, he may not actually carry himself, but utilises sub-contractors both for local pick-up and delivery work, and also for inter-state haulage. Much of the latter class of work is now effected by using the railways as a sub-contractor, using special " piggy-back " railway trucks to carry road trailers and also removable containers.

36   The liability of the freight forwarder in Australia was discussed in the recent case of *Thomas National Transport (Melbourne) Pty. Ltd. & Pay* v. *May & Baker (Australia) Pty. Ltd.*[30] The appellants, before the High Court of Australia, were a large forwarding organisation in Victoria with associate companies of similar name in other states. They employed about twenty carriers around Melbourne to collect goods and bring them into a central depot where they were sorted for onward movement by road, rail or sea (to Tasmania). In the case of road shipments, they were transported to the state of destination by carriers regularly employed by T.N.T. These were sub-contractors employed, like the local carriers, regularly and exclusively by T.N.T., their vehicles carrying the latter's name, and connected with the depot by two-way radio for directions by T.N.T.

Accordingly, in an action for damage to a shipment by fire whilst in the hands of a sub-carrier, the question arose as to whether T.N.T. could claim to be a mere forwarder, and therefore not liable for the loss, on the grounds that it took place while the shipment was not in their possession. This argument was rejected however by the court on the grounds that T.N.T. had actual possession of the goods as bailees throughout the whole transit, either by their own servants or through a sub-contractor, and were therefore liable as carriers for the acts of their sub-carriers.[31]

37   (iii) *United States and Canada*

The position of the freight forwarder is similar in both countries in respect of domestic forwarding operations, although not yet subject to any special statutory control as such in Canada.[32]

---

[28] See *Thomas National Transport (Melbourne) Pty. Ltd. & Pay* v. *May and Baker (Australia) Pty. Ltd.* [1966] 2 Lloyd's Rep. 347. For the distinction see Chapter 11.
[29] Cll. 1 and 3. Cl. 2 provides that the carrier does not contract as a common carrier. In employing sub-contractors, Standard Conditions of Carriage for Interstate Sub-Contractors will normally be used.
[30] [1966] 2 Lloyd's Rep. 347.
[31] *Per* Windeyer J. at p. 354.
[32] The foreign freight forwarder acts merely as an agent on behalf of a shipper.

38   In the United States, on the other hand, domestic freight forwarding has been strictly controlled since Part IV of the Interstate Commerce Act was enacted in 1942. Prior to that date, the courts consistently held that the domestic freight forwarder was not a common carrier,[33] and this ruling remained even after Part IV became effective. However, by an amending statute of December 20, 1950, section 402 (5) of the Act was amended to provide that "The term 'freight forwarder' means any person which (otherwise than as a common carrier subject to Part I, II and III of the Act) holds itself out to the general public as a common carrier."

The Part IV freight forwarder therefore is no longer in the position of a shipper in relation to the actual carrier, but himself stands in the position of a carrier in relation to the shipper, although not actually carrying any goods himself, hence the term an indirect carrier. He may however effect local pick-up and delivery services himself. Similarly in the case of express companies both in the United States and in Canada, these have consistently been treated as common carriers.[34]

39   (iv) *Conclusion*

It can be seen that the status of the forwarder by land transport will depend upon whether he is in fact actually carrying the goods himself for all or part of the transit. Generally, therefore, he will not normally possess the status of a carrier himself except in so far as he may actually carry goods himself by his own transport, but will remain in the position of a mere agent in relation to the shipper.[35]

40   An important exception to this rule arises where domestic freight forwarding takes place on a large scale, such as in the United States.[36] Here, either by statutory provision or by the decisions of the court, the domestic freight forwarder has been given the status of an indirect carrier, that is, although not necessarily effecting any part of the carriage himself, he is given the legal status of a carrier. Similar provisions have been made in the case of express companies, both in Canada and the United States, where the actual carriage, apart from local delivery and collection services, is completely by rail.[37]

---

[33] See *Acme Fast Freight Inc.* v. *United States* (1940) 309 U.S. 638; *American Transportation Co.* v. *Insurance Co. of North America* (1942) 1 N.W. (2d) 521.
[34] *Dominion Express Co.* v. *Rutenberg* (1909) 18 Que.K.B. 50. An express company which undertakes to forward goods is not a mere intermediary or agent as between shipper and consignee. It is a common carrier and is therefore liable as such. Accordingly, it can therefore limit its liability in a bill of lading. In the earlier case of *Leonard* v. *American Express Co.* (1867) 26 U.C.Q.B. 533, there was some doubt as to whether an express company was a common carrier or not, although really only with regard to the particular commodity in question, that is, fish, in respect of which the express company did not offer common carriage. However it will only be liable as a warehouseman in respect of loss or damage occurring while a shipment is in its warehouse awaiting the documents from the shipper, prior to shipment—*Meyer* v. *American Express Co.* (1921) 61 D.L.R. 548. Similarly when the transit is at an end.
[35] See Chapter 3.
[36] *Supra.*
[37] See note 34, *supra.* For a discussion of the operation of express companies—A. W. Currie, *Economics of Canadian Transportation*, 1959, Toronto, Chapter XII.

However, such rules have little application in those countries where the majority of forwarding business is connected with foreign trade. Consequently, it appears that only if the forwarder engages in those categories of operation which fall within C.M.R. or the draft T.C.M. Convention is such a possibility likely to arise in this country. This question will be discussed in a later chapter though.[38]

3. THE CARRIER BY SEA

41 Where forwarding is effected by means of sea transport, the status of the freight forwarder is rarely in dispute. Whereas domestic freight forwarding merely carries the connotation of grouping and consolidation of small shipments to obtain beneficial freight rates, the foreign freight forwarder performs a wider range of functions, including such complementary services as warehousing, insurance and packing, while often acting as a freight or loading broker and or ship's agent at the same time, although rarely as a carrier.[39]

42 However, as has been discussed already in relation to forwarding by land, a distinction must be drawn between a carrier acting as such under a through bill of lading and a carrier acting as a forwarder for the on-carriage of goods by another carrier. Where, though, a conflict of laws question arises and doubt exists as to whether English or foreign law is to be applied, the question whether a carrier is to be treated as one, or alternatively as a freight forwarder, may depend upon which law is applied.[40]

43 In Australia and Canada where the foreign freight forwarder operates in a similar fashion to this country, the legal position is the same. In the United States, however, the foreign freight forwarder is subject to the regulation of the Federal Maritime Commission. His legal status was described by the Supreme Court in *United States* v. *American Union Transport* [41]: "By engaging in these many activities of the forwarding business independent forwarders—and particularly the appellees—act as agents of the shippers." [42] Consequently, a clear distinction has been drawn between forwarding and carriage in respect of shipments by sea. In an early Canadian case it was emphasised that an undertaking to forward is not necessarily an undertaking to carry. Where, therefore, a warehouse-keeper and wharfinger, having undertaken to forward a box to Montreal, duly delivered it on board to the master of a ship in the

[38] See Chapter 13.
[39] See Sections 5 and 6 of this chapter.
[40] See *Anselme Dewavrin Fils et Cie* v. *Wilsons & N.E.Ry. Shipping Co. Ltd.* (1931) 39 Ll.L.Rep. 289, where the question arose whether a through bill of lading was governed by English law or French law.
[41] 327 U.S. 437. See Ullman, *Ocean Freight Forwarder*, Cornell, 1967.
[42] *Ibid.* at p. 443. " The Express Company which handled details of shipments, procured overseas transportation by carrier, and paid all charges therefor, and which received reimbursement from owner of cargo and payment of fee for its services, was not a carrier but was merely a forwarding agent for owner and, as such was liable only for its own negligence ": *J. C. Penny Co.* v. *A.E.C.*, U.S. Ct.App. Docket 22549.

carrying trade to this city, it was held that he had performed his duty and was not liable as a common carrier for its loss.[43] Generally the foreign freight forwarder both in Canada and the United States acts merely as an agent on behalf of his client the shipper or consignee, and does not assume the role of an indirect carrier unless he participates in domestic freight forwarding in addition.

Finally, in other countries where either the export trade does not warrant a forwarding trade, or else historical accident has decreed it so, that is, where the export trade is largely in bulk commodities not suitable for handling by a forwarder, most inward shipments are handled by clearing, landing or dock agents, the name but not the function differing from country to country. These are more fully discussed in a later section of this chapter.[44]

4. THE CARRIER BY AIR

44   Airfreight forwarding

Freight forwarding by air transport is a recent phenomenon which has largely grown up since 1945 with the post-war development of airfreight as a recognised method of transporting goods in quantity. As in the case of regular international airlines, the freight forwarder has come under the control of the International Air Transport Association (I.A.T.A.) and uniform regulations have been agreed upon by the member airline companies to govern those freight forwarders wishing to forward and consolidate shipments on their behalf in return for remuneration in the form of commission paid by the airline concerned.[45]

Where a forwarder is an I.A.T.A. approved cargo sales agent, his relationship with the air carrier by whom he is appointed is laid down in the relevant I.A.T.A. Resolutions. These place him in the position of an agent in relation to his principal the carrier, and lay down certain defined duties.[46] In addition, the forwarder may also act as an agent on behalf of a shipper, thus in many cases being both the agent of the carrier and the shipper. He will not under any circumstances fulfil the function of an air carrier himself, while operating under I.A.T.A. Resolutions.[47]

45   As regards the question of carriage by successive carriers, and the status of a carrier arranging for on-carriage under a through bill, the problem of deciding whether an air carrier is acting as a mere forwarder

---

[43] *Beckett* v. *Urquart* (1844) 1 U.C.Q.B. 188. *Cf. Harris* v. *McPherson* at note 14, *supra*.

[44] See §§ 51 *et seq*.

[45] A forwarder who is not an I.A.T.A. sales agent cannot claim commission for business obtained, and will merely be treated as any other consignor. He can of course get the benefit of bulk rates, and to some extent forwarders have continued to function as non-I.A.T.A. consolidators, their profits being obtained from the difference between rates paid to the carrier and that charged to their customer, as in the case of domestic freight forwarding in the United States and other countries.

[46] See I.A.T.A. Resolutions, 800 *et seq.*; *Perishables Transport Co. Ltd.* v. *N. Spyropoulos Ltd.* [1964] 2 Lloyd's Rep. 379. See § 427.

[47] There are special provisions for the appointment of non-I.A.T.A. air carriers as cargo sales agents—Resolution 810b (K). However the position of the airfreight forwarder in the United States has created some problems owing to attempts by the Civil Aeronautics Board to give him the status of an indirect carrier—see Sundberg, *Air Charter*, Stockholm, 1962, for a discussion of the problem.

or else as a carrier himself no longer arises, as it has recently been settled by international convention.[48]

5. THE LOADING BROKER

46 Types of broker

Having considered the relationship between the forwarder and the carrier both at common law and under the civil law, it is now necessary to turn to those intermediaries in transportation whose operations complement those of the forwarder. The term shipbroker is one that is loosely used to cover several different categories of intermediary engaged in the shipping market. On the Baltic Exchange in London, the following categories exist.[49]

First, there are those engaged in the chartering of ships, that is negotiating a charterparty on behalf of either one or both of the parties concerned, in the former case two brokers usually being involved, each representing a party to the contract.

Secondly, there is the broker engaged in sale and purchase of vessels, a function which may also be combined with that of chartering.

Thirdly, there is the ship's agency side of the trade where the carrier does not have a branch office or other form of representation, which is the usual situation except in the home port. He attends to the various formalities including customs, payments on behalf of the owner, etc. This category will be discussed more fully later.[50]

47 Loading broker and forwarder

The fourth category is the loading broker, who is employed by the shipowner to handle the loading and discharge of his vessels. As the former's function is to advertise for and obtain shipments to fill a vessel to capacity, his operations are complementary to and often overlap those of a forwarder. Consequently it is common to find the same company acting as both loading broker and forwarder, and in some countries, particularly the United States, this is common practice. Although, however, their functions often intermingle, it is necessary to differentiate between them, because when acting as a loading broker, the agent is acting on behalf of the shipowner, whereas in respect of forwarding operations, his principal is the shipper.

48 Distinction

The problem arose in *Heskell* v. *Continental Express Ltd.*,[51] where Devlin J. distinguished between them as follows:

---

[48] See McNair, *Air Law*, pp. 227 *et seq.* As to problems common to both air and sea transportation, see C. E. Manion, *Law of the Air, Cases and Materials*, Chapter 6. For the historical development of commercial air transport, see R. E. G. Davies, *A History of the World's Airlines*. For the American position see J. M. Lindsey, " The Legislative Development of Civil Aviation 1938–58," *Journal of Air Law and Commerce*, Winter 1961–62, and I.A.T.A. Bulletin 21, 1955, pp. 55–58.
   Cf. the position in relation to carriage by land—see Chapter 11.
[49] See generally E. J. Edward, *Shipbrokers and the Law*, London, 1957; C. H. F. Cufley, *Ocean Freights and Chartering*, London, 1962.
[50] See § 49.
[51] (1950) 83 Ll.L.Rep. 438.

"The shipper frequently employs a forwarding agent and the shipowner a loading broker. The forwarding agent's normal duties are to ascertain the date and place of sailing, obtain a space allocation ... and prepare the bill of lading ... and send [it] to the loading broker. [He arranges] for the goods to be brought alongside, making the customs entry and paying any dues on the cargo. After shipment he collects the completed bill of lading and sends it to the shipper. All the regular shipping lines operating from the United Kingdom appear to entrust the business of arranging for cargo to a loading broker. He advertises the date of sailings in shipping papers ... and prepares and circulates to his customers a sailing card. It is his business to supervise the arrangements for loading, though the actual stowage is decided upon by the cargo superintendent, who is in the direct service of the shipowner. It is the broker's business also to sign the bill of lading and issue it to the shipper or his agent in exchange for the freight. His remuneration is ... by way of commission on freight, and that is doubtless an inducement to him to carry out his primary function ... of securing enough cargo to fill the ship. ... [They] discharge well-defined and separate functions. But in practice the same firm is often both the loading broker and the forwarding agent, though two sets of dealings may be kept in separate compartments of the business. The firm generally acts as loading broker only for one line and does all that line's business, so that it is free in respect of other business to act as it will. But even in the case of the same transaction it appears to be customary for the firm to act both as loading broker and as forwarding agent." [52]

It can be seen that to differentiate the two categories of activity is not always easy, as in such circumstances the agent is usually fulfilling both functions simultaneously, and acting on behalf of the respective parties to a differing degree in various transactions depending upon the services required by the parties concerned. A similar problem occurs in the case of airfreight forwarding where the forwarder is both an appointed agent on behalf of the airline, that is, he fulfils a similar position to the loading broker in water transport, while in both cases he acts as a forwarder on behalf of his client, the shipper.

From the commercial angle, though, it is obviously desirable that such functions should be carried out by the one operator, as although the legal status of the latter is twofold, the economic one is in fact that of a single continuous process. Such a problem means however that to establish the status at law the economic function must be carefully analysed and compartmented, so as to ensure that a correct legal classification is arrived at.

[52] *Ibid.* at p. 449.

6. THE SHIP'S AGENT
49 Confusion of terminology

A further source of confusion in defining the forwarder is the use of the name "shipping and forwarding agent." As already discussed, the nomenclature has resulted from the blending of the continental forwarder with the indigenous shipping agents. Such unfortunate terminology has been largely to blame for vagueness and inaccuracy in defining the forwarder's activities and role in commerce. Often, however, the name has been shortened to that of "shipping agent," instead of the more accurate term "forwarding agent." In many cases it can be seen that for the courts the two terms are, if not synonymous, at least interchangeable. Such a practice in itself would have been perfectly acceptable if the matter had not been taken a stage further and the term "shipping agent" used either to mean a shipbroker or ship's agent as well.[53]

The resultant confusion in terminology has meant that it is very difficult in tracing the various precedents on the subject to decide whether a particular case is concerned with forwarding at all, or whether it is merely concerned with ship-broking or agency work. Such statements as that of Branson J. that "In the present case the Continental Lines were employed to do the ordinary work of a shipbroker or a shipping agent"[54] illustrate the loose thought among the judiciary on the subject, as from the facts it is quite clear that the plaintiffs were in fact acting as forwarders, even if the term "shipping" agent was used. Similarly in *Anglo African Shipping Co. of New York Inc.* v. *J. Mortner Ltd.*[55] the distinction was drawn between a confirming house and a shipping agent, whereas the operation in question was rather that of forwarding.

The net result has been that the terms shipping agent and shipbroker have tended to become interchangeable both with each other and also with that of forwarder and ship's agent, whereas as pointed out above, the functions of each are quite clearly defined. The few points of light such as Devlin J.'s distinction between loading broker and forwarder partially redeem this unsatisfactory state of affairs, but an ambiguous body of case law still remains, the true meaning of which can only be ascertained by a careful study of relevant facts, where such are included, to establish the exact relationship in question.

50 Ship's agent and forwarder

The ship's agent, although loosely termed a shipping agent in a number of cases, differs from the forwarder in that, like the loading broker, the former acts as the agent of the shipowner and not of any other party, be he shipper or supplier of goods. His function is purely

---

[53] A "Standard Liner Agency Agreement" has been drawn up in 1970 by the Federation of National Associations of Ship Brokers and Agents as a basis for agency agreements with owners, which lays down the principal functions and rates of remuneration.
[54] *Continental Lines S.A.* v. *W. H. Holt & Sons Ltd.* (1932) 43 Ll.L.Rep. 392.
[55] [1962] 1 Lloyd's Rep. 610.

to represent the shipowner in ports where he has no local office, associate company, or other form of representation. Obviously the cost of maintaining such an organisation would be costly, and to appoint a local agent to act under a regular scale of charges as and when required is a more economic alternative. Such agents normally act for more than one line, dependent upon the size of the port, and often carry on forwarding and other complementary operations at the same time.

However, the two operations are quite separate from the viewpoint of legal relationships. The ship's agent is responsible for paying all necessary outgoings on behalf of the shipowner, from whom he will obtain reimbursement. This will cover paying for supplies, and other dues, and the arranging of customs formalities and other documentation. He will also be responsible for arranging the loading and discharge of a vessel, but this must be distinguished from any function he may fulfil as a loading broker, which although often complementary and also performed on behalf of the shipowner, is concerned with obtaining freight, whereas the ship's agent is concerned with servicing the ship as such, and not in obtaining cargo.

7. Customs Agent, Clearing and Landing Agent

51   Distinction

The forwarder is essentially the product of a developed economy, where there is a large flow of exports. Where however there are but few, and most goods are imported, and exports are merely of primary commodities, he does not exist, his place being filled by the customs agent or broker, who will normally forward what few outgoing shipments may exist, and will handle the reception of shipments, clear them through customs and if required will forward them to a further inland destination.

52   The customs broker in many countries is licensed, and is the only medium whereby customs clearance can be obtained. In some countries, where no such requirements exist, the agent may fulfil on a non-mandatory basis the same functions.

53   In other countries, where although a system of registered customs brokers exists, such as the United States and Canada, there is a developed economy, agents are often both custom-house brokers and forwarders. This, although economically desirable, is not legally necessary, and it is possible for a forwarder to be registered under the Federal Maritime Commission as a foreign freight forwarder, but not as a custom-house broker, or vice versa. Similarly in Canada, where a registration system exists for custom-house brokers, but not for forwarders, many forwarders are registered as custom-house brokers, and many registered custom-house brokers act as forwarders, but this practice is far from universal.

[30]

Confusion can accordingly arise as to which function is being performed, but apart from the fact that certain functions can only be performed by a licensed customs broker, where a licensing system exists, and not by a forwarder or other agent, in both cases the agent is acting on behalf of the shipper and not for the carrier.

54 United Kingdom

In this country, however, no system of customs broker exists, consignees being free to clear shipments through customs themselves if they so wish, or through any appointed agent, without any particular formalities being required. Accordingly, such a differentiation is not relevant here, until such date as a system of licensed brokers is introduced.[56]

55 South Africa

In South Africa, the intermediary who is responsible for handling shipments imported by sea will normally fulfil a multiplicity of functions. Irrespective however of the particular operation performed, he is commonly referred to as a dock agent, although his actual function will either be that of a landing agent or delivery agent. Accordingly his exact rights and liabilities will depend upon which category he falls in.

The courts have considered the position on several occasions, and have stated that a landing agent is required, "when he lands goods to receive them, to store them . . ., to give a receipt to the ship for the goods; and . . . put them on the consignee's wagon."[57] The landing agent is therefore a mere agent acting on behalf of a consignee and is only liable as such, although he may of course be acting as the agent of the carrier too, that is, as a ship's agent.

A dock agent may however be appointed both as a landing agent and as a delivery agent acting on behalf of the consignee, that is, to receive the goods for the purpose of delivery. In his former capacity, he will be liable for cargo received by him for which he is unable to account. Accordingly, if the landing agent cannot prove that a consignment has been deposited in the harbour board store he will be liable for their loss.[58] On the other hand, if he can prove that he has so deposited the goods, he will escape further liability for them[59]: "He is not in the position of a warehouseman, who must keep the goods safe, nor is he entrusted with them as a common carrier."[60] He merely has a certain duty conferred upon him as a landing agent, and if he is not negligent in performing it he will not be liable for any loss which results.[61]

---

[56] See Chapter 16.
[57] *Isaacs & Co.* v. *McKenzie & Co.* (1901) 18 S.C. 362 at p. 370, *per* Buchanan Acting C.J.
[58] *Lister* v. *McKenzie & Co.* (1900) 17 S.C. 368.
[59] *McKenzie & Co.* v. *Tuchton, Moss & Co.* (1901) 18 S.C. 54.
[60] *Lister* v. *McKenzie & Co.* (1900) 17 S.C. at p. 370.
[61] *i.e.* "A certain amount of responsibility is undertaken by the dock agent who undertakes to receive goods on behalf of consignees, and that he is responsible when he receives goods to account for them, and he must also show that he has done all he is required to do, and authorised to do, under the dock regulations": *Isaacs & Co.* v. *McKenzie & Co.* (1901) 18 S.C. 362 at p. 368, *per* Buchanan Acting C.J.

Accordingly, where a consignment of non-perishable goods, which were not usually put in the Harbour Board store, were damaged by rain, a landing agent was held not liable for having deposited them in the open as required by the Harbour Board to await removal by the consignees.[62] If however a dock agent is also appointed as a delivery agent by the consignee, he will be bound to hand over the goods to the consignee in the condition in which he received them, and cannot therefore avoid liability in the circumstances discussed above.[63]

56   It should be noted that although stevedoring is a closely allied occupation, as the court pointed out in the case of *McKenzie & Co.* v. *Johnson*,[64] where the plaintiff was "a stevedore, landing and forwarding agent" suing a shipmaster for stevedoring services, that" stevedoring is quite a different thing from dock agency" and rejected a defence argument that the two were "exactly the same work."[65] Accordingly, where a landing agent agrees to land and tranship a cargo, it is not his duty to bring it out of the hold to the ship's rail which is in fact a stevedoring operation which can therefore be the subject of a separate charge.

57 Landing agent defined
    However the term landing agent does not necessarily carry the same connotation in all countries, as elsewhere it has been used to cover either an agent acting on behalf of the consignee, as in the case of South Africa, or else an agent acting solely on behalf of the shipowner. It may also connote an intermediary who acts on behalf of consignee and shipowner as agent for both of them. The ambiguous position of the landing agent was discussed at the beginning of the century in the Privy Council by Lord MacNaughten in a judgment which illustrates clearly the problems that can arise in attempting to define the exact nature of such an intermediary.[66] He stated that

"It is the practice for the owners of steamers calling at Penang to appoint landing agents at that port. The business of the landing agents is to send lighters to meet an incoming vessel belonging to their employers on being furnished with a copy of the ship's manifesto. The goods are discharged from the ship's tackle into lighters. The landing agents give the master a clean receipt, if they are received in good order. The goods are then carried to jetty sheds ... landed there, and assorted by the landing agents ready for delivery to the consignees on production of the bill of lading indorsed by the ship's agents with a delivery order.... The landing agents make out their account of the landing charges and storage rent, if any, according to a scale of charges exhibited in the offices

[62] *McKenzie & Co.* v. *Tuchton, Moss & Co.* (1901) 18 S.C. 54.
[63] *Ibid.*
[64] (1901) 18 S.C. 276.
[65] *Ibid.* at p. 278. See Bamford, *Law of Shipping in South Africa*, 1961.
[66] *Chartered Bank* v. *B.I.S.N. Co. Ltd.* [1909] A.C. 369 at p. 372.

of the ship's agents. They receive payment direct from the consignees. The endorsement of the bill of lading by the ship's agents is required as a release of the ship's lien for freight and expenses incurred on the shipment. Without such indorsement the landing agents are not at liberty to deliver goods to consignees. This practice [is] the subject of much controversy in Penang. The shipowners contend that the landing agents are the agents of the merchants. The merchants insist that they are . . . the agents of the shipowners. Neither view is quite accurate. These landing agents rather seem to be in the position of *intermediaries owing duties to both parties*—agents for the shipowners as long as the contract of affreightment remains unexhausted, agents for the consignees as soon as the bill of lading is produced with delivery order indorsed."

It is therefore necessary, where the term " landing agent " is used, to analyse carefully the relationships involved to arrive at a true assessment of his rights and liabilities. It should be noted that the harbour authorities may perform such functions itself.[67]

8. FORWARDER OR FINANCIER

58 The forwarder's function is principally that of an intermediary between a shipper and supplier of transportation. The duties performed by him in carrying out this function are numerous and have already been outlined in the previous chapter. Among the larger and financially stronger forwarding companies, there has been a tendency to expand into other fields of activity closely allied to their original one of forwarding. Paramount among these is that of finance, as to expand the forwarding trade an increase in exports is necessary, and for that credit or other financial support is usually a prerequisite for expansion in this field. As a result in many continental countries and in the United States the forwarder has offered credit facilities as an adjunct to his forwarding operations. Obviously relatively few freight forwarders have the capital available for such purposes, but a forwarder may advance the invoice price of a consignment, which he will collect by means of banker's drafts or other forms of bill financing. In the United Kingdom, though, such a practice is extremely unusual, as forwarders normally avoid involvement in financial operations. Such a double function does sometimes occur though in reverse, where a confirming house or export

---

[67] See also *Ebrahim* v. *B.I.S.N.* [1928] S.S.L.R. 14, discussed in Chapter 3, note 48. Equally where the Harbour Board itself fulfils this function or receives imported goods instead of the landing agent, it will normally do so as agents for the shipowners, and can thus obtain the protection of the bill of lading. In *Hardial Singh & Sons Ltd.* v. *P. & O. Navigation Co. and Singapore Harbour Board* (1955) 21 M.L.J. 242, the court therefore held that it was impossible to imply a contract between the Harbour Board and the plaintiff (shippers/consignees) to the effect that the Board undertook to store the goods safely, there was no contractual relationship between them. N.B. Under the particular bill of lading the consignee was to take delivery alongside the steamer, or if not, the shipowner had the option of delivery to the Harbour Board at the consignee's risk, it being the practice to do so in Singapore without special instructions on the matter.

[33]

merchant offers a forwarding service in addition to credit facilities, often drawing little distinction between the two aspects of the business. Such a distinction is necessary though to establish the exact extent of the legal liability and duties of the parties concerned. This problem arose in the case of *Anglo African Shipping Co. of New York Inc. v. J. Mortner Ltd.*[68] where both at first instance and in the Court of Appeal the distinction between confirming operations and forwarding of goods was discussed in some detail. The question was whether there had been a breach of obligation by the agent in the performance of his multiple functions, as the duties of a forwarder are perforce less onerous than those of a confirming house. This question however is outside the scope of this work.

9. THE COURTIER MARITIME IN THE CIVIL LAW

59   The position of the shipbroker on the Continent is generally rather different from that in this country, where the intermediary in shipping circles has been left completely untrammelled by governmental control of one sort or another.

60   In France, for instance, which provides a particularly interesting comparison with this country, the courtier or broker held a privileged position in all fields of commerce until 1866, when all such privileges were withdrawn, with the particular exception of the courtier maritime and the courtier d'assurances maritimes, who both retained their traditional privileged status.[69] Arguments have been put forward as to the merits and demerits of the continuance of such a monopoly, which makes their services compulsory for all foreign ships in those ports where they still operate. However, as an intermediary between foreign ship captains and the administration, they are able to offer guarantees which a " courtier libre " could not, because, as has been pointed out, the national tradition is not really conducive of such confidence in a broker who does not have official recognition.[70] Furthermore, it is a moot point as to whether or not the system in fact increases costs in respect of the services performed by the courtier maritime. Much of their importance has now disappeared though, as in the field of freight broking, which is one of the most lucrative fields of operation in ship-broking, much of the business is carried on in Paris, to which the system has never extended, and where most of the big shipping offices are found. This trade is

---

[68] [1962] 1 Lloyd's Rep. 610.

[69] *Cf.* in Austria a similar system of official shipbroker exists. In Portugal they are named by the government, being subject to regulation in respect of their commercial books and tariff charges. In other countries the brokers are formed into a corporation, and often have a similar status as a public official, but do not possess a monopoly. In this category are included Spain (Arts. 88 *et seq.* C.com.) Netherlands (Arts. 62 *et seq.* C.com.) and Sweden (Law of June 9, 1893). In other countries shipbroking is free. In Belgium the Law of 1867 established their freedom in all respects. In Germany, the Schiffsmakler operates as a free broker, as Art. 36, Gewerbeordnung, has established the freedom of brokerage generally. In Norway the Law of June 5, 1869, suppressed the official broker. Argentina also allows free brokerage, not having followed the Spanish pattern in this respect.

[70] Ripert, *Droit Maritime*, Vol. 2, s. 1387.

therefore carried on by courtiers libres. Furthermore, other exceptions to the compulsory use of the courtier maritime have further eroded their position, and in any case, they do not operate outside certain old-established ports, and not in respect of land or air transportation at all.

61 Definition of courtier maritime

From the legal viewpoint, the courtier maritime possesses a double character. First, he has the status of an " officier ministeriel," that is a public official named by decree, and cannot therefore trade on his own account, though if in fact he does so, his acts will be valid, but will render him liable to both penal and disciplinary sanctions.[71] Secondly, he is also a " commerçant " as Article 632, C.com. renders all brokerage operations "actes de commerce," with the consequent obligation to keep the required commercial books, etc., and makes them subject to the jurisdiction of the commercial courts.[72] The extent of a courtier's operations have been defined by Article 80, C.com., and include freight broking, charterparties, bills of lading, contracts, appearance in litigation, customs matters, etc. Where a courtier maritime maintains an office, that is, in the port in respect of which he holds a licence, he has a monopoly of freight broking, otherwise, as mentioned above, such services are not subject to governmental control. The courtier's position is that of an intermediary between the shipowner and the shipper of goods. In addition, however, a commissionnaire may act as a further intermediary between the courtier himself and the shipper, as an agent d'affretement on behalf of the latter, by whom he is paid, without any official status, a practice which the courtiers not only tolerate, but also make use of themselves. Where they conclude a contract of affreightment, they usually draft the charterparty, but this does not constitute part of their official duties. In certain ports they also act as loading brokers and as marine forwarders.[73] One of the most important aspects of the courtier's operations is that of inward and outward customs clearance. Although a particular courtier may not be engaged to carry out both functions, as they are considered to be indivisible aspects of the same operation, a captain cannot charge a courtier with only part thereof though. An Ordinance of November 14, 1835 (Art. 2) enumerates in detail the operations in question, which include, *inter alia*, depositing the ship's protest, manifest and declaration in customs, the payment of navigation dues, details of imports and exports, etc.

62   Although the captain of all foreign ships must engage a courtier to effect clearance for them, he is free to choose which courtier he wishes to employ. However, the charterparty and bill of lading will often

---

[71] Art. 85, C.com., prohibits the courtier maritime from trading on his own account or having any interest in any other commercial enterprise. This also applied to the courtier d'assurances maritimes until recently, but by Law No. 65-546 of July 8, 1965, under certain conditions the latter can act as a broker for non-marine insurance and re-insurance. See Cass. Req., Feb. 5, 1868, D. 1868, 1, 387.

[72] See Ripert, *Droit Maritime*, Vol. 2, pp. 770–771.

[73] Bordeaux, Dec. 10, 1874, D. 1876, 5, 145.

specify a particular courtier by name, in a clause d'addresse, which will oblige the captain to use the courtier named to avoid liability to the shipper for non-compliance.[74] This monopoly is however subject to certain important exceptions, as clearance can be effected without the intervention of a courtier by the captain himself, provided he speaks fluent French, by the shipper of goods and the shipowner. The latter can be represented by an agent de l'armement who will thus replace the courtier in effecting clearance of the ship.[75] Such representation is however only permitted by a representative who is actually resident in the port in question, and who normally represents this shipowner for all purposes. The courts have not permitted fictitious branch offices to be created to avoid using a courtier maritime.[76] In addition, by the Ordinance of 1681 consignees are permitted to clear their own shipments themselves, which has since been confirmed by a circular of October 25, 1817, and which is supported by the majority of jurists. Where however the consignee of the actual ship is not also consignee of the cargo in it, it seems that the former cannot effect clearance himself.[77] This restriction has in practice mitigated against the inward clearance of the cargo by its consignee, together with the fact that when outward clearance is eventually effected, certain fees will be payable to the courtier concerned even if one has not been employed for inward clearance. Furthermore, even if the consignee of the ship is also the consignee of the cargo, and therefore can effect inward clearance, he cannot effect outward clearance in his former capacity. Likewise the relevant tariffs charged by the courtier mitigate against the intervention of the consignee of the cargo too,[78] and no other class of agent can carry out these functions without laying themselves open to both civil and penal sanctions. Finally, even where commercial treaties exist giving equality to French and foreign ship captains, the courts have rejected the plea that this will give the consul a right to effect clearance on the latter's behalf in place of a courtier,[79] so that the position of the courtier maritime, although increasingly circumscribed, still retains its strongly monopolistic character, which the civil law perpetuates in strong contrast with the spirit of the common law.

[74] Fecamp, March 18, 1896, Rev. int. droit maritime, 11, 161. In Belgium, the courts have given the courtier a direct right of action against a ship's captain for non-compliance with a clause d'addresse, which is treated as a stipulation in favour of a third party—Brussels, June 21, 1884, Jur. Anvers. 1, 330.

[75] Cass. Crim. May 10, 1889, D. 1889, 1, 270.

[76] Cass. Crim. Jan. 31, 1852, 1, 153.

[77] Cass. Civ., Feb. 25, 1895, D. 1895, 1, 393, Rev. int. droit maritime, XI, 772—the decisions conflict on this point however.

[78] Tariffs are fixed from time to time by decree. The conduit of the ship is considered to be indivisible, even if a courtier only covers part of the operations, and therefore the full rate is charged. (Cass. Req. May 2, 1887, D. 1887, 1, 300.) There is some uncertainty whether at law the courtier can claim less than the tariff rates (see Ripert, *Droit Maritime*, Vol. 2, p. 778), although he cannot claim more (Bordeaux, July 10, 1831, D. 1832, 2, 172). Only the tribunaux judiciaires are competent to interpret brokerage tariffs (Cons. d'Etat, June 26, 1874, Rec. Lebon, 603). On the question of charges generally see Chapter 14.

[79] Cass. Civ. Feb. 25, 1895, D. 1895, 1, 393.

10. CONCLUSIONS

63 From the distinctions drawn in this chapter between the various categories of intermediary in transportation, it can clearly be seen that the status of the freight forwarder is inextricably interwoven with that of the carrier, the landing agent and the shipbroker. This overlap is emphasised by the general commercial practice for an intermediary to perform as many associated operations as are economically viable, without attempting to draw any clear distinction between them as they may in practice be one continuous transaction, although from a legal viewpoint quite distinct, creating quite different rights and liabilities between the parties. Between the common law and many civil law countries a sharp distinction can be drawn between the *laissez-faire* attitude to such relationships in the former, with the notable exception of the United States, and the formalistic methods of control and allocation of functions practised in the latter. Similarly, the uneasy distinction between principal and agent at common law and the consequent allocation of all functions to one or other of these legal categories has created considerable uncertainty as to the exact status of the various intermediaries in transportation. This, however, has been overcome to some extent in many civil law countries by the concept of the contract of *Commission*, which offers a third category midway between the simple principal or agent distinction as a useful compromise between them, which enables more clear cut distinctions to be drawn, and therefore more certainty as to the exact status of a particular intermediary or a particular act in question. Even so, in the civil law juristic concepts tend to lag behind commercial reality and still may be unable to reflect accurately the commercial act in respect of which it is required to offer a legal framework.[80] The problem of accurately assessing the true juridical nature of the various aspects of a forwarder's work will therefore be discussed in detail in the next chapter.

---

[80] See §§ 102 *et seq.*

CHAPTER 3

THE FORWARDER—HIS LEGAL STATUS

1. INTRODUCTION

64 WITH the ever-growing complexity of multiple relationships in the world of commerce, commercial agents, who at common law would not be personally liable upon a contract, have to a large extent become principals themselves when entering into contractual relationships. Alternatively by the growth of custom in a particular trade they have accepted personal liability on behalf of their principal either for the payment of the price in a contract of sale, or else for some other aspect of the performance of the contract. In this country the courts have been singularly loath to treat a person as being an agent and at the same time solely liable in a contract to a third party.[1] There has therefore been considerable difficulty in establishing the true position at law of various commercial intermediaries, and of the forwarder in particular. He is in fact the agent of anyone wishing to use his services in arranging the transportation of goods.

65 Commissionnaire de transport

On the Continent, the question is more easily solved, as the forwarder is classified as a commissionnaire or commission merchant, and is, in many cases, subject to special statutory provisions concerning his rights and obligations. To be recognised by the law as a special category of commercial intermediary has both advantages, and disadvantages, inasmuch as freedom of action may be restricted, and stringent rules concerning the licensing of forwarders may exist.[2] However, the fact that there is considerable certainty as to the forwarder's legal position does offer a positive advantage over the vague status held in this country. Here, apart from the distinction already drawn before between the forwarder and a carrier, and other categories of closely allied commercial intermediaries, one is forced to fit the forwarder into the category of principal or agent, when so often he is in fact acting as both simultaneously to varying degrees in particular cases.

In civil law countries, *i.e.* those subject to Roman law-based codes, the commissionnaire, of which the forwarder is one category, is acknowledged to be both.[3] His status requires that he must transact business for the account of his principal, like any other agent, but will do so in his own name, that is, he will accept personal liability for any

---

[1] See D. J. Hill, " The Commission Merchant at Common Law " (1968) 31 M.L.R. 623.
[2] See Chapter 4.
[3] See § 86.

[38]

contracts he enters into for his principal, who will generally not be directly liable to the carrier. On the exact extent of liability in such cases different countries have slightly differing rules, which are discussed in detail elsewhere, so that it suffices to acknowledge that the continental forwarder, unlike his English counterpart, is a recognised commercial intermediary in the eyes of the law in Europe.

2. AT COMMON LAW

(i) *The Forwarder as a Principal*

66 In this country, the situation is very different. The position of the forwarder as an intermediary between carrier and shipper is not always easily ascertained, and must often depend upon a careful analysis of the facts in each individual set of circumstances.[4] To achieve an accurate analysis of the law on this point therefore requires a detailed consideration of the various precedents.

67 First, where a forwarder employs a carrier to effect forwarding operations by road on his behalf, unless it is clearly proved to the contrary, the forwarder will normally adopt the position of a principal in relation to the carrier,[5] and to his client also, particularly where his contract with the latter is subject to Standard Trading Conditions.[6] Similarly where a forwarder undertakes a collection service he will be liable as a principal even though he never in fact effects the actual carriage himself.[7]

68 Where a forwarder employs a carrier on a regular contract basis to carry such goods as he may be employed to forward, he will be in the position of a principal—for example, where a carrier contracted with a forwarder to carry " such quantities of certain copper ingot bars for the carriage of which they had available from time to time sufficient transport," the contract was treated as between principals, the forwarders having also entered into similar agreements with other carriers.[8]

69 Equally, where a forwarder is employed to collect and forward goods for onward transit, even though they may have been employed as agents to do so, if they are entitled to sub-contract and make a profit on so doing they will be in the position of a principal in relation to the

---

4 It is for this reason that S.T.C. are perforce silent on the question of whether the forwarder is in fact an agent or a principal inasmuch as these Conditions must be operative in respect of all aspects of a forwarder's activities. *Cf.* Arts. 1, 11 (6), D.F.C.; Arts. 1, 2, 18, N.F.C.; Art. 1, N.Y.F.F.; Arts. 1–5, C.G. (Belgium); Art. 1, C.G. (Swiss); Art. 2, A.D.S.P.

5 *Lee Cooper Ltd.* v. *C. H. Jeakins & Sons Ltd.* [1964] 1 Lloyd's Rep. 300, at p. 309. N.B. Merely because a party is described as " forwarding agents " does not constitute them agents at law—it may merely be descriptive of the specialised services they provide: *ibid.* at p. 308, *per* Marshall J.

6 *Harris* v. *Continental Express Ltd.* [1961] 1 Lloyd's Rep. 251, see § 269.

7 *Colverd & Co. Ltd.* v. *Anglo Overseas Transport Co. Ltd.*—see § 269. See also Chapter 2, note 14.

8 *John Rigby (Haulage) Ltd.* v. *Reliance Marine Insurance Co. Ltd.* [1956] 2 Lloyd's Rep. 10 at pp. 12, 14.

carrier. Accordingly, where a forwarder charged a higher price to his client for effecting the carriage of a shipment, far in excess of any notional commission, it was held that the forwarders

"... were to collect and forward this cloth for transit to Paris. They were entitled to sub-contract, and that is what they did. I cannot infer that they were really doing what was unlawful to make a profit on their bargain as *agents*. They were doing what they had a right to do—get the work done at any price [7s. 6d.] they could and charge their customer 10s. 6d. I do not think there was any contract between the [shipper and the carrier]."[9]

70   Where a forwarder issues a bill of lading in his own name, he cannot claim to be acting merely as an agent on behalf of his client in effecting transit. As Bankes L.J. explained,

"... this is not a case of principal and agent at all. It is a case of two independent contracting parties, one of whom described themselves as forwarding agents, but although in certain circumstances and/or occasions they might act as mere agents, in this case they did not act or purport to act as mere agents, carrying out their principal's instructions ... and by issuing a through bill of lading they made manifest the fact in reference to this particular transaction that they were an independent contracting party."[10]

71 Personal liability as an agent

In other circumstances, although perhaps still in the position of an agent in relation to his client, a forwarder may be treated as being personally liable to a third party, that is as a principal in respect of certain aspects of a transaction. For instance, in one of the very few cases before the English courts where the activities of the forwarder in relation to airfreight was discussed, the court recognised that airfreight

[9] *Colley* v. *Brewer's Wharf and Transport Ltd.* (1921) 9 Ll.L.Rep. 5 at p. 7. As to the implications of C.M.R. in such a situation see Chapter 13.

[10] *Troy* v. *The Eastern Company of Warehouses* (1921) 8 Ll.L.Rep. 17 at p. 19. See Chap. 13 for facts of these and other cases on the point. This question has come before the U.S.A. courts with particular reference to whether a Pt. IV freight forwarder or express company are to be considered as common carriers within s. 15 of the Shipping Act which requires that agreements between forwarders and carriers to fix prices must be lodged for approval if the parties concerned are subject to the Act. Such approval will exempt them from anti-monopoly restraint of trade laws. If, however, a party is only a freight forwarder he will not be eligible to file any such agreements, and therefore cannot in turn claim the protection of s. 15. Thus it has been held by the Federal Maritime Board that where freight forwarders and express companies undertake to ship personal property and household goods overseas and issue their own through bill of lading to the shipper, thus assuming responsibility from door-to-door, they will be considered common carriers within s. 15 of the Act. If however full responsibility is not assumed for safe water transportation of the goods, the party concerned will only be treated as a freight forwarder, and not as a common carrier who can claim the protection of s. 15. *Non-Vessel Carriers, s. 15* [1961] A.M.C. 1024 at p. 1029. " Where a party undertakes to transport from door to door, it is a common carrier over the entire limits of its routes, both the portion over land and the portion over sea "— F.M.C. Following this decision, Railway Express and Weaver issued modified through bills of lading, thereby assuming door-to-door responsibility. Both companies were therefore held to be " common carriers by water " subject to and protected by the Shipping Act, s. 15—*Non-Vessel Carriers, s. 15* [1963] A.M.C. 1069.

agents are personally liable for freight to the carrier, whether their principal the shipper is disclosed or not, this custom being incorporated into I.A.T.A. Resolutions.[11] The court stated that the latter represents general practice among airfreight agents and merchants in various parts of the world. Irrespective of actual knowledge or not, the shippers were deemed to know of this custom, and were liable to indemnify the forwarders, who paid the carrier the freight dues owed them by the shipper without the latter's authority.[12] This liability remains the same even though the forwarder reveals to the carrier the identity of his principal, the shipper, on whom primary liability really falls.

In *Anglo Overseas Transport Ltd.* v. *Titan Industrial Corp. Ltd.* the courts recognised the custom of the London freight market that forwarders (and shipping brokers) undertake personal liability for freight space to ships agents with whom they deal on behalf of their clients.[13] Such a custom, the court considered, was essential, as without it, it would be impossible to transact business, as a shipowner would never be sure whether he would get a full cargo or not, and furthermore would have no recourse against the forwarder whose credit-standing he knew, but would have to have recourse to an unknown shipper whose financial position might be quite unknown to him. The court refused to accept that the forwarder was a mere agent on behalf of the shipper with no personal liability. In such circumstances though, the agent can in turn recover from the shipper the cost of guaranteeing the taking up of cargo space, and also the actual freight for which they are liable.

It should also be noted that the forwarder accepts personal liability for carrier's [14] and port authorities' charges,[15] dead freight [16] and misdeclaration resulting in the wrong freight being paid, as for instance if the forwarder misdescribes the category of goods being shipped.[17] Such liability to third parties is, however, fairly limited, as the forwarder does not accept personal liability for customs dues in respect of goods which he is clearing on behalf of a client. Nor does he accept liability for insurance premiums of goods in respect of which he effects insurance on behalf of the shipper. In such a case he is merely acting as the shipper's agent in transmitting instructions to the broker or underwriter concerned. It should be observed, however, that in many large multiple groups of transportation and forwarders, the group may have its own

---

[11] *Perishables Transport Co. Ltd.* v. *N. Spyropoulos Ltd.* [1964] 2 Lloyd's Rep. 379.

[12] As to other aspects of indemnity see Chapter 11.

[13] [1959] 2 Lloyd's Rep. 152.

[14] *Lee Cooper Ltd.* v. *C. H. Jeakins & Sons Ltd.*, *supra*.

[15] *P.S.A. Transport Ltd.* v. *Newton Lansdowne & Co. Ltd.* [1956] 1 Lloyd's Rep. 121. Under the forwarder's mandate to collect goods and load them on a ship, etc., he accepts liability to the port authority and has a right to be indemnified by his principal. *Cf. Halal Shipping Co. Ltd.* v. *Aden Port Trustees* [1962] E.A. 97, where the shipping agents were held liable for port storage charges as the Port Trust Ordinance placed liability on the owner of the goods, and the owner as defined in s. 2 of the Ordinance included the shipping agent. The charges became due when debited to the agent's deposit account, and not merely on removal. Similar provisions are found throughout the Commonwealth.

[16] *Anglo Overseas Transport Ltd.* v. *Titan Industrial Corp. Ltd.* [1959] 2 Lloyd's Rep. 152.

[17] But see Cl. 13 (ii) & (iv) S.T.C.

insurance broking company, which in fact means that the liability of the insurance broker for premiums, at Lloyd's generally, and in all cases in respect of marine insurance, will still be present though this will not of course be in the capacity of a forwarder.[18]

72   A forwarder will also be personally liable where he undertakes additional functions such as confirming the actual shipment of goods on the strength of which payment will be made by the buyer,[19] or in countersigning official weight or quality certificates in respect of a shipment.[20] Such functions however are special ones which a forwarder only accepts if he wishes to, and are more common in continental forwarding practice. The mere fact though that a party to a contract of sale guarantees that his forwarder will load as soon as possible after arrival does not mean that the latter is liable for his failure to do so except in his capacity of an agent acting on behalf of his principal the shipper.[21] It should be clearly understood however that in such multiple functions, the forwarder may virtually lose his identity as such, although still operating as one in name, and in fact be operating as an export merchant or confirming house instead.

It should be noted, however, that the liability of a forwarder when contracting as a principal with a carrier [22] should not be confused with the fact that a forwarder will be absolutely liable at common law to the carrier as consignor for any damage caused by goods delivered by him to the carrier. In such circumstances, there is a consignor's warranty of fitness.[23]

73   (ii) *The Forwarder as an Agent*
The forwarder as described by Rowlatt J. in *Jones* v. *European and General Express Co. Ltd.* is the forwarder in the strict sense of the word, that is a mere agent acting on behalf of his principal the shipper, either to forward goods or to receive them on his behalf or on behalf of the consignee.[24] He also states erroneously that the forwarder does not obtain possession of the goods,[25] but even if such a statement was accurate forty years ago, which is to be doubted, as forwarding practice has not changed radically since then, it is certainly not true today. It is just as common in large commercial centres for a forwarder to operate a collection and delivery service as for a shipment to be forwarded without him actually handling it either personally or through a sub-contractor for whose driver he may be vicariously liable.[26] However, he can merely forward or collect goods in respect of transit by

---

[18] See Chapter 17.
[19] *Sphinx Export Co. Ltd.* v. *Specialist Shippers Ltd.* [1954] 1 Lloyd's Rep. 407.
[20] *Heisler* v. *Anglo-Dal Ltd.* [1954] 2 Lloyd's Rep. 5.
[21] See *Sphinx Export Co. Ltd.* v. *Specialist Shippers Ltd., supra.*
[22] See *Lee Cooper Ltd.* v. *C. H. Jeakins & Sons Ltd.* [1964] 1 Lloyd's Rep. 300.
[23] *G.N.R.* v. *L.E.P. Transport Ltd.* (1922) 11 Ll.L.Rep. 133. The forwarder can of course obtain an indemnity from his principal. See Chapter 9.
[24] See § 21. *Marston Excelsior Ltd.* v. *Arbuckle Smith & Co. Ltd.* [1971] 2 Lloyd's Rep. 306.
[25] *Ibid.*
[26] *Colverd & Co. Ltd.* v. *Anglo Overseas Transport Co. Ltd., supra.*

land employing a carrier whilst acting as an agent for his principal,[27] and in forwarding by sea, unless, as discussed earlier, a bill of lading is issued by a forwarder in his own name,[28] he will have the status of an agent in relation to both shipper and carrier. The airfreight forwarder who operates as an I.A.T.A. approved cargo sales agent has his status clearly defined by the I.A.T.A. Resolutions.[29] Under them he is an agent acting on behalf of his principal the carrier, though with certain defined duties. Where a forwarder dispatches goods on his principal's behalf by rail, he will not be liable except as an agent in respect of the transit. By contracting with British Rail, he establishes a direct contractual relationship between the consignor and the Board, and thereby avoids personal responsibility.

74 Function

As Somervell L.J. said in *Von Traubenberg* v. *Davies, Turner & Co. Ltd.*, "one of the things that has to be determined is the part the forwarding agents played in the transaction." [30] Although in their function as mere forwarders they will only have the obligations of an agent, that is, to act with the reasonable care and promptness expected from one, it is not easy to distinguish their function as a mere agent in respect of forwarding operations from any other functions not connected with forwarding which may be carried out as part of the same operation.[31]

An example of this is to be found where a party acts both as a confirming house and forwarder in respect of the same shipment. Here, although the party may be placed in the position of a principal in respect of confirming operations, he will still be an agent to the extent that he merely operates as a forwarder. In other words, his status as a forwarder will not be affected by the simultaneous performance of other operations in relation to either a particular shipment or customer.[32] Equally, a forwarder may be both forwarder and carrier in respect of the same shipment at the same time, retaining his status of agent in respect of his operations in the former capacity.[33]

75 Normal rules of agency apply

The position of the forwarder when operating as a mere agent is subject to the normal rules of agency and will not generally differ from those of any other agent.[34] Consequently, his principal will be liable for

[27] *Coe* v. *Motley* (1926) 24 Ll.L.Rep. 131.
[28] *Troy* v. *The Eastern Company of Warehouses* (1921) 8 Ll.L.Rep. 17 at p. 19. Subject of course to the exceptional circumstances above. Similarly in the U.S.A.—*United States* v. *American Union Transport* (1945) 327 U.S. 437 at p. 443.
[29] See Chapter 2.
[30] [1951] 1 Lloyd's Rep. 462 at p. 465.
[31] *Anglo African Shipping Company of New York Inc.* v. *J. Mortner Ltd.* [1962] 1 Lloyd's Rep. 610 at p. 617.
[32] *Ibid.*
[33] *Harris* v. *Continental Express Ltd.* [1961] 1 Lloyd's Rep. 251 at p. 256.
[34] There are no English cases which turn specifically on the duties of the forwarding agent in this respect, but he is presumably subject to the usual duties of exercising due care and skill, not to let his interests conflict with his duty, etc. See Powell, *Law of Agency*, 2nd ed., p. 302. U.S.A. authorities on these points do exist, though.

his wrongful acts or omissions committed within the scope of his authority. Where, therefore, the agent underpays wharfage charges, the owner will be liable to the port authority even though he has paid his agent the correct charges. These common law rights may however be reinforced by a statutory provision to this effect.[35]

The problem however is to ascertain in any particular set of circumstances or transaction whether the forwarder is in fact contracting as a mere agent or else as a principal, as already discussed earlier. The categories of commercial act discussed in the first two sections of this chapter are quite clearly distinguishable and therefore capable of categorisation. The problem lies in analysing the multitude of operations which do not fall squarely in one category or another or, more often, combine the essentials of several of them. Accordingly, although the existing precedents can be grouped to establish an outline classification upon which to base the forwarder's liability in respect of most aspects of his operations, there will still remain some uncertainty in subsequent litigation as to whether the transaction in respect of which the dispute has arisen, will fall clearly into any one or more of the available categories described above.

76   (iii) *The Forwarder—Whose Agent?*
So far the question under discussion has been whether the forwarder is acting as a principal or as an agent. However a problem that has perhaps created more uncertainty is to decide on whose behalf the forwarder is actually acting when he is functioning in the latter capacity. In other words, the problem of whose agent a forwarder is at any particular moment is one that has taxed the courts to a considerable degree.

77   The position of the forwarder as an intermediary between carrier and shipper is not always easily ascertained, and must often depend on a careful analysis of the facts in each case. For instance, where a forwarder is acting as a receiving agent it is often difficult to decide who is his principal, the consignor or the consignee of a shipment. To take a hypothetical example, a consignment may be shipped from Singapore, with instructions from the sending agent to the receiving agent only to release the goods against proof of payment of the seller's invoice. This would normally be achieved by a letter from a bank certifying that the price had been remitted to Singapore. Fortuitously, however, the consignee is also a regular customer of the London receiving agent. However, he does not know of any such restrictions on delivery and therefore does not possess such a letter of authority. He has paid the supplier and wishes the receiving agent to clear the shipment and deliver it to him, and accordingly gives instructions to him to do so. The shipment is in the receiving agent's possession in London, so that he is physically in a position to follow the importer's instructions without difficulty. On

[35] *Haji Khamishe Juma Essale* v. *High Commissioner for Transport*, 20 (1) K.L.R. 1.

the other hand, owing to the sending agent's instructions, it seems that no release of the goods can take place except against a letter of authority from a bank. The receiving agent cannot therefore follow the importer's instructions even if, in fact, he is acting as his agent in doing so, until such a letter is forthcoming. He finds himself in the invidious position of acting as an agent for a possibly unknown consignor in Singapore, and also acting for a regular consignee who is not able to give him instructions because he has no apparent title to the goods. The receiving agent is therefore not able to accept his instructions until either a letter of authorisation is produced or the " stop " is otherwise lifted. In other words, he is powerless to assist his client.

78 A further problem that arises in forwarding operations is that a forwarder often cannot know the terms of sale in a particular transaction. He may therefore act under instructions given by an exporter, even though he has no right to give them. Standard Trading Conditions expressly provide for this point. By Clause 2 of the Conditions, any clients contracting with a forwarder warrant expressly that they are either the owner or the authorised agents thereof, and by entering into the transaction they accept the conditions therein both for themselves and as agents for and on behalf of all other persons who are or may thereafter become interested in the goods. Further, as a corollary to Clause 2, Clause 9 provides that the customer warrants the accuracy of all particulars supplied.[36]

79 The forwarder must always establish for whom he is acting at any one point. Instructions are generally accepted from the person giving them, provided there is no reason for not doing so. If for example a consignment is shipped f.o.b., the consignee will usually give the routing order.[37] Where there is an export order the forwarder will often act for the overseas buyer in any case. However, the warranty in Clause 9 of Standard Trading Conditions does ensure that the forwarder will be indemnified against any loss resulting from this cause. Returning to the

---

[36] See also Cl. 22, S.T.C., which attempts to reinforce the forwarder's rights by subrogating him to the rights of his client against third parties.

[37] *Jobson* v. *Eppenheim & Co.* (1905) 21 T.L.R. 468. Here the plaintiff sold a consignment of brass to the defendant, which was to be delivered to a forwarder to Goole. The defendant wrote to the forwarder instructing him to receive the brass and to forward it by steamer to Hamburg. The plaintiff dispatched the brass to Goole, not knowing of the further destination, except that it was to be forwarded by steamer. The forwarder shipped the goods to Hamburg, and as the plaintiff remained unpaid he instructed the forwarder's Hamburg branch not to deliver the goods to the defendant. The court held that as the plaintiff only had instructions to deliver to the forwarder at Goole, the goods were received by him as the defendant's agent, fresh instructions being necessary for onwards transit. The transit therefore ended at Goole, and the plaintiff could not thereafter exercise his right of stoppage *in transitu* under the Sale of Goods Act 1893, s. 45 (1). See also *Dixon* v. *Baldwen* (1804) 5 East 175, where stoppage *in transitu* was effected too late as the goods had already reached the forwarder's warehouse. *Cf. Bethell* v. *Clark* (1888) 19 Q.B.D. 553; 20 Q.B.D. 615, where a railway company was merely held to be an agent to forward the goods and not to hold them for the purpose of ending transit. Stoppage *in transitu* was therefore still possible. *Cf. Re Isaacs, ex p. Miles* (1885) 15 Q.B.D. 39 (C.A.). *Cf.* Art. 12, C.M.R., discussed at § 221.

illustration discussed above, as the aim of any commercial agent is to avoid litigation if possible, the importer's instructions to clear the goods received from Singapore would have been accepted if no "stop" had been placed upon them by the sending agent. The forwarder will in practice therefore tend to work upon the chronological order in which agency relationships have come into being, that is, when the instructions in question have been received.

80 The problem stated

The approach of the courts to the problem can best be seen from an examination of the precedents. In the light of these the problem appears to resolve itself into four principal categories. First, where a forwarder is acting on behalf of both the consignor and the consignee simultaneously. Secondly, where a forwarder is acting both as a sub-agent on behalf of the sending forwarder as well as a receiving agent for the consignee. Thirdly, where a forwarder ceases to be the agent of the consignor and instead becomes that of the consignee. Fourthly, where a forwarder acts both as a forwarder and also as an agent for the carrier. Each category will be considered in turn.

81 Forwarder acting as agent for both consignor and consignee

First, a case of some interest where a forwarder acted as agent on behalf of both the consignor and the consignee arose in *J. O. Lund Ltd.* v. *Anglo-Overseas Transport Co. Ltd.*[38] As discussed in a later chapter in relation to the question of the forwarder's lien, the forwarder was acting as the agent for an Italian seller to hold an import shipment pending payment. He was also responsible however as agent for the buyer to warehouse the shipment and to clear it through customs. Subsequently, part of the shipment was delivered by the forwarder to the plaintiff buyer without the required delivery note being presented and counter-signed by a bank as evidence of payment. At common law, a forwarder is offered little protection when acting on behalf of both parties. In *Lund's* case the forwarder would have been both liable to the seller for wrongfully releasing the shipment, and also unable to recover an indemnity from the buyer. The forwarder would therefore have been placed in an invidious position if he had not been trading subject to Standard Trading Conditions, which gave him a contractual right of lien together with the fact that the buyer had agreed to hold the goods he had received on behalf of the forwarder.

The forwarder will also be liable when acting as the agent of several parties, as in a string contract, if he fails to hand over the bill of lading or mate's receipt to the right principal. It is his duty to ascertain this, or else if he delivers it into the wrong hands, he will do so at his own risk.[39]

[38] [1955] 1 Lloyd's Rep. 142; see Chapter 14. *Cf. Duncan Furness & Co. Pty. Ltd.* v. *R. S. Couche & Co.* [1922] V.L.R. 660.
[39] *Brown, McFarlane & Co.* v. *Shaw Lovell* (1921) 7 Ll.L.Rep. 36.

82 Forwarder acting for sending forwarder and consignee

Secondly, the problem of the forwarder acting both as a sub-agent on behalf of a sending forwarder and also as agent to clear and receive goods was discussed in *Von Traubenberg* v. *Davies, Turner & Co. Ltd.*[40] where a suitcase containing valuables was lost after clearance through customs by the forwarder, whilst in transit by train from London to Liverpool. In deciding the duty owed by the forwarder to the owner, it was argued that the former was merely a receiving agent, instructed by the sending forwarder, Schenker, "merely to receive the goods in London, get them through the Customs and ... make any necessary contract with the railway company," rather than " to arrange the transfer of this consignment from Berlin to this country."[41] The court did not consider that such a distinction between the mere receiving and the complete forwarding operation made any difference to the forwarder's liability. The sole question in such a case is exactly what duties has the forwarder undertaken to do? If in contracting to act for the shipper he undertakes more than the sending agent has requested him to do on the former's behalf, he will be liable to the shipper for failing to exercise reasonable care and skill in undertaking that task. In other words at common law he cannot limit his liability merely to the extent of the duties undertaken for the sending forwarder.

83 Change of principal

Thirdly, a problem arises where a forwarder ceases to be the agent of one party and instead becomes that of the other party. As Branson J. said, "there is no reason in commonsense why the same forwarding agents should not, up to a point, act as agents for the sellers and then turn themselves, at the request of the purchasers, into agents for the purchasers."[42] The difficulty is that it is not always clear as to the exact time when this occurs, and whether it in fact ever takes place. For example, a forwarder may be employed by a seller to arrange the transit of goods and be instructed to inquire from the buyer prior to the arrival of the ship, where he requires delivery to be made. If the latter instructs the forwarder to warehouse them pending further instructions, the question can arise as to whom the forwarder represents in so doing, the

---

[40] [1951] 2 Lloyd's Rep. 462 at p. 466.

[41] *Ibid.* at p. 466, *per* Somervell L.J.

[42] *Johann Plischke & Sohne G.m.b.H.* v. *Allison Bros. Ltd.* (1936) 55 Ll.L.Rep. 262 at p. 264. The question of successive agencies was discussed in *Julian Praet & Cie. S.A.* v. *H. G. Poland Ltd.* [1962] 1 Lloyd's Rep. 566, with respect to an insurance agent acting on behalf of one company and then instead becoming the agent of another company. Mocatta J. distinguished the position where an agent acts on behalf of two principals at the same time, from the position where acts are performed by the agent during the existence of Agency A, which in fact relate to Agency B, which is not to operate until Agency A is terminated, such acts not being themselves breaches of Agency A. Hence in such a case as *Praet's* where a broker changed insurers, the court held that there was no duty upon the agent to disclose to his principal that he proposed to do something constituting a breach of contract. Where, however, an agent acts in a dual capacity, that is he accepts employment from another principal which is inconsistent with his duty to the first principal, " he must make the fullest disclosure to both principals of his interest, and obtain the consent of each of them to his double employment ": *ibid.*

buyer or the seller. On the answer to this question will depend whether the seller can still validly exercise his right of stoppage in transit or not.[43] If the forwarder has not been authorised expressly or impliedly by the seller to store the goods, and incur warehouse charges, they can only do so as the agents of the buyer.[44] Accordingly, the right of stoppage in transit will be lost on so doing, as transit will have come to an end.[45]

84   Forwarder acting for merchant and carrier

Fourthly, as discussed in the last chapter, the intermediary in transport may often act simultaneously both for the consignor or consignee and the carrier. In such a case it will be necessary to distinguish his functions both as a forwarder or receiving agent and those as a ship's agent or loading broker, in order to ascertain for whom he is acting in respect of any given action.[46] The question was raised in the pleadings in *C. A. Pisani & Co. Ltd.* v. *Brown Jenkinson & Co. Ltd.*[47] where the plaintiffs, marble importers, sued the defendants for negligent damage to a shipment of marble which was carried in two separate ships. The defendants were both forwarders and ship's agents in respect of one of the ships in question. They put forward two defences claiming either to be the plaintiffs' agents to arrange the clearance and landing of the marble, or alternatively that they were acting as agents for the second defendants who were the stevedores responsible for the loss. Further they claimed that they discharged the slabs as agents for the owners of the ship under the terms of the bill of lading. In the eventuality, the court decided that the defendants were forwarders acting on behalf of the importers and as the damage occurred mainly while the goods were still aboard ship, they were not liable.[48] The court also expressed doubt as to whether the defendants could be held liable in any case as they were merely acting in the capacity of forwarders.[49]

This duality of function can create particular difficulty for the forwarder in relation to the transfer of documents of title. If therefore he expedites a shipment at the request of his principal the consignee, and fails to demand freight, the result may be that his other principal, the

---

[43] *Ibid.*

[44] *Cf.* Cl. 5, S.T.C.

[45] *i.e.* under Sale of Goods Act 1893, s. 45 (2), transit ends as soon as the goods are held by the forwarder as agent for the buyer. See also cases discussed in note 37 above.

[46] *Heskell* v. *Continental Express Ltd.* (1950) 83 Ll.L.Rep. 438. See Chapter 2 above. See also *Kershaw* v. *British Rhineland Nav. Co.* (1922) 10 Ll.L.Rep. 128. As to road carriage see *Lee Cooper Ltd.* v. *C. H. Jeakins & Sons Ltd.* [1964] 1 Lloyd's Rep. 300.

[47] (1939) 64 Ll.L.Rep. 340. See also *Maynards, Walker & Co.* v. *Southey* (1867) 5 Searles Rep. 325 (S. Africa).

[48] *Cf. Ebrahim* v. *B.I.S.N.* [1928] S.S.L.R. 14, where it was held that a landing agent is the agent or servant of the shipowner and that he remained so until the bill of lading was exhausted by delivery according to the exigency of its terms. He was therefore covered by the exemption clauses in the bill of lading in respect of damage to cargo which resulted during a storm when the goods were in the agent's lighters—the agent did not take " delivery " himself.

[49] However, there is nothing to prevent a forwarder from being held liable in the capacity of ship's agent if either the bill of lading does not protect him, or else he is subject to a statutory liability in receiving and discharging cargo from a ship: *Keith Ramsay* v. *Bing Harris & Co. Ltd.* [1925] N.Z.L.R. 1230.

carrier, for whom he is acting as ship's agent, loses his right of lien. Consequently the forwarder may find himself liable to the carrier for the freight, and not reimbursed by the consignee. In such a case, providing he has expressly or impliedly been authorised to pay freight or else the carrier has ceded his right of action to him, he will be able to recover from the consignee. An example of such a cession occurred in the South African case of *Mitchell Cotts* v. *Commissioner for Railways* [50] where the plaintiffs were shipping and landing agents acting in a dual capacity both for consignee and shipowner. The court held that the plaintiffs were not personally liable for freight as they did not hold the bill of lading for value, but simply as an agent for the defendants who had claimed delivery through them and had asked for the goods to be expedited. Consequently they were able to recover from the owner of the goods under their ceded rights.

Finally, where a forwarder is acting both on behalf of a shipper and as ship's agent, if the question arises as to whether reasonable notice of standard trading conditions has been given to a shipper, it will be no defence for the shipper to plead that although the agent has acquired knowledge of them, it was not acquired in the course of their agency on behalf of the shipper, but long before.[51] The shipper will therefore be bound by the knowledge of the forwarder of any Dock Regulations, etc., which the latter has obtained during previous dealings with the Dock Board.[52]

85
(iv) *Conclusion*

From the preceding discussions it can be seen that although a forwarder may consider himself to be acting as the agent of a particular party or of both parties, such a relationship may only exist in the general commercial sense of the word, and in fact he may find himself personally liable as a principal, as in *Harris's* case.[53] Conversely, another party to a transaction, whether shipper or carrier, may find himself laid defenceless, if the forwarder whom he may consider to be acting as his agent, is treated in the eyes of the law as a principal, as in *Lee Cooper's* case.[54] Neither do Standard Trading Conditions offer any assistance on this point, as by their failure to state categorically whether the forwarder is in fact acting as an agent or principal, they do not control this aspect of the relationship between shipper, forwarder and third parties, to any significant degree. Such a relationship will therefore vary from one transaction to another and even from one particular aspect of a transaction to another. Only by investigating the specific dealings of the parties and then applying common law principles to them can the exact relationship of the parties be established.[55]

[50] [1905] T.S. 349.
[51] *Pedro Roca & Co.* v. *British Transport Commission* [1954] 2 Lloyd's Rep. 591 at p. 598.
[52] *Ibid.*
[53] See Chapter 11.
[54] *Ibid.*
[55] See Cl. 1, S.T.C.

3. THE CONTRACT OF COMMISSION IN THE CIVIL LAW

86   (i) *Definition*

Whereas at common law no distinction is drawn between commercial and non-commercial transactions or persons, in all civil law countries a sharp distinction is usually drawn between them, resulting either in a separate commercial code or special provision in the civil code for such matters. For the purpose of classification, it is convenient to divide the civil law jurisdictions into three distinct groups. First, the French group, which includes Belgium and Holland. Secondly, the German group, which includes Switzerland and to some extent the Scandinavian countries. Thirdly, Spain and Italy, who do not fit very clearly into either of the two other groups.

Provision is made in civil law systems for the ordinary agent under the heading of mandate, which governs the relationships of parties where there is direct representation, that is, where the agent acts in the name of his principal when contracting with third parties.[56] Such provisions will almost always be found in the civil code or code of obligations and govern both non-commercial and commercial relationships. At common law such relationships are covered by the normal agency provisions and rules found in the case law. Unlike the common law though, a special category of commercial intermediary is generally recognised under the civil law which is called the contract of commission.[57] This contract is only applicable to certain categories of commercial agent whom the law specifically permits to contract in such a form. Generally this covers those independent intermediaries on the various exchanges and commodity markets who buy and sell commodities or services, etc. However, in a number of civil law jurisdictions a special category of commission has been created under the name of the Contract of Commission de Transport or Spediteur, dependent upon the linguistic group in question.[58]

87 **Contract of commission**

Commission is a contract of indirect representation, under which the essential characteristics are that the commissionnaire acts in his own name for the account of his principal. In other words he is in the position of an agent in relation to his principal, the consignor or consignee, and a principal in relation to the carrier. He is defined in Article 94 of the French Code de Commerce as "celui qui agit en son propre nom ou sous un nom social pour le compte d'un commettant." The Belgian Code de Commerce defines him in identical words.[59] Under neither code

---

[56] See § 93.

[57] For a general discussion on the subject see J. Hamel, *Contrat de commission*, 1949; Baumbach-Duden, *Handel-gesetzbuch*, 1968.

[58] The following are the principal terms in use: France—Commissionniare de transport or Commissionnaire-expéditeur; Germany—Spediteur; Belgium—Commissionnaire-expéditeur; Italy—Speditioniere; Spain—Comisionista de transportes; Holland—Expediteur; Scandinavia—Speditör.

[59] Liv. I, Tit. VII, Art. 12, C.com. (Belgium); *cf.* Holland, below.

is the commissionnaire de transport specifically defined as such though, although at least in the French code there are additional provisions as to his duties which are supplementary to those applicable to the contract of commission generally.[60]

88 Germany

The German HGB does define the forwarder however as "a person who in regular course of his trade undertakes the forwarding of goods by the agency of carriers by land or sea in his own name but for the account of another,"[61] and provides rules supplementary to those on commission generally, which will otherwise apply.[62] The Dutch commercial code likewise defines the forwarder as "somebody who occupies himself with arranging the carrying of merchandise and goods by land and by water."[63] Otherwise most of the provisions on forwarding are the same as those in the French and Belgian codes referred to above.[64]

89 Switzerland

The Swiss provisions are similar to the HGB except that they are found in the Code des Obligations, together with a similar specific provision that the forwarder is to be remunerated, which is merely implied in the other codes.[65] The forwarder is subject to both the general rules on agency in Articles 399–406 C.O. which are supplemented by the rules on commission in Articles 425–438 C.O. There are no special provisions governing the forwarder otherwise.

90 Italy

Italy similarly defines the forwarder or speditioniere, but without any reference to remuneration. No provision existed in the former Italian commercial code in respect of the forwarder, the present provisions being introduced in the new Civil Code in 1942.[66] In addition to these special provisions governing forwarding, the general rules relating to mandate also apply.[67] The Spanish commercial code makes provision similar to the French Code, merely making the forwarder subject to the general rules on commission,[68] together with supplementary rules relating to forwarding, but without specifically defining the forwarder as such.[69]

---

[60] Arts. 96–120, C.com. (France). In the case of Belgium there are only the ordinary provisions covering all contracts of commission—Liv. I, Tit. VII, Arts. 12–15, C.com. See Fredericq, *Traité de droit commercial Belge*, Vol. I, p. 306.
[61] Art. 407, HGB. The identical provision is found in the Austrian HGB.
[62] Arts. 383–406, HGB; Arts. 407–415, HGB. In particular Arts. 388–390, HGB, which deal with the receipt, safe-keeping and insurance of goods.
[63] Art. 86, Com.C. (Holland).
[64] Arts. 86–90, Com.C. (Holland).
[65] Art. 439, C.O.; Art. 409, HGB.
[66] Arts. 1737–1741, C.C. (Italy).
[67] Arts. 1703–1730, C.C. (Italy).
[68] Arts. 244–280, Codigo Com. (Spain).
[69] Art. 378, Codigo Com. (Spain).

91 Scandinavia

Finally, in Scandinavia there are no unified laws relating to forwarding, such as were proposed in 1912 in respect of the contract of commission, the reason given being that to draft such provisions would require the existence of a uniform set of rules relating to bills of lading as a necessary prerequisite, which did not exist at that time. Only in Denmark is the forwarder given a statutory definition.[70] In none of the Scandinavian countries is there any proper statutory regulation of the forwarding trade as such.[71]

92 Commissionnaire acts in his own name

In all cases it is a requirement that the forwarder must contract in his own name, except Scandinavia, Holland and Spain.[72] Under Dutch law, the expediteur is treated under a separate head from the commissionnaire, and there is no requirement that the former must act in his own name.[73] However, it appears that the forwarder will normally contract in his own name. Under Article 86, C.com., anyone who occupies[74] himself with arranging the carrying of merchandise and goods by land or water is considered to be a forwarder, although if he does contract in his own name important rights will attach which he would otherwise not possess. Similarly, under Spanish law the forwarder can act either in the name of his principal or else in his own name,[75] as can any other category of comisionista, the forwarder being governed by the general rules relating to the contract of commission, which permit this.[76] However, if the forwarder does intend to contract in the name of his principal, this intention must be clearly manifest. In a case of doubt, he will be considered to have contracted in his own name.[77]

93 Commissionnaire and broker

Generally, therefore, if a forwarder does not act in his own name he will be treated only as a broker, and not subject to the contract of commission, who merely acts as an intermediary to establish privity of contract between the shipper and the carrier, and who only signs a

---

[70] Naeringsloven, Art. 61. Northern Forwarding Conditions give the following definition: " The task of the Forwarding Agent is to attend against remuneration for the account of clients but in his own name, to the transportation of goods and everything connected therewith. . . .": Art. 1.

[71] The Speditör must be distinguished from the Ekspeditör who is an intermediary between shipper and carrier, who regularly concludes freight contracts for the account of and in the name of shipping companies, and who accepts and delivers goods on the latter's behalf, and takes care of them before and after transit. In other words he is a loading broker, although he may in fact also act on occasion on behalf of the shipper as a forwarder. See § 125.

[72] Art. 94, C.com. (France); Liv. I, Tit. VII, Art. 12, C.com. (Belgium); Art. 407, HGB (Germany); Art. 439, C.O. (Switzerland); Art. 1737, C.C. (Italy).

[73] Arts. 86–90, Com.C. (Holland); see note 63 above.

[74] *Cf.* Art. 415, HGB, which expressly provides that the rules on forwarding will apply to any merchant forwarding goods by land or sea for another in his own name, even if he does not ordinarily do so, but merely does so on one occasion.

[75] Art. 245, Codigo Com. (Spain).

[76] Arts. 244–280, Codigo Com. The only special provision appears in Art. 378, whereby the forwarder must keep a register of the goods which he forwards.

[77] Art. 247, Codigo Com.

contract in his own name if he is specially authorised to do so by the shipper. Consequently if a forwarder contracts with a carrier in the name of his principal, it is assumed that he is acting under a simple contract of mandate.[78] It is interesting to note however that the legal require- ment that the forwarder must act in his own name is under no circum- stances an essential element of the forwarder's commercial practice. In any case, in common law countries the forwarder is subject to the ordinary laws of agency which do not recognise any such distinction between mandate and commission, so that law and practice are more closely *ad idem*. The reason for this anachronism in civil law countries seems to be that the forwarder has traditionally been considered as a particular species of commission.[79] Consequently, the rules of commis- sion, which have generally developed in relation to the buying and sell- ing of goods in markets where it is common for the principal's name not to be revealed, have also been applied to the forwarder.[80] In practice, however, it is common for the shipper and the carrier to be aware of each other's identity, and there is little commercial reason in practice why this should not be so. In the present state of the law though, this is one of the most noticeable distinctions between the common law and civil law relating to freight forwarding.

(ii) *Privity of Contract*

94 Position at common law

The position at common law is that where an agent contracts on behalf of his principal, whether named or unnamed, the latter will acquire all contractual rights in relation to third parties with whom his agent has contracted for him. Where however an agent has contracted in his own name and has not disclosed that he is a mere agent, the third party will have a right to elect whether to hold the later disclosed princi- pal liable or the agent himself.[81] In other words, whether privity of contract is created between principal and third party will depend upon which way the latter elects. If he elects to hold the agent liable, the posi- tion will be similar to that existing under the normal contract of com- mission.[82] However, there is nothing at common law to preclude the simultaneous existence of privity of contract between the agent and the third party in addition to that normally existing between principal and third party.[83] Conversely though, by usage or custom the agent may be placed in sole privity in relation to the third party, while still remaining

---

[78] *Cf.* Art. 94, C.com. (France). See below.

[79] E. Georgiades, " Erreurs d'interprétation et de qualification de la jurisprudence en matière de commission de transport," Rev.dr.franc.comm., maritime et fiscal 1931, p. 113.

[80] The Communist forwarding bodies appear to perpetuate this rule—*cf.* Art. 2, General Conditions of Yugoslav International Forwarders, Belgrade, 1970.

[81] See D. J. Hill, " Some Problems of the Undisclosed Principal " [1967] J.B.L. 122.

[82] *Ibid.* at p. 125.

[83] See D. J. Hill, " The Commission Merchant at Common Law," (1968) 31 M.L.R. 623, note 37; *Sobell Industries* v. *Cory Bros.* [1955] 2 Lloyd's Rep. 82, *per* McNair J.

as an agent in relation to his principal, again creating a relationship analogous to the civil law contract of commission.[84]

95 Position under the civil law

The position under the civil law however is both less flexible and at the same time more complex as regards the legal position of the forwarder, particularly as a result of the special contractual implications arising out of the bill of lading or consignment note under certain codes. The essential characteristic of the normal contract of commission is that no privity of contract will be created by the commissionnaire between his principal and the third party. As regards the commissionnaire de transport, the position is not so clear.

96 France

For instance, under the French Code de Commerce considerable doubt as to the correct position has been caused by the provision in Article 101, whereby the "lettre de voiture" is deemed to create a contract between the shipper and the carrier, or between the shipper, the commissionnaire and the carrier. The shipper therefore acquires direct rights against the carrier under the contract which the commissionnaire has concluded on his behalf with the carrier, and can therefore sue him direct if he so wishes.[85]

Ripert is of the opinion that the Code in fact regards the forwarder as both agent and carrier, with the result that he has been deemed liable both for the actual carriage as well as those activities directly carried out by him.[86] This confusion between the forwarder and the carrier seems to have permeated the French jurisprudence, and it should be noted that at one stage during the nineteenth century the commissionnaire de transport was considered to be no different from a carrier except in name.[87] French law therefore appears to ignore the essential function of the forwarder, that is, to interpose himself between two principals as an intermediary, thus freeing the shipper of all the problems of arranging transportation, under which premise it can be argued that litigation should be possible against the commissionnaire alone. This situation does not affect the relationship existing between the commissionnaire and the carrier, which is the same as that existing between a shipper and carrier where no commissionnaire has interposed himself. It must also be remembered that the carrier himself may be treated as an intermediate agent in so far as he undertakes to deliver the goods to a successive carrier.[88]

---

[84] *Ibid.*
[85] The shipper need not be named in the lettre de voiture—Civ., Dec. 1, 1896, S., 1897. I.189, D., 1897.I.561. Moreover, although not a party to the contract of carriage, the consignee, by benefiting from the "stipulation pour autrui" which the shipper is supposed to make on his behalf, will also have a right of action against the carrier—V. Civ., sect. com., Feb. 1, 1955, D. 1956. 338, note by M. Durand.
[86] Ripert, *Traité élémentaire de droit commercial*, Paris, 1948, pp. 879–881.
[87] See § 103.
[88] *i.e.* the transitaire—see § 110.

97   The provisions in Article 101 of the French Commercial Code are not found elsewhere. No such provision is found in either the Dutch Commercial Code [89] or in the Belgian Commercial Code, under which no direct relationship is established between the shipper and the carrier, [90] although in the latter case certain jurists claim that the shipper can take action directly against the carrier.

98 Germany

Turning to the German HGB, no privity of contract will exist between the shipper and the carrier. If in the event of a claim by the shipper no tortious liability can be established against the carrier, the shipper's only rights will be against the Spediteur. Even if the consignee is in fact the owner of the goods he must generally sue the shipper, who will in turn sue the Spediteur. In this connection though, the latter may be able to argue that the shipper has suffered no damage himself, as, for example, if the shipper has fulfilled his contractual obligation by delivering the goods to the Spediteur in good condition. However the courts have decided that in such a case the shipper can still claim damages from the Spediteur on behalf of the buyer, assuming that the shipper is also contracting in the interests of third parties, and thus adopting their interests as his own. [91] As regards the actual relationship between the Spediteur and the carrier, this will depend upon the particular contract of carriage.

99 Switzerland

Switzerland follows the German provisions closely, no privity being created between shipper and carrier. Similar provisions are also found in the Italian and Spanish Codes, although the latter makes a special provision not found elsewhere, whereby the commissionnaire, when acting in his own name, will be jointly responsible with the carrier in respect of such obligations as would fall upon the latter in respect of carriage by sea or land. [92]

100 Rights of action

Where no privity exists between the parties, as under the German HGB, only if the forwarder becomes bankrupt or cedes his rights to the shipper can a direct action be brought by the latter. This rule seems of general application [93] except under the Italian Code [94] the shipper can substitute himself for the forwarder, and the Swiss Code des Obligations

---

[89] The Dutch courts have held that if a shipper wishes to sue the carrier he can only do so if the forwarder assigns his rights to him. See W. Snijders, " De Expediteur als tussenpersoon bij zeevervoer en de positie van de cognossementshouder," *Rechtsgeleerd Magazijn Themis*, Aflevering 1969 no. I.

[90] Gand, June 17, 1882, P.1883.II.8.

[91] Entscheidungen des Bundesgerichtshofs in Zivilsachen, Band 40. 91. See also E. J. Cohn, *Manual of German Law*, Vol. 1, 2nd ed. (1968), p. 107.

[92] Art. 246, Codigo Com. (Spain); Art. 275, Codigo Com. (Spain).

[93] This rule seems to have extended beyond Europe. N.B. In Japan no right of action exists except by cession—Art. 559, Com.C.—Sup. Ct., June 21, 1907.

The question of a right of direct action against the carrier is discussed in " Réponses parvenues à la date de 15 Juin, 1957, au questionnaire adressé aux experts consultés par l'Institut "—U.D.P. 195 Etudes XXXVI, Commission de Transport—Doc. 19.

[94] Arts. 1705, 1737, C.C. (Italy).

where those rights possessed by the forwarder against the carrier will be automatically transferred to the shipper as soon as he has discharged his contractual duties to his agent the forwarder.[95] However, it is possible for this restriction to be overcome contractually, as under the German forwarding conditions whereby the forwarder undertakes to cede his rights against third parties to his principal at the latter's request, unless the forwarder himself by special agreement undertakes to enforce the claims at his principal's expense and risk.[96]

101   Forwarder contracting in his principal's name

Up till now the position of the forwarder who contracts in his own name has been the subject of discussion. What however is the position of the forwarder who contracts in the name of his principal the shipper? It seems that under all civil law systems in such a case two consequences will result. First, privity of contract will be established directly between the shipper and the carrier. In other words it will be a contract of direct representation, the forwarder not being a party to the contract at all.[97] Secondly, the forwarder's relationship with the carrier will be governed by the rules of mandate alone, or else by a contract of work or service, and not by the rules of commission.[98] In this respect however the position under French law requires special consideration. Under the normal contract of commission the fact that the commissionnaire has contracted in his principal's name will enable him to hide behind his principal under the normal rules of mandate.[99] However, the fact that a commissionnaire de transport contracts in his principal's name appears to have little effect on his position in relation to the carrier owing to the provision in Article 101, C.com., whereby the bill of lading is deemed to constitute a contract between all three parties.[1] Hamel states that there is no "rideau de fer dans la commission de transport,"[2] consequently the forwarder's relationship with the carrier will remain the same in both cases, as will that of the shipper and the carrier, who are already in direct contractual relationship as a result of Article 101 discussed above.[3] Similarly, the forwarder's obligation to his principal will remain the same whether the former contracts in his own name or not, except that whereas under other systems the del credere guarantee is voluntary in all cases, under French law the commissionnaire de transport is subject to a mandatory guarantee subject to contractual limitation.[4]

---

[95] Arts. 439, 425, 401, C.O. (Swiss). The Turkish Code follows suit. *Cf.* Art. 1705, C.C. (Italy).

[96] Art. 52 (*a*), A.D.S.P. and A.Ö.S.P. (Austria). *Cf.* Art. 11 (5), D.F.C.

[97] See Hamel, *op. cit.*, at pp. 8–10. Angers, March 17, 1936, Gaz.Pal., 1936.II.11. Van Ryn, *Principes de Droit commercial*, s. 1849, where other useful references are given.

[98] Liv. I., Tit. VII., Art. 13, C.com. (Belgium). Art. 675, BGB (Germany).

[99] Art. 94, C.com. (France).

[1] Rodière, *Droit des transports*, s. 1331.   [2] Hamel, *op. cit.*, p. 17.

[3] Art. 94, C.com. Another instance of confusion results from the arrete of June 29, 1942, making the courtier de fret liable for loading, insurance and non-delivery of goods shipped under a connaissement fluvial, thus giving him the responsibilities of a commissionnaire de transport in this respect—Rodière, *op. cit.*, s. 531.

[4] Art. 98, C.com. For the duties of the forwarder in Scandinavia see the judgment of the Sup.Ct. of Norway, Dec. 1933 (*Neils P. Hoyer & Son A/S* v. *And. Smith*).

102

(iii) *The Forwarder as a Carrier*

In the normal course of forwarding operations the situation will probably arise under which a forwarder may wish, or be forced, to effect a
contract of carriage, or at least part of it, by his own means of transport.
The question therefore arises as to his exact legal status in so doing, and
whether in fact he is free to do so. Consequently, the various codes all
recognise the rights of the parties to regulate such a situation in the
forwarding contract, but with some variation from code to code.
Where carriage is not performed by a third party, but by the forwarder
himself, two possibilities can arise. First the law may consider him as
still possessing the status of a forwarder simultaneously in respect of
certain ancillary functions which he performs. Alternatively he may be
treated as a carrier in all respects.

103 France

For a long time, considerable confusion existed in French juristic
writings as to the distinction between the carrier and the commissionnaire de transport, as many writers during the nineteenth century took
the view that the difference between them was merely a matter of terminology, and was not of any practical effect as to their respective legal
positions.[5] The problem has largely arisen because in practice the carrier
often acts as a commissionnaire in respect of part of the transit, and
conversely the commissionnaire de transport may often act as a
carrier in respect of part or all of the transit without any change of
name or designation.

The distinction however is not merely one of legal theory. This point
was clearly made in a judgment by the Cour d'appel de Lyon,[6] where
it was held that:

"Le voiturier exécute un fait purement matériel et se borne a
vehiculer et déplacer des marchandises, tandis que le commissionnaire, d'après la définition de l'article 94 du Code de commerce,
agit pour le compte du commettant et fait des actes juridiques pour
lui, son rôle étant de soigner un transport. Il opère non par ses
propres moyens, mais emploie les services de différents voituriers
. . . avec lesquels il passe des contrats. La qualité de commissionnaire se distingue et se caractérise par la complexité des opérations
effectuées, l'absence de règlement après chacune d'elles. . . . "

In other words, the carrier is responsible for the physical execution of
transit, the commissionnaire for the legal execution thereof.

104 Transporteur mixte

Even so, with the complexity of modern transportation methods, it
has not proved easy to categorise all acts and intermediaries engaged in
transporting or arranging the transportation of goods. A particularly

---

[5] Rodière, " Etudes sur la commission de transport: ler étude: La définition de la commission de transport de marchandises," Rev.trim.dr.com., 1957, p. 1.
[6] March 13, 1953: S. 1933, 2, 45; D.P. 1933, 2, 60; Rodière, *Droit des transports*, Vol. 3,
ss. 1324 *et seq.*

difficult example in French law is found in the transporteur mixte, who engages in the carriage of goods by road and rail as a regular method of combined transportation.[7] In practice moreover he rarely actually effects any part of the road/rail transit himself. Consequently he has been compared to the commissionnaire on the principle that he fulfils the same function as one, and at the most, merely effects the initial road transit to the rail head, which may be but an insignificant part of the complete transit.

Such an assimilation of the transporteur mixte and the commissionnaire de transport has however been rejected by the jurists as being fallacious.[8] Where a shipper contracts with a commissionnaire de transport, he is generally indifferent as to the means of transportation utilised to carry out the transit. The intention of the shipper is merely to enter into a contract of commission de transport, and not into a contract of transport proper. In the case of the transporteur mixte though, the shipper intends to, and does in fact, enter into a contract of transport with the former, who is a road carrier duly inscribed in the relevant transport register.[9] The mere fact that the latter may not carry out the actual transportation or part thereof himself does not concern the shipper, and does not therefore affect the creation of a contract of transport between the transporteur mixte and the shipper. Furthermore, the commissionnaire de transport is subject to a system of licensing as a commissionnaire, which does not apply to the operations of the transporteur mixte unless he also wishes to operate as one in addition to his other operations.[10]

---

[7] See § 110.

[8] Peyrefitte, *Les transports mixtes rail route*, 1962, pp. 196–197.

[9] See Chapter 4 as to the statutory provisions relating to carriers.

[10] See Chapter 4. There has been a dispute among the jurists as to whether the true legal status of the transporteur mixte, although that of a voiturier principally, is secondarily in the position of a commissionnaire chargeur to whom Art. 99, C.com., applies, on the ground that " where there are several carriers, the one necessarily plays the role of a commissionnaire "—*per* Josserand, *Les transports*, s. 709. Rodière, however, disagrees with this view on the grounds that such a relationship need not automatically result where there are successive carriers, that is, several carriers each in turn carrying out part of the transit. See note 6.
  It appears that a distinction can be drawn between the transporteur mixte and the commissionnaire on the grounds that the former does not of necessity use another carrier as a substitute for him, as he has legal authority as a carrier (as a transporteur public de zone longue) to carry to all points within the country. The latter, however, must perforce use the services of another carrier, for instance where a road or rail forwarder is required to forward overseas. As Rodière points out, the key to the distinction lies in the " connaissance de la substitution " by the shipper in the case of the commissionnaire de transport: Rodière, " Etudes sur la commission de transport, 2ième étude: La responsabilité du commissionnaire de transport en marchandises," Rev.trim.dr.com., 1957, p. 535. In other words, although the latter has accepted responsibility for the whole " deplacement " the former has clear knowledge and realisation that another party will actually effect the transit.
  It has also been put forward that the fact that there is a disparity of objects between the contracts entered into by the transporteur mixte with the shipper and the carrier respectively, that is, between a " corps certain " and " un chose de genre," does not allow the former to be equated with the commissionnaire de transport, and that he will therefore not be subject to Art. 101, C.com., which would otherwise create a single contract between all three parties. See Peyrefitte, *op.cit.* His intervention as an intermediary in transportation is not therefore an " interposition fictive," unlike that of the commissionnaire de transport between the shipper and the carrier, so that the

105 Status of forwarder who carries goods

There have been considerable differences of opinion between the jurists and the courts as to the position of the commissionnaire where he also acts as a carrier during the execution of the forwarding contract. Two possible theories have been put forward. First, to consider what is the principal function of the commissionnaire. In other words it can be argued that the contract of commission cannot be subdivided, and that any ancillary carriage which may be effected is merely one aspect of the whole.[11] Alternatively, it may be considered necessary to analyse and separate the successive functions of the commissionnaire, allocating them in turn either to the latter category or to that of a carrier, with the consequence that instead of one contract existing, there will in fact be two distinct ones entered into between the parties, with differing rights and liabilities in each case.[12] In practice however the two theories are not in conflict with each other to any marked degree, the courts having adopted both theories on different occasions, depending upon the situation in the particular circumstances.[13]

106 Germany

Similarly under German law the forwarder can also undertake the carriage of goods himself in performance of the forwarding contract provided he is not excluded by the terms of his contract from so doing. In such a case he will be treated as being both a Spediteur and a carrier simultaneously, his status depending on the particular function which he is actually performing at the time.[14] This rule is similar to the second of the two theories discussed in relation to the commissionnaire de transport under French law in the preceding paragraph. Switzerland apparently follows the same rule, as Article 439, C.O., provides that as regards the actual carriage of goods by the forwarder under a forwarding contract, relations will also be subject to the provisions governing the carriage of goods in Articles 440–457, C.O. Under Italian law if the forwarder, even though acting under his mandate, actually effects carriage himself, he will be treated purely as a carrier.[15] Similarly in the case of Spain, although here express permission to carry is required under Article 267, Codigo Com. In Scandinavia although there is no express provision on the matter, it will depend upon either contractual authority, express or implied, being given or else on custom, as to whether the forwarder can actually carry or not.[16]

distinction although very fine in practice is one of practical consequence in determining the rules of law applicable when a dispute arises.

[11] Paris, April 26, 1941, Gaz. Pal.; 1941.II.28. P. Bailly in Hamel, *op. cit.* at p. 249, and *Anselme Dewavrin Fils et Cie* v. *Wilsons and N.E. Ry. Shipping Co. Ltd.,* § 128.
[12] Civ. cass. May 9, 1944, S., 1945.1.22. and note P.L.P. Bull. transp., 1945.16.
[13] Rodière, *op. cit.,* s. 1326.
[14] Art. 412, HGB. *Cf.* Art. 327, Com.C. (Japan), which makes a similar provision.
[15] Art. 1741, C.C. (Italy).
[16] As in other jurisdictions the distinction between commissionnaire and carrier has proved a difficult one; see judgments of the Commercial and Maritime Ct. of Copenhagen, Oct. 2, 1945 (*De Private Assurander* v. *Fr. Christiansen*), and Sept. 24, 1946 (*Handels Co. Nordropa* v. *Paul Lehmann*). However Art. 18, N.F.C., provides that

107 Belgium

In the case of Belgium [17] a distinction must be drawn between the commissionnaire de transport (affréteur routier) who is assimilated to the carrier by statute, their obligations being the same, and the commissionnaire-expéditeur.[18] The difference lies in the fact that the commissionnaire de transport undertakes to transport the goods himself,[19] though not with his own transport, whereas the commissionnaire-expéditeur undertakes merely to forward in his own name for the account of his principal.[20] The latter's function is a comprehensive one, all his functions being part of the contract of commission, and not separate ones, that is, of commission, bailment and carriage.[21] Both are now defined by Article I of the law of June 26, 1967.

108 In practice though the forwarder may limit his liability by means of his trading conditions contractually, irrespective of whether he is in fact acting as a commissionnaire, broker or carrier. This however is subject to any limitations which the law may impose upon him in attempting to restrict his liability to his client, particularly if he is in fact acting as a carrier. For instance, Dutch Forwarding Conditions provide that "Even in the event of taking over transport, the forwarding agent shall be liable under the present conditions and not as a carrier." [22]

109 Remuneration

The actual status of the forwarder will depend in certain circumstances upon the actual method whereby he is remunerated. If for example under Dutch law the forwarder contracts subject to an inclusive price covering all expenses, instead of by commission, he could be treated as a transport contractor (transport ondernemer)[23] who is distinguished from the actual carrier (vervoerder) who performs the carriage himself. In the case of carriage by sea though, the contractor

" When forwarding goods, the Forwarding Agent is not responsible as a carrier unless he himself executes the transportation." It seems that the German rule that the forwarder is liable as a carrier will apply in Finnish law, where the shipper has not been informed of the identity of the carrier. Alarick Hernberg, " Rättshandbok," s. 64.

[17] Fredericq, *op. cit.*, Vol. I, s. 180; Vol. 3, s. 375.

[18] Liv. I, Tit. VII *bis*, Arts. 2 *et seq.*

[19] It is because of these differences of terminology in Belgium that Unidroit has recommended that the formula " commission en matière de transport " be used instead of " commission de transport ": Commentary on the draft Convention relating to the International Forwarding of Goods, U.D.P. 1966—Études: XXXVI Comm. de Transport—Doc. 42.

[20] Comm. Anvers, March 8, 1952, J.P.A., 141. To confuse the issue though, in a decision of the Cour de Cassation of Nov. 5, 1936 (Pas., 1936, 1, 408), it appears that the court considered that the commissionnaire-expéditeur was a commissionnaire who acted in the name of the shipper, which is not true: Van Ryn, *op. cit.*, s. 1800. The distinction lies not in terminology used by the parties, but in the judicial nature of their duties—Hof van Beroep te Brusel, June 23, 1966 (1967) E.T.L., p. 1006.

[21] Brussels, July 14, 1933, J.P.A., 1934, 44. *Contra*: Brussels, July 3, 1954, J.P.A., 1955, 141.

[22] Art. 11 (6), D.F.C. *Cf.* Art. 33, C.G. (Belgium).

[23] *i.e.* where he offers an " all-in " tariff for carriage and auxiliary services. N.B. It appears that the transport ondernemer would not be liable for damage caused during the carriage—his position is not recognised by the Dutch Com.C. though, and there has been dispute as to whether he should be treated as a commissionnaire or as a carrier—Molengraaf, *Principes de droit commercial néerlandais*, 1931, p. 169.

may be treated as a carrier under the law of December 22, 1924, if he undertakes to effect carriage himself. No such regulation exists in the case of carriage by land though. The distinction is important, however, because like French law a distinction is drawn between the liability of the forwarder and the carrier.[24]

Under German law where the forwarder can simultaneously exist as a carrier at the same time, he will have a right to both the commission and the usual freight charges.[25] If however a forwarder charges a fixed rate to the shipper his rights and liabilities will be those of a carrier exclusively, in which case he cannot claim a forwarder's commission in the absence of an express stipulation.[26] Similarly if he consolidates the shipments of several shippers for carriage under a single contract, he will also be treated solely as a carrier, whether he has agreed to charge a fixed rate or not, although the charge actually made must be a reasonable one and no higher than the normal rate had the goods been forwarded separately, and again no commission is payable, unless there is an express stipulation to the contrary.[27] However the German forwarding conditions expressly provide that even where Articles 412 and 413 HGB apply, the forwarder's liability will still be subject to the limitations prescribed by the conditions.[28] Under French law however there are no such restrictions on the method of remuneration of the forwarder, who may either charge commission or a fixed sum.[29] The method of remuneration will not therefore affect the forwarder's status.

110

(iv) *Contrat de transit*

In addition to the commissionnaire de transport, French civil law acknowledges a further category of intermediary, the transitaire, whom it is necessary to distinguish carefully from the former, as the legal consequences resulting from the contract of transit differ from those of the contract of commission de transport to a considerable degree. Such a contract will arise where goods have to be re-forwarded to their destination and the shipper uses an intermediary who, for his account, will receive the goods and remit them to another carrier for onward transmission to their destination. The contract between the shipper and the intermediary is known as a " contrat de transit," although its juridical nature has proved of some difficulty for the jurists to establish. Where, for instance, a shipper contracts with an intermediary to re-forward for him in the shipper's name, the latter will be a mandataire ordinaire, and the contract merely one of mandat. If on the other hand the intermediary contracts to re-forward in his own name there may either be a contract of commission de transport or a contract of

---

[24] See Art. 11 (6), D.F.C., referred to in note 22 above.
[25] Art. 412, HGB.
[26] Art. 413 (1), HGB.
[27] Art. 413 (2), HGB.
[28] Art. 52 (c), A.D.S.P. and A.Ö.S.P.
[29] Hemard, *Les contrats commerciaux*, s. 718.

transit. The latter therefore only covers the situation where an inter-mediary called a transitaire receives goods on behalf of a shipper and re-forwards for the latter's account but in his own name. He is therefore a commissionnaire, *i.e.* acting in his own name for the account of his principal, but not a commissionnaire de transport.

111   Distinction between commissionnaire and transitaire

The distinction between the two lies in the fact that the former under-takes to effect a certain transit, but with the right not to carry himself but to substitute the actual carrier, while still retaining the duty to convey the goods to their destination. The transitaire, on the other hand, only undertakes to enter into a contract of transport for the shipper's account. The obligation here is not for the actual physical carriage, but to enter into what has been called " opérations juridiques," that is, the reception of the goods and a contract of re-expedition.[30] In practice of course, a transitaire may enter into a contract of commission de transport and vice versa, which is quite likely in practice as the inter-mediary in transportation usually fulfils many different functions. How-ever, the contracts are quite separate and must not be confused.[31] The duties of the transitaire are first to receive the goods, check them, and make any claims, etc., that may be necessary to prevent any right of recourse against the carrier being lost.[32] Where loss or damage has resulted, he must carry out any formalities which may be required for recovery against an insurer and inform his principal of the loss.[33] He will advise shippers as to the conditions of carriage and customs regulations, and will carry out customs formalities and discharge them in his name for the shippers' account.[34]

112   Re-expedition can be by any method. The transitaire must choose the method which is best for his principal if the decision is left to him. Otherwise he must forward by the method which he has been instructed to employ, in which case he will not be liable for any loss if he has fol-lowed his instructions.[35] He must conclude the freight contract under the usual conditions of the trade, with no exceptional clauses exempting a carrier or other party from liability. He must check the state of the packages, and is bound not to make any false declarations in relation to them. As on reception of the goods, he must carry out all necessary formalities for forwarding, customs, etc.[36] If so instructed, he must insure

[30] See Ripert, *Droit maritimes*, s. 2027–2033.
[31] Such confusion has occurred in the courts—Comp. Trib. Seine, June 7, 1950, D.M.F., 1951, p. 357 (Som.), which has tended to result in their responsibility being added to through equating them with a commissionnaire de transport.
[32] Le Havre, Jan. 12, 1925, Rev. ventes et transports 1925, p. 170.
[33] Cass. Req. July 8, 1924, Rev. ventes et transports 1925, p. 19.
[34] Where a transitaire has undertaken responsibility for customs dues he is given the privilège du trésor by subrogation, Cass. viv., March 23, 1915, D. 1917.1.63. By the law of June 25, 1920, a transitaire must hold a customs book initialled by a juge de paix.
[35] Aix, July 9, 1924, Dor. Sup., 2, 680.
[36] Rabat, Feb. 9, 1949, D.M.F. 1950, 611, Som.

with a reputable insurance company, and under the usual conditions.[37] If no instructions have been given by the shipper on the question of insurance, the case law is uncertain,[38] although the weight of opinion is in favour of the view that no obligation to insure exists, as if the transitaire in fact does so, he may be liable to the shipper for incurring unnecessary charges. This point will however be covered by Article 5 of Conditions Générales where the contract is entered into subject thereto, otherwise the common law will apply.[39]

If re-forwarding is not immediately carried out, the transitaire will be treated as a salaried dépositaire (bailee) and will be liable for any third party who may carry out this function for him. Similarly, if he fails to protect the goods properly against loss or damage, or if he retains them too long as a bailee before re-forwarding them.[40] The precedents differ as to whether the transitaire has a duty to insure during such a period of bailment or not.[41]

113   These general obligations discussed above, which have developed from the general trade usage of the transitaire when effecting a contract of transit, can be modified contractually, and the latter is bound to obey any instructions given by his principal at a later date, even if these modify those given in the original contract. The liability of the transitaire is based upon the non-execution of contractual obligations and in this respect, the problem may arise of the successful exemption of liability by the carrier while that of the transitaire remains. However, the latter is only liable for his own fault, unlike the commissionnaire de transport.   A shipowner or other carrier may on occasion himself act as a transitaire where he has been instructed by a shipper to re-forward after discharge of the shipment.[42] In an action, the transitaire is not subject to a one-year prescription period nor is he the subject of Article 435, C.com. (fin de non-recevoir), as any action will merely be subject to the common law. This will not apply however where a transitaire acts as a commissionnaire de transport.[43] The difficulty, however, in many cases is to decide whether in fact a transitaire has become a commissionnaire de transport or not—in this respect the question of remuneration may be of assistance in deciding the point as a commissionnaire de transport may agree to effect carriage for a fixed price, whereas the transitaire invariably undertakes receipt and expedition of goods in return for commission and reimbursements.[44]

[37] Cass. Civ., Nov. 6, 1929, Dor. Sup., 8, 100,—see Ripert, *Droit maritime*, Vol. 2, p. 914, note 6, and the cases listed therein.
[38] Marseilles, Jan. 24, 1923, J. Marseille, 1924, 1, 359—here a transitaire was admonished for not approaching his principal for instructions as marine insurance is usually obtained where a sea transit is effected.
[39] See Chapter 17.
[40] Rouen, March 27, 1923, Droit maritime française, 1923, 413.
[41] Cass. Civ., June 29, 1927, Dor. Sup., 5, 488.
[42] As to the problems arising in such circumstances see Ripert, *op. cit.*, s. 2027–2028.
[43] Paris, Feb. 7, 1933, Dor. Sup. 11, 157.   Numerous decisions relieve the transitaire of liability where there is no personal fault—Le Havre, Nov. 14, 1893, Rev.int.droit maritime, IX, 528.
[44] Rodière, *op. cit.*, s. 1370.

4. CONCLUSIONS

114 From the preceding discussion it can be clearly seen that the forwarder has a strongly contrasting position under the two systems of law. The key to the distinction is the differing approach to privity of contract between the various parties. The common law permits the forwarder to contract at will either as a mere agent or as an independent principal without losing his character as a forwarder, but it offers little guidance as to his correct status in any particular set of circumstances.[45] The principal reason for this is that the status of a forwarder does not depend upon the creation or non-creation of privity of contract by the forwarder between his client and the carrier.

115 Civil law

The civil law, on the other hand, places commercial relationships in strict categories, each subject to its particular sets of rights and liabilities.[46] In particular the vacillating approach of the common law on the question of indirect representation is markedly absent under the civil law, as the contract of commission is the cornerstone of the whole concept of commercial representation. The latter has given a legal form to the various forms of indirect representation which are commonplace in commercial transactions and in forwarding and allied operations in particular. Unlike the common law, the whole concept of the forwarder is based upon the principle that privity of contract will not be created between client and carrier by the forwarder. It is the absence of a native contract of commission at common law that has prevented the forwarder from achieving a firm juridical basis, although unconsciously such a concept has developed in respect of the commission merchant who engages in the buying and selling of goods.

It must be emphasised however that the mere existence of a contract of commission has not in itself solved the problem of finding a uniform status for the forwarder in different countries. Difficulties do occur in attempting to relate the various provisions in the different codes relating to the commissionnaire de transport, as not only does the terminology differ from one country to another, but the unfortunate del credere concept which imbues the French provisions has resulted in the forwarder and the carrier being constantly confused in a series of conflicting decisions in the case law.[47] This confusion has been avoided in the other codes, particularly those which are based on the German HGB.[48]

However the result of this confusion does mean that in practice it may not be any easier for the forwarder to establish his exact legal status under the civil law, particularly in France, than it is at present under the common law, with its completely *laissez-faire* spirit. In other

[45] See Section 2 of this chapter.
[46] See Section 3 of this chapter.
[47] See § 96.
[48] See § 98.

words a paradox has resulted whereby the very fact of the Continental lawyers attempting to formalise and provide for the various categories of commercial relationship in respect of the carriage of goods has been to some extent nullified by the complexity of trading relationships and practices in this field and has produced a similar state of uncertainty as at present faces the forwarding community in this country.

116   Unidroit

The recent attempt by Unidroit to prepare a draft Convention for the International Forwarding of Goods was intended to overcome some of these problems.[49] Unfortunately, however, the rapid development of containerisation and through carriage, together with the other rapid advances currently being made in the field of transportation techniques and the resultant uncertainty as to the ultimate form such developments will take, has rendered such conventions potentially obsolescent, and therefore the subject of some criticism among the forwarding community. It therefore seems that any attempt at unification of the rules relating to international forwarding will not bear fruit until there is greater stabilisation in the transport industry generally.

[49] U.P.L. 1965—Paper XXXVI, Forwarding Agency—Doc. 41.

CHAPTER 4

GOVERNMENTAL REGULATION AND THE
CONFLICT OF LAWS

1. GOVERNMENTAL REGULATION

117 THE forwarding industry, like other operational aspects of the transportation field, is one that may be capable of abuse and inefficient operation if not subjected to a uniform system of control. Consequently, in many countries where forwarding is carried on, some form of control of a governmental nature has been introduced. This is in addition to the regulation of customs clearance, which is discussed in another chapter, and which is invariably subjected to a licensing system, owing to the fiduciary nature of the work.[1]

118 United Kingdom

The notable exception where a large forwarding industry exists without any form of control is in the United Kingdom, where as yet no form of licensing or other restrictions have been placed upon the operations of the trade. The only form of control that does exist is that of the Institute of Freight Forwarders, which offers both a code of conduct and Standard Trading Conditions for its members, but as membership is not compulsory, it is possible for forwarding to be carried on by anyone who wishes to do so.

119 Commonwealth

No form of licensing exists in any of the Commonwealth countries in respect of forwarding operations either, but in the United States a very comprehensive system exists in respect of forwarding by land, sea and air, administered respectively by the Inter-state Commerce Commission, the Federal Maritime Commission and the Civil Aeronautics Board. Discussion of these organisations is outside the scope of this chapter.

120 Categories

In most European countries, in keeping with the civil law tendency to formalise all aspects of commercial enterprise, licensing and other forms of regulation have been introduced. These can be divided into two categories. First, those countries not subject to any special administrative licensing system for forwarders, other than that which may be applicable to any other form of business enterprise, but with specific civil law provisions in respect of forwarding operations and the rights and duties of those engaged in the trade. Secondly, those countries

[1] See Chapter 16.

[66]

which have both in addition, or as an alternative, an administrative system for the licensing of those wishing to practise as freight forwarders.

121 Belgium and Holland

The Netherlands does not make any special provision for the licensing of forwarders in respect of inland forwarders, whether by road, rail, inland waterways, or by sea. In Belgium a system of licensing for all auxiliaries in transport including forwarders was enacted by a law of June 26, 1967 (not as yet operative). The forwarder is also subject to the general provisions relating to the contract of commission in Liv. I, Tit. VII, C.com., which deals with the rights and duties of commissionnaires in relation to their clients. These rules apply to all forwarding operations whether by road, rail or water. Similar provisions are contained in Articles 86–90, C.com. of the Netherlands. In both countries there are also special provisions in respect of inland water transport. In the case of Belgium, an Act of May 5, 1936, regulates intermediaries concluding freight contracts by this means of transport and establishes their rate of remuneration. In the Netherlands, voyage-charters of inland waterway vessels are subject to special regulations, which provide that only brokers given Ministry of Transport approval as scheepsbevrachters can operate as such.[2]

122 Germany

Generally no licence is required in Germany. However, special regulations apply to the Abfertigungsspediteur, who is a special category of forwarder recognised by the Road Haulage Act who engages in forwarding by road.[3] In this case the forwarder is appointed by the senior land transport authority, and only those forwarders registered in the Commercial Register who are both experienced and financially reliable will be appointed. This appointment can be cancelled for various breaches of duty, especially concerning statutory trunk haulage offences. The Abfertigungsspediteur is entitled to remuneration from the road haulier, unlike the forwarder who does not hold such a position. However, both are entitled to a commission from their clients under Articles 407–415, HGB. The forwarder must be distinguished from the freight agent who acts either for the haulier or the shipper. The freight agent is entitled to remuneration from either the haulier or the shipper for procuring loads or space on a road vehicle, if such a function is exercised in the normal course of the agent's business.

123 France

In the second category, the French provisions for the licensing of forwarders are laid down in some detail, as are the Italian regulations also. The former provisions are found in a decree of June 30, 1961,

---

[2] Regulations for contracts for non-scheduled transport by inland waterway vessel.

[3] He procures goods for forwarding, places them with a carrier and deals with documentation and charges relating to them. Arts. 33 *et seq.*, Güterkraftverkehrsgesetz 1952 (BGBl I, 697).

as amended by that of December 6, 1963, which requires that forwarders must obtain a permit from the Minister of Public Works and Transport subject to conditions laid down by the decree.[4]

Article 1 distinguishes three categories of forwarding business. First, groupage operations by rail and road carriers, that is, where a forwarder consolidates shipments from or to several consignors or consignees by land transport. Secondly, road transport freighting operations, that is, the forwarding of previously consolidated shipments by means of public road carriers. Thirdly, urban depot operations, whereby the forwarder receives individual shipments or parcels and hands them over without consolidating them to road or rail carriers or other forwarders. To operate the latter a licence must be obtained from the prefect of the department where it lies.

Also for handling all goods a licence must be obtained from the Minister of Public Works and Transport.[5] These are divided into two classes. Under Licence "A" the holder can carry out all three classes of operations in all departments of the country. Under Licence "B," on the other hand, the scope of operation is more restricted, only permitting grouping from a place within a specified area, as defined by the licence, and urban depots to be operated therein also.[6] Road transport freighting is restricted to transits on which at least one terminal is situated within the area. No licence however is required where a forwarder (or freight broker) merely operates in a particular road haulage area by road transport alone.[7] Similarly, a licence is not required where a public road carrier transfers goods for onward transmission beyond his own transit, providing he has actually carried out part thereof himself. In other words, where successive carriers are concerned, the decree does not apply in this respect.

Whereas, in the case of the countries in the first category, that is, Belgium, Netherlands and Germany, there is no differentiation between nationals and foreign nationals, licences will only be granted to the latter in France where reciprocal rights are available. Licences are issued for a period of ten years, but are renewable provided the required conditions continue to be fulfilled. As they are non-transferable, if a business changes hands a new one must be applied for. Permits can also be withdrawn by the prefect of the department wherein lies the registered office, for failure to maintain a statutory bond required as a guarantee for satisfactory performance as a forwarder and by the Minister of Transport in certain other cases.[8] In all cases the opinion of the Disciplinary Council of forwarders, which is elected by licensed

---

[4] See also decree of Nov. 14, 1949, as amended, and decree of July 28, 1965, as amended.
[5] N.B. A special one is required for perishable foodstuffs.
[6] Art. 6 of the decree of June 30, 1961.
[7] Art. 7 of the decree of June 30, 1961.
[8] Art. 19 of the 1961 decree also requires membership of a Guarantee Fund in addition to a cash bond, which is financed by a levy on commission or turnover. The Fund may refuse to guarantee a forwarder at its discretion, in which case the Ministry of Transport must decide whether his licence is to be withdrawn or not.

forwarders, is called for, before a licence is withdrawn, whether temporarily or permanently.

The decree of June 30, 1961, also applies to freight brokers as well as forwarders. The former are defined by Article 3 as any person who, not acting as a commissionnaire de transport, brings together a consignor and public road carrier for the purpose of them entering into a contract of carriage, to which he will not be party himself, unlike the commissionnaire. Their licence will only be valid for the department of issue. Both forwarders and freight brokers are bound moreover to satisfy themselves that any road carrier to whom they transfer goods is authorised to effect the carriage in question.[9]

124 Italy

In Italy, apart from the provisions in Article 1737, C.C., relating to forwarders, detailed provisions concerning their licensing are made in Act 1442 of November 14, 1941. Article 1 provides that all forwarders whether by land, sea or air are subject to the decree, whether the latter offers to contract with the carrier in his own name or on behalf of his customer and any subsidiary transactions. It also provides that customs brokers are subject separately to special customs legislation.[10]

Article 2 provides that all forwarders must be registered on an official register maintained by the provincial Chamber of Commerce. For a forwarder to be entered in the register, he must obtain various certificates as to his integrity, including a police permit together with proof of his financial and technical ability.[11] In respect of each provincial register, a provincial committee is to be set up, representing various economic interests, which is responsible for vetting applications for enrolment, and the suspension or cancellation thereof. Article 10 (6) further provides for the examination by the committee of any complaints in respect of professional relations between a forwarder and his client, and to consider the applicability of the sanctions listed in Article 11 which include the revocation, etc., of a licence and payment of a penalty to a local charity. If a forwarder operates either without a licence or after suspension or revocation, he will be liable to punishment under Article 348, Penal Code. In the latter case the prefect of the province has the power to close the office, but a right of appeal lies to the Ministry of the Interior.[12]

125 Scandinavia

In Scandinavia no form of government control or licensing exists at present, the co-ordinating element in forwarding operations being

---

[9] The decree also applies to the operation of parcels depots. By Article 5 this is defined as the receipt of parcels for forwarding and holding them available for forwarders and road and rail carriers. A permit is required from the prefect of the department concerned, the issue of which is subject to the conditions described above in respect of forwarders and freight brokers.

[10] Act No. 1612 of Dec. 22, 1960, introduced a special register of customs brokers authorised as such by the customs authorities.

[11] Art. 4, Act 1442 of Nov. 14, 1941.

[12] Art. 21, *ibid.*

the Northern Forwarding Agents Association through their General Rules. However, in Finland, Norway and Sweden forwarders may now obtain authorisation from the Chambers of Commerce. Most forwarders have now obtained such authorisation. As regards Eastern Europe, as discussed in an earlier chapter, the forwarding bodies there are all state corporations so that the question of governmental control does not really arise. In other parts of the world as the forwarding of goods is usually a subordinate function of customs brokerage operations, there is again an absence of regulatory controls.

126   In conclusion therefore, the extent to which the forwarder is subject to control differs from country to country. Only in the United States where all types of forwarding are subject to strict governmental control is there a clear-cut distinction drawn between the three categories of forwarding operations, although this merely reflects the particular federal structure of the country with its proliferation of federal agencies covering all aspects of commercial activities. As regards the United Kingdom, although suggestions have been put forward from time to time as to the desirability of a system of licensing, no action in this direction appears likely in the near future. However, membership of the Common Market may result in a greater degree of formalisation in relation to transportation.

2. CONFLICT OF LAWS

127 Theory

Although the problem of conflict of laws has rarely come before the courts in relation to forwarding contracts, the question could prove a very complex one. From the viewpoint of the English courts there are three possibilities as to the proper law of the contract. First, there is the express choice of law as laid down in the *Vita Products* case.[13] The drawback to permitting the parties complete freedom of choice is obvious in that it might be completely unrelated to the contract in any way. Secondly, there is the implied choice of law such as by selection of an arbitral forum.[14] The third possibility is, "where their intention is neither expressed nor to be inferred from the circumstances, the system of law with which the transaction has its closest and most real connection."[14a] Owing to the complexity of forwarding operations, to decide which law is applicable, it is advisable to make an express choice of law in the trading conditions concerned by the insertion of a choice of law clause and/or an arbitration clause. However, this will usually be the law which would be also applicable as having the " closest and most real connection " owing to the very nature of the forwarding trade.

[13] *Vita Food Products Inc.* v. *Unus Shipping Co. Ltd.* [1939] A.C. 277.
[14] *Cie d'Armement Maritime S.A.* v. *Cie Tunisienne de Navigation S.A.* [1971] A.C. 572.
[14a] Dicey and Morris, *Conflict of Laws*, 8th ed., p. 691. See also *The Assunzione* [1953] 2 Lloyd's Rep. 716, C.A.; *Rossano* v. *Manufacturers Life Insurance Co.* [1962] 1 Lloyd's Rep. 187; *Whitworth Street Estates Ltd.* v. *J. Miller & Ptnrs. Ltd.* [1970] A.C. 583.

128   Cheshire is of the opinion that frequently the proper law of an agent's contract is the place where the agent acts.[15] In practice however the choice of law will probably be governed by a choice of law or arbitration clause in the contract. Furthermore, dependent upon the resolution of the conflictual question, it appears that the contractual status of the forwarder may differ significantly dependent upon whether the forwarding contract is subject to common law or civil law, as only in the latter case will it be subject to a contract of commission.[16]

129 United Kingdom

Most forwarders in Europe contract subject to the standard trading conditions of their particular national trade association. Under Clause 25, Standard Trading Conditions, all agreements are "governed by English law and within the exclusive jurisdiction of the English courts." Such a position means that owing to the rule *qui elegit judicem elegit jus*, the express choice of the tribunal prima facie creates an implied choice of law. However, the proviso that the contract is subject to English law is not entirely superfluous as this rule is rebuttable.[17] However, this would not preclude the mode of performance of the various stages of an international forwarding operation being governed by the *lex loci solutionis* of the particular part of the operation in question.[18] In particular this would mean that local regulations and trade custom would apply, subject to which the rights and liabilities of the parties under the principal contract must be read.

130 Other contractual provisions

Similar provisions are made in the forwarding conditions of other continental countries which are generally similar in effect to Standard Trading Conditions.[19] Two provisions do warrant attention though, which could create difficulties in a dispute before the English courts. Firstly, under the Austrian A.Ö.S.P., all disputes, whether settled by arbitration or the ordinary courts, are subject to the proviso in Article 66 that international forwarding contracts are governed by the law applying in the country where the contract was entered into.[20] If under such a provision the arbitrators apply the conflictual rules of the *lex loci contractus* this would achieve a reasonable solution, but if this merely results in the domestic law of the *lex loci contractus* being applied, the result would not necessarily be in harmony with the English precedents. Similarly under Dutch Forwarding Conditions, Article 23 (1)

---

[15] Cheshire, *Private International Law*, 8th ed., p. 234.
[16] *Anselme Dewavrin Fils et Cie* v. *Wilsons and N.E. Ry. Shipping Co. Ltd.* (1931) 39 Ll.L.Rep. 289. The question is of particular importance in the case of successive carriage by sea or land, as whether the intermediary will be treated as a forwarder or as a carrier may depend upon the choice of law governing the contract of carriage.
[17] *Cie d'Armement Maritime S.A.* v. *Cie. Tunisienne de Navigation S.A.* [1971] A.C. 572 at p. 609.
[18] Cheshire, *op. cit.*, at p. 234.
[19] Art. 27, N.F.C.; Art. 8, C.G. (France); Art. 18, C.G. (Switzerland); Arts. 60–61, C.G. (Belgium); Arts. 20–23, D.F.C.; Art. 65, A.D.S.P.; Art. 20, N.Y.F.F.
[20] *Cf.* A.D.S.P.

provides that "All disputes which may arise between the forwarder
and the other party shall be decided by three arbitrators to the exclusion
of the ordinary courts of law and their decision shall be final." Here it
is doubtful whether the English courts would enforce such an arbitral
award under the provisions of the Arbitration Act 1950, or alternatively
whether they would be prepared to stay proceedings in such a case.
There appear to be no direct decisions on this point however, and it
seems that the Act leaves this question largely to the discretion of the
court.[21]

131 Performance of forwarding contract

As regards the performance of the forwarding contract, the very
nature of forwarding operations may involve a number of different
jurisdictions. Here, therefore, a conflict may arise between the proper
law of the contract and the *lex loci solutionis* where these are not identical. It appears however since the case of *Jacobs* v. *Crédit Lyonnais* [22]
that the *lex loci solutionis* will not be permitted to alter the essence of
the contract as defined by the proper law. However, such ancillary
questions such as the forwarder's right of lien or sale may be governed
by the *lex situs* of the goods.[23] Also third parties will be governed by the
law of the country with which the forwarder, or his particular branch
office, is most closely connected.[24]

132 International conventions

In practice, however, the desire of the forwarding trade to avoid
adverse publicity by litigation has precluded many such disputes ever
reaching the courts. The forwarder generally contents himself with
counsel's opinion, and if any complication arises, the loss will be
covered by insurance wherever possible. Perhaps the best solution to the
problem of conflict of laws in forwarding and carriage contracts lies in
the development of the international convention, such as C.M.R. and
the proposed T.C.M. Convention in respect of combined transport, and
the Warsaw and Guadalajara Conventions relating to the carriage of
goods by air, under which such problems are removed from the realm
of conflict completely. In particular the conflictual problems that are
latent in containerised transport point to the need for the extension of
the existing conventions on international carriage into this field of
operations, although the current uncertainty as to the direction such
developments will ultimately take render such a possibility rather
remote in the near future.

---

[21] See Russell, *Arbitration*, 18th ed., pp. 322 *et seq.*
[22] (1884) 12 Q.B.D. 589.
[23] See Chapter 14.
[24] *Chatenay* v. *Brazilian Submarine Telegraph Co.* [1891] 1 Q.B. 79 at p. 82, *per* Lord
Esher. See Cheshire, *op. cit.*, at p. 234.

PART III
THE OBLIGATIONS OF A FORWARDER

CHAPTER 5

THE FORWARDER'S LIABILITY IN NEGLIGENCE

1. INTRODUCTION

133 Form of contract

Having considered the status of the forwarder, it is now necessary to turn to his obligations in respect of the various aspects of his activities.

In his capacity as an agent, the forwarder is subject to the same rights and liabilities at common law in relation to his principal as any other class of agent. He has no special status at law, unlike auctioneers and certain other commercial agents, although the courts have recognised the existence of certain customs in the trade.[1] Also in practice most forwarders contract subject to special conditions in respect of which the forwarder has complete contractual freedom.

The contract of forwarding can be entered into without any special formalities, and in many cases it is entered into orally over the telephone. Swift J.[2] rejected the contention that where a forwarder " acted upon verbal instructions given over the telephone . . . that it was a breach of duty or negligence on the part of [the forwarder] to go on with a matter like this on instructions over the telephone without having anything in writing." The learned judge considered that " it would be going a long way to hold that, because a businessman did not have a telephone message confirmed in writing, he was guilty of negligence which rendered him liable in damages to the person whose servant had sent the telephone message and who was complaining that his servant had acted outside the scope of his authority." [3] The problem though in such a situation is to ascertain whether, if a standard form of written contract is customarily used by the forwarder, it will be binding in any given transaction particularly if a new client is involved with whom no trading pattern has, as yet, been established.[4]

134 Duties of forwarder

The extent of the duties of a forwarder will vary according to the particular operation undertaken.[5] Accordingly, no uniform test can

---

[1] See § 71.
[2] *Comptoir Franco-Anglais d'Exportation* v. *Van Oppen & Co.* (1922) 13 Ll.L.Rep. 59. No direct restriction is imposed by S.T.C., but *cf.* Art. 9, Y.F.C.; Art. 2, C.G. (Switzerland); Art. 6, A.D.S.P.; Art. 4, C.G. (Italy); Art. 16, C.G. (Belgium); all of which require written confirmation. *Cf.* Art. 1, F.B.L.
[3] *Ibid.*, at p. 60, *per* Swift J.
[4] See D. J. Hill, " Standard Trading Conditions—How effective are they? " *Quarterly Journal of the Institute of Shipping and Forwarding Agents*, June 1966. Also *McCutcheon* v. *David MacBrayne Ltd.* [1964] 1 W.L.R. 125; [1965] J.B.L. 53—note by D. J. Hill. *Transmotors Ltd.* v. *Robertson Buckley & Co. Ltd.* [1970] 1 Lloyd's Rep. 224.
[5] *Cliffe* v. *The Hull and Netherlands S.S. Co. Ltd.* (1921) 6 Ll.L.Rep. 136—a forwarder " must act with reasonable diligence," *per* Bankes L.J. at p. 137. See also *Heskell* v. *Continental Express Ltd.* (1950) 83 Ll.L.Rep. 438 at p. 449, discussed in Chapter 2.

be laid down to ascertain either the extent of a forwarder's duty or what will constitute a breach in any particular circumstances. In any case the importance of establishing such a test has been considerably lessened by the increasing use of exemption clauses in written contracts, and of Standard Trading Conditions and R.H.A. Conditions in particular.

These trading conditions define the obligations of the parties in some detail as regards those matters where liability is likely to fall upon the forwarder in the event of any default on his part. The factor common to both Standard Trading Conditions and R.H.A. Conditions 1961 is that liability is excluded for all loss due to negligence unless wilful whether caused by the act or omission of the forwarder himself or by an agent or a sub-contractor.[6] Thus, where a contract is subject to such a condition, a shipper may in practice, be deprived of a remedy both in tort and contract against a forwarder whom he has employed to effect a contract of carriage for him.

This has produced two noticeable trends in litigation. First, there has been an increasing tendency to plead fundamental breach of contract wherever possible, although only with limited success owing to the restrictive interpretation given to the doctrine by the courts whenever it has been pleaded.[7] A second feature of current litigation is the practice whereby the shipper sues the sub-contracting carrier who is actually responsible for the loss instead of suing the forwarder whom he has employed to act for him. In such circumstances the action will be brought by the shipper in tort to avoid any contractual limitations imposed upon him under the terms of his contract with the forwarder.[8]

2. COMPARISON OF THE DUTY OF CARE REQUIRED OF A FORWARDER AND OTHER INTERMEDIARIES

135 **Confirming houses**

To define the forwarder's obligations to his client, it is necessary to distinguish him from associated commercial intermediaries in addition to analysing the various aspects of forwarding operations. The distinction between the forwarder and the carrier has already been discussed in an earlier chapter, and it is obvious that forwarding operations can be carried on in conjunction with a number of other occupations. In particular it is commonly an ancillary function to that of confirming house operations.

In *Anglo African Shipping Company of New York Inc.* v. *J. Mortner Ltd.*[9] the court carefully distinguished the forwarder from the confirming house to establish their respective duties, in order to determine whether the defendant had been negligent in the performance of his

---

[6] See §§ 151 *et seq. Cf.* R.H.A. Conditions 1967, B.R.S. Conditions.
[7] See § 158.
[8] *Lee Cooper Ltd.* v. *C. H. Jeakins & Sons Ltd.* [1964] 1 Lloyd's Rep. 300. *Cf. Morris* v. *C. W. Martin & Sons Ltd.* [1965] 2 Lloyd's Rep. 63, 73, *per* Denning M.R. See also Chapter 11 where this problem is discussed in detail. It has been effectively solved by the inclusion of indemnity clauses in both carriage and forwarding contracts. See Cl. 3 (4), R.H.A. Conditions 1967, and Cl. 24, S.T.C.
[9] [1962] 1 Lloyd's Rep. 610.

duties in one capacity or another. Accordingly, the obligation of a confirming house as such may be an absolute one, in the sense that, when performing a particular commercial transaction which it has undertaken, involving *inter alia* the international sale of goods, it will be bound to carry it out and will be liable if it fails to do so.

The exact extent of this duty will depend upon the type of obligation undertaken. If a confirming house places itself in the position of a principal in a transaction, the obligation will be an absolute one. On the other hand, if a confirming house merely undertakes the obligations of an agent towards one or more parties in a transaction, the obligation will not be an absolute one, but only that of an agent and it will therefore be subject to no greater obligation than a forwarder, who is only bound " to exercise reasonable care and diligence in carrying out their mandate." [10]

136 Carrier

The carrier, like the confirmer, may also be subject to a more extensive duty of care than a mere forwarder, as his duty does not cease with the execution of his mandate in arranging transit, but must extend to the actual execution of the transit itself. Accordingly, the carrier will be liable in respect of any section of the transit which he either carries out himself or for which he has accepted responsibility, in which case he will be equally liable for the acts of any sub-contractor he may employ. If, however, as regards on-carriage, he merely undertakes to forward the goods by another carrier he will only need to show the same degree of care as would be required of a forwarder.[11] It therefore follows that to establish what will constitute a negligent breach of duty by a forwarder it is first necessary to ascertain whether the act in question has been performed by the forwarder himself or by a third party employed by him, and in the latter case the extent to which the forwarder is liable for the third party's acts and omissions.[12] If, however, the contract is subject to C.M.R., the parties will be governed by the provisions thereof as regards successive carriage.[13]

137 Ship's agent

Next, the duty of a forwarder when acting as such must be distinguished from those complementary duties performed when acting simultaneously as an agent for a shipping line. Inasmuch as he is only acting in the capacity of a ship's agent, the forwarder's duty is only " to give the necessary instructions either upon express direction from the shipper himself, or from what they could gather from the documents themselves, as to the destination of the goods and the course they were to take." [14]

---

[10] *Ibid.* at 616, *per* Sellers L.J.
[11] As to the distinction see *Anselme Dewavrin Fils et Cie* v. *Wilsons and N.E. Ry. Shipping Co. Ltd.* (1931) 39 Ll.L.Rep. 289.
[12] See Chapter 11.
[13] See §§ 289 *et seq.*
[14] *Thrige* v. *United Shipping Co. Ltd.* (1924) 18 Ll.L.Rep. 6 at p. 8, *per* Bankes L.J. For the distinction between the forwarder and the loading broker see *Heskell* v. *Continental Express Ltd.* (1950) 83 Ll.L.Rep. 438 at p. 449, discussed in Chapter 2.

In such a situation a forwarder will have performed his whole duty provided he gives such instructions to an on-carrier as may be required under the terms of the bill of lading, even if he independently becomes aware that the seller has ceased to give credit to the buyer. In the absence of any instructions by the seller to the contrary, which he receives either direct as the carrier's agent or else from the carrier himself, concerning any change in trading terms between the seller and buyer in question where prior transactions have taken place, the forwarder is not obliged to check what provisions the seller has taken to protect himself to ensure that he obtains payment in exchange for the bill of lading.[15] If a forwarder does not receive any notification of such changes, no duty of care will attach, irrespective of whether he has any knowledge of matters affecting the parties' commercial standing or not.

138 Agent for both parties

If, in addition to acting on behalf of a carrier, a forwarder undertakes to act simultaneously on behalf of the consignor or consignee of goods, he will also be subject to a duty of care to protect his client's interests.[16] For example, where a forwarder undertook to arrange shipping space for a client whilst also acting as a steamship agent, he could not provide the necessary space for his client, which he had advertised as having available. Consequently he failed to forward his client's shipment, and pleaded as a defence that a rail forwarding certificate required to ship the goods across France to Italy was not available. This the court rejected on the grounds that the absence of such a certificate could be no defence to a claim for non-performance of the London–Havre section of a London–Milan transit.[17]

In other words, if in performing his obligations to one party a forwarder fails to perform those due to another party, either owing to a conflict of interests or an inability to fulfil both at the same time, he will be liable for his breach of duty. Fulfilment of his obligations to one party can be no defence to an action for breach of duty to another, neither it seems can the plea of inability to effect a later section of a transit offer an adequate defence for failure to carry out an earlier section thereof. However, it appears more probable, in the present state of international trade, that if a forwarder is unable to effect the complete transit of a shipment where successive carriage is involved, owing to the absence of the necessary documentary authority, it would equally be within his discretion to suspend shipment until such documents are forthcoming, thus avoiding liability for breach of duty.

---

15 *Thrige* v. *United Shipping Co. Ltd.* (1924) 18 Ll.L.Rep. 6 at p. 7.
16 *Mitchell, Cotts* v. *Commissioner for Railways* [1905] T.S. 349. As to the duty of a forwarder when acting on behalf of two principals in succession see *Julien Praet et Cie S.A.* v. *H. G. Poland Ltd.* [1962] 1 Lloyd's Rep. 566.
17 *Luigi Riva Di Fernando* v. *Simon Smits & Co. Ltd.* (1920) 2 Ll.L.Rep. 279 at p. 281.

3. The Forwarder's Liability for Negligence in Relation to the Contract of Carriage

(i) *Alternative Tariff Rates*

139 Where alternative terms of contract are available, as under British Rail and National Carriers Conditions, a distinction must be drawn between the obligations accepted by the carrier in each case.[18] Where carriage is at " owner's risk " a lower scale of charges is applicable than under "carrier's risk," as under the former, liability for loss, etc., is only accepted by the carrier where it results from the wilful misconduct of the carrier or his servants. Otherwise where carriage is at " carrier's risk " liability is accepted by the carrier for all loss whether resulting from his negligence or not, subject to certain limitations discussed below.[19] Consequently, where a choice of rates is left to the forwarder, he must consider his client's interests in making a decision.

Accordingly, if goods are consigned at "owner's risk" to the knowledge of a forwarder, he will be liable if loss results because of his failure to take such steps as may be necessary to ensure safe delivery. In such a case he is bound either to inform his client of the fact, or else to inquire whether insurance has been effected to cover the goods in transit.[20] Furthermore, a common carrier can either limit his financial liability under the Carrier's Act 1830 or else for an extra charge accept liability for an amount in excess of that recoverable under the Act. The Act will also be contractually applicable to the private carrier where R.H.A. Conditions 1961 are in use.[21] Consequently, a forwarder will be liable if he fails to ascertain whether the value of the goods in question warrants the payment of the higher rate to cover adequately any loss or not.

In *Von Traubenberg* v. *Davies, Turner & Co. Ltd.* the Court of Appeal rejected the argument that such an obligation would place an undue burden on a forwarder as " it is (only) requiring them to do what I should have thought was the whole object of the employment of forwarding agents to effect."[22] Consequently if a forwarder decides the matter without referring it to his client, he will do so at his own risk. Conversely if a forwarder or carrier is instructed to forward or carry goods by a direct route without transhipment, but instead effects transit by means of a cheaper route, partly by sea and partly by land, contrary to instructions, he will be liable to the shipper for the difference

---

[18] N.B. Neither B.R.S. nor private hauliers offer Owner's Risk rates except in special circumstances, such as where goods are highly susceptible to damage or pilferage. B.R.S. Parcels do so on request where goods are not properly protected by packing.

[19] For a historical discussion of " the fair alternative " see Kahn-Freund, *Law of Inland Transport*, 3rd ed., 1956, at p. 211. Cll. 5A, 5B, British Rail Conditions.

[20] See Chapter 17 as to the obligations of a forwarder in effecting insurance of goods.

[21] Cl. 7, R.H.A. Conditions 1961; *Von Traubenberg* v. *Davies, Turner & Co. Ltd.* [1951] 2 Lloyd's Rep. 462 at p. 467, *per* Somervell L.J.

[22] *Ibid.* at p. 467. *Cf.* Cl. 21, S.T.C.

in freight, even though the actual transit effected may be both faster and more efficient.[23]

To protect the forwarder against such liability provision has been made in Clause 16 (*b*), Standard Trading Conditions, whereby the forwarder will always ship goods at owner's risk or other minimum charges, unless expressly instructed in writing to the contrary by the client.

(ii) *The Negligent Performance of Forwarding Operations*

140   The forwarder is obliged as an agent to carry out the particular transaction which he has undertaken on behalf of his principal. If he has only undertaken to forward goods, that is merely to arrange transportation, but not actually to carry it out himself, his obligation will only be to follow the terms of his authority and to exercise due care and skill in executing it.[24] A forwarder has a duty to forward goods without delay unless he has received instructions to the contrary. He therefore has an implied authority to do so. Accordingly, where goods were shipped inland from their port of arrival and later returned there on the client's instructions, the forwarder responsible for handling the goods was entitled to retain them until his client had reimbursed him in respect of railway charges which he had had to pay to obtain delivery of the goods. He did not need any further special instructions before performing his duties, and had acted in accordance with the ordinary duty of a forwarder in railing the goods inland without delay.[25]

141 **Description of goods**

A question of importance is the extent to which a forwarder will be responsible for any inaccuracy etc. relating to the description of goods in a shipment.[26] The question divides itself into two parts. First, is there any discrepancy which points either to a shortage or to the possibility that the goods are not in fact those which the forwarder was instructed to handle. The basic rule appears to be that a forwarder will be liable for breach of duty if he fails to ensure that both the quantity and the description of a consignment match his original instructions. Where, however, a forwarder finds a discrepancy in the description of a consignment, which can reasonably be ascribed to a cause other than the actual one, in the customary performance of his forwarding operations, he will not be liable for negligence in failing to discover the true position if nothing further occurs to put him on inquiry.

For instance, in *George Pulman & Sons Ltd.* v. *F. E. Crowe*[27] a forwarder was instructed to collect three cartons of postcards from a customs house in Milan by the consignor on the consignee's failure to obtain an import licence. Owing to the markings being identical on

---

[23] *Charles Weis & Co. Ltd.* v. *Northern Traffic Ltd.* (1919) 1 Ll.**L.Rep. 241.**
[24] *Cf. Lynch Bros.* v. *Edwards & Fase* (1921) 6 Ll.L.Rep. 371.
[25] *Patel* v. *Keeler & Co.* [1923] A.D. 506.
[26] *Cf.* Cl. 9, S.T.C., discussed in § 219.
[27] (1920) 3 Ll.L.Rep. 100.

this consignment and a similar one from another client to the consignee, which was also handled by the forwarder, the latter returned the other client's goods to the consignor by mistake, a fact they did not discover till they opened the packages some weeks after receipt. In the ensuing action by the consignor, Bailhache J. did not consider that such a mistake in itself constituted negligence on the part of the forwarder, although an additional factor to be considered was the fact that packages returned did not correspond in weight with those in the plaintiff's shipment. The question therefore arose as to whether this discrepancy should have put the forwarders on inquiry as to their identity, when they discovered the loss in weight, which they erroneously ascribed to pilferage. However, as there were no other factors, except for the shortage in weight, to put them on inquiry, the court did not consider the defendant's omission constituted negligence.

142   Quality of goods
Secondly, a forwarder does not customarily hold himself out as accepting responsibility for the quality of goods nor that their specification is that agreed upon by the parties to the contract of sale. This was confirmed where a forwarder was instructed by a buyer to arrange shipment of a consignment of batteries to England from Antwerp, and passed his instructions on to his sub-agent. Neither the forwarder nor his sub-agent was held responsible for the inferior quality of the batteries shipped.[28] Under Clause 13 (iv), Standard Trading Conditions, the forwarder does not accept any liability for "any loss, damage or expense arising from or in any way connected with marks, weights, numbers, brands, contents, quality or description of any goods however caused." This really only appears to restate the position at common law.[29]

143   Duty to inform client of loss
It is the duty of a forwarder to give his client the fullest information regarding any loss that may occur, whether responsibility for it falls on him or on the actual carrier or other bailee. If both the forwarder and the carrier concerned fail to give such information to the shipper, and as a consequence they are joined together in any resulting action by the consignor, the forwarder may forfeit any costs due to him in the case, as he is in breach of his duty to his client as an agent, in circumstances where he would not otherwise be personally liable for the loss.[30]
Roche J. considered the extent of the forwarder's duty to his client in this respect in the interesting case of *G. Peereboom* v. *World Transport Agency Ltd.*[31] He explained that
"A person in the position of a forwarding agent is bound to give such information to his principal as is necessary for the principal to protect his interest in the goods. That is a duty which is entirely

---

[28] *Margolis* v. *Newson Bros. Ltd.* (1941) 71 Ll.L.Rep. 47, *per* Humphreys J.
[29] *Cf.* Art. 11, C.M.R.
[30] *Carl Osterberg* v. *Shipping & Transport Co.* (1922) 13 Ll.L.Rep. 562.
[31] (1921) 6 Ll.L.Rep. 170 at p. 172.

independent of whether the forwarding agent has actual possession of the goods or not. He is managing a certain transaction with regard to them, and if anything arises during the conduct of that transaction which affects the goods or their value or the interest of the plaintiff in them, it is impliedly the duty of the forwarding agent to tell his principal about it."

Accordingly, where a forwarder gave his client a delivery note in respect of a shipment, and failed to inform him that the goods in question were the subject of a dispute between the wharfinger and the ship as to whether they had in fact been shipped or not, he was in breach of his duty to his client, as by his action he deprived his client of an opportunity to take appropriate action.[32]

144   Negligent selection of a carrier

If a forwarder is negligent in selecting a carrier he will be liable to his client for any loss that may result from such a choice.

For example, in *Gillette Industries Ltd.* v. *W. H. Martin Ltd.*[33] the defendant forwarder was responsible for clearing a consignment of razor frames through Liverpool docks and forwarding them by road to Reading. Customs clearance however was to take place at Reading on a nominated day. Consequently, through the need to adhere to this date and being prior to Christmas when thieves were especially active, it was desirable that the goods should be shipped to a place of safety in Reading as soon as possible. The normal procedure was to employ one of a number of regular carriers to carry the goods, which was done in respect of sixteen containers which reached Reading safely. Owing, however to a seasonal shortage of transport, the remaining three containers could not be shipped by this method. The defendants' Liverpool manager, urged by his London office, and probably by the docks also, adopted the same procedure that he had used for the past thirty years in similar circumstances. He sent an assistant to a lorry pool near the docks, which in the words of the court was "organised like a taxi rank." The assistant persuaded a driver and mate to take the load to Reading, and in accordance with his routine went to check the vehicle. He found it had an "A" Licence giving the registration number and the owner's name, Stenton Transport, with an East London address, which he noted. He then took the lorry crew to be interviewed by his manager, who, being satisfied with their credentials, instructed them to carry the consignment to Reading. Accordingly they loaded next day, the empty trailer being subsequently found at West Ham, with part of the load missing, which was never recovered. The court considered the forwarder's manager had failed to exercise such care as might be expected of a professional forwarder in the circumstances.[34] Merely because the procedure had been successfully carried out for a number of years

---

[32] *Ibid.* See § 177 for a fuller discussion of the facts.
[33] [1966] 1 Lloyd's Rep. 57; [1966] J.B.L. 152, note by D. J. Hill.
[34] *Cf. Marston Excelsior Ltd.* v. *Arbuckle Smith & Co. Ltd.* [1971] 2 Lloyd's Rep. 306.

did not in itself prove that it was reasonable. Furthermore, the fact that the manager had failed to make any further check upon the driver's credentials amounted to negligence on his part. Accordingly, the forwarder was guilty of a breach of his duty of care to his client, although in the event as the contract was subject to Standard Trading Conditions which excluded liability for negligent loss, the forwarder escaped liability.

145 C.M.R.

Where a carrier is shipping goods subject to C.M.R., in respect of which he is the first carrier,[35] he will be bound to check two things. First, the accuracy of the statements in the consignment note as to the number of packages, their marks and numbers.[36] Where however he has no reasonable means to check this he must enter his reservations on the note together with the grounds upon which they are based.[37] Secondly, he must check the apparent condition of the goods and their packaging and enter any reservations in respect thereof in the note.[38] Such reservations will not bind the consignor unless he has expressly agreed to be bound by them in the consignment note.[39]

Thirdly, if the consignor so wishes, he can require the carrier to check the gross weight or the quantity of the goods, and the contents to be checked. The results are to be entered in the consignment note, and the carrier can claim payment for expenses incurred in doing so.[40]

If, however, there are no specific reservations by the carrier in the consignment note, it will be presumed, unless the contrary is proved, that both the goods and the packing appeared to be in good condition at the moment when the carrier took them over, and that the number of packages, their marks and numbers, correspond with those in the note.[41] However, the presumption laid down in Article 9 (2) only applies to the check carried out under Article 8 (1), but not to the optional checks permitted under Article 8 (3). As discussed in a later chapter, the Convention only makes the consignment note prima facie evidence of the contract terms of carriage and the receipt of the goods by the carrier.[42]

Article 35 similarly provides that where a successive carrier takes over the goods from a previous carrier, he must both give the latter a dated and signed receipt for the goods, and enter his name and address on the second copy of the note. In addition, any reservations must be entered on both documents [43] and the presumptions in Article 9 (1) and

---

[35] See § 351 on the first carrier, and § 289 on successive carriage.
[36] Art. 8 (1) (*a*), C.M.R.
[37] Art. 8 (2).
[38] Art. 8 (2).
[39] Art. 8 (2).
[40] Art. 8 (3).
[41] Art. 9 (2).
[42] Art. 9 (1).
[43] Art. 35 (1).

(2) referred to above will also apply to the relationships between successive carriers.[44]

It can therefore be seen that the forwarder of goods may be subject to the above provisions either in the capacity of a consignor, a first carrier, or a successive carrier, and to the rights and liabilities arising therefrom. If, therefore, there is any doubt as to his actual status in a particular transaction, it seems highly desirable that he should ensure that the documentary requirements of the Convention as to the reception and forwarding of goods are complied with in all international transits, whether on the face of it subject to the Convention or not.

146   (iii) *Conclusions*

The forwarder is expected to have a thorough knowledge of forwarding procedures. The extent of such knowledge must depend of course on the particular usages and customs of the port or city in question,[45] but certain obligations appear to be common factors in the trade irrespective of the actual place of operation. First, the forwarder will be bound to exercise a duty of care in relation to the various tariffs which may be available for the carriage of goods, and in selecting the most suitable, must bear in mind the value of the commodity and what insurance arrangements, if any, have been made.[46] Secondly, a forwarder is bound to furnish his principal with all available information concerning not only any loss or damage that occurs,[47] but also such information that he may have which will enable his principal to avoid or mitigate possible loss in the future.[48] This obligation is not merely a negative one to transmit any information which the forwarder may receive from third parties, but also imposes a duty to make such inquiries as are relevant where the forwarder is put on inquiry by irregular circumstances.[49] It will be a question of fact in each case as to what will constitute sufficient to put the forwarder on inquiry, and in establishing this all relevant factors must be taken into consideration bearing in mind the actual conditions and local practices where the operation took place.[50] It is therefore not easy to establish more than the broadest guide lines to assist in delineating the duty of care required by the courts in respect of pure forwarding operations. Furthermore, it must be remembered that it is rarely easy in practice to separate one function from another satisfactorily, a factor which the courts have often reflected by the absence of clarity in their judgments, However with the advent of C.M.R. a more careful delineation of the various operations will be necessary to ascertain whether a particular dispute is subject to the Convention or not.

[44] Art. 35 (2).
[45] See § 170.
[46] *Von Traubenberg* v. *Davies Turner & Co. Ltd., supra,* § 139.
[47] *Carl Osterberg* v. *Shipping & Transport Co., supra,* § 143.
[48] *G. Peereboom* v. *World Transport Agency Ltd., supra,* § 143.
[49] *George Pulman & Sons Ltd.* v. *F. E. Crowe, supra,* § 141.
[50] *Gillette Industries Ltd.* v. *W. H. Martin Ltd., supra,* § 144.

4. THE FORWARDER'S LIABILITY FOR NEGLIGENCE IN RELATION TO THE LANDING AND CLEARANCE OF GOODS

147 The obligations of a forwarder when making customs declarations merely extend to such consignments in respect of which he has received specific instructions. Failure to carry out customs clearance in such a case will amount to a breach of duty, but if no instructions have been given to effect clearance, a forwarder will not be negligent in failing to do so.[51] Where loss or damage occurs to goods while they are in the hands of the customs authorities this will not amount to any fault upon the part of a forwarder engaged to effect customs clearance, if goods must be discharged into the custody of customs in the ordinary course of business.[52] Consequently, provided no further act of delay or other default on the part of the forwarder occurs, the latter will not be liable to his client in respect of such a loss.[53] Nor will the fact that clearance has been delayed through the detention of goods by the customs authorities render a forwarder liable for negligence unless this has resulted from his own act or default.[54]

148 Where a forwarder is responsible for landing and clearing goods and receives a package in apparently undamaged condition he is not bound to weigh it to see if it corresponds with the invoiced weight. Therefore, providing goods are in good condition externally on clearing them through customs, a forwarder will not be liable, when they are found to be damaged on arrival at an inland destination and part of their contents missing, unless he has undertaken special contractual liability to this effect.[55]

149 If goods are lost whilst in a forwarder's custody, the burden of proof is on him to explain it.[56] If however they are not in the actual custody of the forwarder when the loss occurs, the latter will only be liable if guilty of some actual default, such as delay, etc., or is liable for the actions of a third party, as where part of the operation has been sub-contracted.[57] Accordingly, where a forwarder was authorised to collect

[51] *World Transport Agency Ltd.* v. *Royte (England) Ltd.* [1957] 1 Lloyd's Rep. 381—see § 462. *Cf.* Art. 11, C.M.R.
[52] *Wessely* v. *Rosenberg, Loewe & Co. Ltd.* (1940) 67 Ll.L.Rep. 16.
[53] See Chapter 7.
[54] *Donner* v. *London & Hamburg Agency* (1923) 15 Ll.L.Rep. 63.
[55] *Jaffer Esmail & Co.* v. *Sorabjee M. Hooker*, 6 E.A.L.R. 35. See also *Lavington Bros. Ltd.* v. *Cooper & Co.*, *Worlds Carriers*, Oct. 16, 1922, Mayor's Ct. *Cf.* Art. 9 (2), C.M.R.; Cl. 6, S.T.C.
[56] Although in *Wessely* v. *Rosenberg, Loewe & Co. Ltd.* (1940) 67 Ll.L.Rep. 16 at p. 18, Atkinson J. considered that the forwarder could discharge this duty by giving an explanation which is equally consistent with the absence or presence of negligence, it appears since the recent case of *Swan* v. *Salisbury Construction Co. Ltd.* [1966] 1 W.L.R. 204 at p. 209, *per* Lord Morris that it is necessary for a forwarder to prove that he has taken all proper and reasonable care with regard to the goods. *Cf. W.L.R. Traders Ltd.* v. *B. & N. Shipping Agency Ltd.* [1955] 1 Lloyd's Rep. 554, where Pilcher J. held that the onus was on the bailee to show that the loss occurred without negligence. *Cf. Transmotors Ltd.* v. *Robertson Buckley & Co. Ltd.* [1970] 1 Lloyd's Rep. 224 at p. 227.
[57] Harbour board regulations may require a landing agent to hand goods over to the board for warehousing, etc., pending clearance. In *Cook & Sons* v. *MacKenzie & Co.* (1902) 19 S.C. 50, the courts held that where goods were landed by a landing agent from a ship in Cape Town docks, the agent ceased to be liable for them on handing

and deliver a package on arrival by ship, and it was discharged directly into a bonded warehouse pending customs clearance, the forwarder was held not liable for the loss of part of the contents, as on the facts it disappeared before the forwarder actually took possession. Furthermore, even though the latter had been guilty of delay in collecting the package, this did not affect the position, as the loss had not taken place during a period when he could be at fault.[58] In performing his obligation to land a shipment for a client, a forwarder is bound to do so within a reasonable time and to take proper care of it, bearing in mind whether the goods in question are of a perishable nature or not. However, his obligation in respect of lighterage and warehousing operations is merely to do what is reasonable and with such dispatch as is reasonable in the circumstances prevailing at the time unless otherwise agreed.[59] Accordingly, it has been held that it did not constitute negligence on the part of a forwarder who was handling a shipment of hides where he could not employ an experienced contractor who specialised in hides as none was available, but instead employed a reasonably competent wharfinger who did not normally handle hides and who was over-committed in respect of other shipments, with the result that the goods were damaged.[60]

150 Forged delivery note

A related problem is that of the forged delivery note. The question that arises here is on whom should liability and consequent loss fall when an unauthorised party has obtained possession of goods by means of a forged or unauthorised delivery or collection note. The decided cases seem to favour the forwarder or landing agent in such a situation unless there has been actual negligence on his part. For instance, in a recent American case, a terminal operator who was bailee of a shipment misdelivered goods in reliance on a forged delivery note purporting to be issued by a customs broker who was responsible for clearing the goods.[61] Here the court were faced with the question whether the broker and his principal, the owner of the goods, were estopped from claiming against the terminal operator on the grounds that the forgery and theft had been carried out by one of the broker's employees. In the event, the court held that as customs house procedure was properly carried out and the broker had not been negligent in hiring the fraudulent employee, no estoppel could arise, as the latter acted outside the scope of his employment in removing the delivery order from his employer's office.[62] Similarly, where a thief stole a consignment note from a forwarder and

them over in accordance with the harbour board regulations. In many cases, however, landing operations are being taken over by the boards themselves, thus placing the complete operation in the hands of one party.

58 *Wessely* v. *Rosenberg, Loewe & Co. Ltd.* (1940) 67 Ll.L.Rep. 16.
59 *Club Speciality (Overseas) Inc.* v. *United Marine* [1971] 1 Lloyd's Rep. 482.
60 *G. W. Sheldon & Co. (London) Ltd.* v. *Alfred Young & Co.* (1921) 6 Ll.L.Rep. 466.
61 *David Crystal* v. *Cunard S.S. Co.* [1964] A.M.C. 1292.
62 See *John Carter Ltd.* v. *Hanson Haulage Ltd.* [1965] 1 Lloyd's Rep. 49, concerning the fraudulent employee.

used it to collect a shipment without authority from the railway station, the forwarder was held not liable to his client for the loss at common law.[63] It seems, therefore, that provided the forwarder has not been negligent in his work methods he will not be liable to his client for loss resulting from the fraud or crime of a third party.[64] He is not obliged to take special precautions above the normal expected in the trade to guard against such fraud or crime committed by a third party unless he has contractually bound himself to do so.[65] Ultimately, however, to decide whether a forwarder has been negligent or not, each case will perforce turn largely upon its particular facts.

5. THE FORWARDER'S LIABILITY FOR NEGLIGENCE IN RELATION TO LOSS
IN TRANSIT

(i) *"Wilful Neglect" in the Forwarding Contract—
Interpretation of Clause 13 (i), Standard Trading Conditions*

151 One field of activity where considerable litigation involving forwarders has occurred is where goods have been lost or stolen in transit. This may result from one of two causes. First, it may result from the act or omission of the forwarder or one of his servants in carrying out his duties. Secondly, it may be through the act or omission of a carrier or his servant employed by the forwarder to effect transit on his behalf. The extent of liability in the second category will be discussed in detail in a later chapter, so that further comment here is unnecessary.[66]

As regards the first category, the forwarder's liability as such has already been discussed. Where, however, a forwarder effects carriage himself, he will be liable as a carrier. In other words, if he undertakes liability as a common carrier, he will be liable for any loss whether he has been negligent or not, subject to those limits on his liability discussed in an earlier chapter.[67] Otherwise, whether fulfilling the functions of a forwarder or of a private carrier, it will be necessary to prove actual negligence on his part or in respect of which he has a duty of care. Conversely, where a carrier acts as a forwarder, his duty will not be that of a carrier, but will be that of a mere forwarder of goods. In other words, "they must act with reasonable diligence," and to quote but one example discussed in an earlier chapter, a sea carrier forwarding goods by rail will not be liable for the failure of the railway company to provide the necessary transport.[68]

152 Standard Trading Conditions

In practice if a forwarder contracts subject to Standard Trading Conditions, he specifically avoids liability as a common carrier,[69] so

---

[63] *Pringle of Scotland Ltd.* v. *Continental Express Ltd.* [1962] 2 Lloyd's Rep. 80.
[64] *Cf. Gillette Industries Ltd.* v. *W. H. Martin Ltd.* [1966] 1 Lloyd's Rep. 57.
[65] As to the effect of illegality on loss in transit see *Archbold Ltd.* v. *Spanglett* [1961] 1 Q.B. 374 (defective road licence) and *Pye Ltd.* v. *B. G. Transport Ltd.* [1966] 2 Lloyd's Rep. 300 (falsification of export invoices).
[66] See Chapter 11.   [67] See §§ 26 *et seq.*
[68] *Cliffe* v. *Hull & Netherlands S.S. Co. Ltd.* (1921) 6 Ll.L.Rep. 136 at p. 137, *per* Bankes L.J. See Chapter 2.
[69] Cl. 1, S.T.C.

that his liability, apart from any special contractual obligations undertaken, will be principally in respect of the negligent performance of his
obligations as a forwarder.

In respect of such loss the forwarder restricts his liability severely
to loss or damage to the goods which occurs "whilst they are in its
actual custody, and under its actual control and . . . was due to the wilful neglect or default of the Company or its own servants."[70] Similarly
Clause 8 of R.H.A. Conditions 1961 provides that "The contractor
shall not be liable for delay or detention of goods or for any loss, damage
or deterioration arising therefrom except on proof that the delay etc.
was due solely to the wilful negligence of the Contractor or the Contractor's servants." Consequently, as forwarders may operate under
either set of Conditions, it is of value to compare the respective provisions in detail.

153 "Wilful negligence"

First, it appears that the words "neglect" and "negligence" in the
respective clauses are virtually synonymous, and that the addition of
the words "or default" in Standard Trading Conditions does not really
alter the extent of the circumstances under which liability for loss is
accepted by the forwarder. On the assumption therefore that the provision in Standard Trading Conditions is the factor synonymous with
that in R.H.A. Conditions 1961, it is desirable to consider the meaning
of the phrase "wilful negligence," as used in the latter Conditions, as
this has been the subject-matter of some discussion by the courts and
jurists as to its meaning, unlike that in Standard Trading Conditions
which has not been the subject of judicial comment at all.

Among the attempts to define "wilful negligence," Kahn-Freund
dismisses it as being a combination or midway point between wilful
misconduct and negligence.[71] He also adds erroneously that the phrase
has not yet been judicially defined, and in turn makes no further attempt
to do so. Charlesworth, on the other hand, briefly discusses the meaning,
and refers to the case of *Re City Equitable Fire Insurance Co.* which
concerned negligence by the directors of a company. Here at first
instance, with the approval of the Court of Appeal, Romer J. defined
it as follows[72]:

> "An act, or an omission to do an act, is wilful where the person
> of whom we are speaking knows what he is doing and intends to
> do what he is doing. But if that act or omission amounts to a
> breach of his duty, and therefore to negligence, is the person guilty
> of wilful negligence? In my opinion, that question must be

---

[70] Cl. 13 (i), S.T.C. *Cf.* Art. 11 (4), D.F.C.; Arts. 17–19, 23, 24, N.F.C.; Art. 10,
N.Y.F.F.; Arts. 33, 35, 41, C.G. (Belgium); Arts. 28, 29, 53, Y.F.C.; Art. 8, C.G.
(France); Art. 8, C.G. (Switzerland); Arts. 37–45, C.G. (Italy); Arts. 51–53, 57–63,
A.D.S.P.; Art. 6, F.B.L.
[71] Kahn-Freund, *Law of Inland Transport*, 4th ed., pp. 272, 368.
[72] [1925] Ch. 407, at p. 434. *Cf. Emblen* v. *Myers* (1860) 6 H. & N. 54. See also Charlesworth, *Negligence*, 4th ed., p. 12.

answered in the negative unless he knows that he is committing, and intends to commit, a breach of his duty, or is recklessly careless in the sense of not caring whether his act or omission is or is not a breach of duty. . . . A wilful act, which amounts to negligence, is not wilful negligence unless there is a will to be negligent. "

154   " Wilful negligence " and " wilful misconduct "

What therefore is the relationship between " wilful negligence " and " wilful misconduct, " in relation to which Kahn-Freund attempts to define the former, and which is the basis of liability where goods are carried at Owner's Risk by British Rail under General Conditions of Carriage?[73] A recent definition has been given by Barry J. in the following terms[74]:

" In order to establish wilful misconduct the plaintiff must satisfy you that the person who did the act knew at the time that he was doing something wrong and yet did it notwithstanding, or alternatively, that he did it quite recklessly, not caring whether he was doing the right thing or the wrong thing, quite regardless of the effects on the safety of the [thing] . . . for which . . . he was responsible. "

Comparing the two definitions, it appears that they are both based upon the concept of a duty owed by one party to another, a breach of which is either intentionally or recklessly committed by the party at fault. The question therefore arises as to wherein lies the difference between the two phrases, if any? Two answers appear possible. First, if these dicta accurately define the meaning of these two phrases, one conclusion that can be drawn is that both "wilful negligence" and "wilful misconduct " have virtually the same meaning. In other words the emphasis must be placed upon the " wilful " intention of the party in performing the act, rather than upon the actual nature of the act. However, another alternative interpretation is that as " negligence " is wider in scope than " misconduct, " liability for " wilful negligence " must also include liability for " wilful misconduct. " There appear to be no judicial dicta on this point, but this premise would appear to be a logical deduction.

Support is to be found for this premise in the dicta of Johnson J. in *Graham* v. *Belfast & Northern Counties Ry. Co.,*[75] where he stated that " wilful misconduct . . . is far beyond any negligence, even gross or culpable negligence. . . . " It can therefore be argued that " wilful negligence " must be intended to cover such gross omissions and acts, which although " wilful " would not amount to " misconduct. " This however raises the further question of whether " gross negligence " differs in any way from " wilful negligence, " or are the two phrases

---

[73] See Cl. 5B, British Rail Conditions.

[74] *Horabin* v. *B.O.A.C.* [1952] 2 All E.R. 1016 at p. 1020, *per* Barry J. *Cf. Hartstoke* v. *L.M.S.* [1942] 2 All E.R. 488 at p. 490, *per* Hallett J.

[75] [1901] 2 I.R. 13—quoted by Hallett J. in *Hartstoke Fruiterers Ltd.* v. *L.M.S., supra* at p. 490.

synonymous? Although there are no dicta on this point, it can be argued that a difference does exist inasmuch as " gross negligence " is not necessarily " wilful " in its execution.

155 Classification

To offer any conclusions therefore, a twofold distinction must be drawn. First, inasmuch as an action is brought in the tort of negligence, there are no degrees of negligence, and the concept of " wilful misconduct, " " wilful negligence " and " gross negligence " are all meaningless. In other words, there is only one duty of care in negligence. Secondly, when considering negligence as an element in an action for breach of a forwarding or carriage contract, there appears to be no reason why varying degrees of negligence should not be recognised, as the action is in assumpsit, in which the test of duty outside the framework of a contractual undertaking is irrelevant.

The following classification could therefore be adopted in defining negligence as an element in an action for breach of contract. First, simple negligence, in respect of which little or no culpable fault exists. Secondly, " gross negligence " would cover those acts of negligence which although not " wilful, " are the result of such a degree of culpable fault as to be considered by a merchant as warranting more severe treatment than simple negligence. Thirdly, " wilful negligence " in the sense of " gross negligence " which has been performed " wilfully. " Fourthly, " wilful misconduct " in the sense laid down by Johnson J. above.

156   If such a classification scheme was adopted, legal form and recognition would thereby be given to the various provisions at present extant in various forms of standard contracts which are in use in various trades. In particular, as regards the forwarder, it must be emphasised that this is not a mere academic point any longer, as with the increasing number of cases before the courts involving contracts subject to Standard Trading Conditions, it is necessary both from the viewpoint of the shipper and the operator to establish what must be proved for a breach to constitute more than mere negligence to render the protection given to the forwarder in Clause 13 (i) ineffective. This is particularly needed, as the courts have been loth to accept a plea of fundamental breach in respect of such tortious acts, where a shipper has endeavoured to avoid contractual limitations on his right of recovery. Furthermore, now that the *Suisse Atlantique* decision[76] throws a cloak of uncertainty on the validity of the doctrine, the need to establish the exact meaning of " wilful negligence " becomes important. If the courts take the view that such a provision is a contradiction in terms and therefore meaningless, it will be necessary for Standard Trading Conditions to recast this form of limitation, as has recently been done in R.H.A. Conditions 1967.[77]

[76] See § 162.
[77] See § 163.

157   Clause 13 (i), Standard Trading Conditions, further provides that the forwarder will only be responsible for the goods,

> " whilst they are in its actual custody and under its actual control and the Company shall not be liable for loss of or damage to goods or failure to deliver the goods unless it is proved that such loss or damage or failure to deliver the goods occurred whilst the goods were in the actual custody of the Company and under its actual control. . . ."

The apparent effect of this proviso is to exempt the forwarder from all liability for goods which are merely in his control, but not in his actual custody. Furthermore the client must prove that the loss, etc., occurred whilst the goods were in the actual " custody " *and* " control " of the forwarder. This latter provision has recently been inserted in the 1970 edition of Standard Trading Conditions to further protect the forwarder from liability. The extent of the forwarder's liability in practice is therefore even more limited than ever.

(ii) *Fundamental Breach and the Forwarding Contract*

158   Several decisions concerning the forwarding of goods have been discussed by the courts in relation to fundamental breach of contract, so that it seems desirable to consider to what extent the doctrine has been relevant to this field of case law prior to the *Suisse Atlantique* case. First, as mentioned above, Clause 13 of Standard Trading Conditions provides almost identical protection in respect of negligent loss for a forwarder as does Clause 8, R.H.A. Conditions 1961, if he operates under them.[78] Accordingly, for this purpose it is not material which set of conditions a forwarder is operating under. However, such protection will only avail for those breaches of contract or tortious acts within the scope of the exemption clauses, which in fact constitute an actual performance of the contract. If therefore the actual method of performance is such that there is a total failure of consideration, or else the breach is so fundamental as to destroy the very basis of the contract, the forwarder will be deprived of all protection under the contract, and will therefore be laid open to whatever common law remedy is appropriate.[79]

The doctrine of fundamental breach of contract has been widely discussed elsewhere, and any further consideration of its nature is outside the scope of this work.[80] Accordingly, the problem will only be further considered in relation to what circumstances will ground a successful plea of fundamental breach of contract. Obviously each case must turn upon its particular facts, but an analysis of those cases involving forwarding transactions where the doctrine has been pleaded, successfully or otherwise, will serve as a guide to its relevance in practical

---

[78] See § 152. *Kenyon Ltd.* v. *Baxter, Hoare & Co. Ltd.* [1971] 1 W.L.R. 519.
[79] *Gillette Industries Ltd.* v. *W. H. Martin Ltd.* [1966] 1 Lloyd's Rep. 57 at p. 65.
[80] See C. D. Drake, " Fundamentalism in Contract " (1967) 30 M.L.R. 531.

terms as a method of overcoming onerous exemption clauses in forwarding contracts.

159   The question divides itself into two parts. First, is there a fundamental breach by the forwarder under his contract with the shipper? Secondly, is there a fundamental breach on the part of the carrier under his contract with the forwarder in the latter's capacity of either principal or agent acting on behalf of his client the shipper?

160 **Fundamental breach by the forwarder**

As regards the first category, such a plea has only been raised in three cases. In *Gillette's* case, discussed earlier,[81] the court rejected the plea that the failure of the forwarder to check the carrier's credentials with sufficient care could constitute a fundamental breach. Similarly in *Pringle of Scotland Ltd.* v. *Continental Express Ltd.*[82] it was held that the fact that a thief was allowed to obtain a blank collection note and fraudulently collect a consignment did not constitute a fundamental breach so as to preclude the forwarder from relying on an exemption clause relieving him of liability for the loss of the goods in question. Finally, in *Colverd & Co. Ltd.* v. *Anglo Overseas Transport Co. Ltd.*[83] where the forwarders were sued on a similar set of facts to those in *Lee Cooper Ltd.* v. *C. H. Jeakins & Sons Ltd.*,[84] although the forwarders were held vicariously liable for the driver's negligence, the court considered that the forwarders were entitled to rely on the carrier employed by them to instruct his driver appropriately on locking the vehicle while left unattended, and were not obliged to supplement these instructions by any of their own. The court refused to treat the driver's action as amounting to a fundamental breach of the forwarder's contract with his client, as the forwarders were not "reckless or indifferent to the safety of the goods entrusted to them."[85] In all these cases, therefore, the common factor is that, without exception, the courts were not prepared

---

[81] [1966] 1 Lloyd's Rep. 57 at p. 67. *Cf. Garnham, Harris & Elton Ltd.* v. *Alfred W. Ellis Ltd.* [1967] 2 Lloyd's Rep. 22, discussed at § 287. In both cases the loss arose from a failure to check the credentials of the sub-contractor. Looking at the facts it is difficult to discover any difference in the degree of negligence displayed by the defendants. However, whereas the court emphatically accepted the plea of fundamental breach of contract in *Garnham* they equally emphatically rejected it in *Gillette's* case. Whether a fine distinction can be drawn between the cases based upon the particular facts is debatable. It therefore raises the possibility of whether the duty of care expected of a forwarder when employing a carrier is less stringent than that required of a carrier when employing a sub-contractor. There has, as yet, been no judicial comment on this point, but in any case it merely offers a purely legal distinction rather than a practical one, as many large transportation and forwarding groups operate under both sets of conditions depending upon the class of business concerned, but without necessarily being able to draw a clear distinction between the varying categories of transaction. In future however, it may be necessary for more care to be taken in defining the respective spheres of operation to avoid such difficulties.

[82] [1962] 2 Lloyd's Rep. 80 at p. 88—Cl. 4 of the forwarder's contract exempted him from liability for any " loss . . . however any of the same may be caused . . . or for loss . . . which may take place in relation to the goods after their acceptance by the Agency and previous to their delivery."

[83] [1961] 2 Lloyd's Rep. 352. For the facts see § 269.

[84] For the facts see § 161.

[85] *Colverd & Co. Ltd.* v. *Anglo Overseas Transport Co. Ltd.*, *supra* at p. 363, *per* Barry J.

to treat the default as amounting to more than mere negligence, no matter how reprehensible the act or omission might seem. Consequently, there is no instance where fundamental breach of contract has been successfully pleaded in respect of a mere forwarding contract.

161 Fundamental breach by the carrier

As regards the second category, that is, where fundamental breach has been pleaded in respect of the contract between the forwarder and the carrier, the court similarly refused, in *Harris's* case, to accept a plea that the absence of the driver from the carrier's vehicle while collecting goods from a customer's premises, leaving the vehicle inadequately locked, constituted a fundamental breach of contract, where a third party claim was made against the carrier.[86] By contrast though in *Lee Cooper Ltd.* v. *C. H. Jeakins & Sons Ltd.*[87] the court took the contrary view. Here a forwarder, Anglo Overseas Transport, was requested to make all necessary arrangements for the transfer of a shipment of rayon acetate material from London docks to the latter's warehouse eight miles away, pending re-export. The forwarder had hired a number of the defendant carrier's vehicles exclusively for his work. As these were fully occupied, by a standing agreement, a vehicle was hired out by the defendant on a casual basis to the forwarder to transport the plaintiff's goods. During the journey the carrier's driver took a tea break of fifty minutes even though he had been stationary in the docks for the previous eight hours and could have partaken of refreshment during that period at dockside facilities. The driver removed the keys of the vehicle, but it was not proved that he had locked the cab doors, and no other steps were taken to immobilise the vehicle. As might be expected, the vehicle had disappeared on his return, and half its load was never recovered. The length of tea break was motivated by a desire to work overtime. As the action was in negligence by the forwarder's client, the shipper, direct against the carrier, and no contractual relationship existed between them, the latter was liable for breach of duty of care to the shipper.[88] However, Marshall J. added that, although not necessary for the judgment, if there had been a contractual relationship in existence between the carrier and the shipper, whereby the former claimed the protection of various exemption clauses, he considered that the carrier had committed a fundamental breach of contract through their driver's conduct, and could not therefore claim the benefit of any contractual protection at all. The judge considered that in such a case the negligence must go to the root of the contract to ground such a plea.[89]

It is very difficult, however, to see in such circumstances if a high degree of negligence can amount to a fundamental breach why it should not at the same time also constitute "wilful negligence." Seemingly considering the facts of *Lee Cooper Ltd.* v. *C. H. Jeakins & Sons Ltd.*

[86] *Harris* v. *Continental Express Ltd.*, *supra*, at p. 260.
[87] [1964] 1 Lloyd's Rep. 300.
[88] *Ibid.*, at p. 308.
[89] *Ibid.*, at p. 310.

the negligence of the driver must surely be considered as wilful, on the assumption that "wilful negligence" can have any meaning in law at all, and therefore the carrier would not have been protected by R.H.A. Conditions at all. This point was not pleaded though, nor was it discussed by the court. The doctrine therefore seems in practice, considering the methods used in forwarding operations, to have been of singularly little value as a means of avoiding onerous exemption clauses.

162   Suisse Atlantique case

The doctrine has been further considered in the recent decision in the *Suisse Atlantique* [90] case. In a dispute concerning demurrage, the House of Lords appeared to doubt whether a rule of law existed whereby an exemption clause is nullified by a fundamental breach of contract. However, Lord Denning M.R. has since clarified the situation in the following terms.[91] First, a fundamental breach may leave the contract open to be performed, in which case, when the innocent party is aware of the breach, he has the option either to affirm or disaffirm the contract. If he affirms it, it will remain in being for the future on both sides, and each can sue for damages for past or future breaches, but it is a matter of construction whether the guilty party can rely on an exemption clause to escape liability. If however the innocent party disaffirms the contract, that is, accepts the breach, it will be at an end from that moment. Secondly, if the fundamental breach instead brings the contract to an end the innocent party will have no option but to accept it. In neither this case nor where the latter disaffirms the contract can the guilty party rely on any exemption clause to escape liability.

It therefore remains to be seen how the courts will approach such provisions as Clause 13 of Standard Trading Conditions in the future.[91a]

163   Road Carrier's Conditions

As regards R.H.A. Conditions, the revision of 1967 has obviated the problems formerly raised by Clause 8, R.H.A. Conditions 1961. These are now brought into line with B.R.S. Conditions, to overcome the mounting criticism from shippers as to the superiority of the latter. Clause 11, R.H.A. Conditions 1967, therefore provides that, "Subject to these Conditions the Carrier shall be liable for any loss, or misdelivery of or damage to goods occasioned during transit unless the Carrier shall prove that such loss, misdelivery or damage has arisen from [certain excepted perils]. . . ." Liability is therefore accepted for loss whether caused by the carrier's negligence or not under both R.H.A. Conditions 1967 and B.R.S. Conditions.[92]

[90] *Suisse Atlantique Societe* v. *N. V. Rotterdamsche* [1966] 1 Lloyd's Rep. 529.
[91] *Harbutt's Plasticine Ltd.* v. *Wayne Tank & Pump Co.* [1970] 1 Lloyd's Rep. 15 at p. 23.
[91]a See *Kenyon Ltd.* v. *Baxter, Hoare & Co. Ltd.* [1971] 1 W.L.R. 519 at p. 533.
[92] *Cf.* Cl. 5, B.R.S. Conditions. Such problems concerning the extent of recovery, except as regards the financial limit, have hardly existed in relation to carriage under B.R.S. Conditions. It is this general acceptance of liability that has increasingly placed the private haulier at a disadvantage when competing with the nationalised haulage companies.

The present position, therefore, is that it is no longer necessary under any of the three principal sets of land carriage Conditions for the shipper to prove wilful negligence, liability being accepted for all loss subject to certain exceptions providing the correct claims procedure is carried out. It should be noted however that all three Conditions exempt the carrier from liability for what is in effect an expanded version of the "excepted perils" discussed in an earlier chapter in relation to common carriage.[93] This provision is necessary as the latter would not apply at law to R.H.A. and British Rail conditions, as under both the contractor is not a common carrier.[94] Under B.R.S. Conditions on the other hand there is no indication as to whether the contract is subject to common or private carriage, consequently similar provisions are necessary to remedy any uncertainty as to the status of B.R.S.[95]

The principal exceptions listed are act of God, war, civil commotion, etc., seizure under legal process, act or omission of the shipper or owner of the goods, inherent waste or defect, etc., defective packing, defective addressing and non-acceptance of delivery within a reasonable period by the consignee. Under no circumstances will liability be accepted where there has been fraud on the part of the shipper or owner of the goods or their servants or agents.[96] Similar provision is found in R.H.A. Conditions 1961, but there is no reference to the fraud of the shipper or owner of the goods. This would be superfluous as liability is in any case only accepted if resulting from the wilful negligence of the carrier.

164 C.M.R.

Under C.M.R. certain important differences in approach must be noted. Unlike the corresponding provision in Standard Trading Conditions and R.H.A. Conditions 1961, where liability is only accepted if it can be proved that there has been either "wilful neglect or negligence" on the part of the forwarder or carrier, no such defence is permitted under the provisions of C.M.R. Liability is placed upon the carrier for all loss, as in R.H.A. Conditions 1967, B.R.S. and British Rail Conditions, whether resulting from the carrier's negligence or not.[97] Article 17 (1) provides that: "The carrier shall be liable for the total or partial loss of the goods and for damage thereto occurring between the time when he takes over the goods and the time of delivery, as well as for any

---

[93] Cl. 11, R.H.A. Conditions 1967; Cl. 5, B.R.S. Conditions; Cl. 5A, British Rail Conditions. See Chapter 2. However, where a verbal contract for the carriage of goods by road is entered into, and it is agreed that the owner of the goods should " carry his own insurance," it has been held in a recent Australian case that such a stipulation does not exclude the carrier's liability for negligence—*Challenge Transport Pty. Ltd.* v. *South Yarra Car Sales Pty. Ltd.* (1961) 35 A.L.J.R. 249.

[94] See Chapter 2, note 10.

[95] *Hunt & Winterbotham (West of England) Ltd.* v. *B.R.S. (Parcels) Ltd.* [1962] 1 Q.B. 617 at p. 623, where counsel admitted that B.R.S. were common carriers.

[96] See note 93.

[97] The question of delay is discussed in Chapter 7. N.B. A German court has held that Arts. 17 *et seq.* govern liability of the carrier only in so far as loss or damage and delay in delivery is concerned. They do not exonerate the carrier in respect of other faults committed in the execution of the contract. Landgericht Bremen, May 6, 1965, 1 E.T.L. 691. *Cf.* Art. 9, T.C.M.; Art. 27, C.I.M.; Art. 6, F.B.L.

delay in delivery." This is subject however to certain specific exceptions including the claimant's own acts or instructions, inherent defects, packing, etc.[98] Liability can also be avoided where loss, etc., has resulted "through circumstances which the carrier could not avoid and the consequences of which he was unable to prevent." This latter proviso in Article 17 (2) lacks the clarity that a common lawyer might expect in a contract of carriage, and in practice difficulty may arise in its application. Moreover, it places a somewhat greater onus on the carrier than

[98]   Arts. 17 (2), (4). *Cf.* certain recent continental decisions: Where a fire resulted through a deflated tyre, this cannot be imputed to the carrier if the latter can prove that the leak in the tyre was not due to avoidable circumstances, *i.e.* where the driver is proved to have exercised all reasonable diligence to avoid it, both before and during transit. The fact that the driver tested the tyre pressure with a gauge before commencing the journey was sufficient proof. Arrond. te Rotterdam, Jan. 21, 1969, 4 E.T.L. 998. It does not follow that because goods are put in a crate instead of in a case that they are by nature subject to damage so as to relieve the carrier of liability under Art. 17 (4) (*b*): Hof s'Hertogenbosch, Dec. 21, 1965, 1 E.T.L. 698. Under Arts. 17 (2), (4) and 18 (2) it is sufficient for the carrier to prove the " possibility " that the loading by the consignor caused the damage to the goods. "Total proof " of the presumed cause, *i.e.* proof of the exclusion of any other possible causes, is not required by the Convention. "Handling, " " stowage " and " loading " by the consignor are each separate categories under which the carrier can avoid liability: Hof van Beroup te Brussel, Dec. 19, 1968, 4 E.T.L. 953.

To benefit from Art. 17 (4) (*c*) the carrier must prove that the loading and stowage of goods by a forwarder could have been the initial cause of damage sustained and that a possible relationship of cause and effect exists between this fact and the damage: Cour d'Appel de Bruxelles, June 28, 1969, 4 E.T.L. 925.

Avoiding action in traffic is a normal risk today to be taken into account when stowing and shoring goods. Where it can be established that damage could have resulted from the stowage and insufficient shoring of the goods by the consignor/forwarder, although not proved that the damage, in whole or part, resulted from this cause, the carrier can still claim the benefit of the presumption under Arts. 17 (4) (*c*) and 18 (2): Trib. de Commerce de Namur, July 22, 1965, 1 E.T.L. 133. Merely because a carrier is liable to criminal sanctions does not preclude him from relying on Art. 17 (4) (*c*) under which there is a presumption that damage has resulted from bad stowage by the consignor. The carrier will not be liable unless he is shown to be negligent: Rechtbank van Koophandel van Antwerpen, April 4, 1965, 1 E.T.L. 314.

The decisions in continental courts on Art. 17 (4) (*c*) appear to conflict: a carrier is not bound to shore heavy goods when loaded and stowed by the consignor. The carrier can invoke Arts. 17 (4) (*c*) and 18 (2) if the shoring is insufficient: Rechtbank van Koophandel te Antwerpen, March 3, 1969, 4 E.T.L. 1900. *Cf.* Even where loading is by the consignor's servants, the carrier must fix loads by normal partitions to prevent the goods sliding. This is merely a normal precaution in carriage. If the damage to the goods has resulted partly through bad stowage and partly through the absence of partitions, liability will be equally shared by the consignor and the carrier: Art. 17 (5). Arrond. te Roermond, Jan. 2, 1969, 4 E.T.L. 1005. *Cf.* When goods are loaded on a vehicle by a forwarder without checking by the driver, the carrier can rely on the presumption in Art. 17 (4) (*c*) and Art. 18 (2) that the handling and loading were the causes of the loss. However, as the damage also resulted through the driver's excessive speed, the carrier was partly liable under Art. 17 (5); Hof s'Hertogenbosch, Dec. 21, 1965, 1 E.T.L. 684. *Cf.* Where the immediate and certain cause of loss is the negligence or omission of the carrier's servants, who ought previous to transit to have ensured that the load did not exceed the foreseen dimensions, the presumption under Art. 18 (2) will not be taken into consideration (a case of an oversize load): Cour d'Appel de Bruxelles, March 12, 1969, 4 E.T.L. 931. *Cf.* A successive carrier is bound to check the stowage of goods and to make reservations where it is considered to be insufficient, and if necessary to refuse to start: Trib. de Commerce Corbeil-Essones (France), April 18, 1969, 4 E.T.L. 988. To prove that damage resulted through a particular risk inherent in the nature of the goods under Art. 17 (4) (*d*), it was held to be sufficient for the carrier to prove that a load of cauliflowers remained for several days on a lorry during the month of August. This does not prevent the consignee from proving that the damage is partly or totally due to other causes which involve the carrier's liability, *i.e.* such as through non-observation of the consignor's instructions: Arrond. te Roermond Oct. 24, 1968, 4 E.T.L. 1012.

at common law.[99] Also, compared with R.H.A. Conditions, the Convention appears to offer the carrier less protection against consequential loss, a hiatus which could increase the cost of underwriting claims.[1]

The carrier cannot avoid liability on the grounds that the vehicle was defective or that the loss occurred " by reason of the wrongful act or neglect of the person from whom he may have hired the vehicle or of the agents or servants of the latter." [2] In other words, the latter part of this provision merely reiterates the provision in Article 3 making the carrier liable for all servants, agents and sub-contractors.[3] If however the carrier is not liable for some of the factors causing the loss, etc., he will only be liable to the extent that those factors for which he is liable have contributed to the loss, etc.[4]

165 Burden of proof

Specific provision is made in Article 18 as to the burden of proof. If the carrier wishes to avoid liability on the grounds that the loss was caused by one of the causes specified in Article 17 (2), the burden is on him to do so.[5] If on the other hand the carrier can establish that the loss or damage " could be attributed to one or more of the special risks " listed in Article 17 (4), there is a rebuttable presumption to this effect,[6]

---

[99] To avoid liability through " unavoidable circumstances " under Art. 17 (2) the carrier must specify them " *in concreto.*" To decide whether they exist or not in the case of a fire, it is necessary to know the cause of the fire—if it is unknown the carrier will remain liable: Arrond. te Alkmaar, June 5, 1967, 2 E.T.L. 1013. Where a carrier attempts to rely on an extraneous factor under Art. 17 (2), he is not required to prove the existence of a particular set of facts, nor specific circumstances relieving him of liability. The carrier can rely on a number of established facts which, if there is no other explanation, would give rise to a reasonable supposition that the damage arose through " unavoidable circumstances," the effect of which was unescapable. The carrier must, however, show that the external force could not have been noticed or prevented by his employees exercising due care: Gerechtshof Amsterdam, Oct. 21, 1965, 1 E.T.L. 305. The carrier can rely on the exemptions in Art. 17 (2) if it appears that the damage was due to an extraneous cause. The burden is on the carrier to show that the damage results from specific circumstances which relieve him from liability. If there is no such evidence the carrier will be liable, *e.g.* where fire was caused by the bursting of two almost new tyres, side by side, through friction: Arrond. te Amsterdam, Oct. 28, 1964, 1 E.T.L. 718. However, the carrier was protected by Art. 17 (2) where the extraneous factor was the reduction in tyre pressure through a sharp object causing the heating and burning of a tyre, which was in good condition, a check having taken place both before and during transit. Arrond. te Rotterdam, April 20, 1965, 1 E.T.L. 137. The following were not unavoidable circumstances: where a carrier left an unguarded lorry parked at the frontier during the night, he was liable for the theft of its load of cobalt: Bundesgerichtshof, Dec. 21, 1966, 4 E.T.L. 888. Neither were violent and exceptional rains which occurred during transit and which damaged the load—the carrier was therefore liable: Arrond. te Amsterdam, March 14, 1964, 1 E.T.L. 738.

[1] *Cf.* Cl. 12 (2) (*b*), R.H.A. Conditions 1967, with Art. 23 (4) (5), C.M.R.

[2] Art. 17 (3). *Cf.* the carrier was liable for a fire caused through a deflated tyre. He vouches for the condition of his property: Rechtbank van Koophandel te Antwerpen, April 9, 1969, 4 E.T.L. 1028.

[3] See § 289.

[4] Art. 17 (5). See Hof s'Hertogenbosch, Dec. 21, 1965, 1 E.T.L. 684, reported at note 98.

[5] Art. 18 (1). *Cf.* Art. 28, C.I.M.; Art. 9 (4), T.C.M.; Art. 6, F.B.L.

[6] Art. 18 (2). The presumption in Art. 18 (2), notwithstanding any common duties which may be imposed upon a carrier, is included to deal with the difficulties which the carrier may have in proving the possible faults of a third party, when after loss or damage has occurred and as a result thereof, he can no longer reconstruct the circumstances of the accident, but wishes to assert that the loss or damage may have resulted

[97]

subject to certain specific limitations laid down in the Article. In particular, he must prove that "all steps normally incumbent on him in the circumstances were taken and that he complied with any special instructions issued to him." [7] Finally, Article 20 lays down under what circumstances the goods will be considered lost and the procedure in the case of subsequent recovery after compensation has been paid.

166   Wilful misconduct or default

However, irrespective of the basis of the claim, by Article 29, a carrier cannot claim the benefit of any of the provisions listed in Chapter IV of the Convention, "which exclude or limit his liability or which shifts the burden of proof," if the damage or loss results from his wilful misconduct or equivalent default, or that of his agents, servants or sub-contractors when acting within the scope of their employment. This provision seems to cover not only the matters included under the heading of " wilful neglect or negligence," which amount to wilful misconduct, referred to in Standard Trading Conditions and R.H.A. Conditions 1961, but also those events which could be considered as constituting a fundamental breach of contract at common law, which would equally preclude reliance on any exemption clauses in the contract and in particular those limiting financial liability. [8] As a result, in the event of litigation in respect of a contract of carriage entered into subject to the convention, such matters can be dealt with within the framework of the Convention, and a remedy accordingly obtained without the necessity to go outside its provisions and have recourse to general principles of law.

A further proviso to Article 29 (2) states that where a carrier is precluded from relying on the defences in Chapter IV through wilful misconduct or default of his servants or agents, the latter will not be able to avail themselves of these defences either. The implication of this proviso is that, although under the Convention such servants, agents, and others engaged in the contract of carriage, will normally be able to claim the benefit of such defences when an action is brought

from one of the special risks listed in Art. 17 (4), particularly those relating to the handling, loading and stowage or unloading of goods by the consignor or the consignee or their respective agents. Cour d'Appel de Bruxelles, March 12, 1969, 4 E.T.L. 931. The carrier's burden of proof avoiding liability is mitigated under Arts. 17–18. These articles recognise the possible existence of factors exempting him from liability. The burden of proof therefore shifts to the claimant who must show that the loss was not caused by the exempting factor. However, a defect in packing is not such an exempting factor when the goods have been loaded and handled in an unsuitable manner by the carrier. Rechtbank van Koophandel te Antwerpen, March 28, 1966, 1 E.T.L. 712. To benefit from Arts. 17 (4) and 18 (2) the carrier is only required to advance the " possibility " that damage, " may have " resulted from, *e.g.*, the absence of packing. Art. 17 (4) (*b*). Hof van Beroep te Brussel, Dec. 19, 1968, 4 E.T.L. 948. A carrier invoking Art. 18 (2) must show that in the circumstances the loss may have resulted from one of the risks in Art. 17 (4). Cour de Cassation de France, Ch. Commerciale, June 17, 1969, 5 E.T.L. 57.

[7] Art. 18 (3), (4), (5).

[8] *Gillette Industries Ltd.* v. *W. H. Martin Ltd.* [1966] 1 Lloyd's Rep. 57; *Lee Cooper Ltd.* v. *C. H. Jeakins & Sons Ltd.* [1964] 1 Lloyd's Rep. 300. *Cf.* Art. 37, C.I.M.; Art. 12 (2), T.C.M.; Arts. 6, 10, F.B.L.

against them directly, in these circumstances they will be faced with a similar situation as that in such cases as *Adler* v. *Dickson* [9] where the English doctrine of privity of contract precludes a servant from relying on exemption clauses in a contract of carriage entered into by his employer with a third party who was injured by the former's negligence, inasmuch as the Convention will be of no assistance to overcome this rule.[10]

167

(iii) *Conclusions*

The problem of loss in transit where a forwarder is involved as an intermediary between shipper and carrier poses certain problems which arise out of the innate peculiarities of the English common law case system. In particular, two opposing rules work in conflict with each other to provide a useful form of equitable balance between the interests of the various parties concerned. The doctrine of privity of contract offers freedom of action to the shipper against a tortious carrier, provided no contractual relationship is established between them, which commercially seems to be undesirable at the present. As a counterbalance to this, the common law gives complete freedom of contract to parties, which the forwarder takes fullest advantage of by the use of Standard Trading Conditions. In defence of this it must be borne in mind that as an intermediary who performs few functions himself personally, he is placed in a position of considerable responsibility for the actions of third parties employed by him on behalf of his client. This freedom in turn can be kept within a fairly strict control by the concept of fundamental breach of contract, which, both as a rule of law and construction can be used to prevent the forwarder from avoiding liability for total non-performance of his obligations.

168   The courts have to some extent dispelled the uncertainty cast over the whole doctrine of fundamental breach by the decision in the *Suisse Atlantique* case, in recent decisions relating to the question. It is therefore unlikely that any real change will occur in the application of the doctrine to carriage contracts in practice, and it is probable that, as regards contracts involving the forwarding and transportation of goods, the existing precedents will continue to develop along the same lines. There has however been a distinct lacuna in this aspect of the law to date [11] as no attempt has been made to analyse the meaning of " wilful neglect/negligence " in Standard Trading Conditions and R.H.A. Conditions 1961. Unless such an analysis is attempted, along the lines suggested, the correct inter-relationship between exemption clauses in forwarding and carriage contracts and the doctrine of fundamental breach cannot be established. Until this is done, there can be no

[9] [1955] 1 Q.B. 158.
[10] *Cf. Lee Cooper Ltd.* v. *C. H. Jeakins & Sons Ltd.* [1964] 1 Lloyd's Rep. 300.
[11] *Sed*: *Kenyon Ltd.* v. *Baxter, Hoare & Co. Ltd* [1971] 1 W.L.R. 519—in this recent case the question of the S.T.C. provisions was partially discussed in relation to a warehousing contract—no systematic analysis of the problem was attempted however.

certainty that the principal trading conditions as formulated at present are a logical extension of general common law principles.[12]

169 C.M.R.

As regards C.M.R., it seems on the face of it to remove certain anomalous principles of the common law from effective operation in the sphere of international carriage of goods by road. Not however until the courts have been required to consider the various provisions of C.M.R. can any truly definitive statement be made as to its effect. In the light of the provisions discussed above though, it seems that whereas the shipper will be placed in a more favourable position than he enjoys at present under R.H.A. Conditions and Standard Trading Conditions, the burden placed upon the forwarder will be heavier if he is concerned with ferry operations, particularly, bearing in mind the increased use of articulated trailers, that is, goods vehicles that do not possess a permanently attached trailer unit. If therefore a forwarder undertakes the responsibility of forwarding such units, he may become liable as a successive carrier under Chapter VI of the Convention.[13] Much however will depend upon the manner in which the courts interpret Article 17 (2).

6. THE EFFECT OF TRADE USAGE AND CUSTOM

170 Proof of usage

In considering forwarding contracts the custom and usage of the trade must be borne in mind as this may have a considerable bearing upon the liability of the various parties concerned. However, to establish the validity of a custom, the courts have invariably required stringent proof that a custom which is detrimental to a shipper or other party is to be enforced, or that it does exist at all.[14] As De Villiers C.J. observed in rejecting a custom that the removal of goods from a landing agent's custody was proof that goods were in good order and extinguished the latter's liability:

> "I cannot agree . . . that because a certain custom has arisen at the docks by which persons who are in charge of goods, either shipping agents or shipping companies, refuse to be bound, or refuse to hold themselves liable in case the goods are removed in an apparently damaged condition, they are not therefore liable. . . ."

It is a question for the courts in the particular circumstances.[15]

---

[12] Although the introduction of R.H.A. Conditions 1967 has constituted a radical change in approach to the private road haulier's liability, it does not however render the earlier discussion concerning R.H.A. Conditions 1961 purely academic, as at the date of writing it is still far from clear how many road hauliers have in fact adopted the 1967 Conditions, as there has been no compulsion on this matter. In particular, those companies who are engaged in both the forwarding and carrying trade appear to be clinging to the 1961 Conditions, so as to retain some uniformity in their trading conditions irrespective of whether they are forwarding or carrying. It therefore seems that the 1961 Conditions will remain in operation for some time, at least by those who also operate under S.T.C.

[13] See §§ 289 *et seq.*

[14] See *Langley, Beldon & Gaunt Ltd.* v. *Morley* [1965] 1 Lloyd's Rep. 297, at p. 306.

[15] *Duke & Co.* v. *McKenzie & Co.* (1898) S.C. 390 at p. 391.

171   A landing agent must take extreme care when attempting to rely on a trade custom to justify the settlement of claim which would not otherwise be legally enforceable against his principal. For instance, in *Thompson, Watson & Co.* v. *The Poverty Bay Farmers Co.*[16] a landing agent settled pilferage claims for which his principal, the carrier, was not liable under the bill of lading, and attempted to recover the amount from him on the grounds that in Cape Town a custom existed that if no special instructions were given to a landing agent other than those printed on the bill of lading, he could disregard any exemptions clauses therein which limited the carrier's liability. The court considered that such a custom was unreasonable, and could not be relied upon, although the mere fact that it was afterwards discovered that the pilferage claims could have been resisted was not in itself sufficient to prevent the landing agent from recovering the amount paid in satisfaction of the claims. However, as the plaintiff agent had not shown all due diligence in discharging his principal's affairs, that is, he had not thoroughly considered his principal's liability under the bill of lading, he could not claim any right to indemnity for losses resulting from his own negligence or default.[17]

172 Certainty

The position therefore is that for a custom to be of use to a forwarder, either in prosecuting a claim against a third party or else in protecting him from liability which would otherwise accrue at common law, its certainty must be clearly established. This implies not only proof as to its existence, but also as to its reasonableness.[18] Such proof is not easily satisfied by a forwarder, owing to the many variations in local practice and the ever-increasing need for flexibility in operation which modern conditions require.[19]

Merely because a certain procedure is regularly adopted for the convenience of the party doing so will not create a binding custom. For example, where a lighterman kept a tally on goods shipped by him for his own benefit, a forwarder could not rely on this practice to support a claim for loss of goods as the lighterman was under no duty to do so, and could not therefore be liable for failing to keep a tally in respect of the goods lost.[20]

173   Further, for a trade custom to bind the public generally it must be shown that it is known to all whose interests required them to have knowledge of its existence, and in any case, if the terms of a bill of lading are inconsistent with a particular port custom, the former must prevail.[21] Consequently, reliance on trade custom is largely being replaced

[16] (1924) C.P.D. 380.
[17] *Ibid.* at p. 392.
[18] *Ibid.* at p. 395. See also *Anglo Overseas Transport Ltd.* v. *Titan Industrial Corp. Ltd.* [1959] 2 Lloyd's Rep. 152 at p. 160.
[19] On custom generally, see Halsbury's *Laws*, Vol. II, pp. 184 *et seq.*
[20] *Cox's Shipping Agency* v. *Pearce & Ramsden* (1921) 7 Ll.L.Rep. 55.
[21] *Parsons* v. *Hart* (1900) 30 S.C.R. 473 (Canada): A shipment of fruit was discharged on the wharf and not immediately removed by the consignees. It was allowed to remain in a

by reliance on uniform trading conditions, particularly Standard Trading Conditions, which not only incorporate existing custom as contractual terms between the parties, but also extend and vary it as the needs of the trade require from time to time.

7. GENERAL CONCLUSIONS

174 It can be seen that the distinctions drawn in Chapter 2 between the forwarder and other intermediaries and the problems involved in establishing a clearly defined classification of the various duties performed by them, logically projects itself into the complementary problem of establishing the extent of the forwarder's liability in the tort of negligence. In many cases it is far from clear as to whether a forwarder in fact has a duty to his client, the shipper, and to what extent he will be in breach thereof in attempting to fulfil his obligations when acting as an agent for a carrier or other commercial person. Likewise, it may not be clear whether the forwarder is in fact merely bound to fulfil his obligations as such or whether the burden placed upon him will be more onerous if he in fact accepts personal responsibility for carrying, warehousing or packing goods himself, whether or not he does in fact perform this function. It seems therefore that a forwarder's duties may be given a threefold breakdown. First, he may act as a mere forwarder, with a duty solely to his client and to no one else. Secondly, he may fulfil a further obligation to a carrier as a ship's agent, or a corresponding function in other fields of transportation. Thirdly, although basically offering his services as a forwarder he may actually perform part of the transit operation himself or some ancillary function which he has undertaken to get carried out for his client. In this case he will be placed in the position of an actual carrier or other commercial person, such as a packer or warehouseman, and his duty will extend to that of such a person. Fourthly, in addition to offering his services as a forwarder, or possibly instead of so doing, he may offer to perform the actual operations himself. In this case he will be subject to the same obligations as any other commercial person offering such services, that is, as a carrier, etc., although if he in fact sub-contracts the actual performance of the operation, the extent of his obligations for any loss caused through the negligence or other default of the sub-contractor will depend on the ultimate extent to which he is liable at law for the acts of such a party, which will be discussed in a later chapter.[22] The extent therefore to

---

shed by the ship's agents until sold a week later by auction. The holder of the bill of lading claimed for short quantity due to theft on the wharf. The bill provided that when goods were delivered from the deck the shipowner's liability was to cease and the consignee was bound to be ready to receive them. The shipowner had not given the ship's agents authority to constitute the former a warehouseman on behalf of the consignees, written instructions having been given as to their duties. They had no authority to deviate from the terms of the bill of lading, and if they did so they must be personally liable for the loss, and not the shipowner. There was no custom or duty to protect the goods until the consignees had sold them and to deliver them to the buyers after inspection, on the consignee's orders. Such a custom in the Port of Montreal was not proved, and, even if it had been, the bill of lading would have overridden it.

[22] See Chapter 11.

which a forwarder may be liable in negligence must depend on which of these categories his operations will fall into. His liability must therefore be a question of fact in each case, subject to certain broad principles and rules which existing case law has laid down, and in any case subject to any contractual terms which the parties may have agreed upon. In this respect, however, the absence of any guidance from Standard Trading Conditions in their present form as to the forwarder's obligations when fulfilling the more complex functions which he undertakes may create problems in the future with the development of more sophisticated forms of transportation.

CHAPTER 6

THE FORWARDER'S LIABILITY IN RELATION TO CONVERSION

1. CONVERSION, DETINUE AND NEGLIGENCE IN RELATION TO FORWARDING OPERATIONS

175 THE duties of the forwarder in relation to the tort of negligence have already been discussed in the last chapter. In many cases, however, a plea in negligence will only be made as an alternative to one in conversion, where the loss suffered by the consignor or consignee results from the wrongful delivery or detention of a shipment of goods for which the forwarder is responsible in some form or other. Conversion has been defined as "an act of wilful interference, without lawful justification, with any chattel in a manner inconsistent with the right of another, whereby that other is deprived of the use and possession of it."[1] Basically, therefore, the forwarder will be liable in many cases both for negligence and conversion where he fails to exercise the normal care expected of a forwarder in disposing of a shipment, but he may be liable for conversion alone where he innocently and without negligence disposes of goods to a third party who is neither the owner nor has an immediate right of ownership to them, or has not been authorised to act on their behalf in so doing, that is, in a manner "inconsistent with such rights."[2]

176 There are two principal ways in which the forwarder may become liable in conversion. First, by wrongful delivery of goods, that is, by transferring either the title in such goods or some lesser interest in them to a third party. Secondly, he may also be liable for conversion to the owner if he retains possession of the goods with the intention of keeping them "in defiance of" the owner.[3] Such an action may also make the forwarder liable in the tort of detinue, but for practical purposes such an act will at some time normally constitute a conversion, so that it will only be necessary to rely on the tort of detinue where the act complained of does not amount to a dealing contrary to title or to the rights of the plaintiff or where the physical return of a chattel is required. It should be noted that detinue will be of no avail against a forwarder where he has had neither actual possession of the goods nor of the documents of title, as in such a case he will have neither detained the goods nor refused to give them up.[4]

[1] Salmond, *Law of Torts*, 15th ed., p. 125.
[2] *Ibid.* at p. 144.
[3] *Ibid.* at p. 146.
[4] See *G. Peereboom* v. *World Transport Agency Ltd.* (1921) 6 Ll.L.Rep. 170 at p. 172.

177   For a forwarder to be liable for the conversion of a client's goods, mere negligence in the performance of his duties to the latter will not necessarily constitute conversion unless it also amounts to a dealing contrary to the true owner's rights. In such circumstances a remedy will only lie in negligence, but not in conversion.

The problem was discussed in *G. Peereboom* v. *World Transport Agency Ltd.*[5] where a forwarder was entrusted with 500 cases to forward to Antwerp from London, being delivered to a wharf by a third party on the plaintiff seller's instructions to be held to the order of the defendant forwarders. The latter, according to their usual practice as forwarders, sent to the shipping company a bill of lading for them, but this was returned covering 339 cases only, which they passed on to the plaintiffs. The reason given by the shipping company for the discrepancies was that the balance of 161 cases had been shut out and returned to the wharf. Subsequently the plaintiff wished to stop shipment, and the forwarder therefore gave him a delivery order for the 161 cases. The former, however, took no action on it for some months, and on eventual presentation to the wharf it transpired they had been shipped to no known consignee and had disappeared.

In the subsequent action against the forwarder the court rejected a plea that the forwarder was liable for detinue as he had never had possession of the goods which he had refused to give up. On the contrary, the forwarder had given the plaintiff a document which would have given him the right of delivery if the goods had in fact been on the wharf.[6] Neither was the forwarder liable for conversion, as he had not dealt with the goods contrary to his client's title or rights in respect of them. The fact that the forwarder had been negligent in informing his principal that the carrier had been in dispute with the wharfinger as to the actual location of the goods did not affect the issue, and could not of itself constitute conversion.[7]

178 Delivery to a third party

Where an action for wrongful delivery is brought against a forwarder, the question arises as to the extent of the forwarder's liability in conversion, where he innocently delivers the goods to a third party. Here a distinction must be drawn between delivery in the knowledge that it is in pursuance of a sale or other disposition of title in relation to the goods, and delivery without such knowledge. The precedents on the

---

[5] *Ibid.*

[6] *Ibid.* at p. 172.

[7] See § 143 for the negligence aspect of the case. In a Canadian case the plaintiff sent two boxes of trees to his agent, addressed to various buyers. They were shipped by steamer to the defendant forwarder, who opened the boxes and delivered some trees to buyers who collected them. Three days later the agent sent to collect them. Many trees were damaged—the evidence was contradictory whether they were damaged before or after arrival, or whether, as pleaded by the forwarder, it was necessary to open the boxes and deliver without delay. The plaintiff sued in trover, but the court held that whether or not the forwarder was guilty of negligence as a bailee, his actions did not constitute a conversion of the goods: *Lovekin* v. *Podgor*, 24 U.C.Q.B. 156.

subject are sparse, but it appears from the dicta of Blackburn J. in
Hollins v. *Fowler* [8] that,

> " On principle, one who deals with goods at the request of the
> person who has the actual custody of them in the bona fide belief
> that the custodier is the true owner, or has the authority of the
> true owner, should be excused for what he does if the act is of such
> a nature as would be excused if done by the authority of the person
> in possession, if he was . . . entrusted with their custody."

In other words, if a forwarder merely delivers goods to a consignee he
will not be liable in conversion if this delivery is wrongful solely on the
grounds that the transaction constituted an act of conversion on the
part of the consignor. So, for example, where a forwarder packs a shipment of goods and ships them on his principal's instructions, he will
not be liable for conversion. [9]

179   **Knowledge**

Where, however, a forwarder has actual knowledge that his delivery
or forwarding of the goods is part of a transaction which affects the
title to them, and not merely their possession, the state of the law is
uncertain, as the precedents differ. In *National Mercantile Bank* v.
Rymill [10] the Court of Appeal held that an agent who in fact delivered
goods to a third party whilst aware that they were the subject of a
contract of sale to the latter, was not liable in conversion. This, however,
is contrary to the dicta by Blackburn J. in *Hollins* v. *Fowler*, although
the principle has been adopted in the American *Restatement*. [11] The
better opinion seems to be that, provided the forwarder has not himself
been instrumental in effecting the sale or other transaction affecting
the title to goods, as opposed to the mere transfer of possession, then
he will not be liable in conversion even if he has knowledge of the
transaction, provided he is not aware of the true owner's title to the
goods. [12] In other words, the test is not whether the forwarder has
knowledge of the nature of the transaction or not, but whether he has
actual notice of the true owner's title to the goods. [13]

180   **Wilful interference**

There can of course be no conversion without wilful interference.
Consequently where a forwarder permits goods to get into the hands of
a third party accidentally or negligently, he will not be liable in conversion. On the other hand though, if a forwarder wrongfully and mis-
takenly delivers goods to the wrong person, or alternatively, refuses
to deliver them to the right person, the forwarder will be liable in

[8] (1875) L.R. 7 H.L. 757 at p. 766.
[9] *Greenway* v. *Fisher* (1824) 1 C. & P. 190.
[10] (1881) 44 L.T. 767.
[11] *Restatement*, 2nd ed., Torts, s. 233.
[12] *National Mercantile Bank* v. *Rymill, supra.*
[13] See Salmond, *Law of Torts*, 15th ed., pp. 134–135; Powell, *Law of Agency*, 2nd ed.,
p. 278; Street, *Law of Torts*, 4th ed., p. 49.

conversion.[14] In particular, as such liability will be absolute at common law, as in the case of both private and common carriers, it is customary to limit this liability contractually wherever possible.[15]

2. THE FORWARDER'S DUTY TO OBEY THE INSTRUCTIONS OF THE TRUE OWNER

181 In considering the forwarder's liability for conversion, a distinction must be drawn between the forwarder when acting as a carrier's agent and the forwarder when acting on behalf of the consignor. When acting in the former capacity, the forwarder will not be liable in conversion if he delivers goods without requiring the consignee to produce a bill of lading, unless he has been instructed to require the production of one, and is himself in actual possession of the goods.[16] In other words where, as commonly happens, the forwarder's function is merely that of " a conduit pipe or messenger, passing on instructions given him by his principal," he will not be liable for conversion.[17]

182 **Possession of bill of lading**

However, irrespective of whether the forwarder is acting for the carrier or the consignor, he must carefully ascertain whether or not the party giving him instructions is in possession of the bill of lading, and with it title to the goods. Otherwise he may find himself liable in conversion for following instructions which are inconsistent with the true owner's rights. For example, if a forwarder fails to deliver goods to the consignee as a result of instructions given to him by the consignor, he will be liable to the consignee in conversion if the consignor has transferred the bill of lading to him.[18] This will not apply of course where the consignor has validly exercised his right of stoppage in transit.

183 Conversely, where goods have been consigned to a forwarder for him to approach the buyer for instructions as to their disposal, the former will be bound to follow any instructions given him by the consignor as to the disposal of the goods until property has passed to the buyer and may be liable in conversion if he does otherwise. If however, in response to the seller's instructions, the forwarder has obtained instructions from the buyer as to the disposal of the goods, the seller will have lost his right of stoppage in transit under section

[14] *The Arpad* [1934] P. 189 at p. 232.
[15] However it is not possible to restrict liability contractually to the extent that it permits a carrier or his agent to disregard his obligation as to delivery, which is basically to deliver against a bill of lading where one exists. Consequently, such an exemption clause will be inoperative where delivery is effected by the ship's agent without production of the bill of lading, and with knowledge that such was wrongful, merely in exchange for a bank indemnity instead. The carrier and his agent will therefore be liable for conversion: *Sze Hai Bank Ltd.* v. *Rambler Cycle Co. Ltd.* [1959] A.C. 576.
[16] *Thrige* v. *United Shipping Co. Ltd.* (1924) 18 Ll.L.Rep. 6.
[17] *Ibid.* at p. 9, *per* Scrutton L.J. In such a case an agent owes no duty to a vendor who has contracted with the shipowner, his principal, rather than with the agent himself as a forwarder: *per* Scrutton L.J.—see Chapter 5.
[18] *Luigi Riva Di Fernando* v. *Simon Smits & Co. Ltd.* (1920) 2 Ll.L.Rep. 279; 4 Ll.L.Rep. 264 (C.A.).

45 (2) of the Sale of Goods Act and therefore any right to recover in conversion.[19]

184   If the forwarder is himself in possession of the bill of lading or other documents of title, he must ensure that he does not transfer them to a party who has no right to them, or else risk liability to the true owner for conversion of the goods in question. Neither will it be any defence that the forwarder handed over the documents of title to an unauthorised recipient as a result of the latter's misrepresentation. For example, in *Kolbin & Sons* v. *United Shipping Company Ltd.*[20] the defendants were forwarders in Archangel who forwarded a shipment of flax to England during the Bolshevik revolution, and in doing so " in the course of their business as forwarding agents they acted in an emergency as reasonably careful businessmen in shipping them to England and warehousing and in deciding to sell [them]." [21] They then handed over the bill of lading to a certain R. who misrepresented himself to be the shipper's agent in this country. R. then sold the goods, retained the price and became bankrupt. In the ensuing action by the shipper against the forwarder for the conversion of the flax, the House of Lords held that, by handing over the goods to the absolute control of R. on condition that they were paid their charges, and thereby taking no further responsibility for them, the defendants abandoned their charge of the goods and were therefore liable in conversion. The fact that they had been deceived by R.'s misrepresentation was no defence, particularly as they had failed to take steps to verify whether in fact R. was the plaintiff's accredited agent or not. In such circumstances, as Lord Atkin pointed out,[22] the prudent course would have been to employ R. as an agent to sell the goods for them, and to account to them for the price, for which they in turn would have been accountable to the true owner, the shipper. This procedure, although not avoiding the problem of R.'s insolvency, would have saved the forwarder from liability for conversion, and provided he was not negligent in employing R., would have avoided liability for breach of his duties of care too. However, a forwarder will not be liable for obeying oral instructions given by an employee without authorisation, provided the latter has apparent authority to give such an order.[23]

3. CONVERSION AND THE FORWARDER'S LIEN—RIGHT OF INDEMNITY

185   A forwarder who is in possession of a client's goods has a right of lien over them in respect of outstanding charges.[24] Such a right will normally only be a particular lien unless by local custom, contractual

---

[19] *Johann Plischke & Sohne G.m.b.H.* v. *Allison Bros. Ltd.* (1936) 55 Ll.L.Rep. 262.
[20] (1931) 40 Ll.L. Rep. 241.
[21] *Ibid.* at p. 248, *per* Lord Atkin.
[22] *Ibid.*
[23] *Comptoir Franco-Anglais d'Exportation* v. *Van Oppen & Co.* (1922) 13 Ll.L.Rep. 59 at p. 60, *per* Swift J. Nor will the fact that fresh instructions have been given by a different method affect the issue: *ibid.*
[24] See Chapter 14.

agreement or by the dealing of the parties, a general lien has come into existence. If a forwarder attempts to exercise his right of lien against the true owner, not being his client, he will be liable for conversion unless he is in fact a common carrier, when it seems that he can exercise his right of lien even against the true owner.[25]

Similarly, where a forwarder attempts to exercise a right of lien against his principal for outstanding charges, he will be liable in conversion if he has in fact lost possession of the goods. For instance, a forwarder may attempt to exercise his right of lien against his principal the consignor over goods shipped under a c.i.f. contract after they have been placed on board ship, but as property will have passed to the consignee when the goods are placed on board, they will hold the goods under the bill of lading on behalf of the consignee and not on behalf of the forwarder. Consequently the forwarder will be liable to the consignee in conversion for doing so.[26]

Conversely, a forwarder who attempts to exercise a contractual right of general lien over goods against the buyer in respect of a general account will be liable to the seller in conversion and detinue where the buyer has rejected the goods and property has therefore not passed to him, but remains instead in the seller as the true owner.[27] Likewise, where a forwarder exercises a right of lien over another party's goods, he will have a right of action against anyone who commits an act of conversion against his interest, but if he wrongfully parts with possession of them, not only will he lose his right of lien, but it will also in itself constitute an act of conversion which will terminate the bailment and render the forwarder liable to the true owner.[28]

186   Right of indemnity

Where a forwarder delivers goods to a person who has no title, and is found liable to the true owner in conversion, under certain circumstances he will be able to recover an indemnity from the person who instructed him to part with the goods. To obtain an indemnity, an express contractual agreement to this effect may be obtained.[29] Otherwise, there must be an implied contract of indemnity between the parties, which can be inferred from the facts of the case as being created when the instructions were given which resulted in the conversion.

It is not sufficient merely to prove that instructions have been given to the forwarder concerning the disposal of the goods, as this in itself does not imply a contract of indemnity. For example, a forwarder was entrusted with goods by the first seller in a string contract, who had stipulated that property was not to pass until payment was made, which in fact never took place. An intermediate buyer, L., authorised the

[25] *Ibid.*
[26] *Langley, Beldon & Gaunt Ltd.* v. *Morley* [1965] 1 Lloyd's Rep. 297.
[27] *Black & Broom* v. *J. Coppo & Co.* (1922) 13 Ll.L.Rep. 279 at p. 347; (1923) 14 Ll.L.Rep. 391 (C.A.).
[28] *Mulliner* v. *Florence* (1878) 3 Q.B.D. 484.
[29] See Cl. 24, S.T.C. discussed in § 283.

forwarder to deliver the goods to the next buyer, and the latter sent an authority to the forwarder to pack and deliver them to the docks, which the forwarder did. It later transpired that the seller had not in fact authorised this. Consequently, the forwarder was liable in conversion to the seller, and could not claim an indemnity from L. for acting on his instructions, as it was not possible to infer a promise of indemnity in the circumstances.[30]

187   C.M.R.

Under C.M.R., where the consignor or consignee of goods wishes to exercise his right of disposal of goods whilst in transit, under the provisions of Article 12 of the Convention, the carrier has a right of indemnity in respect of all expenses, loss or damage involved in carrying out such instructions.[31] If however, the carrier fails to require the production of the first copy of the consignment note, he will be liable to the person who is " entitled to make a claim for any loss or damage caused thereby." [32]

4. CONTRACTUAL PROVISIONS RELATING TO LIABILITY IN CONVERSION

188   Standard Trading Conditions

Owing to the doctrine of privity of contract, contractual protection against liability for conversion, as in the case of negligence, can only benefit a forwarder in respect of liability to a client with whom he is in direct contractual relationship, together with any other parties on whose behalf the client may contract. Consequently, no contractual provision can protect the forwarder if he is sued by the true owner of goods, unless the latter is in fact his client. However, the forwarder is given some protection by Clause 2, Standard Trading Conditions, which provides that the forwarder's clients,

> " expressly warrant that they are either the owners or the author-
> ised agents of the owners of any goods to which the transaction
> relates and further warrant that they are authorised to accept and
> are accepting these conditions not only for themselves but also as
> agents for and on behalf of all other persons who are or may
> thereafter become interested in the goods."

This means that if the client is not in fact the true owner or his author-ised agent, he will be liable for breach of warranty and must indemnify the forwarder against any loss he may suffer through an action in conversion or detinue by the true owner of the goods.

Accordingly, where a forwarder is liable for conversion through following his client's instructions he will be able to obtain a full indemnity from him. If, however, a forwarder commits an act of conversion of his own volition instead of on his client's instructions, whether

---

[30] *D. Steward & Co.* v. *J. Lofthouse & Co.* (1921) 9 Ll.L.Rep. 386.
[31] Art. 12 (5) (*a*). *Cf.* Arts. 21–25, C.I.M.
[32] Art. 12 (7). See Chapter 8 as to the right of disposal under C.M.R.

innocently or not, he will be liable to the true owner of the goods without any indemnity from his principal. However in an action by his principal against him for conversion he will be protected by Clause 13 (ii) which protects him against any failure to carry out his instructions provided the failure " was not caused by the wilful neglect or default of the [forwarder] or its own servants." The net result therefore seems to be that a forwarder will be protected from liability to his principal for misdelivery howsoever caused unless it is through the forwarder's wilful negligence or default which places his liability in this respect on the same basis as that under Clause 13 (i) for loss or damage to the goods, or non-delivery thereof.

189 Contractual lien

A question that has not come before the courts yet concerns the position of a forwarder who attempts to exercise a particular or general lien over goods under the provisions of Clause 23. This clause provides that the right of lien can be exercised by a forwarder in respect of moneys due from the " Sender, Consignee or Owner to the Company." Such a clause will obviously bind any of these parties specified providing they are either in direct contractual relationship with the forwarder or else the contracting party has also contracted on their behalf in making the forwarding contract—Clause 2 expressly states that the client accepts the conditions of Standard Trading Conditions " not only for themselves but also as agents for and on behalf of all other persons who are or may thereafter become interested in the goods." However, if either the " Sender, Consignee or Owner " is not in contractual relationship with the forwarder, they will not be bound by the contractual right of lien, and whether or not a particular lien may exist, the contractual general lien will not be exercisable. Consequently if a forwarder attempts to exercise such a right under Clause 23 against a " Sender, Consignee or Owner " who is not privy to him, he will be liable either in detinue or conversion or both providing that the party injured has an actionable interest in the goods. It seems therefore that Clause 23 can only be fully operative where privity of contract is established by the forwarder with the debtor in question.[33]

5. CONCLUSION

190 The position of the forwarder at common law, like that of the banks, is an onerous one in relation to the tort of conversion, as he accepts responsibility for shipments whose value is far in excess of the limited reward which he received for services performed. His liability can be classed under three headings. First, he will be liable for wrongful delivery, that is, for delivering goods to a party other than the consignee. Responsibility for such an act is one which the forwarder can normally guard against, and will usually arise when he is acting as a

[33] See Chapter 11.

receiving agent rather than in forwarding operations, where his obligations will normally cease in this respect on handing over the goods to a carrier. Secondly, the forwarder will be liable for conversion to the true owner of goods where he accepts instructions from a third party who is not authorised to give them. Against such liability the forwarder can have little protection, as he is rarely in contractual relationship with the true owner, and can only hope to obtain an indemnity from his principal in respect of such liability, if he has obtained either express or implied agreement by his principal to this effect.

Thirdly, a forwarder must exercise caution in exercising any right of lien he may possess, whether contractual or common law, as unless he is a common carrier he will not be able to exercise such rights against the true owner unless such a right is contractually obtained. Consequently the forwarder must note carefully the particular class of freight contract entered into so as to establish the probable time when property passes in a particular shipment. This is not always easy, and where loss results through such an act of conversion, the forwarder is not normally in a position to claim an indemnity from his principal or any other party. It can therefore be seen that although a forwarder can protect himself fairly successfully against liability for loss or damage resulting from negligence, such protection is less easily obtainable in the case of conversion owing to the very nature of the tort. Only by means of a third-party indemnity insurance policy can the forwarder adequately cover himself against such claims, and such cover is customary for all engaged in forwarding operations.[34]

---

[34] To some extent however the problem is avoided where a forwarder has the status of a carrier under C.M.R., as the question of the right of disposal of goods is separated from that of ownership, and instead based solely upon possession of the consignment note—see Chapter 8.

CHAPTER 7

THE LIABILITY OF THE FORWARDER FOR DELAY

1. INTRODUCTION

191 DELAY is the term given for any failure to transport a shipment of goods within such a period of time as is reasonable in the particular circumstances.

The liability of the forwarder for delay in the transit of goods will depend on the exact function which he fulfils. To the extent to which he acts as a carrier, his liability at common law will merely be to ensure that the goods reach their destination within a reasonable time. This is a question of fact in each case, and will apply whether the forwarder is acting as a common or private carrier. In both cases he will only be liable for loss caused by his own negligence and that of his servants. If on the other hand a forwarder merely acts in his capacity of a forwarder, his liability will depend upon the particular operations which he has undertaken to perform.

2. DELAY IN RELATION TO FORWARDING OPERATIONS

192 Where a forwarder undertakes to arrange shipping space for his client in relation to a contract of sale which stipulates delivery within a certain period of time, he is not obliged to ensure that goods can be brought alongside a ship within that time, as far as shipping arrangements are concerned. In other words, if a ship is not ready so as to preclude this, the forwarder will not be in breach of contract. The sole obligation of the forwarder, even if he is aware of the time stipulation, is merely " to act with all reasonable promptness to arrange for shipping space when they know that the goods are available." This does not, however, preclude the forwarder from entering into a specific contractual undertaking to ensure that goods can be brought alongside a ship within a certain time, but in the absence thereof, no such duty will attach.[1]

If, therefore, a forwarder restricts himself purely within the bounds of forwarding in the narrow sense quoted, and does not act as a carrier, a warehouseman or a bailee, he will cease to be liable on shipment provided he has exercised reasonable care in choosing both method and route of carriage, where such has been left to his discretion.[2] If there are alternative routes whereby goods can be shipped, the forwarder will have fulfilled his duty if he chooses " an ordinary, reasonable and

---

[1] *Anglo-African Shipping Co. of New York Inc.* v. *J. Mortner Ltd.* [1962] 1 Lloyd's Rep. 81 at p. 93, *per* Megaw J.
[2] *Marston Excelsior Ltd.* v. *Arbuckle Smith & Co. Ltd.* [1971] 2 Lloyd's Rep. 306.

commercial route," in the absence of instructions to the contrary.³ For example, if in respect of an inward shipment there is a choice between a transit in bond with inland clearance, and a normal transit requiring customs clearance at the port of arrival, the buyer cannot complain if delay results from the choice of the latter, through his failure to pay customs duty on the goods on being notified of their arrival at the port, provided he has not specifically required the forwarder to ship the goods by the bonded route.⁴

193   Often a forwarder may find that delay in the forwarding of a shipment results from extraneous factors beyond his control. If therefore he wishes to put forward such interruptions as dock strikes, public disturbances, etc., as a defence to an action for compensation for delay in forwarding operations, certain criteria must be established. Devlin J. has explained that if a forwarder

"... desires to put forward an excuse of that kind, it is not enough for him to prove that there were exceptional conditions which may have resulted in a breach of his obligations. It is necessary for him to prove that, exercising due diligence, he was unable, owing to the prevailing conditions, to discharge his contractual obligations. In short he must give evidence, not merely of the existence of those conditions, but of their impact upon the work which he had to do under the contract." ⁵

On the other hand, it is quite common for forwarders to operate under conditions where excessive prudence on their part would cause such delay as to defeat the whole purpose of employing a forwarder, which is to expedite matters. For instance, the question arose in a recent case as to whether a forwarder was liable for loss which resulted from his method of operation which was intended to avoid unnecessary delay in operating a postal collection and delivery service. Here the forwarder did not enter the details of individual parcels in his delivery notes which were used in conjunction with a regular collection service he offered from local railway stations. Consequently a thief got

---

³ *Tiberghien Draperie S.A.* v. *Greenberg & Sons (Mantles) Ltd.* [1953] 2 Lloyd's Rep. 739 at p. 744, *per* Devlin J. *Cf. Crowe & Co. (London) Ltd.* v. *Giunipero & Co.* (1920) 2 Ll.L.Rep. 633, where a forwarder was held not liable for delay in shipping a consignment of perishable goods by following the railway company's instructions as to the route of shipment. See also *Cliffe* v. *Hull & Netherlands S.S. Co. Ltd.* (1921) 6 Ll.L.Rep. 136.
⁴ *Ibid.*
⁵ *Mark Lever & Co. Ltd.* v. *Wingate & Johnston Ltd.* (1950) 84 Ll.L.Rep. 156 at p. 163. As Rowlatt J. observed, the forwarder "... does not obtain possession of the goods and he does not undertake to deliver them ": *Jones* v. *European & General Express Co. Ltd.* (1920) 4 Ll.L.Rep. 127. Where therefore a forwarder made a contract with a firm of hide brokers to lighter goods from a ship to the wharf, and to sort and store them there, his obligation was merely to " do what was reasonable in the circumstances that then prevailed ": *G. W. Sheldon & Co. (London) Ltd.* v. *Alfred Young & Co.* (1921) 6 Ll.L.Rep. 466 at p. 467, *per* Roche J. Accordingly the forwarder was not liable for delay resulting from him employing a wharfinger as a sub-contractor who was crowded out with other shipments owing to the congested state of the docks, and who was not experienced in the hide trade, at a time when all regular hide warehouses were full up.

unauthorised possession of some of the notes, and thereby obtained certain goods by false pretences from the station. The court held that as the forwarder had not been negligent in permitting the thief to get possession of the notes, he was not liable for the loss.[6] As McNair J. stated,

> " I am not satisfied that, on the basis of foreseeability, the defendants were in any way negligent in using the collection note which they had used in its present form satisfactorily for many years and covering thousands of operations. Of course it is true that it is not a conclusive answer to a charge of negligence to say: ' We have done this operation this way for years and have never had any ill result '; but at the same time it is a very formidable reinforcement of an argument that in fact the method is not negligent that the method has proved successful over countless occasions; and it is also relevant, although again not conclusive, . . . that other . . . large forwarding agents who handle traffic in bulk . . . use exactly the same forms when collecting from the railway stations without specifying the details of the parcels." [7]

It therefore seems that, where a forwarder operates in a manner generally accepted in the trade as a reasonable method of avoiding unnecessary delay, if on balance it appears that by so doing the forwarder can offer a better service to his clients, he will not be liable at common law for any resultant loss, even though the loss might have been avoided by more prudent, but tardy, methods of operation.

194 Employment of a receiving agent

A forwarder may find himself liable for loss resulting from delay where he has employed a receiving agent to act on his behalf at the end of transit. Such a procedure is commonly practised, both to de-consolidate bulk shipments where smaller shipments have been consolidated under one bill of lading, and also to give a better service to the ultimate consignee in ensuring that the goods reach their destination. It is necessary therefore to consider two questions. First, to what extent is the forwarder liable for delay resulting from his own actions in failing to co-ordinate operations with his receiving agent, and, secondly, to what extent is the forwarder liable for loss resulting from delay actually caused by the receiving agent? The second category is fully dealt with in a later chapter, so that it is unnecessary to consider the forwarder's liability for his sub-agent any further here.[8]

The position as regards the first question seems to be as follows. If by using the services of a receiving agent a forwarder causes actual delay in transit, he will be liable for any loss which results. For instance, where a forwarder dispatched a shipment and documents to his receiving agent according to his normal practice, instead of to the named

---

[6] *Pringle of Scotland Ltd.* v. *Continental Express Ltd.* [1962] 2 Lloyd's Rep. 80.
[7] *Ibid.* at p. 87.
[8] See Chapter 11.

consignee, the forwarder will be liable to his client if the consignee rejects the goods because of delay in delivery, even if he has contractually exempted himself from liability for delay, if his client has given express instructions for the bill of lading to be sent to the consignee.[9] An exemption clause restricting liability for delay will only assist a forwarder where delay occurs in relation to the actual transit agreed upon, but not where an altogether different one is effected.[10]

195   A forwarder will likewise be liable where he fails to pass on instructions to his receiving agent to enable him to forward the consignment expeditiously to its destination, so that delay results. For example, the situation discussed may arise where a forwarder or carrier who is responsible for the shipment of goods fails to inform the receiving agent who is responsible for re-forwarding the goods to a further destination that freight has been pre-paid to cover the whole transit. If therefore delay results through the receiving agent making further arrangements for the on-carriage which he could have dispensed with if he had been informed that freight had been pre-paid, the original forwarder or carrier will be liable for any loss incurred.[11]

196   Where a forwarder is given instructions by his client which are to be passed on to his receiving agent, and the latter fails to carry them out, the forwarder will be liable if he fails to issue further instructions to remedy the delay, when once he has become aware of the dilatoriness of the receiving agent. This liability will be incurred by the forwarder in addition to any which he may incur in respect of the actual default of the receiving agent. Accordingly, in *Mark Lever & Co. Ltd.* v. *Wingate & Johnston Ltd.*[12] the defendant forwarder was instructed to pass on instructions to his receiving agent in Calcutta to contact certain Indian importers. On the arrival of a shipment of cosmetics the agent was to re-offer it for inspection and acceptance, as it had been previously refused, and if again refused by the importers to re-ship the goods to England. As a result of delay on the part of the receiving agent loss was caused to the plaintiff shippers. The forwarder was held liable on this count, and also for failing to re-instruct the agent as to re-shipment when he became aware of the delay. In such circumstances, therefore, unless a forwarder uses the utmost expedition in amending existing instructions when aware either of their inadequacy owing to changed circumstances or of the failure of the receiving agent to carry out his duties, he will be liable for breach of duty to his client and for any subsequent loss.[13]

---

[9] *Hunt & Winterbotham Ltd.* v. *Morny & Co.* (1922) 12 Ll.L.Rep. 286.
[10] *Cf.* the *Suisse Atlantique* case as to the question of the problem of deviation and fundamental breach of contract. See § 162.
[11] *United Express Co.* v. *J. Leete & Son* (1920) 2 Ll.L.Rep. 106.
[12] See note 5.
[13] See Chapter 8.

197 Demurrage

Finally, another aspect of the problem that may arise is where a forwarder hires a vehicle from a carrier and delay occurs whilst it is being loaded or unloaded. Such a problem is one that is increasingly facing land carriers and forwarders with the growing congestion in ports and cities. If the delay occurs through the forwarder's fault he may be liable to the carrier for any loss suffered, although if the delay is caused by the tardiness of the carrier's own servants in loading or unloading the vehicle, the forwarder will not be liable.[14] However, it is a common practice for provision for demurrage charges to be included in road haulage contracts nowadays to overcome such problems.[15]

3. DELAY IN RELATION TO INWARD CLEARANCE

198 The problem of delay in relation to clearance of inward shipments through customs has come before the courts on several occasions. The question divides itself into two sections. First, there is the liability of the forwarder for increased duties which become payable through delay in clearance. This will be dealt with in a later chapter.[16]

The second aspect of the forwarder's liability in respect of delay in clearance is where loss of market or rejection by a buyer results. If an agreement is made by a forwarder (or a carrier) to clear a shipment through customs, and delay in collection and delivery occurs through the latter's failure to obtain clearance which results in rejection by the buyer and consequent loss of market, the forwarder will be in breach of contract in failing to clear the shipment and will be liable to his client for any loss resulting from the delay in clearance.[17]

To render a forwarder liable for delay in clearance, it is a prerequisite that the consignee must have performed all obligations incumbent upon him, and in particular to have carried out all necessary documentation normal in import procedures. Consequently, a forwarder will not be liable for any loss resulting from delay in transit of a shipment, where it is solely the result of the consignee's failure to obtain an import licence.[18] Nor where a forwarder is instructed to clear an inward shipment and to pay all charges, will he be liable for increased charges if they have resulted from detention of the goods by the customs authorities, unless the forwarder has also been negligent himself.[19] However, if the forwarder has agreed with the carrier that, as between themselves, the former will pay customs duties, and through delay in payment the goods are warehoused instead of being forwarded immediately, liability will only fall on the forwarder for the delay and not on the carrier.[20]

[14] *Glibbery* v. *Martin Benscher*, Lloyd's List, April 29, 1921.
[15] *Cf.* Cl. 14, R.H.A. Conditions 1967; Cl. 8 (3), B.R.S. Conditions.
[16] See Chapter 16.
[17] *Robert Shearer Ltd.* v. *Road Haulage Executive* [1952] 1 Lloyd's Rep. 512.
[18] *George Pulman & Sons Ltd.* v. *F. E. Crowe* (1920) 3 Ll.L.Rep. 100.
[19] *Donner* v. *London & Hamburg Agency* (1923) 15 Ll.L.Rep. 63.
[20] *United Express Co.* v. *J. Leete & Son* (1920) 2 Ll.L.Rep. 106.

4. CONTRACTUAL PROVISIONS RELATING TO DELAY

199 Standard Trading Conditions

To restrict his common law liability for delay the forwarder has made express provision in Standard Trading Conditions to cover such contingencies. Under Clause 4 the forwarder reserves the right to adopt any " means, route or procedure " that he may wish, unless given express instructions to the contrary by his client. Even then these can be departed from " if in the opinion of the Company it is at any stage necessary or desirable in the Customer's interests " to do so. Clause 4 is further reinforced by Clause 13 (iv) which provides that " the Company shall not in any event be under any liability for any delay or consequential loss or loss of market, however caused. . . ." [21] This clause is very widely couched and appears to give protection to the forwarder for delay etc. resulting from failure to observe the customer's express written instructions, irrespective of whether it was in the customer's interests to do so or not. It therefore appears that even if the route chosen is not " an ordinary, reasonable and commercial route," [22] and in fact the whole forwarding operation is negligently carried out, the forwarder will avoid liability unless the injury inflicted amounts to a fundamental breach of contract. [23] This point has not yet been the subject of judicial comment though.

200 R.H.A. Conditions

Similarly under R.H.A. Conditions 1961, the carrier does not accept liability for loss of a particular market under any circumstances nor for indirect or consequential loss. [24] Furthermore Clause 8 restricts the carrier's liability for delay to that resulting from his wilful negligence or that of his servants. [25] Under R.H.A. Conditions 1967, the provision in Clause 5 of the 1961 Conditions is restated in Clause 12 (2)(b), [26] although the provision relating to wilful negligence has been deleted and replaced by the requirement of notice in writing within three days of the claim arising. [27] Prior to this, the discrepancies that existed between Standard Trading Conditions and R.H.A. Conditions 1961, although undesirable, were at least relatively slight in extent. Since R.H.A. Conditions 1967 have come into force, however, the two sets of conditions appear to be totally divorced from each other on these points.

201 C.M.R.

Where a contract of carriage is subject to C.M.R., the carrier will be

---

[21] Arts. 7, 24–26, 29 Y.F.C.; Art. 6, C.G. (Switzerland); Arts. 7, 22, 37, C.G. (Belgium); Arts. 13, 17, A.D.S.P.; Arts. 7, 9 (2), 14, D.F.C.; Arts. 4, 22, N.F.C.; Arts. 6, 7, C.G. (France); Arts. 3, 10, N.Y.F.; Arts. 9, 12, F.B.L.

[22] *Mark Lever & Co. Ltd.* v. *Wingate & Johnston Ltd., per* Devlin J. See note 5.

[23] *Cf.* As to the question of liability for deviation, etc., see *Suisse Atlantique* case at note 10.

[24] Cl. 5, R.H.A. Conditions 1961. *Cf. Hadley* v. *Baxendale* (1854) 9 Ex. 341.

[25] *Cf.* Cl. 5 (2) and 6 (2), B.R.S. Conditions. See Kahn-Freund, *Law of Inland Transport,* 4th ed., pp. 289–290.

[26] *Cf.* Art. 23 (4) (5), C.M.R. *Quaere* whether Cl. 12 (2) (b) applies only if goods are lost or damaged.

[27] Cl. 10 (1) (b), R.H.A. Conditions 1967.

liable for loss resulting from delay under the same circumstances as laid down in Article 17 in respect of loss or damage to the goods, discussed in an earlier chapter.[28] Article 19 defines delay as either non-delivery within an agreed time limit or else if no time limit has been agreed upon, as exceeding " the time it would be reasonable to allow a diligent carrier." However in applying the latter test it is necessary to consider the circumstances of the case, and in the case of part loads, the time required to make up a complete load " in the normal way." [29]

The carrier is also given the same defences as in the case of loss or damage to goods laid down in Articles 17 (2), (4) and (5) and is subject to the same rules of proof as laid down in Article 18. Similarly under Article 13 (1) the consignee can enforce any rights arising under the contract of carriage against the carrier in his own name.

Where a claimant can prove that loss has resulted from delay, the carrier will be liable to pay compensation not exceeding the carriage charges.[30] If, however, a special interest in delivery has been declared by the consignor, and an agreed time limit in delivery agreed upon in return for payment of a surcharge, additional compensation can be claimed for the additional loss proved up to the amount of the interest declared.[31] However, compensation will only be payable if a written reservation is sent to the carrier within twenty-eight days of the goods being placed at the consignee's disposal.[32]

5. PERISHABLE GOODS—SALE AND MEASURE OF DAMAGES

202 Many claims in respect of delay relate to the carriage of perishable goods which have deteriorated as a result of an extended period of transit. At common law the only provision relating to perishable goods is a right of sale under the rules relating to agency of necessity where there is a " commercial necessity." In other words, the goods will be reduced in commercial value if they are not immediately disposed of, although the exercise of this right is subject to the condition that the carrier or forwarder is unable to obtain instructions from his principal as to the disposal of the goods.[33] Contractual provision is therefore made in Clause 18 of Standard Trading Conditions, whereby a forwarder can sell or otherwise dispose of any perishable goods which are either not taken up on arrival by the consignee or else are insufficiently addressed or otherwise unidentifiable. This overcomes the defects of the common law inasmuch as the exercise of the right of sale is not dependent upon a " commercial necessity," but merely on the state of the goods, and there is no obligation on the forwarder to inform either the consignor, consignee or the owner of the goods before doing so. Both at common

[28] See § 164.
[29] Art. 19, C.M.R.
[30] Art. 23 (5), C.M.R.—see § 246.
[31] Art. 26, C.M.R.—see § 247.
[32] Art. 30 (3), C.M.R.—see § 305.
[33] See *Springer* v. *G.W.Ry.* [1921] 1 K.B. 257. See Bowstead, *Agency*, 13th ed., Art. 14.

law and under Clause 18 the forwarder can deduct his charges before accounting for the proceeds. The payment or tender of the balance by the forwarder "shall be equivalent to delivery." The client remains liable though for "all charges and expenses arising in connection with the sale or disposal of the goods." [34]

203 "Perishable goods"

Secondly, the question arises of what are "perishable" goods. No definition is available as to their exact nature, and there is no provision as to whether it is left to the forwarder's discretion if goods are in fact perishable or not. The distinction could be of importance as, although notice is not required prior to the sale of perishable goods, Clause 19 provides that in the case of non-perishable goods, which cannot be delivered or are in the opinion of the forwarder insufficiently or incorrectly addressed for delivery to be effected, the sale cannot take place until twenty-one days after written notice has been sent to the customer. It might therefore be possible for a claim to be made against the forwarder on the grounds that as goods are not perishable as claimed by the forwarder, the latter is in breach of condition for failing to give the requisite notice before effecting the sale, and therefore is liable for any ensuing loss. Whether such a plea would succeed could again turn on whether Clauses 18 and 19 are subject to Clause 13 or whether they are to be read disjunctively. [35]

204 Measure of damages

Finally, as regards the question of measure of damages, it should be noted that where a forwarder is instructed to re-forward goods for sale in an alternative market and is guilty of delay in doing so, if the goods in question are perishables, and it is clear that even without the delay incurred they could still not have been sold in the alternative market before they deteriorated, the forwarder will only be liable to pay nominal damages and not the actual value of the goods. [36] Furthermore, although a carrier or forwarder must recognise the possibility of a sub-sale by the consignor or consignee, his liability will only exceed the value of the goods at their destination if he has actual or implied knowledge of any factor rendering such a measure of damages inadequate. [37]

205 C.M.R.

Where the contract of carriage is subject to C.M.R. the carrier is required to ask for instructions from the person entitled to dispose of the goods in accordance with the provisions of Article 12 if it becomes impossible to carry out the contract in accordance with the terms

[34] Cl. 18, S.T.C. *Cf.* Art. 6, N.F.C.; Art. 13, N.Y.F.F.; Arts. 8, 36, 40, C.G. (Belgium); Art. 44, Y.F.C.

[35] *Cf.* Cl. 4, R.H.A. Conditions 1961; Cl. 8, R.H.A. Conditions 1967. *Cf.* Art. 6, N.F.C.; Arts. 29, 40, C.G. (Belgium).

[36] *Mark Lever & Co. Ltd.* v. *Wingate & Johnston Ltd.* (1950) 84 Ll.L.Rep. 156 at p. 167, *per* Devlin J.

[37] *Heskell* v. *Continental Express Ltd.* (1950) 83 Ll.L.Rep. 438.

laid down in the consignment note before the goods reach the place designated for delivery.[38] Where circumstances prevent the delivery of the goods after their arrival at this place, the carrier must ask the sender for his instructions.[39] In both these cases, however, the carrier can sell the goods if they are perishable or their condition warrants such a course, or if the storage expenses are out of proportion to the value of the goods, without waiting for instructions.[40] In all other cases he can sell the goods if he has not received instructions to the contrary from the person entitled to the goods, within a reasonable time, and which he can reasonably be required to carry out.[41] What is reasonable must depend upon the particular circumstances. After sale, the proceeds are to be placed at the disposal of the person entitled to dispose of the goods. However, all charges due under the consignment note, the cost of the request for instructions and of carrying them out and all other expenses chargeable against the goods are deductible.[42] If they exceed the proceeds of sale, the carrier is entitled to the difference.[43] The actual procedure of sale will depend upon the *lex situs*.[44]

6. CONCLUSION

206 The forwarder's position, as in other aspects of his duties to his client, will vary according to whether he is merely acting as an agent or as a carrier. The obligations in respect of delay seem to fall into two distinct categories, those relating to forwarding operations, and those relating to inward clearance. The duty required of a forwarder in relation to the first category is essentially that of the normal commercial agent who has undertaken to carry out the function of a forwarder. In other words, the degree of skill and care expected cannot be that of a carrier who is actually responsible for effecting transit unless the forwarder, in fact, does so. It is therefore only a duty to ensure that goods are brought alongside at the right time if reasonably possible for loading,[45] and to use the skill and care which a normal forwarder would, where the choice of tariff, route or method of transport is left to his discretion.[46] He must also choose reasonably competent, commercial operators to perform such ancillary operations as are necessary, but will not be liable if conditions in the docks, etc., render such a procedure impossible.[47] Lastly, where a forwarder employs a receiving agent to act on his

---

[38] Art. 14 (1). *Cf.* Art. 24, C.I.M. See also §§ 220–224.
[39] Art. 15 (1). *Cf.* Art. 25, C.I.M.
[40] Art. 16 (3). It is not clear however from the text whether he must attempt to obtain instructions or not. Nor whether the goods can be disposed of merely because they are perishable by nature or whether they must be actually in danger of deteriorating. The French text differs in its construction on this point, and apparently favours the latter interpretation.
[41] Art. 16 (3).
[42] Art. 16 (1), (4).
[43] Art. 16 (4).
[44] Art. 16 (5).
[45] See note 1, *supra*.
[46] See note 3, *supra*.
[47] See note 5, *supra*.

behalf, he is bound to co-ordinate their operations and will be liable if, in using a receiving agent in contravention of his instructions, delay results.[48] Equally if a forwarder fails to remedy the failure of a receiving agent to perform his duty by giving further instructions, the forwarder will be liable for resultant loss which could have been avoided by further action on his part.

207   As regards the various contractual provisions in operation currently, there is a distinct cleavage between Standard Trading Conditions and the newly drafted R.H.A. and B.R.S. Conditions, the tendency being to a greater acceptance of liability for delay by the carrier. C.M.R. has in turn extended this liability even further, although the quantum of damages for delay is likely to be lower under its provisions in practice.[49]

---

[48] See note 9, *supra*.
[49] *Cf.* Art. 23 (5), C.M.R. The Economic Commission for Europe (Inland Transport Committee) have produced a draft Agreement on the International Carriage of Perishable Foodstuffs and on the Special Equipment to be used for such Carriage (ATP) 1970.

CHAPTER 8

OBLIGATIONS OF A FORWARDER IN RESPECT OF INSTRUCTIONS RECEIVED

1. GENERAL DUTIES

208 THE extent to which a forwarder will be liable either to his client or to a third party for loss caused by his failure to obey instructions given him by his principal, or conversely through him following instructions given to him by an unauthorised person, will depend to a large extent upon the particular facts of each case.[1] However, certain distinctions can be drawn from the case law on the subject which permit a limited framework of rules to be laid down in relation to this topic.

209 First, at common law there are no particular formalities required of a shipper as to the manner in which instructions are to be given to a forwarder. They can be oral, written, or implied by the circumstances or the custom of the trade although, as will be discussed later, under Standard Trading Conditions special requirements are laid down as to the method of instructions for various operations.[2] At common law where instructions are given to a forwarder orally by a shipper over the telephone, the courts have held that there is no obligation to confirm them in writing for them to bind the shipper in the terms of their authorisation.[3] Secondly, where a forwarder is instructed in respect of operations which are to be carried out by the latter's foreign correspondent, the forwarder is bound to pass the instructions on to the correspondent accurately, and will be liable to his client if he fails to do so, and also for the correspondent's failure to carry them out.[4] Where a forwarder does not forward a consignment according to his client's instructions, he may be liable for loss at common law if it results from his default. If therefore specific instructions are given to a forwarder with no provision for the exercise of his discretion, he will be bound to carry them out and to account for any profits made through his performance of the contract other than according to his instructions. This rule will apply whether there is an absolute obligation to carry as a principal or merely an obligation as a forwarder in the strict sense of

---

[1] Where a forwarder carries out his instructions he is " prima facie entitled to be paid a proper remuneration for having obeyed those instructions. . . ." *Universal Shipping and Forwarding Co. Ltd.* v. *Commercial and Industrial Co. Ltd.* (1919) 1 Ll.L.Rep. 635 at p. 636, *per* Greer J.

[2] See § 219. *Cf.* note 2, § 133 for the continental trading conditions.

[3] *Comptoir Franco-Anglais d'Exportation* v. *Van Oppen & Co.* (1922) 13 Ll.L.Rep. 59 at p. 60, *per* Swift J. See also *Langley, Beldon & Gaunt* v. *Morley* [1965] 1 Lloyd's Rep. 297 at p. 300, where a typical forwarding operation is described.

[4] *Mark Lever & Co. Ltd.* v. *Wingate & Johnston Ltd.* (1950) 84 Ll.L.Rep. 156.

the word.[5] Thirdly, under certain circumstances a forwarder will be bound to approach his client for instructions as to the action he requires to be taken. For instance, it may be the duty of a forwarder to seek his client's instructions as to whether goods are insured whilst in transit or otherwise bailed to a third party, in particular where there are various alternative tariffs, etc., available with varying degrees of liability accepted. In *Von Traubenberg's* case, Somervell L.J. stated that a forwarder had no "right to decide without getting instructions from the plaintiff or finding out whether the goods were already insured, . . . or finding out whether she wanted to have the goods insured."[6]

210 Equally where a forwarder is instructed by a shipper to ship goods at a through rate, and fails to ensure that the onward transit is so effected, he will be liable for any loss resulting from his failure to carry out his instructions.[7] If, contrary to instructions, the forwarder permits the goods to be warehoused on a through transit, instead of directly forwarding them as instructed, the charges incurred will be for his account, and cannot be debited to his client the shipper. If the delay resulting from non-performance of the contract is such that the shipper is forced to intervene personally and to give direct forwarding instructions himself, the forwarder will be bound to indemnify his principal, although he may be able to recover from a defaulting carrier.[8]

2. AMBIGUOUS INSTRUCTIONS

211 If a forwarder is given instructions which are ambiguous and which he honestly interprets as entitling him to carry out an assignment in the ordinary way of business of the place where he operates, he will not be liable for so doing, and will bind his principal by his acts to any third party with whom he has contracted.[9] However, whether an unintentional failure by a forwarder to carry out his instructions will amount to negligence on his part will be a question of fact in each case.[10]

Two questions must be asked to reach an answer. First, has the forwarder in fact understood his instructions in another sense to that intended by his client? Secondly, might the forwarder reasonably have so understood them without being guilty of negligence? This was the test applied by Roche J., who added that "If both the questions are answered in the affirmative, the principle laid down in *Ireland* v. *Livingston* applies."[11]

---

[5] *Charles Weis & Co. Ltd.* v. *Northern Traffic Ltd.* (1919) 1 Ll.L.Rep. 241.
[6] [1951] 2 Lloyd's Rep. 462 at p. 467. *Contra: W.L.R. Traders Ltd.* v. *B. & N. Shipping Agency Ltd.* [1955] 1 Lloyd's Rep. 554; for the extent of the obligation see Chapter 17.
[7] *United Express Company* v. *J. Leete & Son* (1920) 2 Ll.L.Rep. 106.
[8] *Ibid.*
[9] *Ireland* v. *Livingston* (1872) 5 H.L. 395 at p. 416, *per* Lord Chelmsford.
[10] *Gomer* v. *Pitt & Scott* (1922) 12 Ll.L.Rep. 115, see Chapter 17 for facts.
[11] *James Vale & Co.* v. *Van Oppen & Co. Ltd.* (1921) 6 Ll.L.Rep. 167 at p. 169. For facts see § 473. See also *Robert Rohleder* v. *J. Kendall (London) Ltd., Manchester Guardian*, July 24, 1924, which concerned a dispute as to a forwarder's authority in warehousing goods.

If therefore in misunderstanding his instructions a forwarder is not negligent, his principal will be liable for any resultant damage to a third party. For example, a forwarder was instructed by his principal to forward goods from Vladivostok after the Russian Revolution. He was told to draw his charges forward in the normal commercial manner of that place, as his principal did not supply any money to finance forwarding operations and had no arrangement with the forwarder whereby the latter was bound to provide the money himself. The forwarder honestly interpreted these instructions as entitling him to draw and discount a draft to a local bank to cover forwarding expenses, and at the same time to pledge the goods to the bank in such a way as to give it an independent title to them as pledgees, as this was the only practical method of obtaining money to forward the shipment at that time. The court held that in such circumstances a bank is not bound to inquire as to the correctness of the charges as between the forwarder and his principal, so that the latter was bound by the pledge.[12]

212 Similarly, instructions may be given to a forwarder or carrier only to deliver goods on presentation of documents. Here it seems that if no special instructions have been given to the forwarder or carrier, even though the latter becomes aware that the shipper is no longer prepared to extend credit to a particular consignee, he can still assume that the shipper has purposely taken such precautions as are necessary to protect his interests, in which case the forwarder is within his rights simply to deliver the goods on presentation of documents, without further action.[13]

213 Incomplete instructions

The complementary problem which arises is where a forwarder is given incomplete instructions on which he is expected to act. For example, where a forwarder, acting on behalf of a buyer, has been instructed in general terms as to his duties, but not supplied with full instructions, the question arises as to whether either the forwarder or his principal will be liable for the former's failure to carry out the forwarding operation. For instance, where a contract of sale provides for payment against a signed confirmation by a forwarder that a shipment is at the buyer's disposal, there may be an implied duty on a buyer who employs a forwarder to receive goods on his behalf, to ensure that the latter takes all reasonable steps to ascertain whether the consignment is at his principal's disposal or not. But unless the forwarder's instructions require him to do otherwise, his duty will not require him to take any positive action until some material is placed before him on which to act. In such cases, provided the buyer has issued proper instructions to his forwarder in accordance with the contract of sale, the courts will only imply into the contract a need for the forwarder to co-operate

[12] *Rosenberg* v. *International Banking Corp.* (1923) 14 Ll.L.Rep. 299 at pp. 344 *et seq.*
[13] *Thrige* v. *United Shipping Co. Ltd.* (1924) 18 Ll.L.Rep. 6 at p. 7, *per* Bankes L.J.

with the seller or his agent to such an extent as is necessary to make the contract workable. Therefore, merely because a misunderstanding arises between the seller and the forwarder concerning the transaction in hand, the buyer is not obliged to take steps to remove it, provided again that he has given the forwarder proper instructions as to his duties.

For example, in *Mona Oil Equipment & Supply Co. Ltd.* v. *Rhodesian Railways*,[14] a forwarder acting for the buyer refused to give written confirmation that a shipment of oil tanks was at the buyer's disposal, so as to enable the seller to obtain payment, without the buyer's written instructions to this effect. The seller consequently complained to the buyer's London agent, who then gave the necessary instructions to the forwarder, but without informing the plaintiff seller that he had done so. The latter therefore made no further approach to the forwarder, with the result that the seller's supplier cancelled the contract. The seller therefore claimed against the buyer for breach of contract. This the court rejected on the grounds that as the defendant had given proper instructions to his agent, the forwarder, and there was no refusal by the latter to act, he had done all that was necessary to make the contract workable.

3. Whose Instructions to Obey

214   The obligation of a forwarder to obey his client's instructions can create problems where the forwarder is acting on behalf of both the seller and the buyer. Where conflicting instructions are given, who is he to obey? Where only one party gives instructions, is the forwarder to obey them or not?

These questions are particularly likely to arise where a seller consigns goods to a forwarder, as a receiving agent, and the latter on receipt of the goods requires instructions as to their disposal. In such a situation it is essential that the forwarder ascertains that the instructions he receives have been given him by the right party. Otherwise he may find himself liable either for breach of instructions if they have been validly given where he fails to carry them out, or conversely, liable for carrying them out where he has followed instructions given by an unauthorised party.

215   For instance, the seller may have given instructions that the bill of lading is to be held back by the forwarder. In such circumstances, if the forwarder accepts instructions from the buyer as to the disposition of the goods which contravene the seller's orders, the forwarder will be liable to the seller for failing to comply with his instructions. If on the other hand, the forwarder has not received any instructions from the seller as to the disposition of the goods or documents of title, he will be free to follow any instructions given to him by the buyer.[15]

---

[14] (1950) 83 Ll.L.Rep. 178.
[15] *Miller Gibb & Co.* v. *Ackland & Co.* (1921) 8 Ll.L.Rep. 59.

216 Insolvency of buyer

Another common situation is where the receiving forwarder, to whom the seller has consigned the goods, is instructed by the buyer to warehouse the goods and to await further instructions. In such a situation, if the buyer subsequently becomes insolvent, and the seller gives instructions to the forwarder not to deliver, the question will arise as to whom the forwarder must obey. The answer to this will depend upon whether transit has ended or not. This will in turn depend upon the seller's exact instructions to the forwarder. If for example, the forwarder was only ". . . acting as forwarding agents employed to discharge the seller's obligations to see to the transit of the goods and enquire of [the buyer] where they wanted the goods delivered . . .," [16] he would have fulfilled his obligations to the seller on so doing, and would thereafter be bound to rely upon the buyer for instructions as to the further disposal of the goods, transit having ended. If however transit has not ended, the forwarder may be liable in conversion if he fails to observe the seller's instructions as to stoppage in transit. Conversely, if transit has ended, property will have passed to the buyer, and the forwarder will not be liable to the seller in conversion if he places the goods at the buyer's disposal. Both the questions of conversion and stoppage in transit have been dealt with already in earlier chapters, so that further discussion of these points is unnecessary.[17]

217 Indemnity

Finally, the question arises whether a forwarder can recover an indemnity from the party whose instructions he follows if in so doing he incurs liability to a third party. The mere receipt of instructions to deal with a shipment will not of itself create such an inference. Further proof of an independent promise to indemnify the forwarder must be produced to do so.[18] This question is now covered by special provisions in Standard Trading Conditions.[19]

4. CONTRACTUAL PROVISIONS

218 In practice many problems relating to the validity of instructions received by a forwarder can be avoided where Standard Trading Conditions are used. Two principal methods are used in the Conditions to protect the forwarder in respect of certain important aspects of forwarding operations. First, in certain cases the forwarder is to be given express instructions in writing, saving which he will not be liable in respect of any operations for which this is required. For instance, under Clause 4 the forwarder will not accept any limitation on his freedom of

---

[16] *Johann Plischke & Sohne G.m.b.H.* v. *Allison Bros. Ltd.* (1936) 55 Ll.L.Rep. 262 at p. 263, *per* Branson J.
[17] For cases on stoppage in transit see Chapter 3, note 37. *Cf.* C.M.R. provisions at § 220.
[18] *D. Steward & Co.* v. *J. Lofthouse & Co.* (1921) 9 Ll.L.Rep. 386. See § 186.
[19] Cl. 24, S.T.C. *Cf.* Cl. 3 (4), R.H.A. Conditions 1967.

choice as to routes and procedures to be followed in arranging transportation unless a client gives him express instructions in writing as to
his requirements.[20] Even so, if the forwarder considers it necessary or
desirable in the client's interests to depart from the instructions, he is
free to do so.[21] Similarly, no declarations as to the value of goods will
be made by a forwarder in pursuance of the provisions of the various
carriage acts nor under other tariff options for the purpose of extending
the carrier's liability,[22] nor will a forwarder effect insurance of goods,
without express written instructions being given.[23]

219   Secondly, in certain cases, the forwarder will only accept liability if
special arrangements are previously made in writing between the forwarder and his client. In other words, it is not sufficient merely to give
express instructions, which the forwarder will undertake if possible, as a
normal part of his functions. Here the forwarder must agree with his
client the exact conditions under which he will forward, if at all, otherwise no liability will be accepted by the forwarder for any loss or injury
resulting. This category applies in the case of dangerous goods,[24] which
the forwarder will not accept or deal with at all without prior special
arrangement in writing. Similarly, in the case of certain listed valuables,
etc., the forwarder will neither accept nor deal with them without similar
arrangements being made, nor will he accept liability for them if delivered
to him by the customer without special arrangements being made.[25]

Finally, Clause 9 confirms the usual practice as described by
Humphreys J. above, whereby a forwarder does not accept any responsibility for the description of goods unless otherwise agreed.[26] By this
clause, the client is deemed to be bound by and to warrant the description, etc., of goods furnished to the forwarder for customs and other
purposes, and to indemnify him against any loss resulting from such
inaccuracy, whether arising through negligence on the part of the
former or not. A similar right of indemnity is included in Clause 2 where
instructions have been given to the forwarder by a party who later
transpired not to be the true owner or his authorised agent, as a specific
warranty is included that the forwarder's client either has such authority
or is in fact the owner of the goods in question.[27]

220 C.M.R.
Like the common law, C.M.R. does not make any specific provision
as to the form which instructions must take. However, Article 6 (1) and

---

[20] *Cf. Comptoir Franco-Anglais d'Exportation* v. *Van Oppen & Co.* at note 3. *Cf.* Arts. 7,
9 (2), D.F.C.; Arts. 4, 21, 22, N.F.C.; Art. 3, N.Y.F.F.; Arts. 7, 16, 22, C.G. (Belgium);
Arts. 7, 14, 24, 25, Y.F.C.; Arts. 1, 2 (1), C.G. (Switzerland); Arts. 11–13, A.D.S.P.;
Art. 6, C.G. (France).
[21] Cl. 3, S.T.C.
[22] Cl. 16, S.T.C.
[23] Cl. 12, S.T.C.
[24] Cl. 20, S.T.C.   [25] Cl. 21, S.T.C.; *cf.* Art. 20, N.F.C.
[26] Cl. 9 S.T.C. *Margolis* v. *Newson Bros. Ltd.* (1941) 71 Ll.L.Rep. 47 at p. 50. *Cf.*
Arts. 8, 15 (1), D.F.C.; Art. 5, N.Y.F.F.; Arts. 9, 17, 19, 20, 21, 23, C.G. (Belgium);
Arts. 9–11, 32, Y.F.C.; Art. 3 C.G. (France); Arts. 7–10, 24, A.D.S.P.; Art. 5, F.B.L.
[27] Cl. 2, S.T.C.

(2) does specify certain information which either must or can be included in the consignment note.[28] In particular, instructions as to customs clearance etc., must be included,[29] and where applicable, the sender's instructions as to the insurance of the goods.[30] In certain cases the carrier has a positive duty to seek instructions as to his action. First, where it becomes impossible to carry out the contract in accordance with the terms of the consignment note before the goods reach the place designated for delivery, the carrier must ask instructions from the person entitled to dispose of the goods.[31] If, however, it is possible to effect transit by alternative means, and the carrier has not been able to obtain instructions from the person entitled within a reasonable time, the carrier is free to take such action as he deems in the best interests of the latter.[32] Similarly the carrier must ask instructions of the sender where delivery cannot be effected after the arrival of the goods at the designated place, unless the consignee has obtained a right of disposal under Article 12 (3) and ordered the delivery of the goods to a third party, in which case the carrier is required to approach the consignee as if he were the sender.[33]

If the sender gives the carrier inaccurate or inadequate instructions he will be liable for all expenses, loss and damage which the latter may suffer. This liability covers such details as are necessary to enable the consignment note to be completed.[34]

221 Right of disposal

The question next arises as to whose instructions the carrier should accept. This falls into two categories. First, those circumstances where one of the parties wishes to exercise his right of disposal of the goods, and, secondly, where the carrier finds himself unable to perform the contract in accordance with the terms of the consignment note. Article 12 (1) gives the sender three ways in which he can dispose of the goods: by stoppage in transit, by changing the place of delivery, and by changing the consignee.

To exercise this right of disposal, however, the sender must produce to the carrier the first copy of the consignment note on which the new instructions have been entered.[35] He will lose this right when the second copy of the consignment note (which accompanies the goods) is handed over to the consignee or when after the arrival of the goods at the place of delivery the consignee has required the carrier to deliver to him the second copy of the note and the goods.[36]

[28] See Chapter 13 on the question of the consignment note generally. *Cf.* Art. 6, C.I.M.; Art. 3, T.C.M.
[29] Art. 6 (1) (*j*). *Cf.* Art. 11 and see Chapter 16 on customs procedures. *Cf.* Art. 13, C.I.M.
[30] Art. 6 (2) (*e*).
[31] Art. 14 (1).
[32] Art. 14 (2).
[33] Art. 15 (1), (3). See also § 205.
[34] Art. 7 (1).
[35] Art. 12 (5) (*a*). *Cf.* Arts. 21–25, C.I.M.
[36] Arts. 12 (2), 13 (1).

If on the other hand the sender gives the consignee a right of disposal in the consignment note, the latter will have the right from the time when the note is drawn up,[37] provided he is in possession of the first copy of the consignment note on which the new instructions have been entered.[38] The right of disposal, whether exercised by the sender or the consignee, is subject to certain conditions. First, the carrier must be indemnified against all expenses or loss resulting from carrying out the revised instructions.[39] Secondly, that the performance of the instructions is possible at the time they reach the person who has to perform them, and that they do not interfere with the normal working of the carrier's operations or prejudice the senders or consignees of other consignments.[40] Thirdly, that the instructions will not result in the division of the consignment in question.[41] If the carrier cannot carry out the revised instructions for the reasons listed under the second heading, he must immediately notify the person who has given him them.[42] Otherwise, if the carrier fails to perform any valid instructions as to the disposal of the goods as provided for in Article 12, or has failed to require the production of the first copy of the consignment note, he will be liable for any resultant loss or damage.[43]

Finally, if the consignee instructs the carrier to deliver to a third party, the latter cannot reconsign the goods to another party.[44]

222 Carrier's inability to perform the contract

Turning next to the question of the carrier's inability to perform the contract, this is dealt with in Articles 13, 14 and 15 as discussed above If the contract cannot be performed as laid down by the consignment note, the carrier must approach the person entitled to dispose of the goods as laid down in Article 12.[45] If on the other hand he cannot deliver the goods after arrival at their destination, he is required to approach the sender for instructions, and if the consignee refuses the goods, the sender is not required to produce the first copy of the consignment note.[46] However, even after refusal of the goods the consignee is still free to require delivery, providing the carrier has not yet received contrary instructions from the sender.[47] Finally, if the consignee has a right to dispose of the goods *ab initio* under Article 12 (3) and has instructed delivery to a third party, they will each be respectively treated as if they were sender and consignee.[48]

[37] Art. 12 (3).
[38] Art. 12 (5) (*a*).
[39] *Ibid.*
[40] Art. 12 (5) (*b*).
[41] Art. 12 (5) (*c*).
[42] Art. 12 (6).
[43] Art. 12 (7).
[44] Art. 12 (4).
[45] Art. 14. *Cf.* Art. 24, C.I.M.
[46] Art. 15 (1). *Cf.* Art. 25, C.I.M.
[47] Art. 15 (2).
[48] Art. 15 (3).

5. CONCLUSION

223 The position of the forwarder in relation to instructions given to him either by his principal or by third parties can be analysed as follows. He will be bound to obey the instructions given him by his principal either because he has contractually undertaken to do so, or else because of his common law duty as an agent to obey his principal's instructions. Under certain circumstances he may also be subject to a positive duty to obtain instructions either from his principal or from a third party, as where he is holding goods after transit awaiting disposal instructions. Conversely, he may be in a position to act under a discretionary power without obtaining further instructions. Such powers are extensively retained by the forwarder under Standard Trading Conditions where these are operative. A forwarder may also be in receipt of ambiguous or incomplete instructions which he will be required to interpret. In establishing the reasonableness of his resultant actions, the question of local trade usage must be borne in mind and the twofold test laid down in *Ireland* v. *Livingston* [49] applied. Finally, the forwarder will be liable for failure to transmit instructions to a third party either where he has undertaken to do so, or else where he is employing a sub-agent to act for him in forwarding or receiving operations for whom he is responsible.

The position of the forwarder at common law is therefore one that is not capable of general definition, but must depend upon the interpretation of the particular facts in each case. The factors discussed above will of course be of general application, and give general guidance as to the approximate extent of liability in such circumstances. However, the extent of the uncertainty of the forwarder's position at common law is reflected in the extensive provisions in Standard Trading Conditions whereby the forwarder will only accept responsibility for action in respect of many operations where either express instructions are given or else there has been express agreement in writing beforehand. In practice, therefore, it seems that much of the earlier litigation could have been avoided if Standard Trading Conditions had then been in use, and it is significant that there has been virtually no case law in this field in recent years since Standard Trading Conditions have been more widely in use. Similarly, it can be assumed that where a contract is in future subject to C.M.R., this will assist in clarifying the obligations of the parties, and in particular as regards the right of disposal of goods.

[49] See note 9.

CHAPTER 9

THE FORWARDING OF DANGEROUS GOODS

1. THE POSITION AT COMMON LAW

224 Warranty of fitness

At common law the carrier whether common or private is not obliged to carry dangerous goods, without the protection of a compensatory warranty of fitness by the consignor.[1] Under this warranty the consignor will be liable to compensate the carrier for any damage suffered by him through carrying goods of whose nature he has not been informed. The consignor must therefore give notice to the carrier of any dangerous characteristic which the goods may possess, and if on the surface they are apparently harmless, the consignor will be liable to the carrier for damage which he has no reason to anticipate.[2] This rule applies to any goods that are not fit to be carried and is not restricted to dangerous goods in the strict sense of the word. The forwarder may therefore be placed in a twofold position, as inasmuch as he effects the carriage himself he will be entitled to the benefit of this warranty and his principal will be liable to him for any breach thereof. This right of recovery extends not only to the forwarder in his capacity as a carrier, but also to the forwarder's servants who suffer injury through a breach of the consignor's warranty of fitness.[3] Conversely if a forwarder is merely acting in his capacity as such, he will be liable to the actual carrier under the implied warranty of fitness even though he may have little knowledge of the particular shipment in question.[4]

225 Forwarder's liability

The position of the forwarder when acting as such, therefore, seems to be as follows. First, in *Brass* v. *Maitland*,[5] a majority of the court held that there was a warranty by the forwarder that he would not deliver goods to a shipowner which were packed in such a way that the shipowner's employees could not discover their dangerous nature on reasonable inspection, without giving express notice thereof. Such a warranty is independent of the forwarder's actual knowledge. Consequently, if dangerous goods are delivered by a forwarder to a carrier which do not reveal either visibly or by their name their dangerous nature, the forwarder impliedly gives an absolute warranty that the

---

[1] See Paton, *Bailment in the Common Law*, p. 262.
[2] *G.N.R.* v. *L.E.P. Transport Ltd.* (1922) 11 Ll.L.Rep. 133. *Farrant* v. *Barnes* (1862) 11 C.B.(N.S.) 553 at p. 563, *per* Willes J.
[3] *Ibid.*
[4] " Forwarding agents who deliver goods in fact dangerous to the carrier, without informing him of their danger, are liable for consequent damage sustained through that danger ": *per* Scrutton L.J., *ibid.*
[5] (1856) 6 E. & B. 470.

goods are fit to be carried and if they are not fit he will be liable for
resultant loss. Accordingly, where a forwarder shipped casks of a
noxious chemical by a common carrier which were described by the
documents as " general cargo," the forwarder was held liable for the
carrier's death, as the dangerous character of the goods was not one
which the carrier actually knew of or ought to have known.[6] The fact
that a carrier is informed by the forwarder of the name of the substance
will not necessarily protect the forwarder, as if the contents are, for
example, of a more potent quality than they are described, he will be
liable for breach of warranty,[7] and also presumably if the name given
is so obscure that a mere carrier could not be expected to realise the
potential danger involved or else the dangerous nature of the substance
is not a matter of common knowledge.[8] The forwarder is therefore
placed in the position of requiring exact knowledge of the contents of
every shipment he handles on behalf of a client, and must ensure that
the documents accurately describe the contents. Accordingly, although
in practice a forwarder will rely on his client, the shipper, to a considerable extent for such information, if the latter either deliberately or
inadvertently misinforms him, the forwarder will still be liable for
breach of the warranty.[9] It should be clearly understood however that
liability will only attach to a forwarder where he actually acts as a
forwarder. Where he effects other functions on behalf of his client such
as packing, etc., the mere fact that the goods are collected from the
forwarder's premises will not make him liable.

226   One point upon which there is some academic uncertainty is whether
the implied warranty of fitness only operates in favour of the common
carrier or for the private carrier also. If such a distinction were drawn,
it would restrict the operation of the warranty considerably as common
carriage is increasingly rare in this country. Paton draws attention to
the conflicting dicta and juristic opinions on the matter, but is inclined
to the view that the warranty will operate in favour of private as well as
common carriers.[10] It seems therefore that the rule will apply wherever

[6] *Bamford* v. *Goole & Sheffield Transport Co.* [1910] 2 K.B. 94.
[7] *G.N.R.* v. *L.E.P. Transport Ltd.* (1922) 11 Ll.L.Rep. 133 at p. 137.
[8] *Hoey* v. *Hardie* (1912) 12 S.R. (N.S.W.) 268.   A consignor does not fulfil his obligation
by labelling a drum " Acid—dangerous—with care " if the stopper in the drum is
defective and no warning is given as to this: *Faulkner* v. *Wischer & Co.* [1918] V.L.R. 513.
[9] There is both judicial and academic uncertainty as to whether the right is based on
contract or on tort. Kahn-Freund, *Inland Transport*, 4th ed. at p. 380, favours the
latter. Fleming, *Law of Torts*, 2nd ed. at p. 468, treats it as contractual. Charlesworth,
Negligence, 4th ed., para. 831, treats it as tortious, and apparently distinguishes between dangerous goods where he argues there is an absolute duty, and non-dangerous
goods where there is only a duty of reasonable care that goods will not cause physical
damage. Salmond, *Law of Torts*, 11th ed. at p. 673, reviews the authorities.   In
Burley Ltd. v. *Stepney Corporation* [1947] 1 All E.R. 507 at p. 510, Hallett J. treats it
as a question of contract. It seems therefore that the obligation of the forwarder lies
both in tort and in contract. Certainly from the cases the forwarder seems to be
absolutely liable even if the ordinary consignor may not be.
[10] Paton, *Bailment in the Common Law*, pp. 262–263. *Burley Ltd.* v. *Stepney Corporation*
[1947] 1 All E.R. 507 at p. 510, *per* Hallett J. who discusses the authorities and is of
the opinion that the warranty covers all carriers.

a carrier whether common or private is required to carry goods in respect of which either open inspection is not possible or latent defects cannot be discovered.

227 Carrier's liability

Turning to the liability of the carrier in respect of loss or damage to dangerous goods, his is not an absolute one as it would not be reasonable to require the common carriage of dangerous goods. The position therefore seems to be that where there are no special contractual conditions imposed, a forwarder who is acting as a carrier will be subject to the normal duty of reasonable care required of a private carrier. If, on the other hand, a forwarder is acting as a carrier subject to Standard Trading Conditions or R.H.A. Conditions, his liability will be limited by the respective exemption clauses in these contracts which apply for the carriage of normal goods.[11] The forwarder will therefore either fulfil the requirements of the warranty if he is placed in the position of a consignor or conversely he will benefit from the rule if he undertakes to carry the goods himself. If he fulfils both functions, that is he both effects part of the transit himself and acts as forwarder for on-carriage, he will both benefit and be subjected to the rule

2. CONTRACTUAL VARIATIONS OF THE COMMON LAW RULE

228 Standard Trading Conditions

The forwarder will be effected by contractual variations of the common law in two ways. First, under Clause 20 of Standard Trading Conditions the forwarder only undertakes to accept "any noxious, dangerous, hazardous or inflammable or explosive goods or any goods likely to cause damage" where prior written arrangements have been made to this effect.[12] If such goods are delivered to a forwarder without prior written agreement, the consignor will be liable for all loss or damage resulting from it irrespective of negligence and to indemnify the forwarder in respect of any claims, etc. made by third parties in connection therewith. The forwarder therefore obtains contractual rights similar to those given to the carrier at common law by the implied warranty of fitness, even though he does not fulfil the function of a carrier. In this respect Standard Trading Conditions differ from the trading conditions used by British Rail, B.R.S. and the Road Haulage Association, as these merely expand the common law rights of the carrier, whereas Standard Trading Conditions give the forwarder rights which he would not otherwise possess at common law unless he is in fact acting as a carrier himself. Otherwise his only remedy would be against the consignor in the tort of negligence.

229 Carriage conditions

Secondly, where a forwarder forwards goods by British Rail or

---

[11] In particular Cl. 13, S.T.C., and Cl. 11, R.H.A. Conditions 1967.
[12] For full text see Appendix. *Cf.* Arts. 36, 40, C.G. (Belgium); Art. 44, Y.F.C.; Art. 3, C.G. (France); Art. 5, A.D.S.P.; Art. 4, F.B.L.

B.R.S., he must warrant that all merchandise is "fit to be carried or stored," unless the forwarder gives written notice to the contrary to the carrier on delivery.[13] The forwarder will therefore be liable under this clause if he consigns goods which contravene the common law warranty of fitness. If goods are in fact dangerous, British Rail and B.R.S. will only carry them subject to special conditions of carriage laid down in Clause 19 of the Conditions. Dangerous goods are here defined by reference to the Railway Board's List of Dangerous Goods and "goods of kindred nature." [14] Clause 19 (1) provides that where a carrier accepts dangerous goods for carriage that they will be carried subject to the normal conditions of carriage and in addition to the special conditions laid down in Clause 19 (2), the latter to prevail in case of conflict, although if further conditions are added in the consignment note these in turn will prevail over the special conditions.[15]

Clause 19 (2) requires that previous arrangements shall be made with the carrier for the carriage of the goods, and that when they are tendered to the carrier the sender must supply a written declaration of the nature of the goods. Secondly, the goods must be packed in accordance with any statutory regulations in force applicable to the carriage of goods, and, unless there is written agreement otherwise, also in accordance with the British Rail regulations for the packing, labelling and loading of dangerous goods. Thirdly, the client will be responsible for and indemnify the carrier for loss, damage or injury arising from non-compliance with Clause 19, unless the client can prove that the loss, etc., resulted from the carrier's wilful misconduct. R.H.A. Conditions similarly require a written declaration accompanying dangerous goods as to their nature and contents, correct packing, and give a right of indemnity.[16]

230   It is due to these provisions that Standard Trading Conditions make it a strict requirement that such goods will only be accepted if it has already been agreed in writing before delivery that the forwarder will handle them.[17] Otherwise he might not discover their true nature until they have reached the hands of the carrier, by which time it would be too late for the forwarder to fulfil the above-mentioned requirements relating to dangerous goods to avoid liability in respect thereof.

231   Common law and contractual provisions

One important difference between the common law warranty of fitness and any contractual provision is that, as mentioned above, the former inures for the benefit of the carrier's servants and the owners of goods which are damaged by dangerous goods whilst in the carrier's possession. By contrast, any contractual provision will be subject to privity of contract, and will therefore not benefit the carrier's servants

---

[13] Cl. 4 (1), B.R.S. Conditions.
[14] Cl. 1, B.R.S. Conditions; *cf.* Cl. 1 (*a*) (*b*), R.H.A. Conditions 1967.
[15] Cl. 19 (2) (*d*), B.R.S. Conditions.
[16] Cl. 4, R.H.A. Conditions 1967.
[17] Cl. 20, S.T.C.

or any of the latter's clients whose goods have been damaged, unless some form of agency clause to cover an *Adler* v. *Dickson* type of situation is included.[18] The provisions in Clause 2 (2), B.R.S. Conditions, and Clause 3 (3), R.H.A. Conditions 1967, appear to establish such an agency relationship, which will presumably enable third parties to benefit from the principal contract of carriage.[19] It should be noted however that in the case of a sub-contracting carrier, the latter will have no need to rely upon any contractual provision in relation to dangerous goods, as the common law warranty of fitness apparently extends to any carrier, not being subject to the doctrine of privity of contract.[20]

Standard Trading Conditions, on the other hand, have no such provision, but instead give the forwarder a right of indemnity in respect of any resultant loss or damage for which the latter may be liable.[21] Similarly, no direct protection is given to the forwarder's servants in respect of personal injury, but this again would fall within the general indemnity provisions in Clause 24, Standard Trading Conditions. In both these cases, therefore, if either the owner of damaged property or an injured servant claims from the forwarder himself, he in turn will obtain an indemnity from his client on whose behalf he has handled the dangerous goods. This does not of course preclude any direct action by the injured party against the client in the tort of negligence.[22] A similar right of indemnity is also provided for in both B.R.S. and R.H.A. Conditions.[23]

232   Finally, it should be noted that a carrier can recover under the common law warranty in respect of loss to another client's goods even though he is not contractually liable for the loss or alternatively for its full amount. In such a case he must account to the injured client for the full value and not merely the amount otherwise contractually recoverable by the client from him. However, in the case of the contractual rights of indemnity referred to above, in contrast to the common law rule, the indemnity will only cover the carrier's actual liability to third parties, which will not necessarily be the full amount of the loss.[24]

3. THROUGH CARRIAGE AND THE CONVENTION FOR THE INTERNATIONAL CARRIAGE OF GOODS BY ROAD

233 **C.M.R. and A.D.R.**

Although there are no dicta on this point, it appears that if a party fulfils both the functions of a carrier and a forwarder, that is, he effects

---

[18] [1955] 1 Q.B. 158.
[19] See Chapter 11.
[20] See note 9.
[21] Cl. 20, S.T.C.
[22] Clerk & Lindsell, *Torts*, 13th ed., p. 928.
[23] Cl. 19 (2) (*e*), B.R.S. Conditions; Cl. 4 (2), R.H.A. Conditions 1967.
[24] *Cf.* Art. 22 (2), C.M.R., at § 234 below. Even if there is an indemnity clause in a contract of carriage exempting the carrier from all loss, etc., " arising out of the carriage of " dangerous goods, the carrier will only recover if the loss results from the carriage of the goods, but not if it results from the carrier's own negligence: *Pickfords Ltd.* v. *Perma Products Ltd.* (1947) 80 Ll.L.Rep. 513.

part of the transit himself and then acts as a forwarder in respect of on-carriage, he will benefit from the rule in his former function but will be correspondingly subject to it in respect of forwarding operations. Where, however, the whole transit is subject to the Convention, no such distinction between the functions of a carrier and a forwarder in respect of on-carriage will apply, as each carrier will be liable as an initial or successive carrier within the Convention.[25] Presumably, therefore, a carrier cannot be placed in the position of a mere forwarder in respect of on-carriage under the Convention so that such a distinction will not be relevant. Furthermore, the transit may also be subject to the European Agreement concerning the International Carriage of Dangerous Goods by Road (A.D.R.) 1957, which lays down specific requirements in respect of an extensive range of dangerous goods listed therein.[26] Any discussion of C.M.R. must therefore be subject to the additional requirements of A.D.R., although most of its provisions are concerned with the carriage and packing of dangerous goods rather than with the relationships between the various parties involved in the contract of carriage.[27] As a result C.M.R. and A.D.R. are really complementary in their effect with only a slight overlap. The latter will therefore only be discussed where its provisions in fact overlap with C.M.R. It should not be forgotten however that A.D.R. applies to all international carriage of goods by road whether it falls within C.M.R. or not, and therefore covers carriage by containers also.

234   C.M.R. provisions

The Convention deals with the problem from two aspects. First, it makes provision for dangerous goods as such, secondly, it makes additional provision in respect of the defective packing of goods, which in practice will cover the majority of cases where dangerous goods have caused damage or injury to the carrier or to third parties. These provisions therefore replace both the common law implied warranty of fitness and the relevant B.R.S. or R.H.A. Conditions where international carriage as defined by the Convention is involved. Under the second heading Article 10 provides that:

" The sender shall be liable to the carrier for damage to persons, equipment or other goods, and for any expenses due to defective packing of the goods, unless the defect was apparent or known to the carrier at the time when he took over the goods and he made no reservations concerning it."

As regards loss or injury resulting from defective packing, Article 10 is wider in scope than both the common law warranty and Clause 4 (2), R.H.A. Conditions 1967.[28] It protects the carrier in respect of any type of goods whether technically dangerous or not. R.H.A. Conditions

---

[25] Art. 34, C.M.R.

[26] Published by H.M.S.O., 1967.

[27] See the list of requirements for the carrier to fulfil in relation to transport equipment and transport operations in Cl. 10,000–10,602, Annexe B, A.D.R.

[28] See § 231. *Cf.* Art. 12, C.I.M.

1967 follow suit in extending protection to cover " goods which though not [dangerous] . . . are of a kindred kind." [29] The carrier will only lose protection under the Convention if the defect is *apparent* or known to him at the time of delivery. This seems to offer him a wider protection than the common law warranty as he will lose the protection of the latter if the effect is one of which he *ought* to have known. The word " apparent " used in the Convention seems to have a narrower meaning than this, so that the carrier's liability will be more restricted under the Convention than at common law in this respect. It should also be noted that the Article also gives the carrier a right to make any reservations he thinks fit in respect of such goods though. Under the first heading, Article 22 (1) provides that:

> " When the sender hands goods of a dangerous nature to the carrier, he shall inform the carrier of the exact nature of the danger and indicate, if necessary, the precautions to be taken. If this information has not been entered in the consignment note, the burden of proving, by some other means, that the carrier knew the exact nature of the danger constituted by the carriage of the said goods shall rest upon the sender or the consignee." [30]

235   Where the goods are " of a dangerous nature," Article 22 (1) therefore requires the consignor to inform the carrier of the exact nature of the danger and of any necessary precautions which should be taken by the carrier. The Convention also provides that the generally recognised description of dangerous goods as well as the method of packing must be entered in the consignment note [31] and that the consignor will be liable for "all expenses, loss or damage" sustained by the carrier through any inaccuracy or inadequacy in such information.[32] If the carrier enters the particulars in the note, he will be deemed to have done so on behalf of the consignor unless the contrary is proved.[33] Article 22 (1) further provides that where goods are of a " dangerous nature " the consignor must inform the carrier of the exact nature of the danger and of any necessary precautions which should be taken by him. If the consignor fails to enter such information in the consignment note the burden of proof will be either on him or on the consignee to prove that the carrier knew the " exact nature " of the danger.[34] As in the case of loss, etc., under Article 7, the consignor will similarly be liable for any expenses, loss or damage arising from the delivery of the goods to the carrier for transit, providing the latter was not aware of their dangerous nature.[35] Presumably " dangerous goods " and " goods of a dangerous nature " are one and the same thing, so that it appears that the Articles

---

[29] Cl. 1 (*b*), R.H.A. Conditions 1967.
[30] *Cf.* C.I.M. (R.I.D.); Art. 7, T.C.M.
[31] Art. 6 (1) (*f*), C.M.R.   *Cf.* Art. 12, C.I.M.
[32] Art. 7 (1) (*a*), C.M.R.   *Cf.* Art. 7, C.I.M.
[33] Art. 7 (2), C.M.R.
[34] Art. 22 (1), C.M.R.
[35] Art. 22 (2), C.M.R.

referred to above can be read conjunctively and not disjunctively. Consequently, although Article 7 renders the consignor liable for any loss, etc., through any inaccuracy in the consignment note, as Article 9 expressly provides that it is only prima facie evidence of the terms of the contract, if the consignor can prove. that the carrier knew "the exact nature of the danger," this can presumably be pleaded as a defence to liability under Article 7, as well as under Article 22.

236   However, in practice such a plea is likely to be of limited value as although under C.M.R. a consignment note is not essential, in the case of goods listed in A.D.R., a "transport document" is mandatory. The normal C.M.R. consignment note will be acceptable as such, provided it contains the information required under A.D.R.[36] The transport document must accompany the goods, and also, if appropriate, together with instructions to be carried out in the event of an accident.[37] If the load is to be carried by several transport units, a copy of the documents must accompany each unit.[38] It therefore follows that if the consignor fails to declare goods which are subject to A.D.R. and to ensure that they are correctly packed, the carrier will be exonerated from liability in respect of them, and the consignor will instead be unrestrictedly liable for them under C.M.R. Two problems can arise. First, the Convention does not define the meaning of " a dangerous nature," unlike R.H.A. Conditions which relate it to the Railway Board's list.[39] In practice, however, A.D.R. solves this problem by providing a list which covers the majority of goods which are commonly recognised as being dangerous, although no provision is made for the incorporation of new substances developed after 1957.[40] Otherwise, a dispute could arise as to whether the consignor was under a duty to inform the carrier of the " exact nature " of the goods or not. If the goods do not fall within this definition the general rule under Article 10 discussed above will apply which relieves the consignor of liability, where the defective packing is " apparent " to the carrier at the time of delivery, otherwise if they are of a " dangerous nature " the claimant must prove that the carrier had actual knowledge thereof.[41]

237 Destruction of dangerous goods

Secondly, unlike R.H.A. Conditions, a special provision is made for the dangerous goods to be unloaded, destroyed or rendered harmless by the carrier without any compensation to the owner, provided the carrier did not know of their dangerous nature.[42] However, if there is knowledge, any right of compensation will depend on the particular facts and whether the carrier acted reasonably in the circumstances.[43]

[36] For requirements, see A.D.R.
[37] 2002 (3), A.D.R.
[38] 2002 (4), A.D.R.
[39] Cl. 1 (a), (b), R.H.A. Conditions 1967.
[40] For the list, see Annexe A to A.D.R.   [41] Art. 22 (1), C.M.R.
[42] Art. 22 (2), C.M.R. The sender will be liable for the expense.
[43] See Art. 17 (4) (b) (d), C.M.R. Compare the [provisions of Art. 22 (2), C.M.R. with Cl. 20, S.T.C.

A similar right of destruction is obtained under Standard Trading Conditions which is exercisable at the sole discretion of the forwarder or " any other person in whose custody the goods may be at the relevant time." The forwarder also has a right of indemnity against his client in respect of " all penalties, claims, damages, costs and expenses arising in connection therewith " where no special written arrangements have been made in advance. This does not appear to apply where goods are accepted under prior written arrangements.[44]

238   It should also be noted that the distinction between the common law warranty and contractual trading conditions as to whether servants or agents will have a right of action or not, resulting from the doctrine of privity of contract, disappears under the Convention. Employees and agents of the carrier are specifically subject to the Convention and will therefore have a right of action under it.[45] In granting such a right to agents of the carrier as well as servants, the Convention gives wider coverage than above, but unlike the warranty of fitness it does not give any direct right of action against the consignor of the dangerous goods to a third party whose goods have been damaged by them. Any right of action will therefore be at common law, although it is not immediately apparent whether the Convention precludes reliance on the common law warranty of fitness to enable the owner of goods damaged to claim direct against the consignor of the dangerous goods responsible for it, or whether the carrier would have to claim on the former's behalf or else assign a right of action to him. If this is in fact done, the assignee will also be subject to the provisions of the Convention.[46]

The result is that there is considerable variation between the different trading conditions and the Convention as to the definition of dangerous goods, the various requirements as to the duty of the consignor in relation to them, and in particular whether written notice of the dangerous nature of the goods is required. In practice A.D.R. will cover most international transits so that the problem is more theoretical than real.

4. Conclusion

239 The position of the forwarder in relation to the carriage of dangerous goods is therefore a complex one in which much will depend upon whether he is in fact acting in the capacity of a forwarder or else as a carrier himself. Furthermore, the fact that there are now three differing sets of trading conditions in existence, together with the mandatory provisions under C.M.R./A.D.R., reveals an astonishing lack of uniformity. First, there is no common definition of dangerous goods, which means that the respective conditions do not cover an identical

---

[44] Cl. 20, S.T.C.
[45] Carriage of Goods by Road Act 1965, s. 14 (2) (d)—also successive carriers (Art. 34).
[46] Carriage of Goods by Road Act 1965, s. 14 (2) (e).

range of goods. Secondly, there is no mandatory requirement for the dangerous nature of goods to be entered in a consignment note, the requirements of all the conditions differing on this point, although C.M.R./A.D.R. seem to offer the most satisfactory procedure in this respect. Thirdly, the fact that servants, agents and third parties often cannot rely on the respective conditions of carriage as a result of the doctrine of privity of contract, is highly undesirable, and seems in need of some statutory regulation, preferably to bring it in line with the Convention.[47]

240   Finally, a problem that may occur in the future when containerisation develops more widely in this country, will be to define who is the consignor and who is the carrier of goods, so as to establish who will benefit under the common law warranty of fitness where dangerous goods are included in a consolidated shipment shipped in a container, and conversely on whom the corresponding liability as consignor will fall. The difficulty in this respect will arise in deciding whether the container operator, any forwarder shipping consolidated shipments therein, or the actual shipper of the goods, should be liable on the implied warranty or not.

It is to be hoped therefore that such problems when ultimately resolved in relation to international traffic by the proposed international convention will also be an opportunity to make uniform provisions for inland carriage—a chance regrettably missed in relation to C.M.R.[48]

[47] See Chapter 11.
[48] See Chapter 13.

CHAPTER 10

FINANCIAL LIMITATIONS ON THE FORWARDER'S LIABILITY

1. INTRODUCTION

241 SUBJECT to the limitation discussed in the preceding chapters, a forwarder's client will be able to recover a full indemnity from the forwarder in respect of loss suffered for which the latter is legally liable. Consequently, bearing in mind the relatively high value of consignments handled by a forwarder in relation to the small return for his services in forwarding them, the risk borne by the forwarder is often disproportionately high. Not unnaturally, therefore, it has become general practice for forwarders to limit the extent of their financial liability in respect of any claims for which they may be legally liable. As a result, it will be necessary to consider the extent and effect of those financial limitations used in forwarding and carriage contracts, which restrict the amount recoverable to a certain sum, irrespective of the cause of loss. The question divides itself into two parts. First, the extent of the financial limitations under the various trading conditions. Secondly, the interpretation of such provisions by the courts.

2. FINANCIAL LIMITATION OF THE FORWARDER'S LIABILITY

242 The question will be considered under three headings. First, those limitations of general application. Secondly, those provisions which relate solely to certain categories of goods. Thirdly, the recently introduced provisions under C.M.R. in respect of the international carriage of goods by road.

243 Limitations of general application

As regards those limitations of general application, the most severe limit which is imposed upon a shipper in relation to forwarding operations is that under Standard Trading Conditions where the liability of the forwarder is restricted to £100 per ton in respect of loss for which the Conditions do not totally exclude liability.[1] The limits imposed by the three principal land carriers' Conditions of Carriage are considerably higher, being uniformly at a rate of £800 per ton, although with certain minor variations as to the basis of calculating liability in respect of small losses and associated factors. Likewise, in all cases, if the actual

---

[1] Cl. 14, S.T.C. *Kenyon Ltd.* v. *Baxter, Hoare & Co. Ltd.* [1971] 1 W.L.R. 519. *Cf.* Art. 20, N.F.C.; Art. 8, N.Y.F.F.; Art. 33, C.G. (Belgium); Art. 8, C.G. (France); Arts. 54–56, A.D.S.P.

value of the goods is less than the maximum limit, only the lesser sum will be recoverable.[2]

If a shipper employs a forwarder as such, he will only be able to recover at a rate of £100 per ton from the forwarder if the contract is subject to Standard Trading Conditions.[3] The mere fact that the forwarder has in turn contracted with a land carrier subject to a higher rate of recovery, that is, at £800 per ton, will not affect this limit. Only if a forwarder has contracted with the carrier as the shipper's agent so as to give the shipper the benefit of R.H.A. Conditions, and then only in a direct action by the shipper against the carrier, will the shipper be able to recover at the higher rate. As seen earlier, it is for this reason that shippers endeavour to avoid taking legal action against a forwarder employed by them where the contract is subject to Standard Trading Conditions, if an action will lie against a third party in tort, when the latter's liability will be unlimited.[4]

Only where a forwarder is himself contracting subject to R.H.A. Conditions will a shipper otherwise get the benefit of the higher rate of £800 per ton. This will only occur where a forwarder is in fact carrying out the transport operations himself, or in respect of which he accepts personal responsibility while employing sub-contractors to perform it. In such a case the higher rate of £800 per ton will be commensurate with the greater personal responsibility inherent in this method of operation.[5]

244 Special categories of goods

Turning next to those provisions relating to special categories of goods. Where declarations as to the nature or value of goods or of any special interest in delivery may be made whereby a carrier's liability will be increased under the provisions of the various carriage Acts, Standard Trading Conditions provide that the forwarder will only enter such a declaration on the express instructions of his client in writing.[6]

Similarly, under Clause 16 (b), Standard Trading Conditions, where there is a choice of tariff rates under which a carrier or warehouseman, employed by a forwarder on behalf of this client, offers to undertake a higher degree of liability in return for a higher rate of remuneration, the forwarder will not make any such optional declaration as to the value of the goods for the purpose of extending the carrier's liability, unless otherwise instructed in writing. Instead the forwarder retains the right to ship at owner's risk or other minimum rates unless instructed to the contrary.[7]

---

[2] Cl. 12, R.H.A. Conditions 1967; Cl. 6, B.R.S. Conditions. Similar provision is found in the conditions of virtually all forwarding associations in the currency of the country concerned.
[3] *Lee Cooper Ltd.* v. *C. H. Jeakins & Sons Ltd.* [1964] 1 Lloyd's Rep. 300.
[4] *Ibid.*
[5] See §§ 28, *et seq.*
[6] Cl. 16 (a) and (b), S.T.C. *Cf.* in respect of carriage of goods by sea or rail, Arts. 24, 26, C.M.R.; Art. 34, C.I.M.; Art. 6, N.Y.F.F.; Art. 18, C.G. (Belgium); Arts. 2 (3), 6, C.G. (Switzerland); Art. 8, F.B.L.
[7] Cl. 16 (b), S.T.C. See § 139.

245   The effect of this provision is that where a forwarder employs a common carrier to carry goods by road, he is not bound, unless expressly instructed to the contrary, to make any special declaration under the Carriers Act 1830. The latter provides that where goods shipped are of a valuable or breakable nature and over £10 in value, the carrier is relieved of all liability for loss or injury to the goods if the shipper or forwarder fails to make a special declaration in respect of them. As a result, if no instructions are given by the client to make such a declaration, the forwarder will escape liability under Standard Trading Conditions, even though the shipper will have lost any right of recourse against the carrier.[8]

The practical effect of the Carriers Act is very limited these days, as it only applies to common carriers, and few carriers in fact operate as such.[9] However, this rather archaic piece of legislation was given a new lease of life by being incorporated into R.H.A. Conditions 1961 as a contractual right for private carriers operating under their provisions, thus contractually placing the private carrier in a similar position to that held by the common carrier by virtue of his statutory right in respect of those consignments covered by the Carriers Act.[10] This means that where a forwarder operates under R.H.A. Conditions 1961 his liability will be likewise restricted. This provision has now been deleted from R.H.A. Conditions 1967, bringing them into line with B.R.S. Conditions, which have never utilised such a provision.

However, to the extent that R.H.A. Conditions 1961 are still operative, the protection given to the forwarder by Clause 16 (b), Standard Trading Conditions, will still be of value.[11] Equally it may be of importance in those Commonwealth countries, where the Carriers Act or a local equivalent applies, and where the common carrier by road is still the principal category of operator. It should not be forgotten either that if, for any reason, a contract is entered into by a forwarder which is neither subject to Standard Trading Conditions nor R.H.A. Conditions, and the courts consider that the forwarder's methods of operations constitute him a common carrier, he will obtain the protection of the statute itself.[12]

246   C.M.R.

Finally, provision is made under C.M.R. for a financial limit on claims where carriage is subject to the Convention. Under C.M.R., compensation in respect of total or partial loss of goods is limited by

---

[8] *Cf. Von Traubenberg* v. *Davies Turner & Co. Ltd.* [1951] 2 Lloyd's Rep. 462, where the contract was not subject to S.T.C., the forwarder was held liable for failing to obtain instructions from his principal when he omitted to make such a declaration under the Act in respect of valuable goods. *Cf.* Cl. 21, S.T.C.—see § 219.

[9] *Hunt & Winterbotham (West of England) Ltd.* v. *B.R.S. (Parcels) Ltd.* [1962] 1 Q.B. 617. See also *Date & Cocke* v. *G. W. Sheldon & Co. (London) Ltd.* (1921) 7 Ll.L.Rep. 53 at p. 54.

[10] Cl. 7, R.H.A. Conditions 1961. As to the provisions of the Carriers Act, see Kahn-Freund, *Law of Inland Transport*, 4th ed., p. 342.

[11] *Cf. Lee Cooper Ltd.* v. *C. H. Jeakins & Sons Ltd.* [1964] 1 Lloyd's Rep. 300.

[12] *Cf. Hellaby* v. *Weaver* (1851) 17 L.T.(o.s.) 271.

Article 23 (3) to 25 gold francs per kilo (about £3,400 per ton), which is considerably higher than the customary £800 per ton applicable under inland carriage Conditions.[13] Article 24 however provides that on payment of an extra charge, a value in excess of £3,400 per ton can be declared in the consignment note, in which case the former sum will be the basis of assessment of compensation in respect of any claim. Such a provision is commonly used already by carriers in the United Kingdom as a contractual alternative to their normal rates. In the case of delay, however, if a claimant can prove that loss has resulted therefrom the carrier will be liable to pay compensation in respect thereof, up to, but not exceeding, the value of the carriage charges paid.[14]

247   Special interest in delivery

Furthermore, under Article 26 (1), (2), a consignor can, on payment of a surcharge, declare a special interest in delivery where loss or damage occurs, or for which an agreed time limit is exceeded, by making an express declaration to this effect in the consignment note. Compensation resulting from a claim made under such a declaration for the additional loss or damage can be obtained in addition to the amount otherwise payable, though only up to the amount actually declared as of special interest in the consignment note. Whether such a declaration will be made will depend upon the discretion of the consignor.[15]

248   Refund of charges and duties

Where there is a total or partial loss the carrier, in addition, is required under Article 23 (4) to refund in full or *pro rata* carriage and associated charges and also customs duties paid. It is this latter provision which could prove extremely onerous, as, for example, a shipment of goods such as spirits or tobacco which is to traverse several countries is likely to incur an abnormally high rate of duty in relation to the actual value of the goods and the cost of transporting them. No case law has arisen on the point yet though.[16]

249   Valuation

The value of the goods where there has been total or partial loss is to be calculated by reference to their value at the place and time when they were accepted for carriage.[17] This will be reached by reference to the current commodity exchange price, or, if none, by the current market price, failing which by reference to the normal value of goods of a similar kind and quality.[18] If the goods are merely damaged though, the carrier will be liable for their loss in value, based upon their original

---

[13] *Cf.* the higher C.I.M. limit of £14,000 per ton in Art. 31 (1).   This is to be reduced to £7,000 per ton when it is next altered.
[14] Art. 23 (5), C.M.R. *Cf.* Art. 34, C.I.M.
[15] *Cf.* Art. 20, C.I.M.
[16] *Cf.* Art. 31, C.I.M.
[17] Art. 23 (1), C.M.R.   *Cf.* Art. 31, C.I.M.; Art. 10, T.C.M.; Art. 8, F.B.L.
[18] Art. 23 (2), C.M.R.

value as calculated above.[19] However, the amount cannot exceed that payable in the case of total or partial loss respectively.[20]

250 Wilful misconduct

It should be noted that by Article 29 (1), (2), if the damage was caused by his wilful misconduct or equivalent default or by that of his servants, agents or other third parties whom he has employed to perform the carriage, provided they were acting in the course of their employment, then neither the carrier nor his servants, etc., can avail themselves of any of the provisions in Chapter IV which exclude or limit his liability, and in particular the financial restrictions discussed above. In such circumstances, therefore, liability will be unlimited.[21]

251 Combined carriage

However, where the vehicle containing the goods is carried over part of the journey by sea, rail, inland waterway or air and liability is to be determined by that other means of transport within the provisions of Article 2, then the financial limitation will be likewise determined. The amount recoverable will therefore depend upon the provisions of the relevant convention or contractual trading conditions, which may be more or less than that recoverable under C.M.R.[22]

3. THE INTERPRETATION OF FINANCIAL LIMITATION CLAUSES

252 A problem that is coming increasingly before the courts is the interpretation of financial limitation clauses in respect of claims for the loss of part of a ton or hundredweight. The question was discussed at some length in *F. S. Stowell Ltd.* v. *Nicholls & Co. (Brighton) Ltd.*,[23] where a consignment of cherry brandy weighing 1 ton 3 quarters 12 lb. was lost. The point at issue before the court was the meaning of a clause in the Conditions of Carriage whereby liability was " limited to £200 per ton of their gross weight." Judge Block observed that the clause was ambiguous and was capable of three different interpretations. It could mean that liability for loss or damage was limited to £200 per complete ton of the gross weight, in which case damages would be assessed at £200. Secondly, it could be interpreted as meaning £200 per ton of the gross weight *pro rata*, as argued by the defendant carriers, resulting in damages of £248·57½ (£248 11s. 6d.). The third interpretation, which was put forward by the plaintiff shippers, was that the clause should be read to mean £200 per ton or part of a ton, *i.e.* giving damages of £400.

---

[19] Art. 25 (1), C.M.R.
[20] Art. 25 (2), C.M.R. Art. 27 deals with the question of interest and exchange rates.
[21] See § 166. *Cf.* Art. 37, C.I.M.; Art. 12 (2), T.C.M.
[22] *e.g.* £14,000 per ton, Art. 31, C.I.M.; £7,000 per ton, Art. 22 (2), Warsaw Convention; £200 per package, Hague Rules.
[23] [1963] 2 Lloyd's Rep. 275. *Cf. Spaner Bros.* v. *Central Canadian Express Co.* (1918) 43 D.L.R. 400, where the English authorities were distinguished. It was held that where a contract of carriage fixes the value of goods shipped, and limits the carrier's liability to that value, if there is part loss the shipper can recover the real value of the property lost, not exceeding the contractual limit, and is not limited to a proportion.

Following an earlier decision of Sellers J. where the facts were very similar,[24] judgment was given for the plaintiffs on the basis of the third interpretation and damages assessed at £400. The court considered that in a contract of carriage such an onerous clause should be construed as a whole, and " as favourably to the owner of the goods as the clause will permit." Here of course the value of the lost goods exceeded the maximum limit of liability of £200 per ton. If their value had been less than £200, only the true value would be recoverable, according to the general principle of restitution applicable in the law of damages. To overcome this problem R.H.A. and Standard Trading Conditions make special provision that the amount recoverable is to be calculated on a *pro rata* basis, which is of course the most logical solution. These problems can therefore only occur in respect of those contracts not entered into subject to R.H.A. Conditions or Standard Trading Conditions which make similar provision.[25]

253 C.M.R.

The problem is dealt with in a simpler fashion by C.M.R., as this provides that compensation shall not exceed " 25 francs per kilogram of gross weight short." [26] This overcomes the problem of *pro rata* calculations based on large units of weight such as the hundredweight or ton. It should be noted that the basis of calculation is the value of the goods at the place and time when they are accepted for dispatch. No similar provision is found in the respective English conditions. Such a clause however could be very useful where devaluation takes place in the country of destination whilst the goods are in transit or on a falling market.[27]

254 Quotation based upon weight/measurement rate

A complementary problem which arises is that of incorrect charging for loads which a forwarder has quoted his client on a weight/measurement ratio. This question appears to affect forwarders more than carriers as the former rarely see the goods themselves or have an opportunity of checking the accuracy of the dimensions of each load. Three guiding rules have emerged from the recent case law on the subject.

255

First, it is clear from the case of *Zimmerman & Son (Merchants) Ltd.* v. *Baxter, Hoare & Co. Ltd.*[28] that merely because a quotation is made by a forwarder on the basis of a minimum quantity per load, this will not be interpreted as a guarantee by the shipper that the quantity in question can be loaded on a lorry of that capacity. Here the plaintiffs contracted with the defendant forwarders to ship a quantity of tentage,

[24] *Kilroy Thompson Ltd.* v. *Perkins & Homer Ltd.* [1956] 2 Lloyd's Rep. 49.
[25] Cl. 14, S.T.C. provides for recovery " *at the rate of* £100 per ton of 20 cwt." *i.e.* a *pro rata* assessment. *Cf.* Cl. 12, R.H.A. Conditions 1967; Cl. 6, B.R.S. Conditions; see also *David Taylor & Son Ltd.* v. *Bowden Transport Ltd.* [1966] 1 Lloyd's Rep. 287.
[26] Art. 23 (3), C.M.R.
[27] Art. 23 (1), C.M.R. *Cf.* Art. 31, C.I.M.
[28] [1965] 1 Lloyd's Rep. 88.

etc., from Germany to London, on the basis of the latters' quotation of "minimum ten tons per lorry delivered 165s. per ton including all charges, but excluding insurance." In the execution of the transaction it transpired that the tentage was awkward to handle and that owing to the bulky nature of the shipment, sixteen lorries were required to carry the sixty-five-ton load as it was not possible to load the expected ten-ton load on each vehicle. Accordingly, when the shipment arrived in London, the forwarders claimed £1,320 instead of the agreed rate of £536 5s. (£536·25), on the grounds that on the true construction of the contract, it was warranted that the goods should be such that ten tons weight could be carried in a ten-ton lorry, whereas in fact sixteen vehicles were required. McNair J. held that the words "minimum ten tons per load" could not be so construed, and therefore no warranty as to the bulk/weight ratio could be read into the contract. Accordingly the forwarders could only claim the original quoted price, and were therefore themselves liable to the carrier for the balance.

Neither can a forwarder expect to rely on previous dealings with a party in respect of internal domestic carriage as a basis for interpretation of a contract involving international carriage. Therefore merely because a weight/bulk ratio of eighty cubic feet equalling one ton has been the basis of domestic carriage contracts, it does not necessarily follow that such a construction will apply to an export shipment.[29]

256 Customary method of calculation

Secondly, the mere existence of a customary method of calculation will not help the forwarder if his client does not realise that the quotation in question has been made upon the basis of the custom. For example, in a case before the Mayor's Court, a forwarder sued for freight on a shipment of furniture.[30] The rate agreed was "£15 per ton weight or measurement," whichever was the greater. However, it was a shipping custom that where goods were bulky, a weight/measurement ratio applied, forty cubic feet counting as one ton. Accordingly, although the goods only weighed sixteen hundredweight, on this basis they measured seven to eight tons. The forwarder failed in his claim for freight based upon this ratio. The court held that as there was a misunderstanding between the parties as to the basis of charging, the shipper was only liable for the lower rate. It was for the forwarder to ensure that his client was aware of the custom, and as the client had been misled by the forwarder's quotation, the loss must fall on the latter.

257 Goods in excess of specification

Thirdly, if a forwarder makes a quotation for a shipment based upon a certain measurement and weight which has been supplied by the shipper on request, if it later transpires that the goods in question are

---

[29] *Ibid.*
[30] *Alliance Transportation Co. Ltd.* v. *Pike Ltd., Lloyd's List,* Jan. 18, 1922, Mayor's Court.

CHAPTER 11

THE LIABILITY OF THE FORWARDER
FOR THIRD PARTIES

1. INTRODUCTION

260 In the preceding chapters the obligations of a forwarder for his own acts have been the subject of discussion. However, the forwarder, in his capacity as such, does not often actually carry out more than a small part of the forwarding operation himself. He merely offers to effect it by a suitable method of transport which is conveniently available. It is therefore necessary to consider to what extent a forwarder will be liable for the acts of third parties whom he employs to carry out all or part of the forwarding contract. This can be divided into two distinct categories. First, the forwarder's liability for any carrier whom he employs to effect the actual transit of the goods. Secondly, there is the forwarder's liability for any correspondent or sub-agent whom he may use either to forward or receive goods on his behalf at a point of dispatch or arrival where he does not operate in person. Each will be dealt with in turn.

2. THE FORWARDER'S LIABILITY FOR CARRIAGE BY SEA

261 Where a forwarder arranges to forward goods by sea, he will invariably contract as an agent on behalf of his principal the shipper, and will accept no responsibility for the acts of the sea carrier. The rights and liabilities of his principal will therefore depend solely upon the terms of the bill of lading. This does not mean however that the forwarder will not be liable as an agent to his principal, but this aspect of his liability has already been discussed in the preceding chapters.[1]

262 Contract not subject to a bill of lading

Where the contract in question is not subject to a bill of lading, it is not easy to establish to what extent the forwarder accepts liability for transit operations. The position can be more clearly seen from the case of *Lynch Bros.* v. *Edwards & Fase* [2] where a forwarder was employed to " convey or get conveyed " goods belonging to the plaintiff export merchants to a ship in London River. This involved local cartage to a wharf used by the defendant forwarder, and then lighterage to the ship's side. Unfortunately, though, owing to the lighter being left unattended by the lighterman's watchman, the goods in question, tin slabs, were stolen. The question in this case, as Rowlatt J. put it, was "with what

---

[1] See Chapter 3.
[2] (1921) 6 Ll.L.Rep. 371.

responsibilities did the defendants undertake this business?"[3] However, as the defendants had been paid a flat rate for the transit, as in previous similar transactions between the parties, there was some doubt as to their exact status. Rowlatt J. analysed the situation in the following terms:

> "... it is clear the defendants did not act strictly as shipping agents, that is to say, they did not undertake to find space on a cart or in a lighter for these goods upon the terms that they should be remunerated for their ' out-of-pockets ' in making a contract on behalf of the plaintiffs with carter and lightermen, and be paid a percentage for their trouble. . . . I think the defendants are probably best described as contractors . . . to employ carriers at a contract rate to themselves out of which they could make what they could. . . . "[4]

The court therefore held that the forwarders were not liable for loss incurred by the plaintiffs as they had not undertaken the obligation of a common carrier. As they had not contracted upon any specific terms, but upon the "usual terms," they could only be considered to have contracted under such terms as are usual when employing lightermen. In other words, as the latter had excluded liability for negligence, which were the only terms under which a lighterman would operate, the shipper had no remedy against either party.

263   Contract subject to a bill of lading

Where however a shipment is subject to a bill of lading, the forwarder will not be liable in respect of any loss caused by the carrier unless he has himself issued a house bill of lading covering either the specific goods in question or has included them in a consolidated shipment belonging to several consignors or consignees.[5] Such a document may take one of two forms. It may either be in the form of a normal ocean bill of lading merely covering marine transit, or alternatively it may be a through bill of lading covering both sea and land transit.[6] Where a forwarder does issue a house bill in his own name, he will invariably incorporate the terms of the carrier's ocean bill of lading, so as to ensure that his own liability will not exceed that of the carrier actually performing the transit.[7]

Equally, a forwarder may either charter a vessel or space therein, so that he either issues the bill of lading himself, or else accepts responsibility for the form in which it is issued. In such circumstances, he may be liable for any loss due to the carrier's default, under the bill of lading itself, to the extent that he has not excluded his liability. Alternatively,

---

[3] *Ibid.* at p. 372.
[4] *Ibid.*
[5] See Chapter 13.
[6] See *Midland Rubber Co.* v. *Robert Park & Co.* (1922) 11 Ll.L.Rep. 119, discussed in Chapter 13. *Cf.* the converse situation where a carrier merely acts as a forwarder in respect of on-carriage: *Cliffe* v. *Hull & Netherlands S.S. Co. Ltd.* (1921) 6 Ll.L.Rep. 136 —see § 31.
[7] *Ibid.* A similar provision is found in the F.I.A.T.A. Forwarder's Receipt for Transport, see Chapter 13.

he may be liable for the carrier's default where he has not entered into the correct form of bill of lading as originally agreed with the shipper, thus enabling the carrier to exempt himself from liability in respect of the shipment in question.[8]

In the event of such liability, the forwarder will not be able to recover any indemnity from the carrier, unless he has also acted in the capacity of agent for the carrier in signing the bill of lading.[9] Even then, if the actual loss incurred by the shipper does not flow from any act which the forwarder has performed as agent for the carrier, but has only resulted from the forwarder's own breach of an independent contract with the shipper, the forwarder cannot claim any indemnity from the carrier if the latter is in no way responsible for the relationship established.[10]

264   Standard Trading Conditions

In an attempt to solve such problems, the forwarder's liability in respect of carriage by sea has been largely regularised in the past few years by the increasing number of forwarders contracting subject to Standard Trading Conditions. As discussed elsewhere, these provisions give the forwarder considerable protection in respect of loss caused by any carrier whom he may employ to carry goods by sea. Consequently, liability is only likely to arise if a forwarder either operates without using Standard Trading Conditions or the breach in question raises the issue of whether it is of a fundamental nature or not.[11] Only, therefore, if the forwarder carries out functions which are really outside the scope of orthodox forwarding operations, such as confirming house work, will any problems really arise in this respect.

3. The Forwarder's Liability for Carriage by Road

(i) *Introduction*

265   The liability of the forwarder in respect of carriage by road has been the subject of ever-increasing litigation within the last few years. It is a problem which becomes more important with the development of the forwarding of export and import shipments between inland centres and the docks, instead of by rail which was formerly more common.

The common factor in all these cases is generally whether the forwarder can be held liable for theft from a van, belonging to a carrier whom he has employed, where there has been negligence on the part of the van driver in leaving the vehicle unattended. Such a class of contract naturally cannot be considered as a personal obligation,

---

[8] *John Tulloch* v. *Cox's Shipping Agency Ltd.* (1923) 14 Ll.L.Rep. 118. For facts see Chapter 13.
[9] *B. & J. Shaw, etc.* v. *Cox's Shipping Agency Ltd.* (1923) 16 Ll.L.Rep. 216 at p. 219— *i.e.* here the documents signed were not sub-bills of lading signed by the forwarder as agent for the carrier, even though they purported to sign them on behalf of the master of the ship.
[10] *Ibid.*
[11] See § 158.

which the forwarder cannot sub-contract. If it was treated as such, a forwarder would find himself automatically liable for employing a carrier, which would defeat the whole purpose of employing him.[12]

However, the exact position of the forwarder will differ depending upon his particular status in relationship to the actual carrier. For practical purposes this resolves itself into two possibilities. First, the position where a forwarder is acting merely as the agent of the shipper in arranging carriage. Secondly, where the forwarder is acting as an intermediate principal in doing so. This latter category can again be subdivided into those cases where the forwarder is placed in a vicarious relationship with the carrier's driver, thus establishing a master and servant relationship between them, and secondly, where the relationship remains that of independent contractors, the forwarder having no direct responsibility for the carrier's own driver. Each category will therefore be discussed in turn.

(ii) *The Forwarder as an Agent*

266   If the forwarder is acting in the capacity of a mere agent on behalf of his principal, and has not failed in his duty as such, he will not normally be liable for any loss caused by the carrier or his servants. For instance, in *W.L.R. Traders Ltd.* v. *B. & N. Shipping Agency Ltd.*[13] the driver of the vehicle left it unattended for a few minutes to buy a hammer for his own private needs, during which time it disappeared. The plaintiff shippers, who had lost three cartons of nylon stockings, pleaded, *inter alia*, that the forwarder had a duty to ensure that the goods were carried under a contract with the carrier which adequately protected the shipper's interests. The court rejected this argument, emphasising that there is no obligation on a forwarder dealing in the ordinary course of business with commercial goods either to insure them or to inquire whether his client has done so.[14] Consequently, providing the forwarder exercises normal care and skill in arranging a contract of carriage on behalf of the shipper such as would meet the normal requirements of the trade, he will not be liable for any loss caused by the carrier.

267   Standard Trading Conditions

The form of Standard Trading Conditions, however, expressly omits to limit the forwarder to the status of a mere agent, as this would be against the wishes of the forwarding trade generally who do not wish to be considered merely as brokers or non-operating intermediaries. Particularly, as Marshall J. pointed out, if a forwarder hires "a number of vehicles exclusively . . . to be used to transport the goods of any of their customers . . .," such a provision will be quite inconsistent with the concept of the forwarder as the agent of either party.[15]

---

[12] *Cf.* the position of the sub-contracting carrier.
[13] [1955] 1 Lloyd's Rep. 554.
[14] *Ibid.* at p. 557. *Cf. Von Traubenberg* v. *Davies Turner & Co. Ltd.* [1951] 2 Lloyd's Rep. 462—see Chapter 17.
[15] *Lee Cooper Ltd.* v. *C. H. Jeakins & Sons Ltd.* [1964] 1 Lloyd's Rep. 300 at p. 309.

(iii) *The Forwarder as a Principal: Vicarious Liability*

268   Where a forwarder places himself in the position of a principal in relation to his client he will carry the full responsibility of an independent contractor. Consequently, if a forwarder undertakes to perform the contract of carriage himself, or part of it, or at least does not contract as a mere agent in arranging it, he may be liable for any loss caused whether actually resulting from the default of the carrier employed to effect the transit or that of his own servant. However, the forwarder's liability, at least in tort, may depend upon his relationship with the driver of the vehicle from which the theft took place. If in fact the carrier's driver is placed in the position of being under the forwarder's direct control, so as to establish what is, in reality, a master and servant relationship, the forwarder will be vicariously liable for his torts, irrespective of whether the forwarder has himself been negligent or not.

269   **Proof of vicarious relationship**

The problem though is to decide whether in fact such a relationship has been established or not. A comparison between two cases will illustrate this point. In *Colverd & Co. Ltd.* v. *Anglo Overseas Transport Co. Ltd.*[16] a consignment of watches was stolen from an unattended vehicle through the negligence of the driver. The contract between the forwarders and the shipper was a mixed contract, covering not only transport of the goods from London Airport to the plaintiff's offices, but also customs clearance and import licence formalities. The court concluded from the facts, that the forwarders had contracted to transport and deliver the goods from the airport to the plaintiff's offices. They were therefore under a duty to fulfil this obligation, and could not excuse themselves by using sub-contractors to carry it out.[17] The forwarders were, therefore, vicariously liable for the driver's negligence even though not negligent themselves.[18]

By contrast, in *Harris* v. *Continental Express Ltd.*[19] where the facts were similar, the defendant forwarder offered a particular service called Postal Services, in relation to which they offered a collection service. The goods in question were stolen on the journey from the plaintiff's premises to the forwarder's depot, whilst in the carrier's van. The arrangement between the forwarder and the carrier was for the supply of a driver and a van incognito, the latter being marked and coloured in a similar fashion to one actually owned by the forwarder. In the consignment note under which the goods were carried, Clause 1 provided that the forwarder was ". . . not a carrier and reserves the right to

---

[16] [1961] 2 Lloyd's Rep. 352.
[17] *Ibid.* at p. 363, *per* Barry J.
[18] *Cf. Date & Cocke* v. *G. W. Sheldon & Co.* (*London*) *Ltd.* (1921) 7 Ll.L.Rep. 53. When their own vehicles were fully occupied the defendants hired one from a third party, but as Bailhache J. observed, " The fact that they hired this horse and van makes no difference in this case—it must be treated as though it was their own," as the defendants had agreed to carry a shipment from the plaintiff's premises to the docks themselves. See also *F. T. James Co.* v. *Dominion Express Co.* (1907) 13 O.L.R. 211.
[19] [1961] 1 Lloyd's Rep. 251.

refuse to accept any goods offered to it. It will act solely as Forwarding Agent and will only accept and arrange for the transport of the goods . . . subject to all the conditions . . . of . . . any . . . Carrier . . . by or through whom they may be conveyed." Clause 4 also stated that the "Agency shall not be liable under any circumstances whatsoever for any . . . theft . . . of the goods. . . ." The plaintiff therefore argued that the defence in Clause 4 could not be relied upon in the present case, as it was inapplicable to the actual collection of the goods as owing to the wording of Clause 1 the terms did not apply when the forwarder was himself purporting to act as a carrier, but only when he was acting strictly as a forwarder in arranging the transit of goods to their ultimate destination. It was therefore argued that the present arrangement between the forwarder and the carrier was not within the protection of the conditions set out above, as the goods had been handed over to a driver whom the forwarder was holding out to be his servant.

Paull J. rejected the plaintiff's argument.[20] He said that the functions of the forwarder could not be so split up as to deprive them of the benefit of exemption clauses in their trading conditions. The mere fact that the words " the Agency " were used, and the fact that they claimed not to be acting as a carrier, did not preclude them from relying upon the conditions on those occasions when they were actually carrying goods themselves.[21] Furthermore, notwithstanding the fact that the shipper was not aware that the van did not actually belong to the forwarder, and although " The very wording of the consignment note shows it was within the contemplation (of both parties) that the (forwarders) themselves were to collect the goods. . . ," [22] the court still held that vicarious responsibility for the driver was not transferred from the carrier to the forwarder.

270   Is it therefore possible to establish any juridical distinction between these two situations? Certainly, the dividing line between those cases where the forwarder is deemed to have accepted vicarious liability for a carrier's driver, and those where he has not, is a very fine one, and much will depend upon the particular interpretation of the facts adopted by the court. It is possible, however, to distinguish two distinct categories of act. First, where the forwarder has definitely undertaken to transport the goods from one place to another, whether by his own transport or not, as in *Colverd's* case. Secondly, where the forwarder has merely undertaken to arrange transportation of the goods in question, although without necessarily excluding the possibility that he may carry for part of the journey himself, as in *Harris's* case. Only in the former category does it appear that the forwarder will be vicariously liable for the acts of the carrier's servants.

[20] *Ibid.*
[21] *Ibid.* See also *Gillespie Bros.* v. *Roy Bowles Transport Ltd.* [1971] 2 Lloyd's Rep. 521.
[22] *Ibid.* at p. 259, *per* Paull J.—the words used were " Please collect," and not " Please arrange for the collection of the goods."

271   Standard Trading Conditions

To avoid the consequences of such a categorisation, the provisions made under Standard Trading Conditions offer a solution. Where these Conditions are applicable, the fact that Clause 1 excludes the possibility of the forwarder being treated as a common carrier, but without specifying whether the forwarder is acting as a carrier or not, enables the court to avoid the need for any such discussion as arose in *Harris's* case as to the exact function of a forwarder. In other words, if as in *Colverd's* case, the court accepts that Standard Trading Conditions cover the whole contract, the question of function is irrelevant. The imprudence of operating under such non-standard trading conditions as were in use in *Harris's* case, or else without any at all, as in *W.L.R. Traders'* case, is therefore manifest in these decisions.

272   Vicarious liability of the forwarder excludes that of the carrier

However, irrespective of whether trading conditions are operative or not, one consequence of the forwarder being made vicariously liable for the acts of the carrier's servant is that simultaneously the carrier *ipso facto* ceases to be vicariously liable for his acts. As a result, he will be able to avoid liability if sued directly by the shipper in tort, although he may be liable to indemnify the forwarder in respect of any claims which he has himself satisfied.[23]

273   Finally, it is necessary to consider the position where the driver's action is deemed to amount to a fundamental breach of contract. The problem arose in the case of *Lee Cooper Ltd.* v. *C. H. Jeakins & Sons Ltd.*,[24] the facts of which were outlined in an earlier chapter. In a direct action by the shipper against the carrier, the question arose as to whether the intermediate forwarder had been acting as the agent of either party. This the court rejected, stating that all the parties had acted as principals.[25] Consequently, the carrier could not take advantage of either R.H.A. Conditions which were the basis of his contract with the forwarder, nor of Standard Trading Conditions which were the basis of the relationship between the forwarder and his client. He was therefore fully liable at common law.

However, as an alternative, Marshall J. was prepared to treat the driver's action as constituting a fundamental breach of contract.[26] On

---

[23] Furthermore, it should be noted that if the actual carrier is not himself negligent, and the only act in respect of which he can be made liable is based upon vicarious liability for his servant's actions, he will not be liable either if the act in question is completely outside the scope of employment, *e.g.* if, although all reasonable steps had been taken to ensure the driver's integrity, the latter commits larceny—see *Homecraft Weavers Ltd.* v. *George Welsh Ltd.* (1945) 78 Ll.L.Rep. 496.

[24] [1964] 1 Lloyd's Rep. 300; see § 161 for the facts. As to the fraud of the actual carrier, see *Metal Scrap & By-Products Ltd.* v. *Federated Conveyors Ltd.* [1953] 1 Lloyd's Rep. 221.

[25] *Ibid.* at p. 308.   *Cf.* contracts subject to C.M.R. where the Convention lays down clearly which parties are bound by a contract subject to the Convention, thus avoiding the need for reliance on the uncertainties of the operation of the doctrine of privity of contract and express or implied agency clauses such as may be put forward in a case involving a *Lee Cooper* v. *Jeakins* type of situation.

[26] *Ibid.*

the facts, this would not affect the forwarder's liability to his principal as he was not vicariously liable for the driver's actions. However although not discussed by the court, if there had been such a shift of responsibility, the position would have been different, as the driver's actions as the servant of the forwarder would have been treated as a fundamental breach of the forwarding contract instead of that of the carrier. In such circumstances, therefore, it would be possible for the shipper to recover from the forwarder in full, as the latter could not rely on his trading conditions to limit the right of recovery. Conversely, as already mentioned, the carrier would himself avoid all liability to the shipper.

274 **Extra-vicarious liability**

So far the question of the forwarder's responsibility for the acts of a sub-contractor's servants has been treated from the viewpoint of vicarious liability. In the recent case of *B.R.S. Ltd.* v. *Arthur Crutchley & Co. Ltd.*,[27] however, the Court of Appeal took a different approach to the matter. The facts of the case briefly were that the plaintiff carrier transferred goods to the defendants for transhipment locally to the docks, and which were stolen whilst being stored overnight in the latter's warehouse. The loss was partially the result of inadequate security arrangements on the part of the security company to whom the defendants had sub-contracted the task of guarding their warehouse. The question therefore arose, *inter alia*, whether the defendants could avoid liability for the sub-contractor's negligence. This the court rejected on the grounds that[28]:

> "The bailee is responsible for proper care being taken of the goods and to my mind he cannot escape from that liability merely by employing sub-contractors for that purpose, however reasonable may be his confidence in them. Any contrary decision would make a serious and unjustifiable inroad on the rights of bailors, and for this inroad there does not appear to me to be any authority."

In other words, in this dictum Sachs L.J. puts forward the view that independent of any concept of vicarious liability, the bailee of goods cannot avoid liability merely by employing a sub-contractor to perform all or part of the contract for him. The question that therefore arises is whether this dictum, based upon a series of earlier cases, can be reconciled with the precedents discussed above.

The answer to this question seems to lie in the judgment of Lord Pearson in the same case, who analysed the problem as follows[29]:

> "The bailor could not reasonably be expected to be content with a contractual promise of the bailee to take proper care of the goods or engage a competent contractor to do so. If that were the contractual promise, then in the event of default by a competent

---

[27] [1968] 1 Lloyd's Rep. 271. See also *Gillespie Bros.* v. *Roy Bowles Transport Ltd.* [1971] 2 Lloyd's Rep. 521.
[28] *Ibid.* at p. 289, *per* Sachs L.J.
[29] *Ibid.* at p. 285.

contractor duly selected by the bailee, the bailor would have no remedy against the bailee and would have to rely on the possibility of an action in tort against the contractor. To give business efficacy to the contract, the bailee's implied promise should be that he will himself or through his servants or agents take proper care of the goods."

275 Business efficacy

The key to the problem lies in the test of "business efficacy," as although Lord Pearson is probably correct in stating that warehouse-keepers and certain other bailees should be subject to an implied promise to take proper care of the goods through their "servants or agents," from the very nature of the forwarding trade it is far from essential for such an implied promise to be read into a forwarding contract. The distinction between the forwarder who definitely undertakes to transport the goods and the forwarder who merely undertakes to arrange transportation, already considered in relation to vicarious liability, is, in the opinion of the writer, equally applicable here. Only therefore where the forwarder has actually undertaken to transport the goods himself, whether by his own transport or not, can such an implied promise be read into the forwarding contract to achieve "business efficacy." In other words, in such cases as *Colverd's* case [30] the forwarder would be subject to such an implied promise. Where, however, the forwarder only undertakes to arrange transportation, although without necessarily excluding the possibility that he may carry himself for part of the journey, as in *Harris's* case,[31] his duty will merely be "to take proper care of the goods or engage a competent contractor to do so."

276 Application to forwarding contract

In conclusion, therefore, it is submitted that to distinguish between liability for the servants of a sub-contractor based upon vicarious or non-vicarious principles is irrelevant in relation to the forwarding contract. As Barry J. observed in *Colverd's* case [32]:

". . . they [the forwarders] were under a duty to fulfil this obligation and they were not excused from this duty by carrying it out through a sub-contractor . . . and I am prepared to hold that the [forwarders] are in fact vicariously responsible for the acts of the driver."

In other words, it appears that, as regards forwarding activities, the two concepts are merely different aspects of the same rule, as the vicarious liability only results from the overriding obligation of the bailee forwarder to care for the goods. Consequently, any apparent conflict between the two series of precedents really disappears.

[30] *Supra*; the question did not arise in *Lee Cooper's* case.
[31] [1961] 1 Lloyd's Rep. 251.
[32] [1961] 2 Lloyd's Rep. 352 at p. 363.

(iv) *The Shipper—Alternative Remedies against the Sub-Contractor*

277   In the field of contractual relationships, one of the most important differences between the common law and continental civil law is the doctrine of privity of contract. In other words, at common law a person who is not a party to a contract cannot benefit from any agreement entered into unless one of the parties either expressly or impliedly acts as his agent. Such a restriction does not generally exist on the Continent, thus largely avoiding the problems in this field of contractual relations which from time to time come before the English courts.

278   **Lee Cooper v. Jeakins**

The problem is particularly pertinent though to the question of whether a road haulier, employed by a forwarder to carry goods belonging to his client, can obtain the protection of the exemption clauses limiting the forwarder's liability to his client. In this respect it seems that as a result of *Lee Cooper Ltd.* v. *C. H. Jeakins & Sons Ltd.*,[33] where a forwarder is contracting under Standard Trading Conditions, his status is far from certain. Certainly, the mere fact that he is referred to as a " forwarding agent " seems to have little or no effect whatever on his status, and in the latter case the carrier failed to prove that the forwarder was acting as either party's agent.[34]

The forwarder's client is therefore faced with a choice. If he sues the forwarder, his right of recovery will generally be limited by Standard Trading Conditions if they are the basis of the contract. To avoid this restriction, in *Lee Cooper's* case the shipper brought an action solely against the carrier in the tort of negligence. In his judgment Marshall J. stated that the rule still held good that " our law still knows nothing of a *jus quaesitum tertio*," and rejected the defendant's plea that he could take advantage of exemption clauses in the forwarder's contract with the plaintiff.[35] The court also rejected the defendant's argument that he owed no common law duty of care to the shipper, and was therefore not liable in negligence to him. The court emphasised that no rule exists at common law that if a contractual relationship exists between two parties,

[33] [1964] 1 Lloyd's Rep. 300.
[34] *Ibid.* at p. 308, *per* Marshall J.
[35] *Ibid.* at p. 309. *Cf. Morris* v. *C. W. Martin & Sons Ltd.* [1965] 2 Lloyd's Rep. 63 at p. 73, *per* Denning M.R. In *Allen* v. *C.P.R.* (1910) 21 O.L.R. 416, the plaintiff gave a trunk of valuable samples to the Dominion Express Company for which a receipt was given, but he failed to declare their value so that a $50 limit applied in any claim against the latter, who were an independent company operating on the defendant's lines in Canada under a contract whereby the defendant was liable for all valid claims and was to indemnify the Express Company in respect thereof. The trunk was placed by the Express Company in the defendant's car on the defendant's railway, but in the charge and possession of an Express Company servant, and was destroyed in a subsequent collision, for which the defendant admitted negligence. The court held that the defendant was liable in tort to the plaintiff for negligence and could not rely on the Express Company contract with the plaintiff, as there was no privity of contract between them. Furthermore, the court considered that even if the contract between the plaintiff and the Express Company did apply, the clause " that the stipulation . . . shall extend to and enure to the benefit of each and every company or person to whom through this Company the . . . property may be entrusted or delivered for transportation," did not apply to the defendants, but merely to a successive carrier beyond the defendant's line to whom it might be necessary for the Express Company to part with

as there did between the carrier and the forwarder, and the forwarder and his client, respectively, their rights and duties could only be measured by the terms of this relationship, precluding any action in tort arising out of the same facts.[36]

Quoting Lord Macmillan's famous maxim that " the categories of negligence are never closed," [37] the learned judge stated that where carriers are bailees for reward, albeit contractually bound to a forwarder, and know from an extended period of trading that the latter as a forwarder is continually handling his client's goods and not his own, and that from the terms of the consignment note the carriers are aware who are the real owners of the goods in question, and that they are of value, in such circumstances the latter will owe a duty of care to the shipper, and, being in breach thereof, will be liable for the full value of the goods stolen.[38]

279   Learoyd v. Pope

The implications of this decision have been further developed in the recent case of *Learoyd* v. *Pope*.[39] Here the driver left £5,000-worth of worsted cloth for export, unattended for twenty minutes while he went to the wharf office, during which time it was stolen. The case differed from *Lee Cooper's* case in two respects. First, no forwarder was involved in the transaction, the plaintiff shipper having employed a haulier named Hanson, who had in turn sub-contracted the local delivery service to the defendant carrier Pope. Hanson's liability to the shipper was limited by the terms of their contract with the latter to £1,087 18s. 11d., which was duly paid. The plaintiff therefore sued the defendant for the outstanding balance.

Secondly, in contrast with *Lee Cooper's* case, the defendant carriers did not attempt to rely on the financial limit of liability which Hanson's had imposed upon the plaintiffs, nor did they attempt to plead that

the property in order that it might reach its destination. The implication is that even if a forwarder attempted to protect a carrier in his trading conditions in a *Lee Cooper* v. *Jeakins* type of situation with such a clause, care must be taken to see that both the initial carrier and any on-carrier are covered, otherwise the exercise could be self-defeating. Such a situation as this could easily arise when forwarders expand into the container traffic and commence to consolidate small shipments in containers owned by the initial carrier, but which are handled by successive carriers in transit.

[36] [1964] 1 Lloyd's Rep. 300 at p. 311.

[37] *Donoghue* v. *Stevenson* [1932] A.C. 562.

[38] [1964] 1 Lloyd's Rep. 300 at p. 311. This does not however preclude any carrier employed by a forwarder being a common carrier, even if the forwarder himself is at the most liable as a private carrier himself. If the carrier is subject to a common calling, his liability may be absolute, although the plea of common carriage is rarely pleaded even where it is ostensibly a reasonable one to make. Recently, Pilcher J. drew attention to this point—" In a statement of claim the plaintiffs described the second defendants as private carriers. . . . Such evidence as was called in the case was not directed to the question whether in all the circumstances the second defendants could be said to have been common carriers, [but] . . . on such evidence as was called before me I think that it is at least as likely that the second defendants were common carriers as they were not ": *W.L.R. Traders Ltd.* v. *B. & N. Shipping Agency Ltd.* [1955] 1 Lloyd's Rep. 554 at p. 556. See also *Hunt & Winterbotham (West of England) Ltd.* v. *B.R.S. (Parcels) Ltd.* [1962] 1 Q.B. 617.

[39] [1966] 2 Lloyd's Rep. 142. *Cf. Colley* v. *Brewers Wharf & Transport Ltd.* (1921) 9 Ll.L.Rep. 5; *Gillespie Bros.* v. *Roy Bowles Transport Ltd.* [1971] 2 Lloyd's Rep. 521.

Hanson's had acted as their agents in contracting with the shipper. Instead, Pope argued that they were not carrying the consignment as bailees for the plaintiffs and therefore had no duty to the latter to take care of the goods, and were therefore not liable to them for the loss of the goods which resulted from their driver's negligence.

The question therefore turned upon the true legal position of a carrier who finds himself in charge of a third party's goods, but with whom he has no direct contractual relationship.

Sachs J. commenced by reviewing the various precedents on the subject, the majority of which dealt with the question of a forwarder or carrier sub-contracting all or part of the contract of carriage to another carrier, the latter's driver remaining in charge of the vehicle in all cases. The court then considered the question of the form of the contract, and whether a distinction can be drawn between a long-term contract and one on an hourly basis, the latter being applicable in the present case and *Lee Cooper's* case. This the court emphatically rejected on the grounds that it can be of no concern to a shipper as to what kind of contractual terms are entered into between either a forwarder or carrier whom they have employed and any sub-contractor whose services the latter may have utilised, unless the latter is merely acting as an agent in so doing.

If a shipper's contract is to depend upon the terms of such a subsidiary relationship it would place him in an intolerable position, as he would be subject to the terms of a contractual relationship over which he has neither knowledge nor control.

The court therefore decided that the position of such a sub-contractor is that of a bailee to the shipper, who " can conveniently be described as sub-bailee." [40] In this respect, no distinction can be drawn between a contract for the carriage of specific goods, or only, as in *Learoyd's* case, a contract for the mere hiring of a vehicle. The subrelationship will be the same in both cases. The sub-bailee will owe a duty of care therefore in both cases, and to leave a valuable load unattended without any anti-thief devices in a dockland area amounts to negligence for which the sub-bailee must be liable.

In both the cases under discussion, the actual carrier's contract of carriage with the principal carrier contained a clause limiting liability to a certain sum. Such a limit does not, however, affect the shipper as he is not a party to the contract and can therefore ignore it. [41]

---

[40] [1966] 2 Lloyd's Rep. 142 at p. 148. See also *The Regenstein* [1970] 2 Lloyd's Rep. 1.
[41] *Cf.* Paull J. in *Harris's* case: " The [carriers] therefore, being liable, prima facie for the negligence of their servant, I cannot see that the terms of the contract between the [forwarders] and the [carriers] can in any way affect the plaintiffs. . . . The [forwarders] did not enter into the contract with the [carriers] as the agents of the plaintiffs in order to enable the carriage of the goods to be effected. The contract is a contract entered into by the [forwarders] as principals in order, *inter alia*, to assist the [forwarders] in collecting goods from their customers' premises and bringing them to their depot where the dispatch of the goods begins. It may well be that it was also entered into in order to enable the [forwarders] to lower their costs when sending goods from their depot to, for example, a post office, a station or an airport and so to increase their

280 Future procedures

In future, the tendency may be to sue the sub-bailee alone, as a result of *Lee Cooper's* case and *Learoyd's* case, instead of joining both forwarder and sub-bailee together as joint defendants as in the other cases discussed above. The one drawback to such a course is that if, as in *Colverd & Co. Ltd.* v. *Anglo Overseas Transport Co. Ltd.*,[42] where the action was in fact brought against both, the court is prepared to treat the forwarder as vicariously liable for the acts of the sub-bailee's driver, the sub-bailee will cease to be liable to the shipper for any resultant loss. Consequently, if, as in *Colverd's* case Standard Trading Conditions are the basis of the contract between shipper and forwarder, the former will be virtually without a remedy unless a plea of fundamental breach is accepted. If therefore a situation similar to that in *Colverd's* case occurs again, it will be necessary to join both forwarder and sub-bailee as joint defendants. It should be observed, however, that the worthlessness of a remedy against a forwarder trading under Standard Trading Conditions may in fact persuade counsel to rely solely on success or failure in an action against the sub-bailee, as in *Lee Cooper's* case.

This problem did not arise in *Learoyd* v. *Pope* as the shipper had already recovered the full sum recoverable under their contract with Hanson, and merely sued the sub-bailee for the outstanding balance. In both these cases the shipper would have failed to establish liability if it had been proved that the driver was the vicarious responsibility of the forwarder, but the point was not raised in either case. Such a plea was raised however in *Harris's* case, that is, that under the contract between the sub-bailee and the forwarder the driver was actually in the employment of the latter when the goods were stolen, so that they never came into the possession of the sub-bailee at all. The court rejected this argument, the sub-bailee remaining liable for the acts of the driver, and therefore for the full amount of the loss.[43]

In conclusion, therefore, it is clear that in such cases the sub-bailee will have little protection against third party claims, and must therefore ensure that adequate insurance cover is available to protect him against such claims, whether arising from contracts to carry specific consignments, or merely for a general hiring of a vehicle and driver, whether on contract or on a casual basis. The only other possible opportunity for relief will be if he can claim any form of indemnity from the forwarder or principal carrier. This problem will be dealt with in the next section.

---

profit where an all-in rate was quoted, or, alternatively, to allow them to quote a lower all-in rate. I cannot see that the plaintiffs can be affected by such a contract ": [1961] 1 Lloyd's Rep. 251 at p. 259. *Cf. W.L.R. Traders Ltd.* v. *B. & N. Shipping Agency Ltd., supra*, if the forwarder is acting as agent for one of the parties, the reverse will apply, unless either the carrier or the sub-contractor have failed to incorporate any trading conditions into the contract.

[42] [1961] 2 Lloyd's Rep. 352.

[43] *Cf.* The question was not raised in *W.L.R. Traders* at all.

(v) *The Sub-Contractor's Right of Indemnity*

281   The question arises whether a sub-contracting carrier of goods can
claim an indemnity from a forwarder by whom he is employed in respect
of a successful claim against him by a shipper. This will arise where he
has not been able to avoid full liability by relying on exemptions clauses
in his trading conditions, which can only be effective against the forwarder himself, unless the latter has contracted as the mere agent of the
shipper.[44] Obviously, at common law, the carrier will have no remedy
against the forwarder, unless the latter has in some way been actively
responsible to him for the loss in question. Generally, though, this
situation will only arise where the carrier's servant actually becomes the
vicarious liability of the forwarder, in which case the carrier will be
automatically relieved of liability to the shipper so that no question of
indemnity will arise.[45]

282 Contractual right of indemnity
    Where, however, the driver remains the vicarious liability of the
sub-contractor the latter will only have a remedy against the forwarder
if he has contractually obtained a right of indemnity in respect of any
loss suffered as a result of effecting a transit on behalf of the forwarder.
Such a provision is included in R.H.A. Conditions 1967 in the following
terms: " The Trader shall save harmless and keep the Carrier indemnified against all claims or demands whatsoever by whomsoever made in
excess of the liability of the Carrier under these conditions." [46] The
legal limit referred to will be the sum of £800 per ton as laid down in
Clause 12 of the Conditions, if applicable, otherwise for the full
amount where no privity exists with the shipper.
    Such a provision was included in the contract between the forwarder
and the sub-contractor in *Harris's* case, where the contract, although
not subject to R.H.A. Conditions, included a similar clause whereby the
hirers agreed to indemnify the carrier against all claims arising out of
the hiring.[47] Accordingly, in the third party proceedings which were
dealt with at the same hearing, between the sub-contractor and the
forwarder, the former was able to recover a full indemnity against all
loss. Similarly, in *Lee Cooper's* case the carrier would have been able to
recover from the forwarder the damages paid to the shipper, as their
contract was subject to R.H.A. Conditions. The question did not arise
though, as the forwarder was not made a party to the proceedings,
either as a co-defendant or under third party proceedings.[48] Similarly,
a right of indemnity would have existed in *W.L.R. Traders* case,[49] if

---

44 Cf. *W.L.R. Traders Ltd.* v. *B. & N. Shipping Agency Ltd.* [1955] 1 Lloyd's Rep. 554.
45 Cf. *Colverd & Co. Ltd.* v. *Anglo-Overseas Transport Co. Ltd.* [1961] 2 Lloyd's Rep.
    352.
46 Cl. 3 (4), R.H.A. Conditions 1967 (formerly Cl. 20, R.H.A. Conditions 1961). B.R.S.
    Conditions make no such provision. Reliance is placed solely on an agency clause.
    Gillespie Bros. v. *Roy Bowles Transport Ltd.* [1971] 2 Lloyd's Rep. 521.
47 [1961] 1 Lloyd's Rep. 251 at p. 259.
48 Cf. *Harris* v. *Continental Express Ltd.*, *supra.*
49 *Ibid.*

the carrier had succeeded in proving that the contract in question was subject to R.H.A. Conditions, although in the circumstances the court rejected this plea.[50]

283 Standard Trading Conditions

The fact that carriers in the private sector normally include such a right of indemnity in their trading conditions means that the protection which a forwarder has obtained under Standard Trading Conditions, both as to extent of liability [51] and also as to the amount recoverable,[52] can in practice be largely cancelled out if either the sub-contractor is joined as a second defendant, or else the action is brought against him alone. The forwarder will therefore be forced to pay the amount of the claim indirectly by indemnifying the sub-contractor in respect of the sum paid by him to the shipper. To avoid this difficulty a clause has been included in Standard Trading Conditions 1970, whereby the client agrees to indemnify the forwarder against:

"all liabilities suffered or incurred by the Company arising directly or indirectly from or in connection with the Customer's instructions or their implementation or the goods, and in particular the Customer shall indemnify the Company in respect of any liability it may be under to any servant, agent or sub-contractor, or any haulier, carrier, warehouseman, or other person whatsoever at any time involved with the goods arising out of any claim made directly or indirectly against any such party by the Customer or by any sender, consignee or owner of the goods or by any person interested in the goods or by any other person whatsoever." [53]

This clause is intended to bring the matter full circle and will effectively negative such decisions as *Harris's* case and *Lee Cooper's* case, discussed above. The shipper is in fact effectively deprived of any remedy against either the forwarder or any party whom the latter may employ in performing any part of the transaction, provided a similar indemnity clause has been included in the sub-contract.[54]

284 Contractual protection for the sub-contractor

Finally, the question must be considered of whether there is an alternative approach to the problem of the liability of the sub-contractor and the carrier's own servants or agents. Is it possible for him to be given adequate protection against liability to the shipper of goods? An attempt to do so was made in R.H.A. Conditions 1961 to enable any servant or agent or sub-contractor to obtain the benefit of the principal contract of carriage. Clause 1 (*a*) provides that: "Contractor . . .

[50] *Ibid.* at pp. 558 *et seq.*
[51] Cl. 13, S.T.C.
[52] *Ibid.*
[53] Cl. 24, S.T.C.—no such provision was made in the 1956 edition. *Cf.* Art. 11 (3), D.F.C.; Art. 12, N.Y.F.F.
[54] *Cf.* Other provisions in S.T.C. imposing an indemnity are Cl. 9, in respect of loss resulting from inaccurate particulars, etc., and Cl. 20, in respect of dangerous goods.

includes the Contractor's servants and agents and any person or persons carrying goods under a sub-contract with the Contractor."

It is doubtful though whether this clause in fact fulfils its purpose, although there has been no direct dispute on this point to date.[55]

An attempt to remedy this situation has since been made in R.H.A. Conditions 1967. Clause 3 (3) provides that: "The carrier enters into the Contract for and on behalf of himself and his servants, agents, and for sub-contractors and his sub-contractors' servants, agents and sub-contractors; all of whom shall be entitled to the benefit of the Contract. . . ." This wording is very similar to that employed by British Rail and B.R.S. Conditions, which Kahn-Freund considers establishes an agency relationship. If his view proves acceptable to the courts such third parties will be able to take the benefit of the principal contract of carriage, but again subject to them furnishing consideration.[56]

Standard Trading Conditions, on the other hand, do not grant protection against tortious liability to their servants and agents, nor is any provision made for the benefit of any sub-contractor.

285   It is clear from dicta in *Lee Cooper Ltd.* v. *C. H. Jeakins & Sons Ltd.*[57] that there is nothing to prevent a forwarder or carrier from acting as the agent of either the shipper or the carrier in any transaction. In practice it is not difficult to prove that a particular transaction is in fact entered into on behalf of a shipper. Two possibilities exist, first, an express agency clause may be inserted in the contract, although as already discussed, this is not commercially attractive to the forwarding and haulage trade. Secondly, Lord Denning has laid down that a shipper will be bound by the terms of a sub-contract [58] "if he has expressly or impliedly consented to the bailee making a sub-bailment containing these conditions but not otherwise." The problem here is to decide under what circumstances such consent will be deemed to have been given if it is not express.

It appears to be considerably more difficult, however, to prove that a forwarder or carrier is in fact contracting on behalf of another carrier owing to the independent method of operations currently practised in the field of transportation. In other words, it is not easy to persuade the court that where an intermediary offers to effect transportation either through his own transport or by unspecified means, that where he actually employs a sub-contractor he then intends to lessen his status to that of a mere agent. Such a plea is, in most cases, a mere contradiction in terms. However, as none of these contractual provisions has been the subject of judicial interpretation as yet, their true import will remain a matter for conjecture.

---

[55] *Garnham, Harris & Elton Ltd.* v. *Alfred W. Ellis Ltd.* [1967] 2 Lloyd's Rep. 22.
[56] See Kahn-Freund, *Law of Inland Transport*, 4th ed., pp. 325 *et seq.* Cl. 2 (2), B.R.S. Conditions. *Gillespie Bros.* v. *Roy Bowles Transport Ltd.* [1971] 2 Lloyd's Rep. 521.
[57] [1964] 1 Lloyd's Rep. 300.
[58] *Morris* v. *C. W. Martin & Sons Ltd.* [1965] 2 Lloyd's Rep. 63 at p. 72.

(vi) *The Forwarder's Authority to Sub-contract*

286 Where a contract is subject to Standard Trading Conditions, Clause 3 specifically provides that a third party may be employed to carry out any part of the operation in question.[59] Alternatively, it is not uncommon for a forwarder to contract under R.H.A. Conditions in such circumstances if he is part of a multiple group. Here the problem has arisen as to whether the definition of a " Contractor " in Clause 1 (*a*), R.H.A. Conditions 1961, as including " any . . . person carrying goods under a sub-contract with the Contractor," actually gives a carrier authority to sub-contract to another carrier without further authorisation.

287 The interpretation of this clause has recently been the subject of discussion in *Garnham, Harris & Elton Ltd.* v. *Alfred W. Ellis Ltd.*[60] The facts were simply that the defendant carrier sub-contracted the carriage of a load of copper wire to a third party without checking his bona fides, and gave him a delivery order with which he collected the wire, and then promptly disappeared with it. As the court pointed out, such a commodity is extremely attractive to a thief owing to its value and the absence of any conclusive form of identity marks. On the facts, the plaintiff was not aware that the load in question or any previous ones carried for him by the defendant had been sub-contracted.

The court considered that two questions arise in deciding whether a carrier is liable for loss in such circumstances. First, has the carrier a right to sub-contract without the express consent of the shipper. This the court rejected, disapproving earlier dicta to the effect that this clause gave a general right to sub-contract.[61] Paull J. stated that although such a right might exist in particular circumstances, none could be considered to exist in the case in question. Furthermore, he was "prepared to hold that in any contract for the carriage of such [valuable] goods there must be some express words, preferably in the body of the contract, giving a carrier the right to sub-contract."[62] Secondly, even if such authority does exist without the need for express consent, is the carrier aware, or ought he to be, that such an informal method of sub-contracting would be outside the contemplation of the parties as being quite reckless considering the value of the commodity carried, as was the case here. Here, however, there was no right to sub-contract at all, and in any case the manner thereof amounted to a fundamental breach of contract precluding reliance on R.H.A. Conditions under any circumstances.[63]

---

[59] See *Gillette Industries Ltd.* v. *W. H. Martin Ltd.* [1966] 1 Lloyd's Rep. 57, where a typical forwarding operation is described in detail.
[60] [1967] 2 Lloyd's Rep. 22.
[61] *John Carter Ltd.* v. *Hanson Haulage Ltd.* [1965] 1 Lloyd's Rep. 49 at p. 60, *per* Davies L.J.
[62] [1967] 2 Lloyd's Rep. 22 at p. 27.
[63] The defendant could not, therefore, rely on Cl. 12 (*a*), R.H.A. Conditions 1961, whereby advice of non-delivery of goods is required within 28 days to render the carrier liable. This had not been complied with by the shipper owing to the particular

It therefore seems that an implied right to sub-contract under R.H.A. Conditions 1961 can only exist where trading relations permit it, bearing in mind the commodity in question and current trade usage. However, reliance on such uncertain criteria is not a good basis for certainty in trade relationships, and must in fact lessen the effect of standard conditions of contract as a means of limiting the liability of a carrier or forwarder. If, therefore, a carrier intends to sub-contract, it will be necessary for him to obtain express authorisation for such a procedure, to avoid liability in a situation such as arose in *Garnham's* case.

288   However, to avoid the implications of this decision, a clause has been inserted in R.H.A. Conditions 1967 to the effect that: "The Carrier may employ the services of any other carrier for the purpose of fulfilling the Contract. Any such other carrier shall have the like power to sub-contract on like terms." [64] Such a provision would appear to overcome the problem of express authority to sub-contract which was lacking in *Garnham's* case. However, the carrier will still be left with the question raised by Paull J., as to whether the actual giving of authority to the sub-contractor to collect the goods is itself outside the scope of his own authority. In other words, Clause 3 (2) will not protect a carrier who behaves in such a reckless manner as in *Garnham's* case, so as to amount to a fundamental breach of contract. Consequently, although the new provision overcomes the problem of uncertainty of authority, it does not relieve the carrier of his duty of care in exercising it.

(vii) *The Convention for the International Carriage of Goods by Road*

289   Where carriage is subject to C.M.R. specific provision is made as to the liabilities of the various parties. The position of a forwarder will depend upon whether he is in the position of the sender, the first carrier or of a successive carrier. First, if he is acting as a mere agent on behalf of his client or else merely as the sender of goods, he will not be liable as a carrier under the Convention. [65] If, however, he is in the position of a carrier he will be responsible for "the acts and omissions of his agents and servants and of any other persons of whose services he makes use for the performance of the carriage, when such agents, servants or other persons are acting within the scope of their employment, as if such acts or omissions were his own." [66]

trading methods in use. The court further clarified the application of the concept of fundamental breach of contract to contracts of carriage, emphasising that it cannot arise in such a case unless there has in fact been an actual conversion of the goods, which could not be constituted by mere non-delivery of them. Where a carrier has sub-contracted the actual carriage, conversion can only arise where the giving of authority by a carrier to a sub-contractor to collect goods is in itself outside the scope of any authority which the former might possess as to how he can deal with the goods. The reckless manner in which the defendant in *Garnham's* case had effected the sub-contract amounted to such an act.

[64] Cl. 3 (2), R.H.A. Conditions 1967. *Gillespie Bros.* v. *Roy Bowles Transport Ltd.* [1971] 2 Lloyd's Rep. 521. *Cf.* Cl. 2 (1), B.R.S. Conditions.

[65] N.B. The Convention does not define a carrier. See § 351.

[66] Art. 3, C.M.R.; *cf.* Art. 39, C.I.M.; Art. 2, T.C.M.; Art. 2, F.B.L.

This provision is reinforced by a further one stating that the carrier will be liable for the wrongful act or omission of any person from whom he may hire a vehicle to effect transit, and also for the latter's servants or agents.[67] The position is therefore similar to that at common law. Furthermore, the carrier will be deprived of the defences which the Convention gives him either excluding or limiting his liability or which shift the burden of proof if the damage is caused by the "wilful misconduct or default" of his servants or agents or of any other persons whose services he makes use of in performing the carriage, providing they are acting within the scope of their employment.[68]

290   Secondly, where successive carriers are involved in a contract of carriage which is governed by a single contract (with the sender), each of the carriers will be responsible for the whole transit. However, legal proceedings can only be brought against the first carrier, the last carrier or the carrier performing that part of the transit during which the injurious event occurred, although several of the above may be sued at the same time.[69] The former question relates closely to the question of the issue of the consignment note, and will be dealt with in the next chapter. However, this still leaves the equally important question of whether a sub-contracting carrier is a mere agent for whom the carrier will be liable under Article 3, referred to above, or whether he will be a successive carrier under Article 34.

The latter states that acceptance of the goods *and* the consignment note will constitute a road carrier a successive carrier. However, Article 4 states only that the contract will be "confirmed" by the making of the consignment note, and that the "absence, irregularity or loss of the consignment note shall not affect the existence or the validity of the contract of carriage which shall remain subject to the provisions of this Convention." It is not clear therefore whether acceptance of the goods *without* the consignment note will have the same effect.[70]

291   The question is of more than academic value, as if a sub-contractor is not a successive carrier, there is no provision that he will be directly liable to the sender or any other claimant under the Convention. If a claim is made under the Convention, against the carrier who employed the sub-contractor, the carrier may in turn recover from him. However,

---

[67] Art. 17 (3), C.M.R.
[68] Art. 29 (2), C.M.R.
[69] Art. 36, C.M.R.; *cf*. Art. 43, C.I.M.
[70] Whereas Art. 35 (2), C.M.R., specifically states that the provisions relating to successive carriers are subject to Art. 9, C.M.R. (which also concerns the consignment note), Art. 34 makes no such provision. It is logically arguable that Art. 34 is not therefore subject to Art. 4, particularly as it specifically requires the successive carrier to accept both the goods and the consignment note. However, it is equally arguable that Art. 4 clearly states that even if there is no consignment note the contract of carriage "shall remain subject to the provisions of the Convention." However, the issue in Art. 34 is not whether a contract of carriage exists between the shipper and the first carrier, but whether a successive carrier has become a party to it. The better view is that a successive carrier can only become a party on acceptance of the note *and* the goods. Consequently there can be no successive carriage if the note is lost or never drawn up.

the latter's liability to the carrier will not depend upon the Convention, but upon the particular contractual agreement entered into between the parties. Any direct action therefore against a sub-contractor who is not a successive carrier must be brought at common law. Article 28 (1), on the other hand, makes any "extra-contractual claim" dependent upon "the law applicable," that is, the domestic law of the country where the action is brought, or such other law as would be applicable under the rules of conflict of laws. However, Article 28 (2) does provide that where "the extra-contractual liability for loss, damage or delay of one of the persons for whom the carrier is responsible under the terms of Article 3 is in issue, such person may also avail himself of the provisions of this Convention which exclude the liability of the carrier or which fix or limit the compensation due."[71]

292   Subject therefore to such interpretation as the courts may place upon these provisions, it appears that having commenced the action at common law, it is then possible for the parties on both sides to invoke the provisions of the Convention "which exclude the liability of the carrier or which fix or limit the compensation due."[72]

Here again it is not clear to whom these provisions will apply. The Convention prevents direct action against any successive road carrier who is neither the first or last carrier, nor the one performing the transit when the injurious event occurred. It presumably can only therefore apply to actions in tort against, first, the servants of a carrier, secondly, any sub-contracting road carrier who is not a successive carrier because he does not fulfil the requirements of Article 34, or, thirdly, any agent or sub-contractor employed to perform duties which do not involve the actual carriage of the goods such as forwarding and clearing agents, warehousemen whilst the goods are in transit, and others performing associated ancillary functions. It may also apply to those sub-contracting carriers who are not road carriers, who instead carry by sea, rail, inland waterway or air, within the provisions of Article 2, C.M.R., where they are not subject to "the conditions prescribed by law for the carriage of goods by that means of transport."[73]

Looking at the Convention as a whole though, it is clear that there is a lacuna concerning the status of sub-contractors, the outcome of which must depend either upon judicial interpretation or else the amendment of the Convention itself at some future date. Such a procedure is not likely to commend itself however until more countries have ratified it in its present form, as the prospect of impending revision is likely to delay further accessions indefinitely.

---

[71] Subject to Art. 29 (2), C.M.R.—see § 166. *Cf.* Art 40, C.I.M.; Art 12 (1), T.C.M.; Art. 11, F.B.L.

[72] N.B. It is not clear whether the provisions of Chapter V concerning claims and actions and in particular the period for the limitation of actions laid down in Art. 32 would apply or not. Art. 32 only refers to "an action arising *out of carriage* under this Convention," it does *not* refer to "an action arising *under* the Convention." Logically, as the right of action depends upon the common law, such rights should also do so.

[73] Art. 2, C.M.R.

293 Contribution between carriers

Where a carrier has paid compensation to a third party within the provision of the Convention, he can recover contribution from other carriers who have participated in the carriage, subject to certain provisos.[74] First, the carrier who is responsible for the loss will be solely liable, and must reimburse in full any other carrier who has paid compensation to a third party.[75] Secondly, where the loss has been caused by two or more carriers, each must pay his part if it is possible to apportion liability, but if not, payment will be in proportion to the amount of carriage charges due to each.[76] If it is not possible to ascertain which carrier(s) is/are liable, compensation is to be apportioned as above.[77] In the event of the insolvency of a carrier, his unpaid liability will be apportioned between the remaining carriers in proportion to the amount of carriage charges due to each.[78] However, there is nothing to prevent the carriers from making an agreement at variance with Articles 37 and 38 if they so wish.[79]

Where a carrier who has paid compensation to a third party claims recovery from another carrier, the latter is not permitted to dispute the amount paid, provided it was determined by "judicial authority" and he was given notice of the proceedings and given an opportunity to enter an appearance.[80] Such a claim can be made in the country where one of the carriers is ordinarily resident or has his principal place of business, or branch or agency through which the contract of carriage in question was made. Furthermore, all the carriers concerned in the contract can be joined as defendants in the one action.[81]

On the face of it this appears to be a sensible procedure, but in this country, at least, it could impede the settlement of insurance claims and instead encourage litigation. Insurance underwriters who, at present, normally settle outstanding claims without resort to the courts may instead delay doing so until the amount of compensation has been determined by a court of law so as to prevent any successive carrier against whom they may wish to exercise any rights of subrogation from disputing the validity or amount of the payment. On the other hand, where litigation is inevitable it may encourage successive carriers outside the jurisdiction to enter an appearance and thus render further proceedings unnecessary in foreign jurisdictions to recover an indemnity or contribution.

[74] Art. 37, C.M.R.
[75] Art. 37 (a), C.M.R.
[76] Art. 37 (b), C.M.R.
[77] Art. 37 (c), C.M.R.
[78] Art. 38, C.M.R.
[79] Art. 40, C.M.R.; this provision could cause difficulties through the casual methods used by carriers in drawing attention to their conditions of carriage. Otherwise any attempt to derogate from the provisions of the Convention will be null and void: Art. 41, C.M.R. Cf. Art. 53, C.I.M.; Arts. 11 (c), 17, T.C.M.
[80] Art. 39 (1), C.M.R.
[81] Art. 39 (2), C.M.R.

294   Lacunae in C.M.R.

A further problem that may arise out of Article 37 is that no provision is made by the Convention for compensation of an agent who reimburses a third party in respect of loss suffered under a contract of carriage subject to C.M.R. This problem is particularly likely to arise where a forwarder has paid his client in respect of a claim for loss of goods which he has handled on his behalf. In such circumstances he will have no right of recourse against either the first carrier or any successive carrier under the Convention, as he has no obligation to compensate his client. Obviously, a forwarder is not likely to effect compensation in such circumstances knowingly, but if he does so under the assumption that he is in fact the first carrier but in subsequent litigation he is held to be a mere forwarder, he is likely to find himself without a remedy unless he can persuade his client to assign his rights of recovery under the Convention to him.[82]

4. THE FORWARDER'S LIABILITY FOR SUB-AGENTS

295   In performing his operations a forwarder may act in one of two capacities as regards the consignment of goods. First, he may forward them either direct to the consignee, or alternatively to another forwarder, who will then act in the capacity of a receiving agent. Secondly, he may himself be a receiving agent of goods which have been dispatched by a foreign forwarder to him. The forwarding of goods direct to a consignee does not require further comment, as no question of sub-agency can arise. It is necessary, however, to distinguish the forwarding agent from the receiving agent. Such a distinction was drawn in the case of *Von Traubenberg* v. *Davies Turner & Co. Ltd.*,[83] where the latter's function was described as being " merely to receive the goods . . ., get them through the customs . . . and make any necessary contract with [a carrier] " [84] in respect of a transit arranged by a forwarder abroad. The question therefore arises as to what extent a forwarder is liable for the acts of any receiving agent employed by him to handle the reception of a shipment, or, conversely, the liability of a receiving agent for a forwarder employed to forward a shipment to him.

The general rule in agency is that an agent cannot delegate any of his duties without the authority of his principal—*delegatus non potest*

---

[82] N.B. As the C.M.R. consignment note is a non-negotiable document, the question of ownership does not arise, rights of action merely being vested in the sender and the consignee. In such circumstances the forwarder will always have a right of action in either capacity. If, on the other hand, the contract is not subject to the Convention, but instead to the common law, only the owner of the goods will have a right of action unless the forwarder can bring himself within the rule of *The Winkfield* [1902] P. 42 whereby the bailee of goods has a right of action in respect of negligent loss or damage to them, irrespective of whether he is liable to the owner thereof. In other words, he must take possession of the goods as a carrier or other bailee or else be named as the consignee thereof.

[83] [1951] 2 Lloyd's Rep. 462 at p. 466.

[84] *Ibid.*

delegare.[85] This authority may be either express, which requires no further comment, or else implied by "the conduct of the parties . . ., the usage of the trade, or the nature of the particular business which is the subject of the agency. . . ."[86] Such authority must, it is submitted, be implicit in all forwarding operations, or otherwise the smooth running of the trade would be impossible, although no direct dicta exist upon this point.

296   Types of delegation

Two types of delegation are possible. First, where the forwarder has authority to appoint an agent on behalf of his principal. Secondly, where the forwarder has authority to appoint a sub-agent to carry out part of the operations. Only in the first category will privity of contract be created between the shipper and the second agent, and in such a case the first forwarder will not be liable in respect of their relationship, as he will not be privy to it. However, as Wright J. observed:

"The agent does not, as a rule, escape liability to the principal merely because employment of the sub-agent is contemplated. To create privity it must be established not only that the principal contemplated that a sub-agent would perform part of the contract, but also that the principal authorised the agent to create privity of contract between the principal and the sub-agent, which is a very different matter requiring precise proof."[87]

Under the second category, no privity of contract will be established between the shipper and the receiving agent, the forwarder remaining personally liable for the complete operation.

The difficulty however in any particular transaction is to decide into which of the two categories it will fall. It is therefore necessary to distinguish between a contractual undertaking by a forwarder to perform services on behalf of a shipper through a sub-agent, and a mere offer to introduce the shipper to the receiving agent and to inform him of what the shipper requires to be done.[88] In the latter case any contractual relationship that is established will be directly between the shipper and the receiving agent, and will not concern the forwarder.

297   Liability of the forwarder

In general, where a forwarder employs a receiving agent as a sub-agent, he will normally be liable for his acts and omissions. However, it is necessary to distinguish two categories of liability in respect of sub-agency activities. First, the forwarder may be liable for his own failure to exercise due control over the receiving agent in carrying out his instructions, that is, the forwarder will be liable for his own acts or

[85] For an analysis of the problems relating to sub-agency, see Powell, *Law of Agency*, 2nd ed., pp. 305 *et seq.*
[86] *De Bussche* v. *Alt* (1878) 8 Ch.D. 286 at p. 311, *per* Thesiger L.J.
[87] *Calico Printers Association* v. *Barclays Bank and Anglo-Palestine Co. Ltd.* (1931) 145 L.T. 51 at p. 55.
[88] *Margolis* v. *Newson Bros. Ltd.* (1941) 71 Ll.L.Rep. 47 at p. 52.

omissions.[89] Secondly, the forwarder may be liable for the acts and omissions of the sub-agent whom he has employed to carry out an operation for which he himself has undertaken responsibility. Accordingly, where a forwarder is given instructions as to the reception of a shipment, and these are passed on to the sub-agent who fails to carry them out, the former will be liable to the shipper for this failure.[90]

A forwarder will only be liable for the default of the receiving agent, though, if as a forwarder, he has undertaken responsibility for the action in question himself or through his agents. The problem arose in *Margolis* v. *Newsom Bros. Ltd.*,[91] where the shipper of a consignment of electric batteries claimed that the forwarder had accepted responsibility, either himself or through his agents, for the accuracy of description of the batteries which were being forwarded from Antwerp to London. As Humphreys J. stated:

> "the principal business of the defendants is the shipping of goods abroad from this country or from abroad to this country. So far as the importation of goods is concerned, part of the business must be done by a foreign agent, because as everybody knows shippers cannot go [abroad] to look at [them] . . . and, therefore, they have agents on whom they can call to do that."[92]

However, merely because the foreign agent is acting as a sub-agent for a forwarder in respect of part of the operations does not *per se* render the forwarder liable for the sub-agent's default where he has not in fact undertaken to perform the operation in question either himself or through his sub-agent.[93] Accordingly, it was held that the forwarder was not liable for the sub-agent's failure to inspect the goods, as this was outside the normal scope of the forwarder's duties for which he might be impliedly liable, and he had not undertaken to perform such an operation contractually.[94]

It should be noted at this stage, as can be seen from the cases discussed above, that the principle of liability does not differ whether the forwarder is employing the foreign sub-agent to forward a shipment to him or to receive one which the former has forwarded to him. The same criteria will apply in both cases.[95] Where, therefore, a forwarder offers the "facilities of a network of capable agencies under [its] control and management and general superintendence,"[96] it will be liable to use the same care when acting through these agencies abroad as it would in respect of its own actions performed in this country.

---

[89] *Mark Lever & Co. Ltd.* v. *Wingate & Johnston Ltd.* (1950) 84 Ll.L.Rep. 156 at p. 164: for the facts see § 196.
[90] *Ibid.*
[91] (1941) 71 Ll.L.Rep. 47.
[92] *Ibid.* at p. 49.
[93] *Ibid.* at p. 50.
[94] *Ibid.*
[95] See also *Crowe & Co. (London) Ltd.* v. *Giunipero & Co.* (1920) 2 Ll.L.Rep. 633.
[96] *Landauer & Co.* v. *Smits & Co.* (1921) 6 Ll.L.Rep. 577 at p. 580.

298 Sub-agency distinguished from analogous relationships

The question of sub-agency must be clearly distinguished from certain analogous relationships. First, a receiving agent may be neither a sub-agent, nor appointed through the agency of the forwarder at all. This will arise where he has been appointed independently by the consignor or consignee without the intervention of the forwarder.[97] Here the original forwarder will not be liable for any loss resulting from the receiving agent's default as both transactions are separate and distinct. In other words, the respective contracts between the shipper and the forwarder and the shipper and the receiving agent are only related to each other in a purely commercial sense.

Secondly, a forwarder may employ a carrier to effect a contract of carriage as well as another forwarder to receive a shipment at the termination of transit. Here the forwarder's liability will merely be in respect of the forwarding operation itself and also for any receiving operations if he has in fact undertaken to arrange them. It will not extend to matters arising during and out of the actual contract of carriage, unless the forwarder is placed in the position of a principal in the transaction.[98]

Thirdly, the position of the forwarder who in fact acts as a carrier himself and employs a further carrier for onward transit, must be distinguished from the liability arising out of the employment by a forwarder of a sub-agent. In the former situation the position will depend upon whether the carrying forwarder is employing the sub-carrier as a sub-contractor or whether the latter is subject to a separate contract of carriage with the shipper and therefore not in contractual relationship with the forwarder. This question has been dealt with in an earlier chapter, though.[99]

299 Rights of forwarder against the sub-agent

Finally, it is necessary to consider the rights of the forwarder against the sub-agent where he has been held liable for the latter's defaults. The general rule is that the forwarder will have a right of indemnity against the sub-agent in respect of any loss he has thus incurred. Accordingly, where a Swiss forwarder, the plaintiff, who was responsible for the forwarding of seventy truck-loads of Italian pears to this country, instructed his English agents, the defendants, not to release the goods to the consignee unless all freight charges were paid, the plaintiff was held to have a right of action to recover them, as he was himself liable in respect of such disbursements.[1]

300 Rights of sub-agent against consignee

Where a sub-agent is held to be liable to the forwarder employing

---

[97] *Sphinx Export Co. Ltd.* v. *Specialist Shippers Ltd.* [1954] 1 Lloyd's Rep. 407.
[98] See §§ 268 *et seq.*
[99] See Chapter 2.
[1] *Societa Anonima Angelo Castelletti* v. *Transmaritime Ltd.* [1953] 2 Lloyd's Rep. 440. N.B. Only nominal damages were in fact awarded as the defendants by their action had merely extinguished the plaintiff's possessory lien over the goods, which was virtually valueless as they were in a perished state.

him in respect of any loss suffered by him, he will not be able to claim any right of indemnity from the consignee, unless a separate contractual agreement has been entered into between the latter and the sub-agent in respect of the transaction, as otherwise no privity of contract exists between them. This was made clear by Slade J. in the following words:

> " Now ordinarily, . . . there is no privity of contract between a carrier or a forwarding agent and a consignee. . . . the contract of carriage is made by the consignor and the person who undertakes to carry the consignor's goods. True a person having possession of goods and being willing to deliver them to any other person may, unless that other person is the owner of the goods or entitled to immediate possession of them . . . make any contract he likes with the consignee." [2]

Applying this principle in *Anglo-Overseas Transport Co. Ltd.* v. *David Zanellotti Ltd.*[3] it was held that a forwarder employed in this country by an Italian forwarder to receive and clear a shipment of potatoes from Italy had no right of action against the consignee for freight charges which they refused to pay, as in the absence of any special agreement between them to this effect, no privity existed between them.

It is possible, however, for privity of contract to be created where there has been a course of dealing between the sub-agent and the consignee, so as to create a contractual obligation by conduct. It is of interest to note that in *Zanellotti's* case the court rejected the argument that a contract could be created in such a case by custom.[4] As Slade J. pointed out:

> "I know of no case where a contract is created by custom. I know of a number of cases where custom annexes conditions to an existing contract, but a contract is the creature of an agreement between two or more parties. I have never heard of a contract being thrust upon people by custom; and you cannot have an implied term of a contract unless you have a contract." [5]

Otherwise only where the sub-agent can legally exercise a right of lien against the consignee can he recover an indemnity in respect of payments that he is liable to make. [6]

5. CONCLUSIONS

301 The liability of the forwarder for the acts of third parties and the complementary rights of the shipper against both the forwarder and third parties is an area in which it is extremely difficult to draw hard dividing lines in classifying the relevant principles of law with the

---

[2] *Anglo-Overseas Transport Co. Ltd.* v. *David Zanellotti Ltd.* [1952] 1 Lloyd's Rep. 232 at p. 235.
[3] *Ibid.*
[4] *Ibid.* at p. 236, *per* Slade J.
[5] *Ibid.* at p. 236—nor by circular letter—*ibid.*
[6] See § 360.

decisions of the courts. Certain guiding principles however can be established, within which the rights and liabilities of the parties can to some degree be systematised.

First, a clear distinction can be drawn between the liability of a forwarder for carriage by sea and carriage by land. In the case of sea transit, of the very nature of the transaction, the forwarder will invariably be a mere agent in relation to the shipper, unless he actually charters a vessel,[7] which places him outside the field of forwarding operations in any case, or else he issues a house bill of lading or other document in respect of which he accepts a degree of responsibility in respect of the transit.[8] Although Standard Trading Conditions are not definitive as regards the status of the forwarder, the protection they offer does in practice relieve him of any practical concern as to his legal status, owing to their restrictive nature. It is only when such conditions are not operative that any problem will really arise.

Secondly, the position of the forwarder in relation to carriage by road is more complex as, in practice, forwarders act either as agent or principal or both depending upon the particular type of operations which they are called upon to arrange. In particular, the question of whether the forwarder will be vicariously liable for the default of the driver of the carrier's vehicle in which the goods in question are carried, will in each case depend upon the particular facts.

Thirdly and finally, we must turn to the question of the forwarder's liability for the services of other forwarders whose services he may utilise. Although the question has arisen periodically,[9] it has only been discussed in the few cases referred to in the last section of this chapter. Otherwise, the difficulties inherent in sub-agency relationships have resulted in the question being shelved as unnecessary to reach a decision in the case before the court. It is clear though, from the dicta on the subject, that a forwarder will be liable for the acts of any sub-agent whom he may employ, unless he has in fact created privity of contract between sub-agent and principal. Otherwise, only if the default in question is outside the scope of the forwarding contract can he avoid liability for it. The forwarder will of course have a right of recourse against the defaulting sub-agent for a full indemnity, unless the latter has contractually limited his liability in this respect, although such a procedure is not common.

302 Defects of the common law

In conclusion, therefore, many difficulties relating to the liability of a forwarder for third parties, and the latter's inability adequately to protect himself against claims by a shipper, stem from two peculiarities of English law. First, the absence of a contract of commission at common law, or at least the refusal of the courts to acknowledge the

---

[7] See § 263.
[8] See Chapter 13.
[9] *Cf. Hunt & Winterbotham Ltd.* v. *Morny & Co.* (1922) 12 Ll.L.Rep. 286.

existence of those precedents supporting such a concept. Secondly, the refusal of the courts to permit a contract to be created in favour of a third party. If therefore the Law Commission intends to make any alterations in the law in this sphere, contractual and delictual relationships would be much simplified in the forwarding trade, but in the meantime the difficulty of attempting to resolve the conflicting decisions on the subject will remain unresolved.

CHAPTER 12

CLAIMS AND ACTIONS

303 Standard Trading Conditions

It is customary in most trading conditions relating to the carriage of goods for a provision to be inserted discharging the operator from liability if claims are not made within a certain period of time as laid down. At present there is no uniformity among such provisions in British forwarding and carriage contracts, so that the principal trading conditions must be considered in turn. First, under Standard Trading Conditions, Clause 15 distinguishes two categories. First, loss from a package or unpacked consignment or damage, deviation or misdelivery thereof. Secondly, loss or non-delivery of the whole consignment or of any separate package forming part thereof. In the former case, written notice is required within seven days of the end of transit, where this ends in the British Isles, or fourteen days where it ends elsewhere. In the latter case, written notice is required within twenty-eight days of the date when the goods should have been delivered.[1]

304 Road haulage contracts

As regards R.H.A. Conditions 1967 and B.R.S. Conditions, each make provision in a similar fashion except that both a preliminary written advice of the loss, other than on the transport documents, and a written claim must be submitted. In the case of the first category, together with delay, the periods are three days and seven days from the end of transit respectively. In the second category the periods are twenty-eight days and forty-two days respectively from the date of the commencement of transit.[2] However, B.R.S. Conditions also provide that if the trader can prove that it was not "reasonably possible" to advise the carrier in writing within such a period, and the advice or claim was in fact rendered within a reasonable time, the carrier loses the benefit of Clause 7. Such a provision is absent from R.H.A. Conditions 1967 so that the client must take particular care that any claim is submitted within the specified period or else forfeit all right of recovery.[3] It may be observed that the fact that Standard Trading Conditions do not completely correspond with R.H.A. and B.R.S. Conditions could create problems if a forwarder wished to claim against a sub-contracting carrier either for his own benefit or for the benefit of his client, as the latter might not inform him, following the provisions of Standard

---

[1] Cl. 15, S.T.C.

[2] Cl. 10, R.H.A. Conditions; Cl. 7, B.R.S. Conditions. *Cf.* Art. 26, N.F.C.; Art. 9, N.Y.F.F.; Arts. 58–59, C.G. (Belgium); Art. 52, Y.F.C.; Art. 17, C.G. (Switzerland); Art. 46, C.G. (Italy); Art. 64, A.D.S.P.; Arts. 17, 18, F.B.L.

[3] *Cf.* Cl. 12, R.H.A. Conditions 1961, *Garnham, Harris & Elton Ltd.* v. *Alfred W. Ellis Ltd.* [1967] 2 Lloyd's Rep. 22.

Trading Conditions, until after the time limit for claims had expired under the carriage contract. It would not, however, generally affect his legal liability though, as he would normally only accept liability for loss where goods are "in its actual custody and under its actual control." [4] Actual legal liability will therefore rarely arise in practice.

305 C.M.R.

Where carriage is subject to C.M.R., different provisions will apply. Article 30 requires that the consignee on taking delivery of goods must either check their condition with the carrier or send him reservations of a general indication of the loss or damage. This must be no later than the time of delivery in the case of apparent loss, and within seven days, excluding public holidays, in the case of loss or damage which is not apparent. If the consignee fails to follow such a course of action, the fact that he has taken delivery will be treated as prima facie evidence that he has received the goods in the condition described in the consignment note. However, only in the case of loss or damage which is not apparent must the reservations be in writing. [5]

Where both the carrier and the consignee have checked the condition of the goods, contradictory evidence will only be admissible in the case of loss or damage which is not apparent, and where written reservations have been sent to the carrier by the consignee within seven days from the date of checking, public holidays excepted. [6] In the case of a claim for delay in delivery, a written reservation must be sent to the carrier within twenty-one days of the goods being placed at the disposal of the consignee. [7] In all cases the Convention requires both consignee and carrier to give each other reasonable facility to make the requisite checks. [8]

306 Procedures

Whereas, under Standard Trading Conditions, provision is made that all contracts entered into by the forwarder with his clients will be subject to English law and within the exclusive jurisdiction of the English courts, [9] the Convention provides that the plaintiff can bring an action in any court or tribunal of a contracting country, which they may agree upon, or else where the defendant is ordinarily resident or has his place of business or the branch or agency where the contract of carriage in question was made, or in the place where the goods were taken over by the carrier or the place of delivery. Litigation cannot be commenced in any other courts or tribunals. [10] Furthermore, no fresh action can be started between the same parties on the same

---

[4] Cl. 13 (i), S.T.C.
[5] Art. 30 (1), C.M.R.; *Cf.* Arts. 45–46, C.I.M.; Art. 8, T.C.M.
[6] Art. 30 (2), C.M.R.
[7] Art. 30 (3), C.M.R.
[8] Art. 30 (5), C.M.R.   In calculating time limits, dates of delivery, checking, or placing at disposal of consignee will not be included: Art. 30 (4), C.M.R.
[9] Cl. 25, S.T.C.   R.H.A. Conditions make no provision.   *Cf.* Art. 19, F.B.L.
[10] Art. 31 (1), C.M.R.   *Cf.* Art. 44, C.I.M.; Art. 44, T.C.M.

grounds where either an action is pending or judgment has been entered in a court or tribunal competent under Article 31 (1) unless such a judgment is not enforceable in the country where the fresh proceedings are commenced.[11] Where a judgment of a court or tribunal of a contracting country has become enforceable therein, it will then become similarly enforceable in all other contracting states, subject to the formalities thereof being complied with. Such formalities shall not permit the merits of the case to be re-opened.[12] This provision includes judgments after trial, or by default, and settlements confirmed by court order, but not to interim judgments or to awards of damages, in addition to costs, against a plaintiff who wholly or partly fails in his action.[13] Finally, it should be noted that security for costs is not required in proceedings under the Convention from nationals of contracting countries resident or having their places of business in one of those countries.[14] Security for costs will presumably still be required in respect of nationals not resident or without a place of business, and conversely of non-nationals possessing a residence or place of business in a contracting country, and in all other cases.

307   Joinder of parties

In practice, however, in this country at least, the tendency is to join all successive carriers and other parties on whom liability may be placed, whether under the Convention or otherwise, to avoid the need for such extra-territorial enforcement of judgments. This also has the advantage of establishing which party is actually liable in successive carriage where either the first or last carrier has been sued, and enables the underwriters to decide more readily whether, in a particular case, it is better to settle out of court or to pursue the action. To date, although there have been some cases on the Continent, in all cases final judgment has yet to be entered in an English court in a case subject to the Convention.

308   Limitation of actions

As regards the bringing of a court action, in respect of a claim arising under the Convention, the normal period of limitation in respect of claims in contract and in tort of six years is shortened to that of one year, unless there is wilful misconduct or such default as the court may consider to be equivalent thereto, when the period is extended to three years.[15] Time will begin to run, in the case of partial loss, damage or delay, from the date of delivery. In the case of total loss it will run from the thirtieth day after the expiry of any time limit, or, if none, from the sixtieth day after the goods were taken over by the carrier. In all other

---

[11] Art. 31 (2), C.M.R.
[12] Art. 31 (3), C.M.R.
[13] Art. 31 (4), C.M.R.
[14] Art. 31 (5), C.M.R.
[15] Art. 32 (1), C.M.R.   *Cf.* Art. 47, C.I.M.; Art. 14, T.C.M.

cases time will begin to run from a date three months after the making of the contract of carriage.[16]

If, however, the plaintiff makes a written claim, time will be suspended until such date as the carrier rejects the claim in writing and returns the documents attached thereto. If part of the claim is admitted, time will only start to run again in respect of that part of the claim still in dispute. The burden of proof of receipt of claim, reply and return of documents, rests on the party relying on these facts. Time will not be suspended, however, by further claims having the same object.[17] Subject to the above provisions, the extension of any period of limitation and the fresh accrual of rights of action will be governed by the law of the court or tribunal seised of the case.[18] In other words, where a case subject to the Convention comes before the English courts, domestic rules will apply. Finally, a right of action which has become time-barred cannot be exercised by way of counterclaim or set-off.[19]

309   Arbitration clauses

The Convention permits an arbitration clause to be inserted in the contract of carriage, but in conferring competence on an arbitration tribunal, it must also provide that the tribunal shall apply the Convention.[20] In practice many existing arbitration clauses do not include such a provision, so that where transit is subject to the Convention, the provision will be devoid of effect and arbitration procedure therefore not possible.

---

[16] Art. 32 (1), (a), (b), (c), C.M.R. The first day is not included in the period: Art. 32 (1), C.M.R.
[17] Art. 32 (2), C.M.R.
[18] Art. 32 (3), C.M.R.
[19] Art. 32 (4), C.M.R.
[20] Art. 33, C.M.R. Cf. Art. 61, C.I.M.; Art. 15, T.C.M.

PART IV
DOCUMENTS OF TITLE AND PAYMENT

CHAPTER 13

THE FORWARDER IN RELATION TO BILLS OF LADING AND OTHER DOCUMENTS OF TITLE AND CARRIAGE

1. THE DUTIES OF THE FORWARDER IN RELATION TO DOCUMENTS OF TITLE

(i) *Introduction*

310 ONE of the essential functions of the forwarder is to ensure the safe arrival of a shipment forwarded, and although he does not generally guarantee the safe arrival of goods, his function in ensuring the safe transfer of goods to the consignee or other authorised recipient is of paramount importance. This function is to a considerable extent performed by the control of the bill of lading issued in respect of the goods in question, or else through other documents of title or of transit. The forwarder can therefore ensure, first, that the goods have been dispatched either by the method and route specified, or by the most suitable route, and, secondly, that the documents of title are not handed over to any unauthorised party, nor the goods themselves handed over to anyone except the true owner or his accredited agent.

The forwarder as such, subject to the exceptions to be discussed below, does not usually issue bills of lading in his own name, as this is not part of his function, being merely the agent of his client, and not the agent of the carrier or one himself. Where he does issue bills of lading, it will normally be in a different capacity. In other words, as discussed in an earlier chapter, the forwarder often acts as a loading broker or ship's agent as a field of operations complementary to those of forwarding, and it is in this capacity that he will issue bills of lading on behalf of a carrier.[1] This must not of course be confused with the merely mechanical function of preparing bills on behalf of either his client or the carrier to expedite the paper-work in relation to the transportation of goods and to avoid needless duplication thereof. The fact, however, that the forwarder as such does not issue bills of lading does not preclude him from issuing one if he also operates in the capacity of a carrier himself. Such a procedure may enable the forwarder to avail himself of protective clauses in a bill of lading which he would not otherwise be able to do.[2]

(ii) *The Bill of Lading Distinguished from other Documents*

311 There are three principal elements which constitute a bill of lading. First, it is a formal receipt by a shipowner acknowledging shipment,

---

[1] See *Luigi Riva Di Fernando* v. *Simon Smits & Co. Ltd.* (1920) 2 Ll.L.Rep. 279. See Chapter 2.

[2] *Scruttons Ltd.* v. *Midland Silicones Ltd.* [1962] A.C. 446.

or received for shipment, of goods from the shipper. Secondly, it is a memorandum of the contract of carriage. Thirdly, it is a document of title enabling the ownership of goods to be transferred by indorsement and delivery. As such it is subject to the provisions of the Carriage of Goods by Sea Act 1924 as to the rights and duties of the parties. There are many complexities concerning the various categories of documents which may be issued purporting to be bills of lading, but a discussion thereof is outside the scope of this chapter. However, if a document relating to the carriage of goods does not enable title of goods to be transferred it will not constitute a bill of lading. The bill of lading is therefore of considerable use in trade to enable a buyer to obtain credit in relation to the goods which it represents. Consequently, the acceptability of the bill of lading in financial circles becomes of paramount importance.

312 Mate's receipt

In particular, it is necessary to distinguish it from two other common documents of carriage. The mate's receipt is a document which a shipper may be given by a ship's agent when goods are received by him for shipment.[3] This will be exchanged for a bill of lading when the goods are actually shipped on board. Even though it is not a document of title it is sometimes used as a security for advances. Increasingly, though, it is dispensed with where a forwarder is employed to arrange shipment.[4] The delivery order, on the other hand, is supplied where the goods in question are only part of a larger parcel shipped under a single bill of lading.[5] Again it is not a document of title, although in these circumstances there is no way of issuing the shipper with a bill of lading. Turning however to forwarding operations, it is now necessary to consider the various forms of document commonly in use.

313 Consignment note

The short-sea trade, that is, cross-Channel services, and all services operated by British Rail, are generally transacted on the basis of consignment notes, rather than bills of lading. The former are not accepted as documents of title, and their acceptability by banks as a document for which credit will be granted will depend purely on the personal standing of the parties involved. The same applies in the case of air waybills issued under the Carriage of Goods by Air Act 1961 where carriage is effected by air freight.[6]

314 Forwarder's documentation

It is normal practice for a forwarder to issue various types of carriage document, either to signify that he has taken possession of a

---

[3] *Nippon Yusen Kaisha* v. *Ramjiban Serowgee* [1938] A.C. 429 at p. 445.
[4] *Heskell* v. *Continental Express Ltd.* (1950) 83 Ll.L.Rep. 438 where the procedures are explained.
[5] *Comptoir d'Achat* v. *Luis de Ridder Ltda.* [1949] A.C. 293.
[6] As to the unsuccessful attempts to make the air waybill negotiable, see K. M. Beaumont, *Negotiability of the Air Waybill* [1957] J.B.L. 130.

shipment of goods, or to enable the goods to be handled during transit operations, issued usually prior to a bill of lading being drawn up. This problem was discussed in the Commercial Court by Bailhache J. in a case involving Davies, Turner & Co., the forwarding agents.[7] This was an action by the buyer against the seller for the return of the purchase price of fifteen tons of caustic soda, which was part of a larger contract quantity. Owing to difficulties in shipping c.i.f. London–Genoa direct, it was agreed to ship the goods to Calais and then overland to Turin. The defendant sellers therefore put the goods in the hands of the forwarders who gave them a document against which the buyers' bank paid the price. It later transpired that the shipping licence had expired before the goods were ready for shipment, so that they were never shipped. They remained in the hands of the forwarders, and were ultimately sold to pay heavy warehouse charges. The forwarders paid the balance to the defendants who received it under protest claiming that they were not concerned in the matter. Under a c.i.f. contract, the seller is bound to deliver the correct documents, which are an invoice, a marine policy, and a bill of lading.[8] Other documents such as a certificate of origin may be required, but these represent the bare minimum. If, therefore, the seller has failed to deliver, *inter alia*, a bill of lading, he will be in breach of contract and will be liable to repay the price to the buyer.

The principal question in the case was therefore whether the document actually presented to the bank for payment constituted a valid document for this purpose or not. The court rejected the sellers' plea that the buyers' bank was justified in paying the price. Bailhache J. explained that the document in question "was not a bill of lading, . . . but it was what they called a reception order, and purports to say, received in good order so and so goods for shipment to so and so, and it goes on to say, they only undertake to forward the goods from London, and having so forwarded the goods are not under any responsibility whatever."[9] As the sellers had therefore not presented the required documents of title, they were liable to repay the purchase price.

315 Cartage note

In respect of other aspects of his operations, a forwarder may issue certain other categories of document to his client which will not give any title to the goods, but are merely intended to grant possessory rights.[10] To enable goods to be collected either from a customer for onward transit, or else from a carrier terminal for local delivery, it is customary for a forwarder to issue cartage orders or consignment notes. For instance, if a forwarder is instructed to collect goods from

---

[7] *Emilio Clot & Co.* v. *Compagnie Commerciale du Nord S.A.* (1921) 8 Ll.L.Rep. 380.
[8] *Biddell Brothers* v. *E. Clemens Horst Co.* [1911] 1 K.B. 214 at p. 220.
[9] (1921) 8 Ll.L.Rep. 380. *Cf. Luigi Riva Di Fernando* v. *Simon Smits & Co. Ltd.*, *supra.*
[10] *Cf. D. Steward & Co.* v. *J. Lofthouse & Co.* (1921) 9 Ll.L.Rep. 386.

a client's premises, he may issue a cartage note to a sub-contracting carrier for the purpose.

316 Forwarder's consignment note

A forwarder may also accept goods for forwarding under consignment notes issued in his own name, to be followed up in due course by bills of lading issued by or on behalf of the carrier in question where sea transit is involved.[11] However, where sea and land transit is to be effected, as in the case of most continental shipments, this may either be by means of a through bill of lading covering the whole transit,[12] or else by a bill in respect of the sea transit, together with a waybill or consignment note in respect of the land part of the carriage. Where a waybill is issued by a forwarder for an international transit, it will usually be forwarded to the latter's receiving agent, who will in turn prepare delivery notes to enable the consignees to obtain possession of the goods.[13]

It can therefore be seen that where documents relating to the possession or ownership of goods are issued by a forwarder in the course of his operations, it is essential to determine the exact nature of the document, or else none of the parties will be able to determine wherein lies the property to the goods, nor who has a right of possession to them. On the answer to such a question will depend not only the question of right to payment, particularly where this is effected through a bank in exchange for documents, but also the associated question of liability in conversion or detinue where there is a refusal by the forwarder or a party to part with either the documents of title or the actual goods themselves where a demand to this effect is made by a third party.[14]

(iii) *The Forwarder's Duties in relation to the correct Documentation of Shipments*

317 Correct documents

Where a forwarder acts on behalf of his client in carrying out a forwarding operation, he must ensure that the correct documents in relation to the goods are presented to the carrier for signature, where the forwarder is responsible for preparing them. Consequently, where a forwarder contracts to ship under a specified type of bill of lading, he will be liable if he ships under a different one.[15]

He must also ensure, either where he presents documents of title or carriage to a carrier for signature, or else where he requests the carrier to prepare them himself, that the documents which he obtains

---

[11] *Cf. Crowe & Co. (London) Ltd.* v. *Giunipero & Co.* (1920) 2 Ll.L.Rep. 633.
[12] *Ibid.*
[13] For a typical forwarding transaction, see *Anglo-Overseas Transport Co. Ltd.* v. *David Zanellotti Ltd.* [1952] 1 Lloyd's Rep. 232, at pp. 233 *et seq.*
[14] See Chapter 6.
[15] *B. & J. Shaw, etc.* v. *Cox's Shipping Agency Ltd.* (1922) 13 Ll.L.Rep. 387, *per* Bailhache J.

from the carrier are in fact according to the same tenor, and do not significantly vary in any detail. Consequently if a forwarder has undertaken to arrange for shipment under a bill of lading he will be liable if he permits carriage to take place under any other documents.[16]

318 Transfer to the right person

Where a forwarder is in possession of documents of title or carriage it is incumbent upon him to ensure that he transfers them to the right person. Such a problem can particularly arise in relation to the complexities of a string contract, that is, a contract where there are several successive buyers and sellers transacting their business through the medium of the documents of title or carriage, rather than through actual possession of the goods themselves. This of its very nature is a typical transaction in which a buyer or seller will employ the services of a forwarder to ensure that the documents of title in fact reach the correct person entitled to them. Accordingly where a forwarder is engaged by a series of sellers to put goods on board ship, normally he will only get a mate's receipt at first from the carrier or his agent, which will later be exchanged for a bill of lading. Consequently, if the forwarder fails to ask his successive employers what he is required to do with the mate's receipt, and permits it to get into the wrong hands, or alternatively exchanges it for a bill of lading, which he then passes on to a later party in the string, who is not at that moment entitled to it, he will be liable for any loss thereby arising.[17]

Similarly if a party to whom the forwarder transfers the bill misrepresents himself to be the consignor's agent, when in fact he has no authority to take possession of the bill of lading, the forwarder will be liable for so doing if he has failed to verify the truth of this claim before making delivery.[18] If a forwarder delivers goods to a consignee without requiring the production of a bill of lading he may be liable in negligence to his principal the consignor.[19]

Where a forwarder regularly uses a particular form of consignment note for collecting shipments from a railway terminal, he will be liable if unauthorised use is made of one so as to permit a consignment to be fraudulently obtained by a third party. However, the mere omission to enter full details of every consignment on the notes to avoid unwanted delay, such being the normal trade procedure, will not

[16] *G. Peereboom* v. *World Transport Agency Ltd.* (1921) 6 Ll.L.Rep. 170, discussed at §§ 143 (negligence) and 177 (conversion).
[17] Local custom or usage may be relevant in considering the forwarder's duties in the matter. *E.g.* in *Kapadia* v. *Laxmidas* [1964] E.A. 378, by the customs of the Old Port of Mombasa delivery is given to shipper's agent merely on presentation of invoices, and although the owner believed that by retaining possession of the bills of lading he retained the ownership and control of the goods he was estopped from denying the agent's authority to deal with the goods.
[18] *Kolbin* v. *Kinnear & Co.* (1931) 40 Ll.L.Rep. 241—for the facts see § 184, *sub nom. Kolbin & Sons* v. *United Shipping Co. Ltd.*
[19] *M. L. Kopschinsky* v. *Thomas Meadows & Co. Ltd.* (1920) 4 Ll.L.Rep. 235; *cf. Midland Rubber Co.* v. *Robert Park & Co.* (1922) 11 Ll.L.Rep. 119 at p. 260.

constitute negligence so as to render the forwarder liable for any ensuing loss.[20]

319   Documents made out to the correct party

The forwarder is also faced with the complementary problem of ensuring that he has in fact made out the bill of lading in favour of the right person.

If a forwarder has not been expressly instructed to make the bill of lading out in the consignee's name, he will not necessarily be liable for loss incurred through delay in presentation of documents to the consignee, unless he has acted without due care in his operations. However, if the forwarder is instructed to make out the bill in the consignee's name, he will be liable for any loss incurred if he makes it out in the name of his receiving agent at the port of arrival, contrary to instructions, merely because this is his usual method of operation.[21] If a client fraudulently misrepresents to a forwarder that he is entitled to the goods, or that a third party is so entitled and the bill should be made out in the latter's name, it is difficult for a forwarder to avoid liability in conversion to the true owner.[22] This problem is again likely to arise in string contracts, as the forwarder is placed in the position of having to obey the orders of the various intermediate parties, without necessarily being in a position, commercially speaking, to check the exact extent of their authority.

320   Contract of indemnity

Where, however, as a result of such unauthorised instructions, a forwarder deals with goods inconsistently with the rights of the true owner resulting in liability for conversion, by transferring the bill of lading, dock warrant or other document enabling a third party to obtain possession, the courts have sometimes been prepared to imply a contract of indemnity against the intermediate seller in a string contract.[23] However the Court of Appeal have made it quite clear that "it is a question for the jury on the facts in each case to say whether they can imply an indemnity or not."[24] Accordingly, in the only authority on the subject actually involving a forwarder, the court were not prepared to imply such a contract. In practice though, where Standard Trading Conditions are used, the forwarder is amply covered by Clause 24, which gives the forwarder a contractual right of indemnity in respect of third party claims.[25]

20 *Pringle of Scotland Ltd.* v. *Continental Express Ltd.* [1962] 2 Lloyd's Rep. 80.
21 *Hunt & Winterbotham Ltd.* v. *Morny & Co.* (1922) 12 Ll.L.Rep. 286; *cf. M. L. Kopschinsky* v. *Thomas Meadows & Co. Ltd.* (1920) 4 Ll.L.Rep. 235.
22 For an illustration of some of the problems that can occur see *Martin* v. *London & Cologne S.S. Co., Lloyd's List,* Nov. 25, 1921.
23 See *Dugdale* v. *Lovering* (1875) L.R. 10 C.P. 196.
24 *D. Steward & Co.* v. *J. Lofthouse & Co.* (1921) 9 Ll.L.Rep. 386 at p. 387, *per* Bankes L.J.
25 See § 283. Cl. 2, S.T.C. further reinforces this by imposing an express warranty that the client is either the owner or the authorised agent thereof, in respect of any goods which are the subject-matter of the contract: see § 188.

(iv) *The Forwarder's Duties in relation to the Presentation of Documents for Payment*

321 Although the question of presentation of documents to enable payment to be obtained is much too wide to be discussed within the limited scope of this chapter, the following observations are relevant in considering the position of the forwarder in relation to the question of payment, whether by confirmed credit or by any other means.

First, where a confirmed credit or other financial arrangement is in existence, and the forwarder is aware of it, he is bound to present the correct documents to the bank which are required under the terms of the credit, and will be failing in his obligations to his principal if he does not follow his instructions on this point.[26]

Particular care must be exercised where there has been a change in arrangements as to the documents to be presented for payment. For example, a credit will often be opened "in exchange for shipping documents." This will mean that payment will be made on presentation of a bill of lading or other document of title. If, however, the terms of the credit are altered, for instance, to "payment against forwarder's weight receipts and invoices," payment will then be made on the basis of non-property-passing documents, in respect of which, unlike the bill of lading, the forwarder may be liable in case of inaccuracy as regards weights, etc., if he has personally certified their accuracy.[27]

In other circumstances, if the forwarder is aware of the change in arrangements, he must present the necessary documents in accordance with the amended schedule, and if the documents in question are those which he is required to draw up himself, such as a " received for shipment" receipt,[28] confirmation of actual shipment of goods, or countersignature of official weight and quality certificates,[29] he will fail in his duty if he presents an incomplete set for payment.

Finally, it is possible for a complementary obligation to lie on the forwarder himself, if he has undertaken to pay the seller personally where, as in continental practice, he involves himself in the financing of operations. Here the forwarder, like a banker, will be bound to pay according to the terms of the credit opened, and if documents of title are presented in accordance with the credit, he will be liable for refusing payment on the grounds that the goods had first to be analysed or otherwise processed to ensure that they were up to the contract standard, where such a provision had not been included in the terms of the credit.[30]

---

[26] *Cf. M. L. Kopschinsky* v. *Thomas Meadows & Co. Ltd.* (1920) 4 Ll.L.Rep. 235.
[27] *Société Metallurgique d'Aubrives et Villerupt* v. *British Bank for Foreign Trade* (1922) 11 Ll.L.Rep. 168.
[28] *Sphinx Export Co. Ltd.* v. *Specialist Shippers Ltd.* [1954] 1 Lloyd's Rep. 407.
[29] *Heisler* v. *Anglo-Dal Ltd.* [1954] 2 Lloyd's Rep. 5 at p. 6.
[30] *Dexters Ltd.* v. *Schenker & Co.* (1923) 14 Ll.L.Rep. 586, *per* Greer J.

(v) *The Duties of a Receiving Agent in relation to the Presentation of Documents of Title*

322   It is not uncommon for a forwarder to deliver the documents of title relating to a shipment for which he is responsible to his own agent at the place of destination, instead of to the named consignee. This will both facilitate inwards clearance and other allied matters, and will also enable freight and other charges to be collected from the consignee, where such are chargeable to his account. Alternatively a forwarder may actually make out the bill of lading in the name of his receiving agent instead of the consignee. This may be done for commercial convenience, or else as part of a consolidated shipment, which will be discussed in the next section of this chapter. Where a shipper arranges with a forwarder for a bill of lading to be taken out in his own name and to his own order and that the consignee is to pay cash against shipping documents, if the forwarder permits the bill to be drawn in the name of his correspondent, the receiving agent, and fails to instruct the latter that he is only to deliver it for cash against documents, he will be liable to his client the shipper if the consignee fails to pay.[31]

Where a forwarder employs a sub-agent to receive goods, the latter will be liable if he delivers a shipment without the correct documents of title being presented to him by the consignee. To avoid unnecessary delay, though, if the required documents are not available on the arrival of the goods, it is not uncommon for a receiving agent to deliver the shipment in exchange for a written undertaking by the consignee to indemnify him against all claims resulting from the delivery of the goods without the production of the shipping documents. In addition, the agent will usually require the indorsement of the consignee's banker as a further security.[32]

Similarly, where a receiving agent is instructed by the forwarder to arrange for the transfer of possession of a shipment of goods to a consignee, he will be bound to follow any instructions which may be included in the waybill or other documents of carriage used where a bill of lading is not issued in respect of the goods in question. If he fails to do so he will be liable to the sending forwarder in negligence. The normal instructions in such a case would be "payment against documents," which would preclude a consignee from being given a delivery note by the receiving agent to enable him to obtain possession of the goods without effecting payment, unless otherwise agreed.[33]

323   Unauthorised acts

Where a receiving agent in so doing acts outside the scope of the authority given him by the forwarder who has forwarded the shipment to him, the latter will be liable to the shipper who has employed him

---

[31] *Kolbin* v. *Kinnear & Co.* (1931) 40 Ll.L.Rep. 241, *supra.*
[32] *Union Bank of Australia Ltd.* v. *Rudder* (1911) 13 C.L.R. 152 at p. 160.
[33] *Anglo-Overseas Transport Co. Ltd.* v. *David Zanellotti Ltd.* [1952] 1 Lloyd's Rep. 232 at p. 234.   See Chapter 14.

for the breach, although he will be able to claim an indemnity from the receiving agent. The latter in turn may have a right of action against any guarantors.[34] If, however, the receiving agent's principals, that is, the sending forwarder and/or the shipper, with full knowledge of the facts ratify his act and approve the delivery without the correct presentation of the relevant shipping documents, he will be relieved of all liability in respect of his unauthorised delivery. Likewise, any letter of guarantee intending to indemnify him against such claims will in turn become unenforceable, as no cause of action can lie in respect of them.[35]

The situation was discussed in the Australian case of *Union Bank of Australia Ltd.* v. *Rudder*,[36] where the seller of a motor-car in Chicago used the services of an American forwarder and carrier, P. & Co., to forward the vehicle to Sydney, who in turn employed the plaintiffs as their receiving agent in Sydney. P. & Co. issued a through bill of lading covering both the land and sea transit, which in similar transactions had normally been sent with a policy of insurance and a draft, and on payment the through bill of lading would be handed over enabling possession to be obtained of the vehicle. The through bill was not forthcoming. The receiving agent therefore communicated with M., the seller's agent in Sydney, and agreed to hand the vehicle over in return for suitable guarantees as described above. This was later approved by P. & Co. and the shipper, but M., after paying the shipping charges, obtained possession of the car and sold it without accounting to his principal for the proceeds. P. & Co. therefore claimed an indemnity from their receiving agent in Sydney at the instigation of the seller on the ground that he had no authority to deliver the car without the authority of the shipper. The receiving agent in turn sued the defendant bank as guarantors under their indorsement of the letter of guarantee given by M. This claim was rejected by the court however, on the grounds that as there was a subsequent valid ratification of the plaintiff's actions by P. & Co. and the shipper, no enforceable claim could be made against the former so that no cause of action remained.

324   It should be noted that such a problem is particularly likely to face a receiving agent where, as in *Rudder's* case, he receives a ship's bill of lading from the sending forwarder covering a large number of packages, of which the item in question is but one, and in respect of which the former has not received the through bill of lading relating to it. In such circumstances the receiving agent is faced with a dilemma. He has received the shipment in question as consignee under a consolidated ocean bill of lading, and although not wishing to hold on to the item, is faced with the fact that the item in question is intended to be handed over to a person not formally authorised to receive it. As a result he

[34] *Union Bank of Australia Ltd.* v. *Rudder* (1911) 13 C.L.R. 152 at p. 161.
[35] *Ibid.* at p. 163.
[36] *Ibid.*

may lay himself open to an action for conversion by the holder of the through bill, as the non-production thereof leaves the question absolutely open as to the possibility of some claim arising on it.

To avoid the prospect of indefinitely retaining the goods, the safest course for a receiving agent in such circumstances is to obtain a letter of guarantee by way of indemnity. This will normally adequately cover the latter against any claims made upon him by the shipper or by the sending forwarder on his behalf, but it should be noted that unless specifically drawn to cover such contingencies, the guarantee will not cover any loss resulting to the shipper subsequent to delivery through the misappropriation of the proceeds of any sale of the goods by the consignee merely because his duty as an agent was to account for them to his principal the shipper.[37]

325   Equally a forwarder may consign a shipment on behalf of a client under a bill of lading made out to his own order as consignor, and instead of utilising the services of a receiving agent, will indorse the bill and mail it to a local bank in the consignee's country. If he instructs the bank not to surrender the negotiable bills of lading until the consignee has paid for the goods, the bank will be liable in conversion for permitting them to get into the consignee's hands without collecting the amount due.[38] If the forwarder's client has in fact instructed him to obtain payment in exchange for documents, he may himself be liable to his client for the amount of the draft in such circumstances if he has employed a bank or other agent and the latter has failed to effect collection.[39]

2. DOCUMENTS RELATING TO THE FORWARDING AND CARRIAGE OF GOODS

(i) Introduction

326   The relationship of the forwarder and the receiving agent with the shipper and the consignee in respect of the drafting and presentation of bills of lading and allied documents relating to the passing of title to goods and their transportation has been considered in the first part of this chapter. However, the question of the nature and characteristics of the principal types of document with which the forwarder commonly deals in this respect has still to be considered.

Whereas the carrier will either issue a consignment note or waybill if carriage is by land or air, without any intention of creating a document of title, where carriage is by sea the carrier will normally issue

---

[37] *Ibid.* at p. 163, *per* Griffith C.J.; *i.e.* here it was only intended to be an indemnity to the receiving agent against any claims in consequence of " such delivery," that is, of the car without the necessary documents, not to indemnify the shipper against any loss sustained following delivery.

[38] *Danzas* v. *National Bank of Alaska* [1964] A.M.C. 1832, where the client specifically stated in his instructions to the forwarder that payment was to be obtained on receipt of documents.

[39] *Ibid.*

a bill of lading which combines both the functions of a document of title and of carriage. The forwarder therefore is faced with a twofold problem. First, he must offer his client a document whereby carriage can be effected, and, secondly, where carriage is partly by sea, he must supply a document of title also. This can be achieved by obtaining from the actual carrier either a consignment note or bill of lading covering the transit to pass on to his client. In many cases the forwarder will in fact prepare the documentation himself on behalf of the carrier, acting as his agent in doing so. However, both in order to protect the forwarder's status as an independent intermediary, and to solve the practical problem of effecting through documentation where successive carriage is involved, the forwarder has attempted to utilise alternative forms of documentation.

327 Several approaches have been made to the problem. First, the forwarder may take out the bill of lading in his own name, particularly where he is consolidating shipments, and offer his client a forwarding certificate instead, which will merely evidence carriage without fulfilling the function of a document of title. Secondly, certain well-established forwarders have attempted to issue a document which will combine both functions, that is, to issue a "house" bill of lading although not themselves carriers.[40] Thirdly, there is the "through" bill of lading which is increasingly used to provide comprehensive documentation where successive carriage by land, sea or air, is involved.[41] Finally, certain new categories of document have come into existence, which, although not intended to be treated as documents of title, are intended to overcome the problems of international transit, and which may ultimately become as acceptable to the banks as the bill of lading is at present.[42] Each will be considered in turn.

(ii) *Groupage Bills of Lading*

328 A forwarder may consolidate group shipments into one large consignment either to obtain the benefit of bulk freight rates from the carrier, or else for his own convenience where he is required to forward a number of small shipments to the same destination. Where a forwarder does consolidate shipments he will ship them under one consolidated or groupage bill of lading. In such circumstances the bill will usually be made out with the forwarder as consignor.

The groupage bill of lading is commonly used in two situations. First, where a forwarder is required to forward several shipments which are intended for a single consignee, as, for example, where a foreign importer has ordered goods simultaneously from several suppliers, which are to be handled by one forwarder, the latter will forward them under one bill of lading. Secondly, where a number of consignments are

---

[40] See § 332.
[41] See § 333.
[42] See § 343.

destined for different consignees but via the same port of entry, a forwarder who is responsible for handling them all may dispatch them all under the one bill of lading. In the first example the bill of lading may be made out either in the name of the importer himself, or else in the name of the forwarder's local receiving agent as consignee. In the second example the bill will either be made out to the forwarder's own order or else to his receiving agent. Where a receiving agent is employed or the forwarder has a local office at the place of destination, either the agent or the forwarder himself will break bulk and deconsolidate, and distribute the individual consignments in accordance with the forwarder's instructions.

329   Where a forwarder regularly consolidates shipments, whether in respect of small consignments for his own convenience or to take advantage of differential freight rates, certain problems are likely to arise. First, payment for goods shipped under an export transaction will often be effected by means of a banker's commercial credit, under which the buyer is normally expected to produce a bill of lading, in exchange for which the bank will make payment.[43] However, the groupage bill may often cover consignments from a number of shippers to a number of buyers. It is therefore not suitable to be used in conjunction with a banker's credit, as it will never correspond with the terms laid down in the letter of credit as to the documents to be obtained in exchange for payment.[44] To overcome this problem, the practice has developed whereby a forwarder will issue "shipping certificates" in respect of the items listed under a particular letter of credit, which will be drawn to cover the presentation of such a document instead of the customary bill of lading. A proviso may also be included that the certificate must be issued by a certain named forwarder.

330 **Delivery orders**
Where a forwarder consigns goods under a groupage bill, if he consigns the shipment to his receiving agent at the inwards port, he will issue delivery orders for presentation by the buyer or other consignee to the agent in respect of each of the shipments consolidated in the groupage bill of lading. It should be noted that where a groupage bill is issued, the buyer does not have a right of action against the carrier direct under the forwarder's delivery order, which is the only document which he will receive. Any right of action must lie against the forwarder, who in turn must take action himself against the carrier under the bill of lading.

331 **Contractual right to consolidate**
Furthermore, where it is common practice to consolidate shipments on certain routes, a forwarder will often include a clause in his trading conditions whereby he retains the right to consolidate any shipments

---

43 C. M. Schmitthoff, *Export Trade*, 5th ed., Chapter 21.
44 Gutteridge & Megrah, *The Law of Bankers' Commercial Credits*.

he is required to forward under one bill of lading and to consign them to his agents to reduce freight charges. This will not protect him against liability though where he disregards his client's specific instructions to consign the goods direct to the consignee. Consequently, the inclusion of a clause exempting the forwarder from all liability for loss howsoever caused does not protect him against a breach of any special instructions which he may be given as to the drawing up of the bill of lading.[45] However, where Standard Trading Conditions apply, it appears that the forwarder is adequately protected against such contingencies.[46]

(iii) *The House Bill of Lading*

332 Certain of the larger forwarding companies issue documents of control to their clients which are commonly called house bills of lading. They differ from the orthodox bill of lading in that the forwarder does not issue a house bill in the capacity of a carrier, but with the intention of substituting his own documents of control for a carrier's bill of lading to enable the consignor to obtain payment from the consignee or buyer. However, banks are not generally very favourably disposed to accept the house bill of lading in lieu of a carrier's bill, and considerable difficulty may result when a letter of credit requires the presentation of an orthodox bill of lading. Consequently, the acceptability of the house bill of lading in banking circles depends essentially on the reputation of the particular forwarder issuing it. Only house bills issued by a limited number of forwarding companies are recognised as acceptable and even then the letter of credit must be drawn to cover them specifically.[47] As a result, although fairly common in this country, the house bill is not so widely used on the Continent.

What therefore is the position of a forwarder who issues such a document? It seems that where he does issue such a bill in his own name, as opposed to issuing a bill of lading in the name of the carrier to his own order or that of his receiving agent, the forwarder will be placed in virtually the same position as a carrier himself. One of the obvious disadvantages of the house bill to a shipper, however, is that it is not issued by the actual carrier, but merely by a forwarder who generally has neither the means nor the intention to perform any part of the operation himself. Accordingly, virtually all the obligations entered into by the forwarder will be performed by a third party so that any exemption clauses limiting liability in respect of the acts of any agent, carrier, etc., become of basic importance, as they not only limit liability in respect of on-carriage under a through bill of lading, but also in respect of the primary carrier too.[48]

---

[45] *Hunt & Winterbotham Ltd.* v. *Morny & Co.* (1922) 12 Ll.L.Rep. 286 at p. 287.
[46] Cll. 4, 13 (ii), S.T.C. See Chapter 5.
[47] This was agreed at an international bankers' meeting in 1963.
[48] *Midland Rubber Co.* v. *Robert Park & Co.* (1922) 11 Ll.L.Rep. 119.

Furthermore, by issuing his own house bill of lading, a forwarder can restrict his liability as regards the transit without the need to use any further contractual documents. In other words, by issuing a house bill of lading to his client, a forwarder can often obtain the benefits of acting as carrier without necessarily suffering any of the disadvantages thereof. Where, however, the contract of carriage is effected subject to the actual carrier's bill of lading, the forwarder must introduce his own trading conditions as a separate contractual document to limit his liability, or else he will be faced with the problem of ensuring that they are brought to the notice of his client in order to bind him, which in practice is not always easy where a forwarder is dealing with a new client to whom notice of the terms has not been given prior to a forwarding contract being entered into.[49]

(iv) *The Through Bill of Lading*

333   Where carriage is to be effected by several vessels or by different means of transport, the complete journey will often be covered by a through bill of lading. There is no reason in principle why a carrier should not issue a through bill for a transit by any number of different means of transport, but if too complex, such a document may in practice prove too cumbersome for commercial use.[50]

A through bill can, in principle, be issued by any type of carrier. He does not need to be a carrier by sea, although if a land carrier or forwarder does issue such a bill, he will need to accept responsibility for that part of the transit.[51] In practice, however, a through bill will normally be issued by a sea carrier as this will generally constitute the major portion of the journey. Furthermore, a bill of lading issued by a sea carrier will generally be more acceptable to the financial community, as was discussed in the earlier part of this chapter. The through bill is of particular importance in the case of exports and imports to and from inland centres to enable one set of documents to to be used to cover the complete journey.

334   Forwarding contract

Instead of issuing a through bill a carrier may merely contract to forward the goods by a further carrier instead of undertaking to carry himself. In this case the carrier will merely undertake the duties of a forwarder in this respect.[52] In other words, he undertakes to enter into

---

[49] *Von Traubenberg* v. *Davies, Turner & Co. Ltd.* [1951] 2 Lloyd's Rep. 462. *Gillette Industries Ltd.* v. *W. H. Martin Ltd.* [1966] 1 Lloyd's Rep. 57.

[50] With the recent growth of containerised traffic to and from the principal trade centres of the world, it is envisaged that the forwarding functions of the sea carrier, whether by through bill of lading or not, will increase considerably with the development of inland customs clearance, as the sealed containers will be forwarded from the port of entry with the minimum of formality. Only container clearance will be necessary at the port, without reference to the contents, which will be cleared at the inland centre to which the container is consigned. In connection with this development, forwarders are combining to open offices at the various inland centres to facilitate transit operations.

[51] See *Troy* v. *The Eastern Company of Warehouses* at § 335.

[52] *Moore* v. *Harris* (1876) 1 App.Cas. 318. See Chapter 2.

a suitable contract on behalf of the shipper with a successive carrier and to ensure that the goods are delivered to him safely, and to arrange for the performance of any other ancillary operations pertaining to the transit, such as customs clearance, etc. These functions he may either perform himself or arrange for a clearing or customs agent to perform them instead. The actual arrangements will differ in each case as there is no uniform practice in these matters.

The legal position where the first carrier acts in the capacity of a forwarder is that a direct contract is created between the consignor and the successive carrier. Such a relationship is not as common as the alternative one whereby the consignor contracts solely with the first carrier for the complete journey, in which case the latter is personally liable for the on-carriage, all successive carriers being treated as agents of the first carrier in respect of the sections of the journey performed by them.[53] In these circumstances the contract of carriage takes the form of a through bill of lading. Under this the first carrier is liable at common law for the complete performance of the contract, but it is customary for a clause to be included limiting the first carrier's liability to that part of the journey actually performed by him.[54] As a result, the practical difference between a through bill of lading with such a clause inserted and a contract whereby an ordinary bill of lading is issued in respect of the first carrier's part of the journey, together with an obligation to forward the shipment for the remainder of the journey, may not be very great as to the actual obligations undertaken by the parties.[55]

335 Whether the document is a bill of lading or not

Where, therefore, a forwarder purports to issue a through bill of lading, it is first necessary to establish whether the document in question is in fact a bill of lading or not, as it may transpire that a mere consignment note or similar non-negotiable document has in fact been issued.[56]

The question was discussed in *Troy* v. *The Eastern Company of Warehouses*,[57] where the plaintiff shipper unsuccessfully claimed back the freight charges payable in respect of an unperformed section of a through transit. Whether the plaintiff could recover or not depended upon whether the defendants had issued a through bill of lading themselves or whether they had merely contracted as agents on behalf of the shipper in effecting carriage. The shipper claimed that as they had described themselves as "forwarding agents" they had therefore contracted as his agents and were accountable to him. This argument was

[53] See Chapter 2. See Sassoon, *C.I.F. & F.O.B. Contracts*, 1968, §§ 91 *et seq.*
[54] *Ibid.*
[55] As to the distinction, see *Cliffe* v. *Hull & Netherlands S.S. Co. Ltd.* (1921) 6 Ll.L.Rep. 136, where a bill of lading was issued for carriers from Rotterdam to Hull with a clause stating that the goods were "to be forwarded from Hull to Manchester." This was held to be a forwarding contract and not a through bill of lading. See Chapter 2.
[56] *Luigi Riva Di Fernando* v. *Simon Smits & Co. Ltd.* (1920) 2 Ll.L.Rep. 279.
[57] (1921) 8 Ll.L.Rep. 17. See § 418 also.

rejected by the court, which did not consider relevant the name by which the defendants were known nor the fact that they had informed the plaintiff of the method of charging for the carriage. To obtain the business they had had to issue a through bill of lading with all its attendant responsibilities, and the mere fact that they had excluded all liability for loss during on-carriage did not alter the situation. They were not liable, therefore, to refund the unused balance of freight after the consignee took early delivery because of unsettled political conditions.[58]

336   Even where it is established that the document issued by a forwarder is a through bill of lading, the question still arises as to what extent a forwarder can rely on its terms. In other words, the question may arise as to whether a forwarder can in fact rely on its protection in the light of the procedures used in forwarding operations generally.

The question was considered at some length in the case of *Midland Rubber Company* v. *Robert Park & Co.*[59] where the defendant forwarders made out a through bill of lading in respect of goods shipped on behalf of the plaintiffs with instructions that delivery was only to take place against the through bill of lading. The defendants' agents in Zurich permitted the purchaser to collect without presentation of the bill of lading, that is, without having paid the purchase price. The through bill provided that the forwarders were not liable for any loss caused by any carriers, nor by " their specified representatives, or of others for the time being. . . ." Under this clause the defendants pleaded that they were not liable for the acts of their Zurich agents. The plaintiffs in reply argued that the conditions in question only applied to the receiving and carrying of goods under the through bill, but had nothing to do with the handing over of the goods to the purchaser. This argument was rejected by the court, who did not consider that it was possible to separate the varying functions carried out under the contract, as the bill of lading was intended to cover them all. The defendants were therefore protected against liability for the negligence of their agents.[60]

(v) *Containerisation*

337   The rapid development of containerisation in the carriage of goods has created certain difficulties in relation to documentation and the applicability of the various international conventions governing the carriage

---

[58] *Ibid.* at p. 19, *per* Bankes L.J.   *Cf.* the American case of *Penney Co.* v. *American Express Co.* [1952] A.M.C. 901 where the American Express received goods at an inland point in Italy and issued its own " through bill of lading " to deliver the goods at an inland point in the United States. They were held to be acting as a forwarder and not as a carrier.

[59] (1922) 11 Ll.L.Rep. 119, *i.e.* it was made out in the form of a house bill, that is, issued by the forwarder in his own name and not on behalf of a carrier.

[60] *Cf. David Toubkin* v. *Herbert Smart & Co. Ltd.*, *Lloyd's List*, Dec. 10, 1921. The position of a forwarder who purports to issue a through bill of lading may depend upon the choice of law in respect of the contract, as the result may differ from one system to another: *Anselme Dewavrin Fils et Cie* v. *Wilsons & N.E. Ry. Shipping Co. Ltd.* (1931) 39 Ll.L.Rep. 289.   See Rodière, *op. cit.*, Sections 942, 1027, 1348.

of goods. First, a container will invariably be subject to successive carriage and some form of through documentation will be necessary. Consequently, the future development of container transport will result in one legal person accepting responsibility for the whole transit. Such a person could equally be a sea carrier, a road haulier or a forwarder.

As regards the form of documentation suitable for containerised shipments, various proposals have been put forward by interested bodies, any comment on which would be out of date before publication. Suffice it to say that a comprehensive report on this and associated problems has been issued by the U.K. Committee for the Simplification of International Trade Procedures. [61] Although it is too soon to say with certainty what forms will eventually win general acceptance, it is obvious that it could take the form of a through bill of lading, or else a document such as that proposed under the draft T.C.M. Convention. [62] Equally, the container operator, whether he is a forwarder or not, will himself require some form of documentation to cover the actual movement of the container itself. Whether this will take the form of a through bill of lading issued by a sea carrier, or whether some alternative method will be devised, remains to be seen.

338   As a result of such developments, the legal status of the forwarder will alter both in relation to his client and to the carrier. If he operates as a container operator himself he will need to supply a universally acceptable document of title, which the house bill of lading never has been. On the other hand, if the forwarder does not operate as a container operator, it is probable that he will consolidate on behalf of the latter so that the need for the house bill of lading will disappear. Even if the forwarder does continue to consolidate as an independent operator, the fact that an acceptable document of title can be issued by the container operator at the point of dispatch, that is, where the container is loaded, which will usually be a convenient inland trade centre, means that the practical need for the house bill would disappear. Only in the case of a shipment by orthodox shipping techniques would the house bill remain of value, and as it is the very forwarders whose house bills are credit-worthy that are likely to participate in the new containerisation programmes to any extent, its decline will be accentuated. Furthermore, it seems that it is on those routes and in those commodities where the forwarder is most active that containerisation is most likely to replace or supplement orthodox techniques.

[61] SITPRO Report, H.M.S.O., 1970. It has been suggested that banks and finance houses really do not need a document of title to enable them to exercise a right of lien over the actual goods which are often in a place remote from this country. The Board of Trade have recommended that this right could be substituted for an interest in the proceeds of an approved insurance policy which would cover such risks against which a finance house would wish to protect themselves. This question is at present under consideration by both banking and forwarding interests in this country.

[62] See §§ 341 *et seq.* N.B. the Convention is not restricted to containers but applies to any form of combined transport.

339   Certain problems are inherent in the shipment of goods by container. First, there is the inability to check whether goods are damaged or not whilst in transit, thus preventing the annotation of the bill of lading as to the condition of the goods. From the shipper's viewpoint this problem would be largely solved by the concept of the " Combined Transport Operator," proposed by the T.C.M. Convention,[63] who would himself accept responsibility for the contents, irrespective of whether he can in turn recover from the actual carrier responsible or not. However, the container operator will be faced with serious problems where either a shipper loads a container himself with a complete load, without supervision by the container operator, or else a forwarder consolidates smaller shipments himself while acting in an independent capacity, and not as the agent of the container operator. In neither case will he have any proof as to the condition of the goods at loading, so that either a system of inspection will be necessary or else contractual limitation of liability in the case of loss resulting from faulty packing, etc. In such a case considerable care would be necessary to delineate the extent of the container operator's liability, which might be further limited dependent on whether a professional packer is employed or not. It remains, however, to be seen how this problem will be handled in practice.

340   Finally, the question arises as to whether the existing limits of financial liability under the existing international conventions will remain adequate. Previously there was doubt as to the extent of recovery for packages consolidated in a container or on a pallet. However, under the amendments introduced by the Brussels Protocol 1968, where goods are consolidated in a container or pallet, the packages listed on the bill of lading as packed therein are to be treated as individual units, for the purposes of calculating the amount recoverable.[64] As regards the proposed T.C.M. Convention, although no provision has been made as yet as to the financial limits on recovery, this will presumably reflect current requirements.

(vi) T.C.M. Convention

341 The problems of through carriage and containerisation are closely interrelated, and in practice many problems arising are common to both, as most through carriage will in fact result from the use of containerisation.[65] In both cases the problem really resolves itself as one of combined transport by two or more methods of transport. To deal with such problems both the International Maritime Committee (C.M.I.) and Unidroit have for some years studied the problem, and

---

[63] See §§ 341 et seq.
[64] Art. IV, r. 5 (c), Brussels Protocol 1968. See also K. Gronfors, *Container Transport and the Hague Rules* [1967] J.B.L. 298.
[65] On the American position see G. Ullman, " The Role of the American Ocean Freight Forwarder in Intermodal Containerised Transportation " [1971] *Journal of Maritime Law and Commerce* 625.

a jointly sponsored draft Convention sur le Transport International Combiné de Marchandise (T.C.M. Convention) has been produced for consideration by a diplomatic conference in the near future.[66] As there is as yet no firm agreement as to its terms it can be assumed that it will not be adopted in the immediate future. It is therefore only necessary to consider it in outline.

342 Provisions

First, T.C.M. creates a new legal person, the Combined Transport Operator (C.T.O.) who replaces the traditional carrier as the person responsible to the shipper for the operation in question. However, he is only defined by the Convention as a person who issues a Combined Transport (C.T.) document.[67] In other words the Convention will only apply to those contracts of combined carriage where a C.T. document is issued which is headed " Combined Transport Document governed by the T.C.M. Convention," where the place of acceptance and delivery are situated in two states.[68] Unlike other conventions concerning the carriage of goods it is not intended to be mandatory. Forwarders can therefore still issue a house bill of lading and similar documents if they wish. F.I.A.T.A., however, have recently introduced a F.I.A.T.A. C.T. document, which although basically in accord with the T.C.M. document differs in detail.[69] The acceptability of such variants will essentially depend upon their acceptability to the banks, so that any differences will perforce be minor.

Unlike C.M.R., which is specifically non-negotiable,[70] T.C.M. can be either negotiable or non-negotiable, dependent upon the needs of the parties.[71] It can therefore fulfil the needs of both the short sea continental trade and also the deep sea inter-continental trade too.

Finally, liability under the Convention is on a "network," system, that is, once the point of loss or damage is determined, the liability of the C.T.O. will be regulated under the Convention according to the provisions of any other international Convention or national law which is mandatory, or under certain circumstances, the contractual agreement between the C.T.O. and a sub-contractor.[72] In other words, where the contract or any part of it would otherwise be subject to C.M.R., C.I.M., the Warsaw Convention or the Hague Rules, such provisions will still apply.[73]

It remains to be seen, however, how this concept develops in practice.

(vii) *F.I.A.T.A. Documents of Carriage and Warehousing*

343 As mentioned above, the house bill of lading possesses both distinct

[66] See further SITPRO Report, 1970.
[67] Art. 1 (4), (*b*), T.C.M. *Cf.* Arts. 1, 2, F.B.L.
[68] *Cf.* C.M.R. where the existence of the consignment note does not affect the validity of the contract—see § 350.
[69] See Appendix for the provisions of the F.I.A.T.A. F.B.L.
[70] Art. 4, C.M.R.
[71] Arts. 3 (1) (*a*), 6, T.C.M. *Cf.* Art. 3, F.B.L.
[72] *Cf.* Art. 2, C.M.R.; Art. 2, C.I.M.; Art. 6B, F.B.L.
[73] Art. 11, T.C.M.

advantages and disadvantages. Among the latter, perhaps one of the most important is the fact that shipowners and banks do not always accept them and their exact legal status is far from certain. Furthermore, the desire to improve the forwarder's status has given an impetus to the search for an alternative form of document. As a result of much enthusiasm on the part of forwarding organisations in Belgium and Holland, F.I.A.T.A. have introduced two forms of international forwarding documents in the anticipation that they would eventually be adopted by all the principal forwarding organisations throughout the world. These documents are the Forwarding Agents Certificate of Receipt (F.C.R.) and the Forwarding Agents Certificate of Transport (F.C.T.).[74]

The purpose of F.C.R. is to certify the receipt of goods pending their actual carriage. F.C.T., on the other hand, is intended to replace the house bill of lading. A growing problem, particularly on the Continent, is the fact that the through bill of lading and the through consignment note in respect of land carriage, place duties and liabilities on the first carrier in a transit which does not fall within the ambit of his own operations. A carrier may be concerned with transit over a system governed by the Hague Rules, the Warsaw Convention, C.I.M.[75] or C.M.R., dependent on whether transport is by sea, air or land. If he does not wish to concern himself in liabilities arising from outside the standard trading conditions under which he operates himself, the forwarder can offer an alternative by means of an F.C.T. document.

344   Provisions of F.C.T.

F.C.T. can only be drawn up and issued by a forwarder, and is subject to strict security safeguards. First, the national F.I.A.T.A. association is responsible for issuing to forwarders numbered sets of the document for use in international traffic. The forwarder must keep a register of F.C.T.s issued, and any copies must be marked "not negotiable." He is also required to ensure that the consignment in question has been taken over by him or his agent, and that he has the sole rights of disposing of it, and that the goods are in good external order.[76] It is also provided by F.I.A.T.A. rules that any changes or additions to the text which modify the juridical nature of the document invalidate it, but to what extent such a provision would be of effect without some statutory provision in this country is of some doubt.[77] Although F.I.A.T.A. suggest that F.C.T. should be considered negotiable, it is difficult to see how this could be achieved without either legislative provision or a court decision on the matter.

---

[74] R. Th.J.le Cavalier, past President of FENEX, devised the scheme.
[75] Kahn-Freund, *Law of Inland Transport*, 4th ed. For a recent outline of the provisions of C.I.M. see Chapter 20.
[76] F.C.T. introductory paragraph.
[77] *Notice—Issuing of F.C.T. Documents*, FENEX undated, Clause 4.

345   F.C.T. specifically incorporates the standard trading conditions of the national trade association in question, and although not accepted as yet in this country would, if introduced, do likewise here.[78] These are normally printed on the back of the document. Six printed clauses are included which will take precedence in the event of conflict with the national trading conditions.[79]

Provision is made whereby the forwarder is authorised to enter into contractual relations with carriers, etc., subject to the latter's usual trading conditions, which will therefore bind the shipper in respect of that part of the transit in question.[80] Also it is provided that the forwarder only contracts as such, and not as a carrier, and therefore does not assume any liability for the execution of his instructions given to carriers and other third parties engaged in the transit.[81] The only obligation in this respect is for "the careful selection of third parties."[82]

However, Clause 4 limits this disclaimer of liability to a considerable extent by providing that the forwarder accepts full responsibility for the proper delivery of the goods to the holder of the document through the intermediacy of a receiving agent designated by the forwarder.[83] Subject to this proviso though, the forwarder does not accept liability for the acts or omissions of carriers involved in the execution of the transit, nor of any other third parties.[84]

Clause 3 further states that the forwarder will subrogate his claims against any carriers and other parties if so requested. As regards the question of insurance, provision is made for cover to be effected by the forwarder only on express instructions in writing.[85] This merely reiterates the provisions found in most trading conditions already.[86] A deviation clause is also included to cover the occurrence of unforeseen circumstances.[87] Where these occur the forwarder is entitled to deviate from the route or method of transport previously envisaged. A similar provision is found in Standard Trading Conditions.[88] Finally, it should not be forgotten that any provision in the relevant forwarding conditions which do not directly conflict with the provisions of F.C.T. will also apply.[89]

---

[78] The existence of the house bill of lading has mitigated against its introduction.
[79] See Appendix.
[80] Cl. 1, F.C.T. *Cf.* Cl. 1, S.T.C.
[81] Cl. 2, F.C.T.
[82] Cl. 2, F.C.T.
[83] This acceptance of liability for the receiving agent effecting delivery was introduced at the request of the Swiss Association. *Per* F.I.A.T.A. minutes. Doc 410/2, Dec. 9, 1965.
[84] Cl. 3, F.C.T. This proviso, although not as yet the subject matter of judicial comment, is presumably intended to cover the forwarder against any damage or delay in transit, although not exonerating him from liability, in the event of the goods not being delivered at all. It seems that the exact meaning of this clause will depend upon the provision made by the particular national trading conditions which are incorporated into F.C.T. relating to the rights and liabilities of the parties in this respect.
[85] Cl. 4, F.C.T.
[86] See Chapter 17.
[87] Cl. 5, F.C.T.
[88] Cl. 4, S.T.C. See § 199.
[89] F.C.T., introductory paragraph.

346   In using F.C.T. as an international document, there is an obvious drawback in the need to incorporate the trading conditions of each member state, but as the rights and duties of forwarders in different countries differ considerably, such diversity must be recognised until international forwarding conditions are agreed upon.[90]

347 **F.C.R.**

In addition to F.C.T., the Forwarding Agents Certificate of Receipt has become widely used on the Continent, which is intended to certify the receipt of goods pending transit. This makes provision for the incorporation of irrevocable forwarding or disposal instructions, which may be included in the document.[91] Amendment or rescission of these instructions is only possible against surrender of the F.C.R. in question, and is subject to the issuing forwarder still retaining a right of disposal over the shipment.[92] Furthermore if such instructions authorise disposal by a nominated third party, the rescission or amendment will only be effective if they reach the forwarder prior to any disposition by such a third party.[93]

As an F.C.R. does not establish any right to a claim for the surrender of the goods specified, but merely represents a forwarder's receipt for them with certain safeguards, only one original is issued, and if a copy is required, it is to be marked "not negotiable." When other freight documents such as bills of lading are to be issued subsequent to the issue of an F.C.R., care must be taken to ensure that the terms of such documents do not conflict with the obligations undertaken in the F.C.R., and especially that any safeguards therein are not rendered invalid. For instance, if a bill of lading is issued to a party who is debarred by an F.C.R. from exercising a right of disposal, the latter would be placed in the position of being able to dispose of the goods by means of the bill without the need to produce the F.C.R., which would defeat the object of such a document.

348 **Advantages of F.I.A.T.A. documents**

The advantage, at least to the continental forwarder, of both these documents is that they can be issued immediately the shipment has been loaded on a vehicle for collection by the forwarder. Accordingly, if a letter of credit is opened by a buyer against delivery of the shipment to the forwarder, payment can be obtained immediately against presentation of documents. This offers an obvious advantage to the seller, who is not required to await payment until the goods are sent to a seaport or their ultimate destination by the carrier.

In conclusion, although they have been adopted by some European

---

[90] With the rapidly changing development of the trade the introduction of such conditions is not likely in the foreseeable future.
[91] The provisions of F.C.R. are not numbered in separate sections or clauses.
[92] Note to F.C.R., para. 1.
[93] Note to F.C.R., para. 2.

countries, these documents have not as yet proved attractive to the British forwarding community, owing to the widespread use of the house bill of lading for many years, which stands or falls on its individual merit, based upon the commercial standing of the particular forwarder concerned. In any case, it is probable that the proposed T.C.M. document and the F.I.A.T.A. version thereof will ultimately replace F.C.T. In the United States, the question of the unification of shipping documents has delayed development there. It seems therefore at present to be essentially a product of the civil law countries, and may well remain a localised phenomenon there unless political events dictate otherwise.

(viii) *The Convention for the International Carriage of Goods by Road*

349 Where a forwarder is engaged in international carriage by road to and from Europe, whether by his own vehicles, or else by a sub-contracting carrier, he will be subject to the Convention on the Contract for the International Carriage of Goods by Road.[94] This covers the international movement of any motor vehicle or trailer, and as regards cross-Channel traffic, the articulated trailer shipped without any traction unit is an increasingly popular method of transit which a forwarder can operate without the need for an extensive fleet of traction units, as on reaching the Continent a local haulier can haul the trailer to its destination.

Such forms of international carriage whether partly by sea, air or rail will be subject to the Convention in respect of the complete operation provided the vehicle is not unloaded.[95] This is subject to the proviso that any loss, damage, or delay, occurring solely through the other method of transport will be determined by the provisions covering such method, that is the Hague Rules in respect of sea transit, the Warsaw Convention, etc., for air transit, and either the national rail carriage conditions or C.I.M. in respect of rail transit.[96] If there are no prescribed conditions, then the provisions of the Convention will apply.[97]

350 Consignment note

Any contract of carriage entered into subject to the Convention must be confirmed by the making out of a consignment note,[98] which is "prima facie evidence of the making of the contract of carriage, the conditions of the contract and the receipt of the goods by the carrier."[99] In other words it is not intended to be a document of title, but merely a method of laying down standard conditions of contract for international carriage of goods by road. As in the case of the through bill

---

[94] See Chapters 5 and 10.
[95] Art. 2 (1), C.M.R.
[96] See note 72. *Cf.* Art. 2, Guadalajara Convention 1961, which may conflict with Art. 2, C.M.R.
[97] Art. 2 (1), C.M.R. *Cf.* Art. 2, C.I.M.; Art. 11, T.C.M.
[98] Art. 4, C.M.R. *Cf.* Arts. 6, 7, C.I.M.; Art. 3, F.B.L.
[99] Art. 9 (1), C.M.R. *Cf.* Art. 5, T.C.M.

of lading and T.C.M., it is intended to facilitate the movement of goods internationally and, if necessary, by more than one method of transport subject only to one set of conditions for the whole transit. Unlike these two documents, it is not intended to facilitate transfer of title or of payment for goods, restricting itself purely to defining the actual contract of carriage. Furthermore, Article 4 provides that "the absence, irregularity or loss of the consignment note shall not affect the existence or the validity of the contract of carriage which shall remain subject to the provisions of this Convention."[1]

Within the consignment note certain specified information as to parties, destination, C.O.D. charges, insurance, etc., is laid down by Article 6 (1) and (2). The note is to be made out with three original copies and is to be signed by both the consignor and the carrier.[2] One copy goes to each of them and one accompanies the goods.[3] Where the goods are to be loaded in different vehicles, are of different kinds, or to be divided into different lots, either the consignor or carrier can require a separate note to be made out for each vehicle, kind or lot of goods.[4]

351 Who is a carrier

C.M.R. does not say who should draw up the consignment note, although it can be inferred from Article 9 (1) that it will be done after the goods have been received by the carrier. However, if the carrier, or a forwarder acting as such, fills in the consignment note on behalf of the consignor at his request, unless the contrary is proved, he will be deemed to have done so as the agent of the consignor,[5] who will therefore be liable for any inaccuracies therein.[6] The problem, however, is that the Convention does not define who is a carrier. The question of who will constitute a successive carrier has already been discussed in an earlier chapter. This still leaves unsolved the primary question of who is the first carrier. Although the Convention states that the consignment note must contain the names and address of the carrier,[7] any irregularity in the note will be devoid of effect,[8] and will not prevent

---

[1] *Cf.* Art. 9, Warsaw Convention, which provides that in such a case the carrier is precluded from relying on those rules excluding or limiting his liability, although otherwise the contract remains subject to the Convention. Art. 1 (1), C.I.M., requires a consignment note to bring the contract within the Convention.

[2] *Cf.* Arts. 6, 8, C.I.M., where the note must be signed by the consignor together with a duplicate. The forwarding station must certify acceptance by date stamping the note. *Cf.* Art. 5, Warsaw Convention, where the consignor must sign the note and can require the carrier's signature.

[3] Art. 5 (1), C.M.R. Although it does not mention it, presumably the signature of the forwarder as the consignor's agent would be acceptable.

[4] Art. 5 (2), C.M.R.

[5] Art. 7 (2), C.M.R.

[6] Art. 7 (1), C.M.R. The Covention does not deal with the question of the carrier's liability to the consignee for negligence in filling up the consignment note—any such claim would fall under the common law. The note can be drawn up prior to receipt of goods by the carrier and validated by signature at that point.

[7] Art. 6 (1) (c), C.M.R.

[8] Art. 4, C.M.R.

an earlier carrier not named in the note being designated the first carrier, thus making the former a successive carrier. It is therefore far from clear under the Convention what are the exact implications of this provision, and in particular the real status of the forwarder thereunder.

352 Position of the forwarder

It would appear that if a forwarder is consolidating shipments into a carload, to be forwarded in a carrier's vehicle, he may sign the consignment note as sender, and may not give his client a copy, but instead contract with him subject to Standard Trading Conditions. If, on the other hand, he forwards in his own vehicle he will be bound as a carrier to give his client a consignment note subject to the Convention. The real difficulty is likely to occur where he offers a transportation service to the public but either does not carry himself or else does not own any vehicles or merely operates a local pick-up service. The question has already arisen on the Continent, but not as yet in the English courts, and is therefore open to speculation. Similarly where a forwarder also contracts subject to Standard Trading Conditions in respect of matters not covered by the Convention, which is common practice, he is precluded from exempting himself from liability under the Convention, even if he attempts to do so by including a clause to this effect, if in fact he is a carrier subject to the Convention.[9] In other words the use or otherwise of Standard Trading Conditions does not establish a forwarder's status. The real answer to the problem seems to be that both as regards the first and successive carriers there is a gap in the Convention, and until the necessary amendments are effected, it will only be possible to ascertain the status of the parties to a contract of international carriage *ex post facto* and then only in relation to the transaction in question.[10]

3. Conclusions

353 The position of the forwarder in relation to the various documents of title and carriage, as has been seen in this chapter, is a complex one, which does not lay itself open to general statements of principle. Much turns upon the facts of the particular case. However the forwarder's

---

[9] Arts. 6 (1) (*k*), 7 (3), C.M.R. If the note does not contain a statement that the carriage is subject to the Convention the carrier will be liable for all loss sustained by the person entitled to dispose of the goods through it.

[10] This is particularly important bearing in mind the high limit of liability under the Convention (£3,400 per ton) and the fact that under the Convention the carrier is liable for the defaults of his servants and agents and any other person whose services he uses (Arts. 3 and 17 (3)). This therefore runs contrary to the provisions of S.T.C. and R.H.A. Conditions 1961 which exempt the operator from such liability and also to the traditional freedom of contract at common law (see Chapter 5). It may also create problems where underwriters wish to settle a claim without litigation, where a carrier's C.M.R. and R.H.A. liabilities are with different insurers, and there is therefore doubt as to which policy a particular claim should be settled under. See § 289.

position is a vital one and certain common factors do emerge in relation to the various documents currently in use.

First, the traditional bill of lading has been the subject of a considerable amount of litigation, and as seen in the first section of this chapter, the forwarder's position is clearly established in this respect. The forwarder as agent for the shipper must exercise such care as would be normally expected of a professional agent.[11] However if he is also in the position of agent for the carrier he must also fulfil his duties to the latter, whether as loading broker, ship's agent or other functionary.[12] Irrespective of whom he acts for, any documentation that a forwarder undertakes to draw up must be accurate within the confines of the particulars furnished to him.[13] He must also ensure that the documents of title and carriage are transmitted to the correct recipient, and that any financial provisions as to method of payment are complied with and an acceptable form of document is furnished.[14]

354   Outside the field of the traditional bill of lading, however, the forwarder's position has become increasingly complex. In an effort to fulfil the requirements of international trade, semi-official documents such as F.C.T. and F.C.R., and the provisions of C.M.R. have been introduced in recent years in an attempt to offer more flexible methods of documentation. Two issues conflict here which do not find a ready solution. The shipper requires a more sophisticated form of document to cover transport by successive carriers and different methods of transport. Traditionally, though, the finance houses have only accepted the bill of lading as a negotiable document of title. The conflict between these two interests is obvious and not easily solved. It is certain that the bill of lading is proving increasingly inadequate for international transit, but drawbacks exist in obtaining an acceptable document of title. In particular, the person who may be most conveniently placed to issue an alternative document of carriage is often least suited to back a document of title by suitable financial safeguards. At least the carrier by sea usually possesses enough capital assets to cover the normal contingencies which can arise in respect of a bill of lading. Particularly with the development of containerisation and groupage executed by operators who may not have any proprietary interest in the equipment used, but merely leasing facilities, the problem of finding a suitably backed document of title, apart from a bill of lading, becomes increasingly difficult.

In the case of C.M.R. there is no intention to create a negotiable document at all, thus creating an *impasse*.[15]

---

[11] See Chapter 5.
[12] See Chapter 2.
[13] See §§ 317 *et seq*.
[14] See § 321.
[15] Art. 6 (1) C.M.R., requires the consignee to be named in the consignment note. Art. 1 (5) also provides that the use of consignment notes representing a title to goods will be confined to internal traffic only.

355   The draft T.C.M. Convention envisages a new creature called a
" Combined Transport Operator " who would accept full responsibility
for the complete transit.[16] This may solve transportation problems, but
it is far from certain whether such a concept offers a suitable basis for
a negotiable document of title, unless in practice container operators
are in fact shipowners. Otherwise if such persons prove to be men of
straw, financial confidence in such documents could be badly shaken.
The conflict therefore resolves itself into one of confidence versus
convenience.

[16] See § 341.

CHAPTER 14

THE FORWARDER'S RIGHT OF LIEN

1. INTRODUCTION

356 IN the world of commerce, the problem which faces businessmen at some time or another is that of non-payment of charges. For the intermediary, such as the forwarder, this can be a particular problem, as merely offering a service to third parties, he will rarely have the financial resources that a manufacturer or seller of commodities will usually possess. As a result therefore the common law has developed various remedies and procedures to assist a creditor to obtain payment of his dues. Obviously, the ultimate remedy of an action for non-payment will lie, but this may involve unnecessary expense to the creditor, and in any case may prove both slow and time-consuming. However, if a creditor is in a position to retain possession of the goods in respect of which the charges have been incurred, he will be in a much stronger position to obtain prompt payment.[1] Accordingly the principal remedy which has been developed by the common law whereby security can be obtained by retaining possession of goods already held until outstanding payments are made, is the lien or right of retention. The lien as such does not offer any positive rights to a creditor, but merely gives him the right of passively retaining possession of the goods until satisfaction has been obtained. To overcome this limitation, however, it is not uncommon where Standard Trading Conditions are in use for a clause to be inserted giving the creditor an option of exercising a right of sale over the goods if payment is not made, subject to certain specified conditions, a right which the common law does not give under any circumstances.[2]

357 **Types of lien**

Two types of lien can exist at common law. First, there is the special or particular lien, which merely gives to a creditor the right of retention

---

[1] The question of the methods of payment in relation to carriage was discussed in *Esterhuyse* v. *Selection Cartage (Pty.) Ltd.* 1965 (1) S.A. 360. Here a firm of removal contractors agreed to remove household furniture and effects subject to a contractual proviso that " All work *strictly for cash* on delivery unless arrangements made prior to commencement of work." When a driver refused to accept payment by cheque on arrival, it was held that " cash " in such circumstances was used in its ordinary or restricted sense and did not include a cheque. In reaching this decision the court considered that regard had to be had to the fact that if a worthless cheque were accepted the carrier would lose his lien, and that it is not likely in such a case for a carrier to intend the decision whether or not to accept a cheque to be the sole responsibility of the actual driver of the vehicle. The general rule is that the authority of an agent in such a case to receive payment is usually confined to receiving it in cash. *Cf.* Cl. 17, S.T.C. *Cf. McGraw-Edison* v. *Direct Winters Tpt. Ltd.* [1968] 1 O.R. 663.

[2] See § 370.

in respect of charges which are outstanding with regard to the particular shipment over which the lien is actually exercised, but not in respect of any charges outstanding in relation to any other transaction between the parties concerned. Secondly, there is the general lien, which gives a right of retention to a creditor in respect of outstanding charges due on general account between the parties. Such a right of lien cannot exist at common law except it be granted by statute, judicial recognition of a right of general lien in a particular trade, such as bankers possess, or by implication arising from the general dealings between the parties in the past. The only other way in which a right of general lien can be obtained is by a contractual agreement between the parties, and this, like the right of sale mentioned above, is often incorporated in standard forms of contract where such are in use.[3] Finally, it must be clearly understood that the common law lien is to be distinguished from the maritime lien, which is non-possessory and attaches to the property in question irrespective of whose possession it may be in, and whether ownership is transferred to a third party or not. Such a right will not normally be available to a forwarder, and is therefore outside the scope of this chapter.[4]

358 Civil law

In the civil law, however, the rights of security available to creditors in respect of outstanding charges are provided for, in detail, in both civil and commercial codes, and do not correspond at all closely to the remedies available at common law.[5] Two categories of remedy are available. First, the right of retention, which is similar to the particular lien at common law, and secondly the right of privilege. As one writer observed: "The notion of privilege is a curious compound of the English concept of lien, including the possessory lien of the common law and the non-possessory equitable lien, and of the idea of priority between categories of competing creditors."[6] Like the common law lien, the privilege can be either particular or general. However it can vary in concept in the various jurisdictions from being in the nature of a pledge to a combination of the legal and equitable lien. It is therefore necessary to consider the rights of the forwarder both at common law and under the civil law in respect of the various associated remedies available.

2. THE FORWARDER'S RIGHT OF LIEN AT COMMON LAW

359 The common law lien is a very important remedy for the freight forwarder, and it is therefore necessary to consider in some detail the exact extent of the rights which a forwarder can exercise to recover outstanding charges in respect of a client's goods which are in his possession.

[3] *Ibid.*
[4] See Carver, *Carriage by Sea*, 11th ed., para. 777.
[5] See §§ 386 *et seq.*
[6] Amos & Walton, *Introduction to French Law*, 3rd ed., p. 248.

First, in analysing the forwarder's right of lien, it is essential to distinguish between the various activities which the latter may undertake, as it is quite common for a forwarder, as part of his overall operations, to act not only as a forwarder in the strict sense of the word, but also as a carrier, warehouseman and packer, without necessarily differentiating between these functions. However, ignoring for the moment any contractual conditions which may be imposed upon a customer, the position of these four categories of operation differs as to the exact extent of the common law lien available. Consequently, the forwarder may find that his remedy for the recovery of charges due for a particular shipment may differ, dependent upon whether he has packed it, carried it, stored it, or merely forwarded it.

(i) *The Forwarder as Such*

360   The forwarder, when acting simply as such, is given a particular lien in respect of charges incurred on behalf of his principal which arise out of his employment as an agent in performing his duties as a forwarder.[7] This right of lien not only extends to forwarding operations as such, but also to inwards clearance operations, when a forwarder is acting as a receiving agent, either on behalf of the consignor or consignee. However, when possession is lost of the goods over which the possessory lien is being exercised, the forwarder will not be able to exercise any right of lien over any other property of his principal which may later come into his possession, unless a contractual general lien has been established.[8] Where, though, a forwarder is acting as the correspondent or sub-agent of an overseas sending forwarder, the latter will have recourse against him if he causes his lien to be extinguished by releasing the goods contrary to instructions.[9]

However, where a sub-agent is required to indemnify the sending forwarder against any loss he may suffer through the former's actions in releasing a shipment, he cannot claim an indemnity from a consignee to whom a shipment has been released, if he has only entered into a contractual relationship with the latter merely as agent of the sending forwarder, and not on his own behalf, as generally no privity of contract will be established between them. An example in a recent case will serve to illustrate this point. A forwarder in the United Kingdom was acting as a sub-agent for an Italian forwarder, and was instructed not to release an import shipment of pears from Italy until the whole freight was paid. However, the Italian forwarder's lien was extinguished through the sub-agent's failure to obey instructions. In the resultant action the court held that although the forwarder was therefore liable for the freight charges himself, he could not claim any right of indemnity from the British importer to whom he had released the goods, as

---

[7] *Societa Anonima Angelo Castelletti* v. *Transmaritime Ltd.* [1953] 2 Lloyd's Rep. 440 at p. 449, *per* Devlin J.
[8] See § 365.
[9] *Ibid.*

any contractual agreement which the defendant sub-agent had entered into with the importer in respect of payment of the freight was merely as agent of the plaintiff, the Italian forwarder. Consequently he had neither rights nor liabilities under the forwarding contract.[10]

In such circumstances, whether the British forwarder is acting as a sub-agent for a foreign sending forwarder or directly as a receiving agent on behalf of a foreign consignor, he will not have any contractual rights against a consignee unless he enters into an agreement with the latter under which he obtains either a right of lien or of indemnity in respect of disbursements for which the forwarder may be liable.[11] It should be noted moreover, that in such circumstances as in *Societa Anonima Angelo Castelletti* v. *Transmaritime Ltd.*,[12] where a sub-agent is liable to the sending forwarder for the loss of a right of lien, the measure of damages will only be the actual value of the consignment at the time the lien was extinguished. Where, therefore, the shipment in question is a perishable one, the measure of damages will be reduced accordingly, and may merely result in nominal damages being awarded if the goods have ceased to have any commercial value at all.[13]

(ii) *The Forwarder as a Carrier*

361 A forwarder often carries goods himself either for local delivery and pick-up operations, or else when operating as part of a multiple transportation group.[14] When operating as such, his status will not be that of a mere forwarder, but that of a carrier, and as such the rights of lien that he would possess in the latter capacity, if any, must be exercised. First, it is necessary to decide whether, in respect of any particular transit, a forwarder is acting as a common carrier or as a private carrier. In his capacity as the former, it is accepted law since the case of *Skinner* v. *Upshaw*[15] that the common carrier has a particular lien on goods carried by him as against the true owner in respect of freight charges for them. If a forwarder operates as a private carrier, though, there is some uncertainty as to whether he possesses a right of lien at common law or not, in respect of freight. Chitty, in the first edition of his *Treatise on Contracts*, states that " a particular lien may be created by legal relation ... where the law throws an obligation on a party to do a particular act. Upon [this] principle it has been held that common carriers ... have a particular lien for their ... labours and expenses in regard to their ... employment." [16] Kahn-Freund, on the other hand,

---

[10] *Ibid.* at pp. 451–452.
[11] See § 299.
[12] [1953] 2 Lloyd's Rep. 440.
[13] *Ibid.*
[14] See Chapter 1.
[15] (1702) 2 Lord Raymond 752.
[16] Chitty, *Treatise on the Laws of Commerce and Manufactures and the Contracts relating thereto*, 1824, Vol. 3, at p. 539. This is supported in the 22nd ed.: " The common, but not the private, carrier has, at common law, a particular lien upon the goods he carried in respect of his freight ": Vol. 2, para. 466. See also Halsbury's *Laws*, Vol. 4, p. 194, para. 475, which supports this view.

appears to consider that a private carrier also has a particular lien in respect of his charges, although not as against the true owner of the goods unless he is also the consignor.[17]

362   Such a differentiation between the common carrier and the private carrier is justified on the grounds that the former is obliged to carry goods owing to his common calling, but such a line of reasoning appears to be a *non sequitur*, as the common calling only extends to goods offered by a consignor who is prepared to pay his charges in advance, in the absence of which he is not obliged to carry.[18] On the other hand, if he does in fact give credit to the consignor he will then be liable under his common calling, although this would only be by choice and not mandatory, so that there does not appear much reason for such a distinction to be drawn between the two classes of carrier. It is clear therefore that the extent of the lien which a forwarder can exercise at common law when performing the functions of a carrier will differ depending on whether he is acting as a common or private carrier. However, although a forwarder operating a delivery service to and from the local railway station was held to be a common carrier in *Hellaby* v. *Weaver*, it is doubtful as to whether any forwarder would hold himself out nowadays to accept all goods offered him for forwarding.[19] Bearing in mind the uncertainty which is potentially present, it is advisable for a forwarder to ensure that he carries as a private carrier by contracting subject either to Standard Trading Conditions or R.H.A. Conditions if the carriage is more than an incidental part of a routine forwarding operation.

(iii) *The Forwarder as a Warehouseman and Packer*

363   The larger forwarder often combines the function of warehouseman or wharfinger with that of forwarding, both operations being complementary to each other, particularly in this age of specialist transit methods. Here again there is some doubt as to the extent of the warehouseman's lien. The precedents undoubtedly have granted a particular lien to the warehouseman, but uncertainty exists as to whether a general lien is available at common law or not.[20] By contrast, for historical reasons, the packer has been placed in a specially favourable position since the eighteenth century, when his right of general lien was accepted by the courts. This developed by custom of the trade from the practice,

---

[17] Kahn-Freund, *Law of Inland Transport*, 4th ed., pp. 405–406. *Electric Supply Stores* v. *Gaywood* (1909) 100 L.T. 855. *Cf.* Paton, *Bailment*, p. 285, who is less certain on this point: " It is very difficult to find conclusive authority relating to private carriers." For the forwarder's rights of lien against third parties see §§ 371 *et seq.*
[18] On the historical aspects see J. Story, *Law of Bailments*, 9th ed., 1878, pp. 457 *et seq.*
[19] (1851) 17 L.T.(o.s.) 271. See *W.L.R. Traders Ltd.* v. *B. & N. Shipping Agency Ltd.* [1955] 1 Lloyd's Rep. 554.
[20] *Halsbury's Laws*, Vol. 24, pp. 148–149. See also *Vacha* v. *Gillett* (1934) 50 Ll.L.Rep. 67, on the question as to whether a warehouseman is entitled to claim storage charges after having giving notice of his exercise of a lien over the goods.

as in the case of the factor, of giving credit to his clients.[21] As a consequence it can be seen that dependent on the particular operation being carried out by a forwarder, his rights of lien at common law may be either particular or general.

364   The problem is illustrated by the case of *Ahlers* v. *Broome*,[22] where a British agent made advances to foreign tomato growers, and retained the proceeds of sale. The question before the court was whether the plaintiff merchant who had handed over the shipment to the defendant agent on behalf of the growers could claim a general lien as a factor on the proceeds of sale for his advances without notice to the defendant. This the court rejected, holding that the plaintiff was merely "a shipping agent acting for himself and others who had combined to forward goods to this country for sale by the consignees here."[23] It can therefore be seen that this situation could easily create considerable problems in modern commerce, where it is not easy for a dividing line to be drawn between the various operations.[24] The difficulty essentially dates from the time when it was not customary for a forwarder to trade in general account with his customers, although such a practice is now quite normal.

(iv) *General Lien by Trade Usage and by Contractual Agreement*

365   Although historically, "General liens are not favoured by our law, and the courts are in general inclined against them,"[25] a right of general lien can be acquired by general trade usage or by implication of law, as in the case of the packer.[26] The question arose in a recent case as to whether any custom existed in the West Riding of Yorkshire of a general lien in favour of forwarders in the area. The defendant forwarder could not prove such a custom to the satisfaction of the court, nor as a result of the indecisive form of the contract used by the parties, one arising by agreement between them, nor did one arise out of their course of dealing. Accordingly the forwarder failed to justify the exercise of such a right.[27]

366 **Standard Trading Conditions**

As in practice the forwarder is in current account with his client, usually with a credit balance in favour of the forwarder, it is desirable that a right of general lien should be obtainable in case the customer is in financial difficulties. As can be seen from *Langley, Beldon & Gaunt Ltd.* v. *Morley*,[28] extreme difficulty exists in proving the existence of a

---

[21] *Green* v. *Farmer* (1768) 4 Burr. 2214 at p. 2222.   *Re Witt, ex p. Shubrook* (1876) 2 Ch.D. 489, C.A.
[22] (1938) 62 Ll.L.Rep. 163.
[23] *Ibid.* at p. 166, *per* Branson J.
[24] *Cf. Tellrite Ltd.* v. *London Confirmers Ltd.* [1962] 1 Lloyd's Rep. 236.
[25] Chitty, *op. cit.* 1824 at p. 544.
[26] *Ibid.* at p. 545.
[27] *Langley, Beldon & Gaunt Ltd.* v. *Morley* [1965] 1 Lloyd's Rep. 297.
[28] *Ibid.*

trade custom to this effect, as does the proof of a general lien arising from a course of dealing between the parties. The obvious alternative is to incorporate a general lien into the forwarder's standard trading conditions which is increasingly done. Unfortunately, it is by no means universal for all forwarders to be members of the Institute of Freight Forwarders, and thus no certainty that a comprehensive form of contract will be used by all those engaged in the trade, even if a standard form of contract is in fact used at all. However, the Standard Trading Conditions of the Institute do provide a right of general lien in Clause 23 in the following terms:

> "All goods (and documents relating to goods) shall be subject to a particular and general lien and right of detention for monies due either in respect of such goods or for any particular or general balance or other monies due from the Customer or the sender, consignee or owner to the [forwarder]."

Where therefore, forwarders trade under Standard Trading Conditions a contractual right of general lien can be enforced.[29]

367   The right was recognised by the courts in the case of *J. O. Lund Ltd.* v. *Anglo Overseas Transport Co. Ltd.*[30] Here the defendant forwarders were acting as intermediaries between an English buyer, the plaintiff, and an Italian seller in a series of import transactions in respect of various shipments of cloth, for which a running account existed. As stated by the court:

> ". . . there was a kind of tripartite relationship between the parties to this contract. The defendants, as forwarding agents, were acting as agents for the Italian vendors, to hold the goods in their warehouse pending payment by the plaintiffs, and at the same time, they were also acting as agents for the plaintiffs to safeguard and warehouse the goods and to clear them through the customs. So they were an intermediary between both of the principal parties to the contract." [31]

The normal procedure was for the forwarders to retain a consignment until a delivery note, issued by the seller and countersigned by the latter's bank, was presented by the buyer to them. By mistake, on this occasion, part of a shipment was delivered by the forwarders to the buyer against a delivery note that had not been countersigned by the bank. The forwarders therefore contacted the buyer and it was agreed that the latter would hold the parcel in question on behalf of the forwarders pending payment against the delivery order. Feeling themselves morally bound, the forwarders paid their Italian principal the price of the goods, and debited the buyer's account accordingly.

---

[29] *Cf.* Art. 19, D.F.C.; Arts. 16, 25, N.F.C.; Art. 15, N.Y.F.F.; Arts. 55–57, C.G. (Belgium); Arts. 54–55, Y.F.C.; Art. 10, C.G. (France); Art. 16, C.G. (Switzerland); Art. 36, C.G. (Italy); Art. 50, A.D.S.P.; Art. 15, F.B.L.
[30] [1955] 1 Lloyd's Rep. 142.
[31] *Ibid.* at p. 145.

Furthermore, as they had contracted with the buyer subject to Standard Trading Conditions, they attempted to exercise their contractual right of general lien over other goods.

The question therefore arose whether the forwarders were justified in debiting the buyer's account and in exercising their general lien in respect of the sum outstanding. The court held that although the forwarders had committed a breach of their contract with the seller by releasing the goods without proper authorisation, this did not deprive them of their rights against the buyer. Furthermore, a special agreement had been made that the buyer would hold the parcel in question on behalf of the forwarders with the additional implication that the buyer would indemnify the forwarders against any loss they might suffer from having paid the Italian seller and leaving the goods in their possession. The forwarders were therefore entitled to be indemnified by the buyer and had properly debited his account, and were justified in exercising their right of lien.[32]

368 Where, however, a seller of goods delivers them to a forwarder with instructions that he is to hold them to the order of the buyer, as the latter's agent, whether the forwarder will be able to exercise a contractual right of general lien against the buyer in respect of outstanding charges will depend upon whether property in the goods has passed to him or not. If property has passed to the buyer, the forwarder can validly exercise his right of general lien as his principal is now the true owner. If property has not passed, though, the forwarder will be liable to the seller for detention of the goods if he attempts to exercise his general lien. Similarly, if the buyer rejects the goods and this rejection is accepted by the seller so that property never passes, the forwarder is likewise precluded from exercising his general lien.[33] This will of course be a question of fact in each case.

369 **Stoppage in transit**

A problem that must be considered in relation to the exercise of both particular and general liens by forwarders, is whether such rights will take precedence over the seller's right of stoppage *in transitu*.[34] This right arises when the seller's right of lien has been extinguished by the goods leaving his possession. It can be exercised while goods are in the hands of a carrier prior to the buyer obtaining possession of them or transit ending.

The rule at common law is that the carrier's particular lien, and presumably the forwarder's, takes priority over the seller's right of stoppage *in transitu*, although there is no case law on this latter point. Where however there is a contractual right of general lien such as exists under Standard Trading Conditions, this will not have priority

---

[32] *Ibid.*
[33] *Black & Broom* v. *J. Coppo & Co.* (1922) 13 Ll.L.Rep. 279 at p. 347, and 14 Ll.L.Rep. 391 (C.A.). *Cf. O.M.S.A.* v. *Philippens & Co.* (1971) Nederlandse Jur., No. 203.
[34] s. 45, Sale of Goods Act 1893.

over the seller's rights of stoppage *in transitu*, unless there is "a clear agreement, express or implied, upon their part so to do." [35] Such priority seems to be intended by Clause 23 of Standard Trading Conditions, although again this point has not been considered by the courts as yet. However, such a right of general lien can only be invoked by the forwarder when he is in direct contractual relationship with the seller. Otherwise, if he is merely acting on behalf of the buyer or other consignee, there will be no privity of contract between forwarder and seller, and the normal common law rules will apply, that is, the seller's rights of stoppage *in transitu* will take priority. In any case, even where there is privity of contract between the forwarder and the seller, whether the former's contractual general lien takes precedence or not will ultimately depend upon the true construction of the particular contract. Equally, a forwarder may enter into a contract of carriage on behalf of a seller, and then be instructed to effect a stoppage *in transitu*. In such a case the seller will be subject to the carrier's right of particular lien for outstanding charges unless the latter has entered into any contractual agreement waiving such precedence.

370 **Contractual right of sale**

Finally, it should be noted that at common law the lien, whether particular or general, is purely a passive one, giving no right of sale, but merely a right of retention until outstanding charges have been paid.[36] This defect has, in practice, been overcome by the provision in Clause 23, Standard Trading Conditions, of a right of sale by auction or otherwise at the debtor's expense and the proceeds to be applied in total or part satisfaction of the lien. Such a right can be exercised within one month of notice being given to this effect if payment is not made in the meanwhile. A similar provision is found in R.H.A. Conditions under which a forwarder may operate. The sole difference is that no notice is required to be given to the debtor before a sale is effected.[37] Accordingly, provided a forwarder operates under Standard Trading Conditions or R.H.A. Conditions, the defects of the common law right of lien will be avoided, provided the party in question is a party to the contractual agreement.

(v) The Forwarder's Right of Lien in relation to Third Parties

371 The extent to which a forwarder's lien, whether particular or general, extends in relation to third parties is far from certain. The problem can be divided into four categories, dependent upon the particular function the forwarder is performing, that is, carriage, sending forwarder, sub-agent, and receiving agent. Each category will be dealt with in turn.

---

[35] *United States Steel Products Co.* v. *G.W.R.* [1916] 1 A.C. 189 at p. 204, *per* Lord Atkinson.

[36] A statutory right of sale does exist under Railway Clauses Consolidation Act 1845, s. 97, in respect of the Railways Board. In practice, though, General Conditions of Carriage render it unnecessary—Leslie, *Law of Carriage by Railway*, p. 449.

[37] Cl. 13, R.H.A. Conditions 1967. *Cf.* Cl. 15, B.R.S. Conditions.

372   Carrier—common and private

If the forwarder is acting as a common carrier, as mentioned above, a particular lien will exist even against the true owner of the goods, so that if property has passed to the consignee with whom the forwarder is not in contractual relationship if he is only acting on behalf of the seller, the lien will still attach irrespective of the absence of any contractual relationship with the consignee. However, under Standard Trading Conditions the forwarder is specifically stated not to be a common carrier.[38] Such a provision means that the right of particular lien can only be exercised as long as the consignor remains the owner of the goods. Consequently, no right of lien will attach against a buyer where property has passed to him, if the forwarder has the status of a private carrier when acting for the seller.[39] Only if the owner of the goods is in fact his principal, or otherwise a party to the contract, can the forwarder rely upon his contractual right of (general) lien.

373   Forwarding agent

If, on the other hand, the forwarder is to be considered not as a carrier, either common or private, but merely as an agent acting on behalf of the seller, he will only possess a particular lien in respect of debts due from his principal, and in exercising his rights he cannot deprive a third party of his existing rights, except in so far as his principal could have done so.[40] Accordingly it appears that a forwarder's rights of lien when acting simply as an agent will be more restricted than when he is operating as a carrier.

374   Sub-agent

Where a forwarder is a correspondent or sub-agent, he has the same right of lien against his principal as he would have had against the sending agent who employed him if the latter had been his principal.[41] Such a right is not affected by any settlement between the latter two. This will apply whether the lien is particular or general, provided the claims in question have arisen in the course of the sub-agency. Where a general lien is exercised over the principal's goods, although this right can extend to claims not arising from the particular sub-agency *vis-à-vis* the sending agent, the sub-agent's right of lien as against the principal cannot exceed those which the sending forwarder would have had against his principal if the goods had been in his possession instead of in that of the sub-agent.[42]

375   The question also arises whether the buyer or consignee will be subject to the forwarder's contractual right of general lien if the latter's

---

[38] Cl. 1, S.T.C.
[39] *Electric Supply Stores* v. *Gaywood*, note 17, above.
[40] *Brunton* v. *Electrical Engineering Co.* [1892] 1 Ch. 434 and Halsbury's *Laws*, Vol. 1, pp. 205–206.
[41] Bowstead, *Agency*, 13th ed., Art. 81 (2).
[42] *Mildred* v. *Maspons* (1883) 8 App.Cas. 874. *Cf.* Marine Insurance Act 1906, s. 53, and *Near East Relief* v. *King* [1930] 2 K.B. 40.

contract is with the seller. No problem need arise if the forwarder is also acting on behalf of the consignee in the transaction, providing he contracts subject to Standard Trading Conditions with both parties, so as to obtain a contractual general lien and uniformity of conditions of contract. If however the forwarder either fails to obtain a contractual general lien against the consignee or acts solely for the seller, he will not be able to exercise any right of general lien against the consignee, as " owner or consignee," unless the seller is in fact acting as agent for the latter, which will depend upon the particular conditions of sale.[43]

376   Receiving agent

A problem that has not yet come before the higher courts but is faced by forwarders from time to time is the extent of the lien applicable in respect of the clearance and forwarding of inward shipments.[44] A recent example will illustrate the point. A German forwarder was instructed by a client to ship household effects from Germany to England. He arranged with an English forwarder to clear and forward the goods inland to a furniture repository. The German forwarder asked the English receiving agent whether he required prepayment or not, and was told that it was not necessary, and that he would collect the charges himself from the consignee, who was the consignor's wife. This he was unable to do, a dispute then arising as to whether he could exercise a particular lien over the goods in the repository. As often occurs in inward clearance, Standard Trading Conditions had not been used as the basis of the contract, being primarily designed for outwards shipments. The only charges personally due to the English forwarder were his clearance charges,[45] the prime sum being that due to the German forwarder for forwarding and transportation. Accordingly, the English

---

[43] Cl. 2, S.T.C., provides that customers " expressly warrant that they are either the owners or authorised agents of the owners of any goods to which the transaction relates and further warrant that they are authorised to accept and are accepting these conditions not only for themselves but also as agents for and on behalf of all other persons who are or may thereafter become interested in the goods." Under Cl. 13, R.H.A. Conditions 1967, the right of general lien can only be exercised against the owner of goods in respect of moneys due from him. From the *United States Steel* case (note 35 above) it seems that the word " owner " in such cases must also include those with the right to demand delivery under a document of title. Otherwise a *non sequitur* would result if property did not pass until acceptance or delivery, that is, after the right of lien is lost.

[44] The question did come before the Mayor's Court in *Schenkers Ltd.* v. *Betancor & Co. Ltd.* (1939) April 15, *World's Carrier*, p. 318, but was not very adequately reported. However, goods had been consigned by a Belgrade forwarder through the plaintiff forwarder to the defendant consignee. The goods were a rotting shipment of plums, which the forwarder would only hand over to the consignee in return for a promise to pay the proceeds of sale to them less customs duty, to cover freight charges. The court held that the forwarder could enforce this promise. Judge Thomas pointed out that " the plaintiffs . . . insisted on having an express lien for freight . . . they are the receiving agents at this end . . . they do not seem to be in the position of carriers in such a way as would give them a lien . . . and therefore it is essential for them to show that they have got a lien because otherwise they may incur charges and have to pay for freight, etc." It is quite clear therefore that without a specific contractual provision the forwarder will not have any right of lien against a consignee in respect of his charges.

[45] See *Anglo-Overseas Transport Co. Ltd.* v. *David Zanellotti Ltd.* [1952] 1 Lloyd's Rep. 232 at p. 235, *per* Slade J.

forwarder could not claim a lien in respect of those charges not due to him, and no specific contract for C.O.D. had been made. In such a situation it seems that the forwarder is collecting as a sub-agent on behalf of the German forwarder, and therefore any rights of retention which he may have will be dependent on those held by the German forwarder, which are of cource those obtainable at German law. In such a situation it seems that unless a specific contract of C.O.D. is entered into, an English forwarder collecting on behalf of a foreign forwarder will be subject to the rights existing under the proper law of the forwarding contract, which he will exercise as the latter's agent. In this situation it will be necessary to establish whether such rights of retention or privilege are dependent upon the continued possession of the goods either by the foreign forwarder or an agent acting on his behalf, or whether such rights can exist, like the equitable lien, irrespective of continuing possession or not. If continued possession by the forwarder or his agent is necessary to exercise such rights, it will be necessary to establish whether in such a case the carrier or warehouseman holding the goods after transit is doing so as the agent of the consignee or the foreign forwarder, to determine whether the right has been lost or not. It appears however that upon the determination of the rights in question, the English courts would then apply the proper law of the contract, that is to say, those concepts in English law which are most analogous to those which would apply in Germany.[46]

As an alternative though, the problem could be overcome if a uniform practice could be established by the English forwarder not only in respect of debts due to him but also for those debts for which he had accepted the responsibility of collection on behalf of a foreign sending forwarder.[47] Admittedly, difficulties may occur in ensuring that the contract in question is subject to Standard Trading Conditions, that is, whether reasonable notice has been given to the other party, but this problem can usually be solved by a strict documentary procedure when contracting with clients.

(vi) *Unauthorised Carriage Contracts Entered into by a Forwarder*

377 The question must be considered as to whether a forwarder's principal will be subject to a carrier's right of lien where the forwarder has entered into a contract of carriage which is outside the scope of his authority.

---

[46] See Cheshire, *Private International Law*, 8th ed., pp. 231 *et seq.* and Chapter 4 above.
[47] " Now, ordinarily, . . . there is no privity of contract between a carrier or forwarding agent and a consignee. . . . True, a person having possession of goods and being willing to deliver them to any other person may, unless that other person is the owner of the goods or entitled to immediate possession of them—and he would not be entitled to immediate possession of them if the carrier [or forwarder] had a lien on the goods— make any contract he likes with the consignee . . . the contract being that in consideration of the forwarding agent, or the person having possession with or without a lien, parting with the possession of the goods, the consignee will pay the stipulated amount which he has agreed to pay." *Anglo-Overseas Transport Co. Ltd.* v. *David Zanellotti Ltd.* [1952] 1 Lloyd's Rep. 232 at p. 235, *per* Slade J.

No English authorities exist on this point, but the question was discussed in an Australian case on the subject.[48] Here the principle was laid down that if a forwarder is instructed by his principal to arrange a contract of carriage and negotiates a different one from that authorised, the shipper will still be subject to the carrier's right of lien for freight charges, notwithstanding the absence of authority, if the carrier is bound to carry the goods under the revised contract. In other words, following the general rules of agency, provided such an act is within the apparent or ostensible authority of the forwarder, his principal will be bound by his acts. Accordingly, where a forwarder (referred to in this case as a carrying agent) was instructed by the plaintiff's agent to forward goods to the plaintiff at B., he arranged with a carrier to do so, provided the latter could find a mate taking the same route. A waybill was therefore signed by the carrier undertaking to deliver at B. As he could not find a mate, he agreed with the forwarder to take the goods to W. As a result of this unauthorised act the plaintiff refused to pay the freight and sued the carrier for conversion when he attempted to exercise his right of lien in respect of the charges outstanding. The court held that although the forwarder had not been authorised to make a second contract of carriage so as to bind the plaintiff, as the carrier was bound to carry the goods under the new contract, he was consequently entitled to exercise his right of lien.

378   The effectiveness of such a lien must therefore depend upon either the ratification or implied authority of the principal, if express authority has not been given.[49] It is uncertain whether a carrier will be able to enforce his right of lien in the absence of these requirements, although he will be unable to do so in any case if he has notice of the forwarder's lack of authority.[50] At common law, therefore, the principal is placed in a relatively strong position where a forwarder has exceeded his authority. In the United States though, the Uniform Commercial Code places the carrier in a more favourable position by providing that the common carrier can exercise his right of lien " against the consignor or any person entitled to the goods unless the carrier had notice that the consignor lacked authority to subject the goods to such charges and expenses."[51] This provision removes the problem from the realm of agency law and its attendant uncertainties and places it purely on a statutory basis. Similarly under the Code the private carrier will have a valid lien against the consignor or anyone who permits a forwarder

[48] *Gallimore* v. *Moore* (1867) 6 S.C.R.(N.S.W.) 388, N.S.W. Sup.Ct.(F.C.).
[49] *Leaf* v. *Canadian Shipping Co.* (1878) 1 W.N. 220. In this case a bill of lading was signed by the appellants' shipping agent, a condition being that a right of lien existed in respect of the goods to be shipped " for all previous unsatisfied freights and charges due to them by the shippers or consignees." The right was exercised in respect of the shipping agent's debts due in respect of charges for other consignors' shipments. The court held that such a right of lien could not be validly exercised as it was beyond the powers of the shipping agent to bind his principal in such an extensive manner, the plaintiff therefore recovered dues which he had paid under protest.
[50] *Waugh* v. *Denham* (1865) 16 Ir.C.L.R. 405.
[51] S. 7–307, Uniform Commercial Code.

to have control or possession of the goods even if he has no real or implied authority, unless, as in the case of the common carrier above, he had notice of this fact.[52]

(vii) *Analogous Provisions in other Common Law Jurisdictions*

379 U.S.A.

Although the common law lien is found in virtually all other common law jurisdictions, certain differences, whether statutory or otherwise, warrant attention. Where a federal structure exists such as in the United States, the forwarder's lien may vary according to whether a particular transaction is inter-state or intra-state. As regards the former, the Interstate Commerce Act provides that all freight forwarders licensed in interstate commerce have the status of a common carrier.[53] Consequently the rights of lien will be identical to those of a common carrier, which will be either particular, as at common law, or else general if obtained by contractual agreement or by trade usage. There is apparently unanimity as to the extent of the common carrier's right of lien in the courts of England and the United States.[54] In intra-state transactions the Interstate Commerce Act does not apply.[55] The freight forwarder is not therefore treated as a common carrier unless he actually extends his operations so as to acquire the status of one, while still ostensibly acting as a forwarder.[56]

380 In his capacity as a forwarder though, it does not appear certain whether he actually possesses a right of lien analogous to that of the carrier, in the absence of any contractual agreement to this effect. In *Judson Freight Forwarding Co. v. Delaware L. & W. R. Co.*[57] a forwarder shipped goods by rail to New York under a bill of lading which provided that delivery could only be obtained in exchange for the instrument in question. The defendant, a connecting carrier, released the goods to the owner without presentation of the bill of lading issued by the initial carrier, and was subsequently sued by the forwarder for his charges and for freight paid to the carriers. In allowing recovery of the amount in question, the court stated that "Whether the plaintiff . . . be treated as a forwarder or as a common carrier, we think the law is clear that it would have a lien upon the [goods] for its charges and for the railroad's charges advanced by it."[58]

---

[52] *Ibid.*
[53] Part IV, s. 402 (5), Interstate Commerce Act.
[54] *American Jurisprudence*, 2d, Carriage, p. 497.
[55] The definition " interstate commerce " includes transportation "from or to any point in the United States to or from any point outside thereof, but only insofar as such transportation takes place within the United States ": s. 402 (6), Interstate Commerce Act.
[56] *Kettenhofen* v. *Globe Transfer & Storage Co.*, 70 Wash. 645.
[57] (1911) 163 Ill. App. 22.
[58] N.B. Since the enactment of Part IV, Interstate Commerce Act, there would be no distinction in such a case in respect of inter-state commerce, as the freight forwarder is expressly given common carrier status—s. 402 (5)—see § 38. See also *Heath* v. *Judson Freight Forwarding Co.* (1920) 47 Cal. App. 426. " Aside from its lien for lawful charges, a forwarding company cannot be allowed to defeat the owner's right to control the shipment."

This case concerned an interstate forwarding transaction, but in a case relating to a foreign freight forwarder the court made it clear that a forwarder does not possess any right of general lien apart from contract. In *Ettinge & Co.* v. *Atlantic Transport Co.*[59] a forwarder in New York regularly employed the defendant shipping company to transport its shipments to England. It normally received a sea bill of lading in favour of its English correspondent, but on this occasion bills of lading were made out to the order of the forwarder himself. The defendant delivered the bills of lading to the English correspondent who forwarded them in turn to the ultimate consignees. However, although it was not connected with the bills as such, a draft drawn by the plaintiff forwarder on the correspondent was attached to them, which the latter refused to honour. The plaintiff therefore sued the shipping company for breach of its contract of bailment by delivering the goods to the correspondent, instead of holding them to the plaintiff's order as per the bills of lading. The court however dismissed the action, pointing out that the plaintiff was merely a bailee itself, and had no lien upon any part of the shipment in respect of advances or charges due. It had no title to the goods except as a bailee, and suffered no legal damage as a result of the delivery.[60]

In practice though, the problem is largely solved, as in this country, by the use of standard trading conditions incorporating both a contractual right of general lien and a right of sale on non-payment of claims which remain unsatisfied within a certain time after a demand for payment has been made.[61] Consequently, providing such conditions are incorporated as the basis of the contract, there is no need to rely on the few conflicting precedents in this field.

381   Foreign freight forwarder

A peculiar situation has arisen in the case of the foreign freight forwarder. Under the Rules of the Federal Maritime Commission a person cannot obtain or retain a forwarding licence if he has a "beneficial interest" in a shipment to a foreign country. This has been defined as "any lien interest . . . arising by financing of the shipment."[62] In other words a distinction has been drawn between a right or lien in respect of "out-of-pocket expenses," which are specifically excluded from this limitation, and a right in respect of an advance of the invoice price of

---

[59] (1914) 160 App.Div. 635.

[60] In *Green* v. *Clarke* (1855) 12 N.Y. 343, Marvin J. expressed the opinion that where a forwarder of salt was paid freight by means of 90-day term bills, he was not entitled to a lien on the goods.

[61] Art. 15, N.Y.F.F.—" The Company shall have a general lien on any and all property (and documents relating thereto) of the Customer, in its possession, custody or control or en route, for all claims for charges, expenses or advances incurred by the Company in connection with any shipments of the Customer and if such claim remains unsatisfied for thirty (30) days after demand for its payment is made, the Company may sell at public auction or private sale, upon ten (10) days written notice, registered mail (R.R.R.), to the Customer, the goods, wares and/or merchandise, or so much thereof as may be necessary to satisfy such lien, and apply the net proceeds of such sale to the payment of the amount due to the Company. Any surplus from such sale shall be transmitted to the Customer, and the Customer shall be liable for any deficiency in the sale."

[62] Rule 510, 21 (1), F.M.C., General Order 4 and P.L. 87–254.

the goods. This distinction has been upheld by the courts on the grounds that it prevent forwarders from receiving freight discounts in the guise of shippers.[63] However, a forwarder is not in fact prohibited by the Rules from financing shipments, but merely from retaining a right of lien in such a case. Neither does it cover the payment by a forwarder to a supplier of funds advanced to him by letter of credit for the purpose.[64] Similarly, it appears that the guarantee of payment for goods is outside the restriction, but none of these points has as yet been subject to the scrutiny of the courts, and must therefore remain of uncertain outcome at present.

382 Australia

In Australia, which also possesses a federal structure, the domestic freight forwarder has been held to be a carrier, although not necessarily following a common calling, on the ground that although it arranges the transportation of goods between various inter-state points, it is not a mere forwarder because either by its servants or sub-contractors it has actual possession of the goods as a bailee during transit.[65] Foreign freight forwarders however are merely agents in so far as they do not actually carry themselves. The rights of lien will therefore depend on which class of operations are being carried out.[66]

383 South Africa

Finally, the position in South Africa demands individual attention as it is based upon the rules of Roman-Dutch law. Although certain tacit hypothecs, such as are found under the civil law, formerly existed, these disappeared with the passing of the Insolvency Act 1936. The equivalent of the English lien is the *jus retentionis*, which can, like the lien, be either general or particular. The former is only obtainable by a course of dealing or by trade custom. As in English law, the *Factoor* has by custom been given a general right of retention by the Dutch authorities over any goods or the proceeds of sale which are in their possession.[67] The forwarder on the other hand only possesses a particular right of retention according to the decision in *Patel* v. *Keeler & Co.*[68] where it was decided that as a forwarder must forward goods without delay unless instructed to the contrary, he is entitled to exercise a right of retention over them, but only until his principal has indemnified him in respect of carriage charges so incurred.[69]

[63] *New York Foreign Freight Forwarders, etc.* v. *U.S.*, 337 F.2d 289 at p. 297.
[64] Circular Letter, DDF-2, April 29, 1965, Director, *Bureau of Domestic Regulation of the F.M.C.* See Ullman, *Ocean Freight Forwarder*, Cornell, 1967.
[65] *Thomas National Transport (Melbourne) Pty. Ltd. & Pay* v. *May & Baker (Australia) Pty. Ltd.* [1966] 2 Lloyd's Rep. 347—their trading conditions excluded a common calling. See § 36.
[66] As S.T.C. are generally used, the position seems to be the same as in the United Kingdom.
[67] Burge 2–4.
[68] [1923] A.D. 506.
[69] " An agent for the landing . . . of goods has a lien . . . upon the goods for the amount of his reasonable expenses incurred in the landing . . . of the goods . . . and may

384   As regards the actual extent of the right of retention, Roman-Dutch law is not so restricted in its application as is the right of lien at common law. At common law, when the forwarder is merely acting as an agent, he will only possess such rights in the goods as his principal had at the time when the lien attached. In other words, it is subject to all third party equities which existed at that time,[70] with the exception of money and negotiable instruments which can be taken free from equities if the forwarder takes as a holder in due course.[71] Under Roman-Dutch law a distinction is drawn between "necessary" or "useful," and "voluptuous" expenses. In respect of the former, the right is *in rem*, that is, it can be exercised against the whole world. In the case of "voluptuous" expenses, provided they were properly incurred, a right of retention can exist, but only in respect of the agent's principal or those successors in title with whom he retains privity of contract.[72] Consequently, where the expenses incurred are "necessary" expenses, the forwarder possesses a wider right of retention under Roman-Dutch law than does his counterpart at common law.[73] However, if he is acting as a correspondent for another forwarder, his rights of retention as a sub-agent will be restricted to "necessary" and "useful" expenses which have actually benefited his principal, unless privity of contract exists between the parties.[74]

(viii) *Conclusion*

385   From the questions discussed in this section, the principal factor that emerges is the aura of uncertainty that shrouds the right of possessory lien which a forwarder can exercise. There appears to have been a definite reluctance on the part of the courts to define the various categories of lien which the commercial agent can exercise. This has placed the forwarder in a more difficult position than many other commercial intermediaries as the multiplicity of functions that he may be called upon to perform means that the extent of his rights of lien will differ from one part of his operations to another.

In particular, the arbitrary division between those operations which will ground a right of general lien at common law and those which will not, is quite inexplicable except on the basis of the economic quirks which faced the courts in the early decisions on the subject. Much seems to have turned on whether the agent gave financial advances to

---

therefore retain them until (paid) ": *Walker* v. *Durrant & Co.* (1883) 2 S.C. 361 at p. 365, *per* De Villiers C.J.
    As to the carrier's right of lien for freight see *Standard Bank* v. *Wilman, Spithause & Co.* (1886) 6 S.C. 17. See also *Anderson & Co.* v. *Pienaar & Co.* (1922) T.P.D. 435. N.B. The Standard Trading Conditions introduced in 1966 by the South African Shipping and Forwarding Association are very similar to S.T.C.
[70] *Peat* v. *Clayton* [1906] 1 Ch. 659.
[71] *Tindall* v. *Barnett* (1887) 3 T.L.R. 476.
[72] Villiers & Macintosh, *South African Law of Agency*, 1957, p. 204.
[73] *Patel* v. *Keeler & Co., supra.*
[74] See note 72.

his client. This the factor commonly does, but the reasons for extending this right to the packer seems to be extremely tenuous. Likewise, the distinction drawn in *Tellrite Ltd.* v. *London Confirmers Ltd.*[75] between the confirmer and the factor seems to be illogical if the basis of the general lien is the financial responsibility undertaken by the agent. To grant such a right to the latter, while denying it to the former, merely on the grounds of obsolescent precedents point to a system of precedent gone mad.

Similarly, for the modern forwarding organisation with its integrated packing and warehousing facilities to find that on one statement of account for a customer the rights of lien will differ from item to item does not seem to reflect commercial reality on the part of the courts. Admittedly it is possible in many cases to obtain a contractual right of general lien, but the forwarder can never be sure in the case of new accounts whether the initial contract will be subject to Standard Trading Conditions or not owing to the rules concerning reasonable notice. The only valid criterion for a right of general lien seems to be whether the trade in question normally operates in general account with its customers. If the answer is in the affirmative, it is only logical for the agent to be given a right of general lien at common law, without the need for hair-splitting decision based upon outdated precedents. As the forwarder customarily trades on general account such a right should be accorded to him, as it is to the packer, factor and banker, on the grounds that with modern forwarding methods it is a mere anachronism for such a right not to be granted.

3. RIGHTS UNDER THE CIVIL LAW

386 At common law the principal criterion is whether a right of lien exists or not, and if so whether it is particular or general. In the civil law, as mentioned earlier, the position is considerably more complex. The forwarder's rights over his client's goods in respect of outstanding charges fall into two broad categories. First, those preferential rights which are analogous to the pledge or charge, which may either be express or implied by statute. Secondly, there is the right of retention which is essentially the same as the lien at common law. These rights are basically similar in purpose in the various civil law jurisdictions, but may be founded upon different juridical bases. It is therefore necessary to consider the two classes of rights in relation to the principal civil law jurisdictions in turn.

(i) *Rights of Preference*

387 **France**

In considering the rights of preference of the forwarder, it must be noted that the rights of the commissionnaire and the carrier do not always coincide. Such a divergence is particularly noticeable in French law, and is of interest considering the French concept that the commissionnaire

---

[75] See note 24.

de transport is fully responsible for carriage himself.[76] The privilège is defined by Article 2095 C.C. as "un droit que la qualité de la créance donne à un créancier d'être préferé aux autres créanciers, même hypothécaires."

388 Extent of right

It is twofold in effect. First, it offers a preferential right of payment of outstanding debts due to the creditor. Secondly, it is exercisable over the debtor's movables, which can be realised if necessary by means of a judicial sale. One of the most important characteristics of the privilège is the principle that one can only exist where the legislature has created such a right—in other words there can be no privilège *sans texte*.[77] Privilèges can either be general, that is, attaching to a debtor's possessions or else particular, attaching only to certain things. They can either attach to immovables or movables. The latter category, privilèges mobiliers, may be established by special laws. The carrier's right of privilège was established by Article 2102 (6) C.C. That of the commissionnaire de transport is sanctioned by Article 95 C.com., which grants such a right to all classes of commissionnaire in general.[78]

389 Carrier and commissionnaire compared

Whereas the carrier's privilège is specifically defined as covering "les frais de voiture et les dépenses accessoires"[79] the privilège of the commissionnaire extends to virtually all types of charges relating to the contract of commission. It covers payment of commission charges and advances and has developed from the practice of trading on general account.[80] By contrast with the common law lien which is merely passive, both the forwarder's and the carrier's privilège are active, and permit the holder of the privilège to exercise his rights of preference over the proceeds where a judicial sale has been effected, if such proves necessary.

One important difference between the rights of privilège of the commissionnaire and the carrier lies in the subject matter of the charge. The privilège of the commissionnaire can be exercised over any of the debtor's goods which are in his possession in respect of debts arising from the execution of contracts of commission relating to goods other than those over which the right is exercised.[81] In other words, in so far as a comparison is valid, such a right will produce a similar result to

---

[76] See Rodière, *Droit des transports*, Section 1347.

[77] Req. May 18, 1831, *Grands Arrêts*, no. 192.

[78] Rouen, March 7, 1906 (sous Civ. July 27, 1909) D.P. 1910.1.345, note by M. Lacour concerning the early disputes as to whether the commissionnaire de transport was covered or not—Rodière, *op. cit.*, Section 1336.

[79] Art. 2102 (6), C.C.

[80] Art. 95, C.com.; Rodière, *op. cit.*, Section 1337. *Cf.* the position in England.

[81] Agen, March 18, prec. Lyon, March 13, 1933, S., 1934.2.45. Planiol & Ripert, *Traité pratique de droit civil français*, 2nd ed., XII, Section 173 *bis*,—*i.e.* "current account"— a privilege exists on the credit balance which eventually exists in favour of the commissionnaire—Hemard, *Contrats Commercials*, II.731, cass.fr. Nov. 25, 1872, D.P., 1872.I.436.—it is lost however if it is mixed with other credits: *cf.* Belgium, Van Ry *Principes de droit commercial*, Section 1826.

the right of general lien at common law. However, it should be noted that the forwarder only possesses the latter right by contractual agreement, whereas the privilège of the commissionnaire is implied into all contracts of commission by virtue of the statute. By contrast, the carrier's right of privilège is limited by the concept of unité d'expédition, which means that the privilège can only be exercised over such goods as have been shipped under the same lettre de voiture as those in respect of which the charges are outstanding.[82]

The commissionnaire is therefore placed in a more favourable position than the carrier, as he can exercise his rights of privilège over shipments totally unconnected with those in respect of which the debt is due. It was pointed out in one case that this was intended to prevent a commissionnaire from paralysing his client by the need to retain each shipment until all charges relating to it had been paid.[83] If however the commissionnaire actually performs part of the transit himself, the law will then treat him as a carrier and his rights of privilège will be accordingly restricted, in so far as they appertain to the transit actually performed by the commissionnaire.[84]

390 Sub-agent

Where a sub-agent is employed, the latter may claim rights of privilege over a shipment in respect of payment due from the principal commissionnaire. This will be restricted though to charges outstanding in respect of the goods in question and cannot be invoked in respect of charges outstanding for other transactions.[85]

391 Right based upon possession

The right of privilège given by Article 95 C.com., can only be exercised subject to the conditions prescribed by Article 92, C.com. This provides that the commissionnaire must have possession of the goods or they must be held by a third party who is intermediary between the parties. Such possession is deemed to exist when the goods are in transit, in customs or in a public warehouse or by possession of a bill of lading or lettre de voiture.[86] The commissionnaire's privilège will be lost if either he surrenders possession to the consignee, or if the carrier holds them to the latter's order.[87]

392 Priorities

A problem which often faces the commissionnaire in the exercise of his right of privilège occurs where a vendor has consigned goods for

---

[82] Rodière, op. cit., Section 771; Planiol, op. cit., Section 772.

[83] Paris, April 26, 1941, Gaz. Pal., 1941.II.28.

[84] It should be noted that the enterprise de déménagement is in a peculiar position, being treated as a commissionnaire in respect of operations not performed by it. Consequently it enjoys the privilege of Art. 95, C.com., not Art. 2102 (6), C.C.

[85] Rouen, May 15, 1959, J.C.P. 1959.II.192. Cf. Art. 50 (b), A.D.S.P., at note 132.

[86] Art. 92, C.com.

[87] Cf. the captain of a ship has a right of preference over goods for his freight for a period of 15 days after delivery providing they have not passed into the hands of a third party—Art. 307, C.com. As to involuntary loss of possession—see Rodière, op. cit., Section 772.

which he has not been paid. The general rule is that in such a case the commissionnaire's right would take priority over that of the vendor. This follows because the commissionnaire's right of privilège is based upon the concept of a gage or pledge the priority of which is based upon actual possession. However, where such failure has taken place before the goods in question have actually been delivered, the difficulty that faces the commissionnaire in such a situation is the requirement by the courts that he must act *de bonne foi*.[88]

No problem occurs where the commissionnaire has no knowledge concerning the question of payment of the seller, as he can then fulfil the requirement of good faith as a prerequisite to exercising his right of privilège. Where however, as quite often occurs, goods are shipped "contre remboursement" or C.O.D., the commissionnaire is perforce aware that the seller has not been paid by the buyer, and cannot therefore fulfil the requirement of good faith. Consequently, his right of privilège will be deferred to that of the unpaid seller.[89] In such circumstances the commissionnaire's right of privilège will not afford him any satisfactory remedy, so that it will be necessary to exercise his right of retention to secure payment of his charges and commission. This right however will only be particular and not general. The commissionnaire will therefore only be able to retain against those amounts outstanding in respect of the shipment in question, but not for payments due on a general account.[90] Equally, a sub-agent cannot invoke the protection of Article 2279, C.C., against the claim of a consignor, as he is not a holder in good faith within the meaning of the Article, as he is fully aware that the principal commissionnaire from whom he has received the goods has no personal rights over them.[91]

393   Conditions Générales

Provision is also made in Article 10 of the French Conditions Générales des Transitaires whereby a right of retention and preference is imposed on all goods, etc., with which the forwarder is entrusted, in respect of all debts whether related to the goods retained or not. In other words the particular right is extended to secure debts due on general account.

394

Finally, it should be noted that the commissionnaire de transport can only exercise a right of privilège when acting in his own name. If he acts in the name of his principal, he will merely have the rights

---

[88] Civ., sect. com., Dec. 15, 1947, D.1948.112; Art. 2279, C.C.; *cf.* Belgium, Brussels, Nov. 25, 1959, Jur.com.Brux., 1960.26. *Cf.* The Italian Civil Code gives both the carrier and the forwarder a right of privilège for charges due—Art. 2761, C.C. It is also provided that their privilège takes priority over third parties' rights, provided they act in good faith—Art. 2756, C.C. Also a right of sale is given according to the rules for the sale of a pledge.

[89] See Hemard, *Contrats Commerciaux*, II.928.

[90] See Rodière, note J.C.P., 1959.II.192.

[91] Req. Nov. 21, 1927, D.P. 1928.1.172, rapport de M. le conseiller Bricout.

of an ordinary agent under the civil law, that is, subject to the rules of mandat ordinaire, which will only give him the right of retention.[92]

395 Belgium

The position of Belgium closely follows the French rules and classification, but some important differences do exist which warrant discussion. The commissionnaire de transport (affréteur routier) has been assimilated to the position of a carrier by statute.[93] Consequently, in contrast with the French position, the commissionnaire de transport does not possess the privilège of a commissionnaire, but only that of a carrier.[94] The equivalent of the commissionnaire de transport in French law is designated a commissionnaire-expéditeur, who possesses a similar right of privilège.[95] Likewise, he must act in his own name if he does not wish to be treated merely as a mandataire ordinaire.[96] The principal difference therefore seems to be that the forwarder by land is often equated with a carrier as a matter of course in Belgium, whereas in France he can be treated as falling into either category dependent upon the particular operation in question. Upon his particular status, the right of privilège will therefore depend.[97]

Under Belgian law, as in France, the commissionnaire-expéditeur has an advantage over the carrier (and commissionnaire de transport) in as much as he is not subject to the principle of unité d'expédition.[98] However, the Belgian carrier does possess one advantage which his French counterpart does not, as his right of privilège is extended for a period of twenty-four hours after delivery of the goods to their owner or the consignee, unless possession, in the sense of a right to ownership, has been transferred to a third party by the latter within that period.[99]

---

[92] Art. 94, C.com.; Art. 1984, C.C.; Crim. July 24, 1852, D.P. 52.1.255.

[93] Art. 2, etc., law of August 25, 1891. This does not apply to commissionnaires of air or waterway transport. See Fredericq, *Traité de Droit commercial Belge*, Vol. 3, p. 376. See § 107.

[94] For the history of the matter see Rodière, Rev.Trim.dr.comm., 1957, p. 535. Cass., Nov. 5, 1936, Pas. 1936, I.407.

[95] Cass., Nov. 5, 1936, Pas., 1936.I.407, Van Ryn, *op. cit.*, Sections 1822 *et seq.* The Belgian privilège covers all loans, advances and payments made by the commissionnaire and also interest, commission and charges—Liv. I, Tit. VII, Art. 14 (1)–(3), C.com. Cass. Sep. 4, 1958, J.P.A., 1960, 195.

[96] Van Ryn, *op. cit.*, Section 1800.

[97] See Chapter 2.

[98] This means that where there are several shipments under one lettre de voiture, the carrier can exercise his right of privilège over the last shipment in respect of dues due on the whole transaction. Comm. Liège, August 27, 1915, Jur. Liège, 1919.62.

[99] Art. 20, 7 de la loi hypothecaire, Dec. 16, 1851—*i.e.* he has a gage tacit because the value of the goods is increased by transit—Fredericq, *op. cit.*, Vol. 3, p. 451.—*Cf.* the position under Art. 440 HGB, where three days of grace are given. See § 399. *Cf.* The Spanish Commercial Code gives a forwarder a right of privilège over goods either in his actual possession or at his legal disposal for all charges including commission. This right can be exercised up to eight days after the forwarder has given up possession of them. Arts. 276, 375, Codigo Comm. N.B. No trading conditions have been obtainable.

396   Conditions Générales (Belgium)

The Belgian Conditions Générales make specific provisions to protect the forwarder's rights. This is achieved in two distinct ways. First, provision is made in Article 55 of the Conditions that all claims recognised by law are exercisable as a single right, whether in respect of different shipments or goods which are no longer in the commissionnaire's possession. The effect of this condition is to consolidate all rights which the forwarder may possess, whether in the capacity of a commissionnaire-expéditeur or as a carrier. Secondly, in addition to those rights existing at law, as modified by Article 55 above, Article 56 of the Conditions gives a right of gage or pledge which is subject to the rules governing commercial gage. This extends over all goods, documents, etc., which either notionally or literally come into the possession of the commissionnaire after the first forwarding instructions have been given. It can be exercised against both the consignor and the owner of the goods.[1]

397   Holland

The Burgerlijk Wetboek does not explicitly give the forwarder a right of privilège in respect of goods forwarded. This is more restrictive than the French and Belgian provisions, as the privilège of the carrier only covers the cost of freight and related expenses.[2] However, in practice "related expenses" also cover the disbursements of the forwarder but following the text of Articles 1185 (7), 1193, B.W., the forwarder does not possess any right of privilège with regard to his own expenses and commission.[3] Some jurists consider, though, that the forwarder's right of privilège is not based upon Articles 1185 (7) and 1193, B.W., on the grounds that these sections only relate to the carrier's privilège. They therefore argue that the forwarder who has paid the carrier's freight and expenses is subrogated to the latter's rights against the other parties to the affreightment pursuant to Article 1438 (3), B.W.

398   Germany

The German system of preferential rights is similar in concept to those discussed above, but is more clear cut and systematic. Apart from the right of retention, which will be discussed later, the HGB gives a statutory form of pledge to certain categories of commercial agent over goods which they have received from their client to secure the various charges due to them.[4] Accordingly, by Article 410 HGB the

---

[1] *Cf.* Art. 19 (2), D.F.C.; Art. 10, C.G. (France), at note 47 to § 411. Art. 16, C.G. (Switzerland), provides that where goods are remitted to a forwarder to be forwarded or stored and they have already reached him, they will serve as a gage for the balance of all dues outstanding on general account between consignor and forwarder. Art. 36, C.G. (Italy) gives a right of privilège and retention on general account.

[2] Art. 1185 (7), B.W., in conjunction with Art. 1193, B.W. *Cf.* France: Art. 95, C.com.; Germany: Art. 410, HGB; Belgium: Liv. I, Tit. VII, Art. 14 (1–3), C.com.

[3] But see retention at § 413.

[4] " Pfandrecht " (pledge) is a charge on a movable created to secure the performance of an existing or future obligation, the pledgee being entitled to satisfy his claim against the pledgor out of the object pledged.

Spediteur is given a statutory pledge in respect of the goods which he is to forward. Also, as he is himself permitted to carry, and will be treated as a carrier in respect of such part of the transit as he himself may perform, a similar right is available to him as a carrier under Article 412, HGB. Article 410 provides that the Spediteur can exercise his right of pledge over the goods forwarded by way of security for freight, commission, other expenditure and for advances made on the goods.[5] The carrier's right of pledge extends to cover all claims arising out of the contract of carriage, demurrage, duties and any advances made on the security of the goods.[6] However, unlike the French right of privilège, the commercial pledge does not give any rights to secure debts due on general account. The right is merely particular to the goods secured. A sub-agent is also permitted to exercise such rights as the principal Spediteur possesses, and in particular his right of pledge.[7] Also, if the Spediteur's claims have been satisfied by the sub-agent, the latter will be subrogated to his rights. Similarly, if the sub-agent satisfies the carrier's claims in place of the principal Spediteur, he will be subrogated to the carrier's rights himself.[8]

399 Possessory right

The Spediteur's rights of pledge only exist as long as he is in possession of the actual goods, or else can exercise a right of disposal over them by means of a bill of lading or warehouse receipt.[9] However, to protect the claims of Spediteurs and successive carriers, unless otherwise provided by the letter of advice, the last carrier in possession of the goods in a successive carriage must collect any amounts owing to the former. He is therefore permitted to exercise their rights of pledge which will remain in existence until the last carrier's right of pledge is extinguished.[10] This contrasts with the carrier's right of pledge, which can be exercised judicially for a period of three days after delivery to the consignee, provided the goods remain in the latter's possession. If the carrier fails to obtain payment on delivery and does not enforce his right of pledge by judicial process within a period of three days of delivery to the consignee, he will be liable to the Spediteur (and preceding carriers) for any loss suffered.[10a] Conversely, the defaulting carrier will lose any rights of indemnity which he may possess against preceding carriers or Spediteurs, who will be similarly affected in turn. His claim against the consignee will remain unaffected, though.[11]

400 A.D.S.P.

As in the case of the privilège, the pledge is implied by law, and

[5] *Cf.* the position in the U.S.A. at §§ 379 *et seq.*
[6] Art. 440, HGB.
[7] Art. 411, HGB; see. Art. 50 (*b*), A.D.S.P., at note 31 to § 407.
[8] Art. 411 (2), HGB.
[9] Art. 410. The right of disposal by the various documents listed in Art. 410 is a form of possession—see Art. 424, HGB.
[10] Art. 441, HGB.   [10a] Art. 440, HGB.
[11] Art. 442, HGB.

therefore no contractual agreement is necessary for a forwarder to exercise his rights. However, as in the case of the Belgium Conditions Générales, the German A.D.S.P. does make special contractual provision extending the statutory right of pledge, but as the contractual provisions are mainly applicable both to the pledge and the right of retention, the provisions in question will be discussed below in relation to the latter.[12]

401   Exercise of pledge—sale

Unlike the commercial lien, the pledge is a *jus in rem* which can be exercised against the whole world. However, it should be noted that if the Spediteur receives the goods from a person who is neither the owner nor has the right to dispose of them, he will only be able to exercise his legal pledge if he has received the goods in good faith.[13] The forwarder has a right to satisfy his debt by selling the property which forms the subject of it, but whereas under the commercial lien, discussed below,[14] a court order is necessary to authorise such a sale, under the commercial pledge no such authorisation is required. However, before exercising his right of sale the forwarder must notify the owner of the goods where practicable, and by Article 368, HGB, a period of one week must elapse between such notice and the actual sale, or if such notification is impossible, time will run from the date when the right of sale arose.[15] The same rule applies in the case of the carrier, but with the proviso that such notice must normally be given to the consignee, but if the latter cannot be found or refuses to accept the goods, the notification must be sent to the consignor.[16]

402   Priorities

Finally, where competing claims exist over the same goods, they will normally rank inversely to the date of creation, the later rights taking precedence over the earlier ones. However, any rights of pledge which may have arisen out of the activities of commission merchants or warehousemen will give precedence to those rights which pertain to the forwarding or carrying of goods. The latter rights will also take priority over any rights of pledge which a forwarder or carrier may have to secure any advances they may have made.[17] Consequently, if, as often happens, the business of forwarding is combined with that of warehousing or factoring, those rights exercised in the latter capacities will give precedence to those rights exercised as a forwarder or carrier and to any third parties exercising similar rights. A parallel may be seen in

---

[12] See § 405.
[13] See Art. 366, HGB; Arts. 932–935, 1207, BGB. Art. 366 (3), HGB, applied equally to carriers and warehousemen too.
[14] See § 409.
[15] This replaces the period of one month required under Art. 1234, BGB.
[16] Art. 440 (4), HGB.
[17] Art. 443, HGB. These provisions are based upon the reasoning that those bringing goods to their destination have enhanced their value, and therefore deserve greater priority over other creditors.

the position of the forwarder at common law who also acts as a packer or factor, where the reverse situation prevails, the forwarder having more extensive rights in the latter capacity than as a mere forwarder.[18]

(ii) *The Forwarder's Right of Retention at Civil Law*

403　From the discussion in the last section, it can be seen that the right of privilege and the statutory pledge are concepts for which no parallel exists at common law. By contrast, in the right of retention we find a concept which is closely analogous to the common law lien, both particular and general. However, the extent of the right will vary from country to country, being in some jurisdictions wider in application than at common law, and in others of narrower scope. To balance these variations where standard trading conditions are in use, it is customary to extend the right of retention contractually, so that the actual rights of the forwarder do not in fact differ from one country to another in practice. The binding effect of such provisions will depend upon whether a client is bound by the terms of the forwarding contract, which in turn will depend upon the application of the general principles of contract. It is therefore necessary to consider the provisions governing the right of retention in the principal civil law jurisdictions, together with the standard trading conditions of the respective trade associations where these are relevant.

404　Germany

Perhaps the most interesting form of lien is found under German law. This is characterised by the existence of both a civil law and commercial law right of retention, which are dealt with in the BGB and the HGB respectively.[19] Both rights can be exercised over the movable property owned by a debtor to secure the payment of moneys due.[20] The right exercisable under the BGB is analogous to the common law particular lien, as it is only exercisable for claims arising from the same transaction in respect of which the right of retention has been exercised. On the other hand, the right of commercial lien given by Article 369 can be exercised in respect of a general account for all outstanding debts. It can therefore be equated with the common law general lien, except that the forwarder can only obtain the latter contractually, at least, as regards his forwarding operations.[21] However,

---

[18] See § 363.

[19] Arts. 369–372, HGB; Art. 273, BGB: lien=Zurückbehaltungsrecht. Possession can be actual or constructive, that is, through bills of lading, carrier's receipts and warehouse receipts: Art. 369, HGB.

[20] *Cf.* the position in Switzerland where the forwarder has a right of retention upon all goods concerned, as well as on the proceeds of sale thereof—Art. 434, C.O., and Art. 895, C.C. This right covers all charges and the forwarder's commission. It should be noted that in respect of actual transit performed by a forwarder, Art. 439, C.O., provides that he is to be treated as a carrier and not as a commissionnaire, in which case if a consignee contests the charges payable on a consignment, he can only claim delivery if he deposits the amount in question with the court. This will be treated as a substitute for the carrier's right of retention—Art. 451, C.O.

[21] See § 365.

Article 370, HGB, goes further, inasmuch as it permits the commercial lien to be exercised in respect of debts which will accrue *in futuro* as well as those which have already accrued. This is only permitted in two cases though, first, where the debtor has been adjudicated bankrupt or has suspended payments, or secondly, if execution has been levied on the debtor's property, but not satisfied.[22]

405   A.D.S.P.

However, A.D.S.P. extends both the right of pledge and lien to all claims whether matured or *in futuro*, which he may have against the principal in respect of any of the services listed in Article 2 (*a*), A.D.S.P., that is, forwarding, warehousing, carrying, advances, etc.[23] The effect of this provision is that any contract subject to A.D.S.P. will not be restricted by the limits imposed by Articles 369–370, HGB, in respect of future claims. However, the right of lien or pledge can only be exercised where claims, present or future, are not in dispute, or the financial standing of the debtor endangers the forwarder's claims, if they do not relate to the goods in question.[24]

406   Rights against third parties

By contrast with the statutory pledge, discussed above, the lien, whether civil or commercial, is only a *jus in personam*, against the debtor, and not a *jus in rem*.[25] No right of lien can be created over goods which are not owned by the debtor, even if the forwarder has acted in good faith,[26] although if the debtor was the owner of the goods at the time that the forwarder obtained possession of them, he will be deemed to remain so as regards the forwarder's right of satisfaction, until the forwarder is aware that he has ceased to be so.[27] Moreover, if a forwarder obtains an enforceable judgment against his client, it will hold good against any third party who has acquired ownership after the forwarder has obtained possession of the goods, provided that the latter is not aware of the change of ownership at the time when he commenced legal proceedings.[28] Otherwise, the forwarder's right of lien will hold good against a third party if the defences which can be set up against the debtor can also be set up against the third party.[29]

However, A.D.S.P. provides that where a forwarder is instructed to hold goods to the order of a third party or to surrender them to one, the forwarder can only exercise his right of pledge or lien against the third party in respect of claims not relating to the goods in question if this does not cross the instructions of the principal or impair his legitimate interests.[30] In such circumstances therefore the forwarder will

[22] Art. 370 (1), HGB.
[23] Art. 50 (*a*), A.D.S.P.
[24] Art. 50 (*c*), A.D.S.P.
[25] See § 401.
[26] *Cf.* pledge at § 401; Art. 366 (3), HGB; Arts. 932–935, BGB; Art. 1207, BGB.
[27] Art. 372, HGB.
[28] Art. 372 (2), HGB.
[29] Art. 369 (2).
[30] Art. 50 (*d*), A.D.S.P.

only have a particular right of pledge or lien in relation to the third party.

407   As regards the exercise of the extended contractual right of pledge by one forwarder against another, A.D.S.P. has provided that in so far as the rights given under Article 50, A.D.S.P., exceed the legal rights of pledge or lien, the sub-agent can only exercise them in respect of goods which belong to the principal forwarder, or which the sub-agent can consider as belonging to the latter, such as furniture vans, sheets, etc.[31] In other words the sub-agent is prevented from obtaining security on goods belonging to third parties which he is handling on behalf of another forwarder, or those in respect of which reasonable doubt as to ownership may exist. Such a provision helps to prevent an indiscriminate use by a sub-agent of the rights given him by Article 50, A.D.S.P.

408   The forwarder's right of lien will be excluded though if it is inconsistent with any instructions given to the forwarder by the debtor before or at the time of delivery of the goods, or with any obligation on the part of the forwarder to deal with the goods in a specified manner.[32] This restriction will not apply if the fact of the debtor's bankruptcy or unsatisfied execution, as referred to in Article 370 (1), HGB, above,[33] does not become known to the forwarder until after he has taken delivery of the goods or the other obligations referred to have been created.[34] These restrictions have, in practice, been largely overcome by a provision in A.D.S.P. excluding the operation of Article 369 (3), HGB, on all contracts subject to the Conditions.[35]

409 Sale
     The Spediteur has an advantage over his common law colleague inasmuch as a statutory right of sale is given him by Article 371, HGB. In other words the German commercial lien is an active one unlike the common law equivalent, where the right of sale must be obtained contractually.[36] Furthermore, A.D.S.P. makes provision for the forwarder to charge a sales commission on the gross proceeds of sale where a right of sale is exercised under this Article.[37] This right is to be exercised under the procedure laid down for the civil law pledge,[38] although as in the case of the Spediteur's statutory pledge the period of grace is reduced from one month to one week.[39] However, this right, unlike the statutory pledge, can only be exercised if a court order authorising the sale is obtained.[40] No right of sale exists at all under the rules of the civil law lien.[41]

[31] Art. 50 (*b*), A.D.S.P.
[32] Art. 369 (3), HGB.
[33] See note 22 to § 404.
[34] Art. 370 (2), HGB.
[35] Art. 50 (*f*), A.D.S.P.
[36] Cl. 23, S.T.C.
[37] Art. 50 (*h*), A.D.S.P.
[38] Art. 1234, BGB.
[39] Arts. 371 (2), 368, HGB.
[40] Art. 371 (3), HGB.
[41] Art. 273, BGB.

410   One important restriction on the exercise of the commercial lien by a forwarder must be noted. Article 369 (1), HGB, provides that the lien is only applicable in respect of debts due from one merchant to another. No such restriction exists in the application of Article 366, HGB, in relation to the forwarder's statutory pledge, where the contract of forwarding, or carriage, need only be a mercantile contract on one side. As a result the forwarder has been faced with the problem that the HGB does not permit him to exercise a right of commercial lien in respect of a large number of his clients, who through the very nature of his business are not merchants at all. The importance of this limitation lies in the fact that neither the civil law nor the commercial pledge give any rights of preference or retention in respect of debts due on general account.[42] Accordingly, provision has been made in the A.D.S.P. that by contractual agreement the forwarder's rights of commercial lien which the law permits him when dealing with merchants, will be extended to all other categories of client.[43] This avoids the problem in practice, as A.D.S.P. is in almost universal use in Germany.

It can therefore be seen that the distinction between the exercise of the Spediteur's rights of pledge and lien has been blurred to a considerable extent by the application of A.D.S.P. to forwarding transactions. Consequently, although the juridical basis of the pledge and commercial lien are quite distinct in German law, the practical result is much the same.

411   France and Germany—comparison

As in German law so in French law a distinction must be drawn between the preferential rights of privilège and the simple droit de retention. First, the droit de retention only operates in respect of a debt affecting the retained article. It therefore equates with the German civil law lien and the particular lien at common law. It contrasts with the French law privilège and the German commercial lien which are both exercisable on general account, as regards the forwarder.[44] The droit de retention does not give any rights of preference, but is solely based upon possession. The droit de retention is not restricted to the forwarder who acts in his own name as is the right of privilège, which is only granted to the commissionnaire de transport and not to the ordinary mandataire.[45] The reason for this is that the relationship between commissionnaire and principal remains that of a salaried mandat. The right of retention will therefore merely be that of an ordinary mandataire, which is provided for in the Code Civil.[46] The carrier's rights of retention are similar.

---

[42] See § 398.

[43] Art. 50 (f), A.D.S.P.

[44] The distinction between the droit de retention and the privilège was discussed in the judgment of the Cour de Lyon, July 2, 1934, S., 1935.2.11.

[45] See § 393. Art. 94, C.com.

[46] By Art. 1948, C.C., a droit de retention is granted to the dépositaire of goods—this right has been extended by the courts to the contract of mandat—Civ. Jan. 17, 1866, D.P. 1.77.

Unlike privilège, no right of sale exists under the droit de retention —again in this respect it equates with the German civil lien and the common law lien, which are similarly merely passive rights. The privilège can only be exercised against the creditor, being merely a *jus in personam* and not a *jus in rem* as is the right of retention. The latter will cease on loss of possession of the goods unlike the right of privilège. As in the case of A.D.S.P. provision is made in the French Conditions Générales whereby a right of retention is contractually imposed on all goods, etc., with which the forwarder is entrusted, in respect of all debts whether relating to the goods retained or not. In other words the particular right is extended to secure debts due on general account.[47]

412   Belgium

The position in Belgian law accords very closely with that in French law, both in regard to statutory provisions and jurisprudence.[48] It does not therefore warrant further discussion, within the scope of this chapter.

413   Holland

In Holland, Articles 1766 and 1849, B.W., give both the bailee of goods and the mandataire a right of retention over property entrusted to them until payment is forthcoming. The relationship between the forwarder and his client constitutes a mandate as in France, and therefore falls within this category. By Article 19 of Dutch Forwarding Conditions a forwarder has a right of retention over all goods, documents and moneys until sums due have been paid. This right is to be exercised at the principal's expense. Alternatively, if the goods have been forwarded on, the fowarder has a right to collect such amount on subsequent delivery, or to draw a bill for the amount to present with the shipping documents annexed. As under other trading conditions referred to above, the right of retention is stated to be on general account,[49] and in the event of non-payment a contractual right of sale is obtained.[50] The right of retention can be exercised in respect of charges which the consignee is required to pay, such as freight, etc., when the forwarder is acting for the consignor, and is not in fact in direct contractual relationship with the former.[51]

414   Scandinavia

The pattern in other European countries follows a similar pattern to those discussed above. The position in Scandinavia warrants particular mention though, as the General Rules of the Northern Forwarding Agents Association are almost in universal use among

[47] Art. 10, C.G. (France).
[48] See Fredericq, *op. cit.*, Sections 300, 450, and Art. 57, C.G. (Belgium).
[49] Art. 19 (2), D.F.C. *O.M.S.A* v. *Philippens & Co.* (1971) Nederlandse Jur., No. 203.
[50] Art. 19 (3), D.F.C.
[51] The jurists appear to differ on the basis of this relationship, and as to whether a direct or derivative contractual relationship exists. One opinion is that the relationship is

forwarders of the four countries concerned. These do not have statutory sanction, but have been accepted by the courts as being generally known and followed by the commercial community as a whole. This has been particularly so as regards the question of privilege and retention. Article 16, Northern Forwarding Conditions, provides that a right of lien exists in respect of all outstanding charges, including forwarding and storage charges, both for goods retained and on general account. In the event of default, a right of sale by public auction or other suitable means is available, although notice is to be given to the owner and holders of liens on the goods in due time if possible.[52] A provision not found in other standard trading conditions is that in the event of loss or destruction, the forwarder can exercise the same rights over any compensation paid by insurers, carriers, etc. This presumably can only be effected in the event of payment direct to the forwarder, who otherwise would not obtain the necessary possession to exercise his rights.[53]

The binding effect of the contractual right of general lien in the Conditions has been confirmed by the courts in two cases. First, in Denmark, the Court of Appeal of Copenhagen confirmed that such a right existed under the Conditions.[54] Secondly, more recently in Sweden a dispute arose as to whether the right of lien was merely particular or whether it could be exercised in respect of all outstanding debts.[55] Here again the contract was subject to the Conditions, the court holding that the right of general lien was binding on a client's administrator in insolvency, and rejected the plea of absence of knowledge. It therefore appears that although not possessing the mandatory origins of the A.D.S.P. in Germany, the universality of use of Northern Forwarding Conditions has produced virtually the same effect, and that Article 16 will therefore be of general application among the merchant community.

4. CONCLUSIONS

415 It can be seen that the series of rules existing which govern the exercise of rights over a debtor's goods are of considerable complexity, but are present in all legal systems. To state their juridical basis however is less easy. In some respects they relate to the law of obligations, but in

based upon Art. 1353, B.W., which permits a party to a contract to stipulate in favour of a third party, and which is irrevocable when accepted by the third party—per correspondence with FENEX (Dutch Forwarding Association).
[52] Art. 16, N.F.C.
[53] *Ibid.*
[54] Judgment of the Court of Appeal of Copenhagen, Oct. 28, 1921 (*I.P. Jensen* v. *Jorgen P. Madsen A/S*).
[55] Judgment of the Tribunal of Norrköping, May 21, 1953. *Aktiebolaget Prosits Konkursbo* v. *Akt. Transportkompaniet* Svea Ct. of App., June 29, 1962 (unreported). Art. 16, N.F.C.—general lien re earlier commission—commented on in Grönfors-Hagberg, *De nordiska speditionsvillkoren*, Gothenburg, School of Economics and Bus. Admin. Publications, 1963.3, 44–7. *Cf. Langley, Beldon & Gaunt Ltd.* v. *Morley* [1955] 1 Lloyd's Rep. 297

other respects they are concerned with real rights (droits réels). Consequently, each jurisdiction has approached the problem through the medium of differing but interrelated institutions.

416   Under the civil law, two converging approaches have been used. First, the preferential rights available under the statutory right of gage or privilege. Secondly, the possessory right of retention. The common factor between the two concepts is that basically in both cases the forwarder or carrier must have possession of the goods either at or prior to the exercise of his rights. The right of tacit gage is generally based upon actual possession but in some jurisdictions, notably Belgium, Germany and Spain, this period may be extended.[56] Again the rights of tacit gage may be merely particular, or else on general account, as in the case of France.[57] In all cases a right of sale will exist, subject usually to the normal rules relating to the contractual gage. Certain differences may also exist between the tacit gage of the commissionnaire or Spediteur, and the actual carrier.[58] In differing aspects of the exercise of the rights, advantages may accrue to one or the other, a situation which merely adds to the complexity of the relationship, bearing in mind that a forwarder may fall into both categories on differing occasions.

417   The right of retention, on the other hand, has more characteristics which are common to the various systems. For example, the right of retention is merely particular and not general, with the exception of the German commercial lien which can be exercised in respect of a general account.[59] In this respect the common law lien and the civil law right of retention are similar in application, except that, as in the German commercial lien, the forwarder may have a general lien, but only in respect of his packing and factoring activities.[60] Similarly, under all systems, except Germany, the right of lien is merely a passive one, which does not give any right of sale of the goods retained.

Various other lesser differences exist, which have all been discussed in the preceding sections of this chapter. However, it is through the general application of standard trading conditions of the various national forwarding bodies that many of these differences in fact disappear. In particular, in virtually all cases, the rights either of preference or retention are extended from the particular to general account, and a right of sale, where such is not available at law, is invariably included as a contractual right. As a result, what in fact commences as a juridical nightmare generally resolves itself in forwarding practice as a virtually identical system of possessory protection on general

[56] See §§ 395 *et seq.*
[57] See § 389.
[58] See §§ 389, 399.
[59] See § 404.
[60] See § 363.

account with a right of sale in the event of non-settlement of outstanding claims.

CHAPTER 15

CHARGES

1. METHODS OF CHARGING

(i) *General Provisions*

418 THE forwarder may charge his client by various methods. First, he may charge an inclusive rate for forwarding and transit, without giving the client any breakdown of the charges incurred. If a forwarder operates in this method a distinction must be drawn between the situation where a forwarder in fact issues a bill of lading in his own name from the position where he merely quotes an inclusive rate per ton (or other measurement). A dispute involving a through bill of lading arose in *Troy* v. *The Eastern Company of Warehouses*[1] where a forwarder had quoted freight payable in advance for a shipment to Russia, delivery of which had been taken before arrival at destination. The question therefore arose as to whether the forwarder was liable to refund the sum saved owing to the consignee not requiring the contract to be performed in its entirety. The Court of Appeal held that the forwarder was not liable to refund the excess as he did in fact accept the responsibility of issuing a through bill of lading as an independent contracting party, and not as a mere agent on behalf of the carrier. The mere fact that the client had been given a complete breakdown of the charges to be incurred and offered alternative rates did not affect the issue. As Bankes L.J. observed[2]:

"It was a mere accident that the defendants rendered their account in that form. They were under no obligation to do it. They might have charged a lump sum, in which case it would have been very difficult, it seems to me, for the plaintiff to have even formulated a case founded upon their present contention. ..."

On the other hand, though, if a forwarder contracts to forward goods by a particular direct sea route at a certain rate per ton, and in fact ships them by a cheaper route partly by sea and partly by land transport, he will be accountable to his client for the difference in rates. This is so even if the method of transit used is in fact quicker than the method contracted for and the goods arrive quite safely. The application of this rule will depend upon satisfactory proof that the actual route has been specified in the contract with no alternatives given.[3]

[1] (1921) 8 Ll.L.Rep. 17.
[2] *Ibid.* at p. 19.
[3] *Charles Weis & Co. Ltd.* v. *Northern Traffic Ltd.* (1919) 1 Ll.L.Rep. 241.

419   The question next arises whether a forwarder can claim reimbursement where he has contracted to forward goods at a particular rate and additional freight in fact becomes payable. Here the position seems to be that if such an increase results from the negligence of the forwarder he will not be able to claim reimbursement from his client. On the other hand, if the increase results from matters outside the forwarder's control, he can claim an indemnity although this does not appear to entitle him to make a profit therefrom.[4]

420 Standard Trading Conditions

Where, however, the contract is subject to Standard Trading Conditions, provision is made to overcome this problem as Clause 8 provides as follows:

"Quotations are given on the basis of immediate acceptance and subject to the right of withdrawal or revision. If any changes occur in the rates of freight, insurance premiums or other charges applicable to the goods, quotations and charges shall be subject to revision accordingly with or without notice."

As a result there has been a noticeable absence of litigation concerning the revision of charges since the inception of Standard Trading Conditions except where they have not been the basis of the contract or the increase has been due to an error of calculation by the forwarder and not due to any actual alteration of carriage rates.[5]

421   Accordingly, the question arises whether the forwarder will be bound by the rates he has quoted once his client has accepted them if no alteration has taken place. It is not clear from the wording of Clause 8 whether it is intended to permit withdrawal or revision by the forwarder only prior to acceptance, or whether revised rates can be quoted after acceptance by the client. If the former interpretation is correct, it merely restates the common law. If, on the other hand, it is intended to permit the withdrawal or revision of the offer to forward after acceptance, Clause 8 fails to make clear whether it is intended that the forwarder is free not only to withdraw his offer at any time until performance, but whether he can also revise the rates after performance. Such ambiguity is not satisfactory, although to date no dispute has come before the courts as to the interpretation of this particular clause of Standard Trading Conditions.

(ii) *Conference Rates*

422 To overcome unnecessary competition and to stabilise the shipping

---

[4] *Immediate Transportation Co. Ltd.* v. *Speller, Willis & Co.* (1920) 2 Ll.L.Rep. 645 at p. 647.   The question of indemnity is dealt with more fully below at § 430.
[5] See §§ 254 *et seq.*   *Cf.* Arts. 2, 3, 13 (2), 15, D.F.C.; Arts. 14–15, N.F.C.; Art. 4 N.Y.F.F.; Arts. 10, 11, 13, 14, 39, C.G. (Belgium); Art. 2, C.G. (France); Arts. 3–5, 14, Y.F.C.; Arts. 8 (6), 10, 11, C.G. (Switzerland); Arts. 4, 20, A.D.S.P.; Art. 14, F.B.L.

industry on the principal shipping routes of the world, the Conference system of standardised rates developed during the last half of the nineteenth century. Under this system a standard tariff of rates was established, together with a rebate system to encourage shippers not to use non-Conference shipping lines, who offer cheaper rates. The problem facing the forwarder in this respect is how to ensure that rebates are obtained for his client.

423   The freight agreement

Two systems of preferential rates are in use by the various shipping conferences. First, the shipper may enter into a contractual agreement to the effect that he will only ship by a Conference line on that route in return for an immediate rebate on freight paid. The freight agreement is entered into by the shipper with the Conference concerned, and the rebate is payable to him. Secondly, the Conference may offer a system of deferred rebates, payment of which will be deferred until the end of the rebate period, which is normally six months. However, if the shipper uses a non-Conference line during the period for shipping goods to the Conference area, the rebate may be forfeit. Similarly, where he has signed a contract he may be liable to repay the amount of the rebate he has received, by way of liquidated damages, if he breaks it. The rebates vary, but are often up to 10 per cent. Generally speaking the forwarder is not a party to the Conference agreement.[6]

424

The rebate is not payable until the shipper has signed a declaration/claim form at the end of the rebate period to the effect that the relevant shipments during that period have been shipped on Conference line vessels.[7] If it is not claimed it will not be paid by the shipping line. The forwarder cannot sign the rebate form in the case of deep-sea Conferences,[8] so that it is often ignored by the shipper and the forwarder if the amount involved is small, as not being worth the cost of collection. This rule complicates the situation where a forwarder ships goods under a groupage bill of lading. Here for the purposes of the Conference agreement the forwarder still signs as agent for the various shippers. Consequently, where there is a rate rebate, and not a net charge, such as is applicable on some routes, the forwarder will not get the rebate immediately. The forwarder must obtain the signatures of all the shippers of goods shipped under one bill of lading to obtain the rebate.

425

The rebate system therefore causes much work. The forwarder must

---

[6] However, exceptionally, as in the case of the U.K.–Mexico Conference, the freight contract is binding on all parties and on any forwarder acting on behalf of the consignor or consignee.

[7] It does not matter in such a case whether the bill of lading is taken out by the consignor or by the forwarder, as the latter is still the agent of the consignor.

[8] There are a few exceptions such as the U.K./East Africa Conference, which permits the forwarder to sign a freight agreement where he is operating as a principal. On the other hand, it is fairly standard practice for the short-sea (Continental) Conferences to permit forwarders to sign freight agreements.

record it, process claims forms, send them to the shipper for signature, await their return and then forward them to the shipping company. On receiving payment from the latter, the forwarder must record the payment and credit the shipper. Net rates would cause much less trouble, but the rebate system remains a useful weapon of the Conferences to enforce conformity. It is therefore clear that certain advantages may exist for the forwarder to use non-Conference lines, although this is not often practical as the Conferences have a virtual monopoly on a number of routes.

2. LIABILITY OF THE FORWARDER IN RESPECT OF CHARGES

426 As discussed in an earlier chapter, the forwarder may take upon himself the obligations of a principal, in which case he will be personally liable to the carrier for all charges in any case.[9] Where however the forwarder acts as a mere agent on behalf of his principal under certain circumstances he may still be personally liable to third parties for the payment of various charges. This liability may be incurred either by express or implied contract with the third party, which will usually be pursuant to the express authority of his principal, although such authority may also arise out of the custom of the trade. The forwarder may also incur liability by legislative provision. As regards trade custom, this may differ from port to port—for example, the courts have acknowledged the custom in the United Kingdom whereby the forwarder accepts personal liability for dead freight to ship's agents.[10] By custom or regulation the forwarder may also be liable for port authorities' charges. For example, in the Port of London, under the forwarder's mandate to collect goods and to load them on a ship, etc., he accepts liability to the Port Authority and has a right to be indemnified by his principal.[11] It also appears that a forwarder will accept personal liability for any misdeclaration resulting in the wrong freight being paid, e.g. if he misdescribes the category of goods.[12] He does not accept personal liability for customs dues though,[13] and he only places insurance as an agent, merely relaying his principal's instructions to the broker.[14]

427 **I.A.T.A. Resolutions**

Where a forwarder is an I.A.T.A. approved cargo sales agent, his relationship with the carrier is defined by the relevant I.A.T.A. Resolutions.[15] Under them he is an agent acting on behalf of his principal the

---

[9] See Chapter 3.
[10] *Anglo Overseas Transport Ltd.* v. *Titan Ind. Corp. Ltd.* [1959] 2 Lloyd's Rep. 152. See also *British Standard Portland Cement Co. Ltd.* v. *Zim Israel Navigation Co. Ltd.* [1963] E.A. 391—Port of Mombasa. *Contra: Mitchell, Cotts* v. *Commissioner for Railways* [1905] T.S. 349.
[11] *P.S.A. Transport Ltd.* v. *Newton, Landsdowne & Co. Ltd.* [1956] 1 Lloyd's Rep. 121. *Cf. Halal Shipping Co. Ltd.* v. *Aden Port Trustees* [1962] E.A. 97.
[12] *Per* trade source.
[13] See Chapter 16.
[14] See Chapter 17.
[15] I.A.T.A., Resolutions 800 *et seq.*

carrier, with certain defined duties. He must collect and accept payment of pre-paid transportation and other charges. In the recent case of *Perishables Transport Co. Ltd.* v. *N. Spyropoulos Ltd.*[16] Salmond L.J. acknowledged that air forwarders are personally liable for freight to a carrier:

> " It is quite plain that air agents are in the same position as shipping agents: if they arrange for the shipment or air passage, even although they disclose that they are doing so for a principal, even for a named principal, they incur a personal liability to the shipping company or the air company for the freight. This has been so for many years in shipping, it has been so for quite a long time so far as air transport is concerned. The Cargo Sales Agency Rules of the International Air Transport Association . . . apply to all countries in Europe and many parts of the world. I have no doubt that they incorporate the usual practice in the trade among airlines, agents and the merchants in various parts of the world who make use of these transport facilities."[17]

428 C.O.D.

Where a forwarder is instructed to collect charges on behalf of his principal he will also be liable if he fails to do so, but instead surrenders the goods in question to the consignee or his agent without obtaining payment in return.[18] Similarly, if a forwarder acting as a sub-agent is instructed by the principal forwarder to collect charges on his behalf, he will be liable to him if he fails to do so.[19]

Standard Trading Conditions however provide that where a forwarder undertakes to handle a C.O.D. consignment, he will only do so on " condition that the Company in the matter of such collection will be liable for the exercise of reasonable diligence and care only." This really only restates the common law position, though, provided the forwarder does not in fact surrender the goods to the consignee without prior payment, a situation which the clause does not cover.[20] However, if the forwarder is placed in the position of a carrier under C.M.R. he will be liable under Article 21 for any failure to collect "|cash on delivery" charges under the terms of the contract carriage. This duty is " without prejudice to his right of action against the consignee," but as the Convention does not itself give the carrier any right of recovery against the consignee, the question remains to be decided by common law.[21]

---

[16] [1964] 2 Lloyd's Rep. 379.
[17] *Ibid.* at p. 382.
[18] *J. O. Lund Ltd.* v. *Anglo-Overseas Transport Co. Ltd.* [1955] 1 Lloyd's Rep. 142.
[19] *Societa Anonima Angelo Castelletti* v. *Transmaritime Ltd.* [1953] 2 Lloyd's Rep. 440.
[20] Cl. 17, S.T.C.
[21] See §§ 433 *et seq. Cf.* Art. 19, C.I.M.; Cl. 9 (1), R.H.A. Conditions 1967; Cll. 11, 18, R.H.A. Conditions 1961; Cl. 8 (1), B.R.S. Conditions; Art. 1 (5), D.F.C.; Art. 14, N.Y.F.F.; Art. 38, C.G. (Belgium); Art. 12, Y.F.C.; Art. 3, C.G. (France); Art. 34, A.D.S.P.; Arts. 12, 13 C.G. (Switzerland).

429   The position therefore in respect of the forwarder's liability for charges is one that has no discernible pattern, and which will alter according to the exigencies of the trade. It is therefore only possible to state the present position to complete the picture of the forwarder's rights and duties in relation to his overall operations. No further comment seems of value except to add that only in the field of air forwarding is there any formal system of control in existence, the reason for this being the rapid development in this field in the postwar period, since when there has been a marked tendency to impose controls on transportation wherever possible.

3. The Forwarder's Right of Indemnity Against his Principal

430   Under the general rules of the law of agency, a forwarder can render his principal liable for any forwarding charges which he has express authority to incur. Similarly, where a forwarder acts within his implied authority he can also require an indemnity from his principal in respect of expenses properly incurred.

This implied authority will extend to any acts falling within the ordinary duties of a forwarder which will depend upon the particular circumstances.[22] However, in attempting to ascertain whether a forwarder has a right of indemnity or not, it must be noted that the mere fact that a party gives instructions to a forwarder does not necessarily render him liable in respect of them.

For instance, the fact that a buying agent gives shipping instructions to a forwarder, and the latter submits his accounts to him, is not in itself sufficient to render the buying agent liable for freight and insurance charges incurred as a result of his instructions. If, therefore, it is not contemplated or intended that the buying agent should become personally liable to the forwarder for the charges in question, and there is no presumption to this effect in the circumstances, the forwarder will have no recourse against the buying agent, but only against his principal.[23] Here again though the status of the buying agent may be as uncertain as that of the forwarder.

431   On the assumption that the forwarder has authority, either express or implied, to incur charges on behalf of his principal, the question arises as to what extent he can require his principal to indemnify him in respect thereof. Here a distinction must be drawn between those charges which are expressly or impliedly agreed upon, or which are normally incidental to the performance of the forwarding contract, and those charges which have not been agreed upon by the parties at the time the contract was made and are not such as are necessarily within their contemplation.

[22] *Patel* v. *Keeler & Co.* [1923] A.D. 506.
[23] *J. S. Holt & Moseley (London) Ltd.* v. *Sir Charles Cunningham & Partners* (1949) 83 Ll.L.Rep. 141.

As regards those charges falling within the first category, these can be claimed in full, whether arising through agreement between the parties, statutory regulation, such as for port authority charges,[24] or through trade custom.[25] In the case of those charges falling within the second category as Greer J. observed in *Immediate Transportation Co. Ltd.* v. *Speller, Willis & Co.*[26] in relation to a claim for storage charges, a forwarder can claim an indemnity providing " it was reasonably necessary for the plaintiffs, in performing their duty as forwarding agents, to incur the expense of putting these things into store."

Similarly, where such extra disbursements are incurred solely by reason of the client's own actions, they will be presumed to be additional to the forwarder's agreed charges. An example of this occurred where a forwarder was employed to inspect and tranship goods at London docks. Owing to the shipper's delay in instructing the forwarder, the goods were discharged on the quay instead of being lightered, and remained there long enough to incur inward port dues. The shipper was therefore held to be liable for the extra charges.[27] Where, however, the excess charges result from an error in charging on the part of the forwarder, the latter cannot claim an indemnity, although if this has been left to the forwarder's discretion, this will not necessarily apply.[28]

432 Standard Trading Conditions

To overcome the problem, Standard Trading Conditions contain a series of overlapping provisions which appear to give the forwarder extensive protection in this respect. First, Clause 8 renders the client liable if any changes occur as to the rates of charges quoted.[29] Secondly, Clause 10 renders the client liable for any charges etc. imposed by port authorities, etc. Thirdly, Clause 5 provides that, "Pending forwarding or delivery, goods may be warehoused or otherwise held at any place or places at the sole discretion of the Company and the cost thereof shall be for the account of the Customer." [30] Finally, Clause 24 gives the forwarder a general right of indemnity in respect of all third party claims "arising directly or indirectly from or in connection with the Customer's instructions or their implementation."

4. THE POSITION OF THE CONSIGNEE

433 A problem that faces the forwarder is whether a consignee can be liable

---

[24] *P.S.A. Transport Ltd.* v. *Newton Landsdowne & Co. Ltd.* [1956] 1 Lloyd's Rep. 121.
[25] *Anglo Overseas Transport Ltd.* v. *Titan Ind. Corp. Ltd.* [1959] 2 Lloyd's Rep. 152. *Perishables Transport Co. Ltd.* v. *N. Spyropoulos Ltd.* [1964] 2 Lloyd's Rep. 379; see § 427.
[26] (1920) 2 Ll.L.Rep. 645 at p. 647.
[27] *Ibid.*
[28] *E. W. Taylor & Co. (Forwarding) Ltd.* v. *Bell* [1968] 2 Lloyd's Rep. 63. See § 258 for the facts. See also §§ 254 *et seq.*
[29] See § 420.
[30] *Cf.* Art. 25, N.F.C.; Art. 31, C.G. (Belgium); Arts. 36–51, Y.F.C.; Art. 15, C.G. (Switzerland); Arts. 31–35, C.G. (Italy); Arts. 43–49, A.D.S.P.

for freight and under what circumstances. Such a situation will only arise where the forwarder is either acting directly on behalf of the consignor or else as a sub-agent on behalf of the principal forwarder. It therefore resolves itself into two distinct questions.

434   Forwarder's right of indemnity against the consignee

First, if the forwarder has released goods to the consignee without payment of charges being made, he will extinguish the consignor's right of lien and in many cases be liable himself to his principal for the charges in question. If, therefore, the forwarder has reimbursed either the consignor or the principal forwarder the question arises whether he in turn can claim an indemnity from the consignee. Such a right can only arise by contractual agreement. As Slade J. observed,[31] a forwarder can say to a consignee, " if you want possession of these goods, although there is no privity of contract between us and you at the moment, we are only prepared to hand them over to you if you will make a contract with us here and now to pay us the sum stated."

Ordinarily, however, there is no privity between a forwarder and the consignee, merely between the forwarder and the consignor. To establish such a relationship it is necessary for the forwarder to enter into a separate agreement with the consignee to this effect, which is outside the scope of his agency whilst acting on behalf of either the consignor or the principal forwarder. In other words, the mere fact that a forwarder has entered into a contract with the consignee as an agent on behalf of his principal does not entitle him to rely upon any terms therein, if he is not a party thereto.[32]

In such circumstances, therefore, the forwarder cannot claim an indemnity from the consignee. Neither can such a right be obtained by custom of the trade.[33] It therefore appears that for a forwarder to claim a right of indemnity against a consignee, there must be an unambiguous contract to this effect entered into directly by the parties concerned.[34]

435   Liability for charges—consignor or consignee

The second question that arises is the complementary one of whether the consignor of goods can avoid liability to a forwarder for freight charges on the grounds that this is the responsibility of the consignee. The position was made clear by Greer J. in *Universal Shipping and Forwarding Co. Ltd.* v. *Commercial and Industrial Co. Ltd.*[35] Where instructions are given to a forwarder and they are carried out

"prima facie, the plaintiffs [forwarders] are entitled to be paid a

---

[31] *Anglo-Overseas Transport Co. Ltd.* v. *David Zanellotti Ltd.* [1952] 1 Lloyd's Rep. 232 at p. 235. *Cf.* Cl. 15, S.T.C.
[32] *Societa Anonima Angelo Castelletti* v. *Transmaritime Ltd.* [1953] 2 Lloyd's Rep. 440 at p. 451, *per* Devlin J.
[33] *Supra*, at p. 236, *per* Slade J. See § 300.
[34] *J. O. Lund Ltd.* v. *Anglo-Overseas Transport Co. Ltd.* [1955] 1 Lloyd's Rep. 142 exemplifies such an agreement—see § 367.
[35] (1919) 1 Ll.L.Rep. 635 at p. 636.

proper remuneration for having obeyed those instructions—instructions to do work as forwarding agents, to do work which was the usual work of forwarding agents—a great advantage to the defendants [consignors] when taking delivery of the goods at the docks, because of the experience of the forwarding agents and the influence they would have with regard to obtaining contractors to undertake the work and deal with wharfingers, etc."

A consignor who has instructed a forwarder to act on his behalf cannot therefore avoid liability for charges easily. There is nothing to prevent a novation of the debt by the conduct of the parties, whereby the debt is transferred from the consignor to the consignee with the agreement of the forwarder. However, merely because the account is sent by the forwarder to the consignee in the first instance, does not of itself constitute such a novation. This is merely a convenience to all concerned, as ultimately the cost of the charges will partially fall on the consignee, and it is equally convenient for him to apportion the charges as between himself and other parties to the transaction as for the consignor to do so, but without necessarily intending to affect their respective legal liability.[36]

This question has recently come before the courts in *E. W. Taylor & Co. (Forwarding) Ltd.* v. *Bell*.[37] Here a forwarder sought to recover forwarding charges in respect of meat shipments to the Continent from the consignor. The latter disputed the charges and claimed that the consignee was solely liable for the charges, either on the grounds of an implied term arising from the dealings of the parties, or alternatively, that the consignor had merely requested the goods to be forwarded on behalf of the consignee.

This argument was rejected by the court on the grounds that no agency had been pleaded or relied upon in the transaction, nor was there any course of dealing to this effect. Such a course of dealing could not be justified on the grounds, *inter alia*, that prior to the consignments in question, which were the last of many, the defendant had ceased to trade with the Continent on c.i.f. terms and had begun to trade f.o.b. The court considered that merely because the defendant's liability to the buyer ceased on the goods being loaded did not affect his relationship with the forwarder, to whom the defendant's contracts with his buyers were *res inter alios actae*, and did not determine his relationship with the forwarder in any way.[38] Finally, the mere fact that the forwarder sent the invoice to the consignee after the carriage had been effected was not relevant, as this was merely at the request of the consignor, against whom the forwarder retained a right of recourse.

436   It appears therefore that where a forwarder is instructed to effect a

[36] *Ibid. Cf. E. W. Taylor & Co. (Forwarding) Ltd.* v. *Bell* [1968] 2 Lloyd's Rep. 63.
[37] *Ibid.*
[38] *Ibid.* at p. 71.

forwarding operation he will be able to claim payment of all charges reasonably incurred on behalf of the consignor, who will not be able to avoid liability unless he can prove he was acting as a mere agent on behalf of the consignee or a clear contractual agreement to this effect was entered into by the parties.[39] Since this decision however, a new provision, Clause 11, has been inserted into Standard Trading Conditions 1970 and states that:

" When goods are accepted or dealt with upon instructions to collect freight, duties, charges or other expenses from the consignee or any other person the Customer shall remain responsible for the same if they are not paid by such consignee or other person."[40]

This would therefore cover a *Taylor* v. *Bell* type situation in future.

5. REMUNERATION

437 The question of the forwarder's remuneration is one that does not lend itself to academic discussion, but a brief account thereof is necessary. The position is that the law does not place any restriction on the methods whereby a forwarder obtains his remuneration. He is free to charge commission, an inclusive rate, or to profit by groupage rates, or any combination thereof which is economically desirable.

On the question of remuneration by the carrier, the forwarder is not very favourably placed in this country. In the case of carriage by sea, he will receive a commission from short sea Conference lines, that is, for continental traffic, but not generally for deep-sea Conference traffic. Only if the forwarder is also a loading broker or exclusive sales agent will he obtain commission from the carrier in such cases. By contrast, on the Continent the entrenched position of the forwarder in the field of rail transit has enabled him to obtain commission for all classes of sea traffic, which gives him an advantage over his United Kingdom counterparts.

In the case of carriage by air, where a forwarder is subject to I.A.T.A. Resolutions, which most are, he will not charge his client but will be paid commission by the I.A.T.A. carrier.[41] This rule is of general application in most countries throughout the world.

Where forwarding is by land, no commission is paid generally by British Rail, except for international traffic. In the case of carriage by road, the methods of remuneration are infinite, and are not capable of classification.

[39] It is interesting to note that the plaintiff attempted to rely upon Cl. 5, S.T.C. 1956 (new Cl. 7), discussed below, to prove that they had looked throughout the course of their dealing to the consignor for the payment of their charges. The court regrettably failed to comment upon the efficacy of this clause, and contented itself with dealing with the question in general terms: *ibid.* at p. 65.

[40] *Cf.* Art. 1 (5), D.F.C.; Art. 10, N.F.C.; Art. 38, C.G. (Belgium); Art. 12, Y.F.C.; Arts. 3, 7, C.G. (France); Art. 13, C.G. (Switzerland); Art. 34, A.D.S.P.

[41] He is also bound not to accept higher commission rates from non-I.A.T.A. carriers than are payable under I.A.T.A. scheduled rates: Cargo Sales Agency Rules.

438 **Standard Trading Conditions**

To ensure that the forwarder is not accountable for any remuneration he may receive from carriers, etc., and to ensure that any commission he may receive in respect of insurance business, or which the client is due to pay him, is not claimed by the client or withheld by him, Clause 7 of Standard Trading Conditions gives him a contractual right to such " brokerages, commissions, allowances and other remunerations customarily retained by or paid to " forwarders and insurance brokers.[42] Consequently disputes on the question of the forwarder's remuneration are largely avoided.

Finally, although in certain jurisdictions such as the United States the forwarder's rights of remuneration are strictly controlled by governmental bodies, no such control appears desirable or imminent in this country. Only if a system of licensed customs brokers is introduced is such a system likely, and only then in respect of those charges relating to customs clearance itself.

6. CONCLUSIONS

439 In conclusion, it is manifest that the law is prepared to offer considerable latitude to the parties in deciding upon their mutual rights and liabilities in relation to the payment of charges. The only restrictions upon the forwarder are those imposed by such organisations as I.A.T.A. and the various shipping Conferences. However, the forwarder has attempted to safeguard himself in relation to his client by provision in Standard Trading Conditions.

The principal problem relating to forwarding charges is the extent to which a forwarder will be liable personally for them to carriers and other third parties. The case law clearly shows that it is necessary to fall back upon either trade custom or contractual agreement which will differ from port to port and may be fraught with uncertainty. As was discussed in an earlier chapter much of this uncertainty stems from the absence of a contract of commission at common law.[43] If the forwarder were subject to a contract of commission as in continental countries, there would be no doubt as to his liability for charges, as in all cases he would be personally liable to the carrier in all respects, as no privity would be created between the carrier and his client, except under French law, and even then this would not relieve the forwarder of his obligations to third parties.

---

[42] *Cf.* Arts. 11–13, 15, N.F.C.; Art. 16, N.Y.F.F.; Art. 52, Y.F.C.; Arts. 9, 12, C.G. (Switzerland); Arts. 21–23, A.D.S.P.
[43] See Chapter 3.

PART V

THE FORWARDER IN RELATION TO ASSOCIATED COMMERCIAL TRANSACTIONS

CHAPTER 16

THE CUSTOMS BROKER

1. CUSTOMS BROKER AND FORWARDER

440 THE freight forwarder, when operating in relation to export and import shipments, essentially acts as an intermediary in relation to the transportation of goods, and particularly in relation to the forwarding thereof. However, on the import side, which involves the inward clearance of shipments, the forwarder will often act as a receiving agent in respect of goods, whether he reforwards them or not. The one factor common to all inward shipments is that they must all be cleared through customs either at the port of arrival or else at some authorised inwards clearance centre.[1]

This function of clearing goods through customs is one that has long been handled by specialists in the procedure, called either customs brokers, customs agents, or custom-house brokers, dependent on the particular terminology used in the country in question. Such an operation can in itself be considered as completely separate from forwarding as such. In some countries this separation is complete and in others, where the manufacturing industries have not developed to the extent to warrant the growth of a forwarding trade, only the customs broker exists who also transacts what limited forwarding services may be required by exporters.[2]

Such separation, however, does not generally mean that a forwarder cannot be a customs broker as well, and vice versa, but although both functions may be carried out as part of the same commercial operation, they must be considered as being quite distinct from each other. In Canada, for instance, two-thirds of all forwarders are also custom-house brokers, the remaining third carrying on forwarding operations alone, and correspondingly some custom-house brokers do not engage in the foreign forwarding trade, but merely restrict themselves to inward clearance operations ancillary thereto. Moreover, it should be noted that if a forwarder does not also operate as a custom-house broker he is bound to utilise the services of one for customs clearance if such services are required by his client.[3] Equally, in such countries as the United Kingdom, where no organised system of customs broker exists, the forwarder will informally perform these operations on behalf of his client. The absence of a recognised customs brokerage system in this country is however an exception to the general rule in most developed countries.

---

[1] See note 14.
[2] *i.e.* in South America. See Chapter 1.
[3] See § 448.

2. FUNCTIONS OF THE CUSTOMS BROKER

441 Before discussing the legal status of the customs broker in detail, it is necessary to consider briefly the functions he performs. In effecting the clearance of a shipment on receiving the manifest for the goods, the broker must rate the related invoice in respect of the customs tariff in question to arrive at the correct customs duty payable. He will then prepare the formal entry and present it to the customs for approval. It differs from country to country as to whether the consignee or the customs authorities compute the duty due.

In this country the former is still responsible for this operation, but it has been recommended that the latter could suitably take over this function.[4] The broker then pays the duty on behalf of the importer to whom he renders an account for the duty paid, incidental charges, plus brokerage. In respect of such charges prompt payment is normally expected, as it is not part of the customs broker's function to extend credit in respect of such payments. In addition to his main function the broker will offer various ancillary services such as applying for refunds where duty has been overpaid, tracing shipments, and obtaining rulings on tariff classifications in respect of dutiable imports. In some countries certain brokers may also act as tariff consultants and represent their clients before the revenue department in valuation and tariff cases.[5]

442 In the United Kingdom clearance through customs can either be performed by the consignee himself or by an agent for him.[6] As entries have to be reconciled with the ship's manifest, which is prepared by the loading broker at the point of shipment, a sending forwarder must ensure that the bills of lading are prepared and delivered as quickly as possible for the manifest to be prepared, otherwise clearance may be delayed at the port of arrival. It should be noted that where preferential dues are desired and a certificate of origin is required, the forwarder cannot sign such a document, which can only be signed by the actual manufacturer. With the speed of air shipments it is not always possible for the certificate of origin to be made available at the time of entry, and H.M. Customs will often accept a signed declaration of a Commonwealth exporter on his commercial invoices claiming Commonwealth preference. Equally, in the case of air shipments it is advisable for the air waybill to name a clearing agent to facilitate prompt handling on arrival together with the complete documentation attached if possible.

---

[4] See note 14.

[5] *i.e.* Canada. Generally the customs broker must also be able to undertake the actual delivery and distribution of shipments cleared through customs by them, either by means of their own organisation or else by employing a carrier for the purpose. In New Zealand, for example, many customs agents undertake cartage, distribution, storage, packing and general forwarding to and from all parts of the world.

[6] N.B. No power of attorney can be granted though to an agent to carry out clearance of shipment—see § 446.

443   Clearance was formerly only available either at the port of entry or else the airport in the case of air freight, although inland clearance facilities are now being set up at deep-sea container depots. This procedure of inland clearance is at present due for considerable development in the United Kingdom having been immensely stimulated by the rapid growth of containerisation by sea, land and air. Where such a procedure is used, containers travel sealed from the point of loading to the inland depot in question, and are not opened at the point of entry into the country. Increasingly many forwarders have set up receiving points within the clearance depots to enable them to take full advantage of them, and to de-consolidate shipments in containers themselves.[7] Such developments may expand in the future, though, and if they do develop to any extent, the forwarder will involve himself in customs clearance to a considerably greater extent, as the point of unloading and clearance will be one and the same, without any scope for variation.

444 U.S.A.

In the United States the position of the custom-house broker was explained by Frankfurter J. in *Union Cartage Co.* v. *Jensen*[8]:

"We shall outline the nature of this custom-house brokerage business only so far as it is relevant to a consideration of our problem. On Goods shipped . . . into this country the consignee of imported merchandise must 'make entry' of them at the office of the Collector of Customs . . . either in person or by an authorised agent. . . . To make entry the contents and value of the shipment must be declared and the tariff estimated and the production of a certified invoice and bill of lading is generally required.[9] Speed in making entry is vital, because goods cannot proceed to their ultimate destination until its completion. Apart from the fact that importers cannot always or even often make entries in person, the procedure makes demands upon skill and experience. The specialist in these services is the custom-house broker. In addition, he advances the duty in order that the goods may be cleared.[10] The competence of the broker also bears on the efficient collection of customs duties in that the likelihood of additional assessment or refund after final determination of the duty is greatly lessened by accuracy in the tentative computation. But since errors and differences of opinion are inevitable, to insure collection of deficiencies the Government requires a bond prior to release.[11] . . . To protect importers as well as the Treasury, Congress has authorised the Secretary of the Treasury to prescribe rules and regulations governing the licensing as custom-house brokers. . . ."

---

[7] See Chapter 12.
[8] (1944) 322 U.S. 202, 203–205.
[9] 6A Federal Customs Act, tit. 19 at 1484.
[10] 6A Federal Customs Act, tit. 19 at 1505.
[11] 6A Federal Customs Act, tit. 19 at 1499.

The position of the custom-house broker in the United States as described by Frankfurter J. is equally a fair description of his counterpart in other parts of the world. Unlike the United Kingdom, however, a strictly controlled system of licensing exists, to protect both shipper and state.

445 As in the case of the forwarder, the problem of differentiating the custom-house broker's functions from allied operations has come before the American courts, in particular in relationship to remunerations for the various operations carried out. The question of the exact relationship of a custom-house broker with his clients and an express company on whose behalf he was also acting was discussed in a United States case where the broker was the express company's representative at a port of entry into the country.[12] A dispute arose as to which party was entitled to custom-house brokerage fees which had been collected by the express company in respect of shipments for which the broker was the licensed custom-house broker and effected clearance operations. In other words, was the broker merely acting as the express company's agent in the matter or independently for himself as a custom-house broker? It was decided as a question of fact that an express or implied agreement existed that the compensation paid by the express company for running the express business for them did not compensate the broker for the services rendered as a custom-house broker and that fees earned as such belonged to him as an independent broker.

In such circumstances it is therefore essential that a clear agreement should be drawn up as to the exact services which an operator is to perform for the remuneration paid, so that any payment received from other sources will not be the subject of dispute. Such a problem is not likely to arise, of course, where payment is made direct to the custom-house broker himself, but if clearance charges are merely included in general freight charges and in fact collected by a carrier or other party, the question is likely to give rise to dispute unless the respective responsibilities of the parties have been clearly delineated.

3. Classification of the Customs Broker

446 The customs broker can be classified into two distinct types. First, where no licensed system of customs brokers exists at all, as in this country, where a consignee can either clear goods through customs himself or through an agent as he wishes, who may or may not be a customs broker. The position of the agent engaged in customs clearance in the United Kingdom does not differ whether he effects such operations as a professional function or whether he does so as an adjunct to other activities, or merely on behalf of a particular commercial concern. As no licensing system exists the customs broker cannot be considered as a recognised class of commercial intermediary,

---

[12] *Railway Express Co.* v. *MacKay*, 181 Fed. 257.

even though it is a normal adjunct of the forwarder's operations in shipping or receiving goods on behalf of a client.

Whereas in most countries an importer can grant a power of attorney to a customs broker to act for him, such a procedure is not acceptable to H.M. Customs. The obligation is on the importer to make a customs entry, and he may be required to sign the declaration of value on which duty is assessed. However, this does not preclude an importer from employing an agent to act on his behalf for all other aspects of the operation, although if he does so the authorities may require the agent to produce a written authority to act on behalf of his principal in effecting customs clearance: section 300 of the Customs and Excise Act 1952.

Similarly there is no system of credit at present in the United Kingdom whereby dues do not have to be paid at the moment of clearance, but instead debited to a customs broker's account. In fact no system of credit is really possible without a system of licensed customs brokers, as the administration to handle it would otherwise be too vast.[13] The only concession is for a system of bank-guaranteed cheques to avoid the need for cash payments. Anyone can adopt such a procedure, but as the cost of the bank guarantee is high, only the larger importers and clearing agents would normally do so. Such a system does not equate though with that whereby the customs broker accepts responsibility for payments due to customs. However, although his responsibility is not specifically defined by regulation, the position of the forwarder or shipping agent when effecting customs clearance has been discussed in a number of cases and their functions defined to some extent by the courts.

447   The second category is where a customs broker can only operate subject to a governmental licence granted under strict conditions, although generally an importer may, if he wishes, clear a shipment himself, without employing a licensed broker. This category is by far the most widely found, and in this respect it is not unlikely at some time in the future for this country to follow suit and institute a system of licensed customs brokers to speed import and export shipments.[14] All countries in Europe, North America, South America, Australia, New Zealand, South Africa and India have made statutory provision for the licensing of customs brokers. Obviously each country has made provisions that differ considerably in detail, but certain factors are common to all of them. In particular, the customs broker is licensed by the department of customs and excise or the department exercising such functions irrespective of its actual name.

448 Commonwealth countries

In those Commonwealth countries where a system of licensed customs brokers exists, provision is usually made in the Customs Act

[13] N.B. Common Market countries all have a system of licensed customs brokers and a system of four weeks' credit.

[14] See the recommendations in *Through Transport to Europe*, Economic Development Committee for the Movement of Ports, H.M.S.O., 1966.

for the licensing of brokers, with detailed provision being made under subsidiary Customs Regulations.[15] Provision is made either under the principal Act or subsidiary regulations for a broker to give an acceptable security before obtaining a licence. This will either be in the form of a valuable security or otherwise by means of a guarantee policy issued by an insurance company.[16] Although brokers will normally be members of a trade association, membership of which will be restricted to licensed brokers, it is not necessary for a broker in fact to be a member of such an association. Licensing may be to operate as a customs broker generally, as in the case of New Zealand, or it may be only in respect of a specific port, as under Canadian regulations. A licence is not required where an importer or exporter wishes to transact business in a customs house solely on his own account, nor to the employees of such a company acting on behalf of his employer.[17] Express provision is made by the Indian Regulations to this effect, and is implied by the terms of the provisions made by the regulations of the other countries in question. The Indian Regulations also provide that where an agent is only appointed solely to enter and clear certain ships or lines for which he is appointed an agent, that is, in respect of work incidental to his employment in clearing such ships, he will not require a licence. Such a provision is not found elsewhere, and in such a case presumably a licence would be required. In any case, an agent would not normally wish to limit his operations to such an extent by not possessing a licence to act as a customs broker when the need arose.

Provision is also made in the various regulations covering employees of customs brokers acting as such. Such employment may be restricted to such persons as have passed the requisite examinations, though again the actual provisions differ. The effect, however, in all cases is to restrict very severely those acceptable as customs brokers, so as to ensure their absolute integrity, both for the benefit of the customs authorities and also of their clients. In all cases the licence is solely applicable to the actual holder and is not transferable. Licences are normally issued for a period of one year on payment of a fee, and can be revoked by the issuing authority for failure to comply with customs regulations or to comply with the conditions of the bond entered into by him, or for other actions of a fradulent or criminal nature. Provision is made in the case of all the countries under discussion for an appeal to be made by a broker against either revocation or suspension of his licence, and detailed procedures are laid down covering such matters.

---

[15] *i.e.* Australian Customs Acts 1901–65, ss. 183A–183C, and Customs Regulations, reg. 180. New Zealand Customs Act 1966, ss. 231–235, and Customs Regulations 1968, regs. 132–133. Indian Customs Act 1962, s. 146 (2), and Custom House Agents Licensing Regulations, regs. 3 *et seq.* Canadian Customs Act, s. 116, and Custom-House Brokers Licensing Regulations 1969.

[16] In the case of New Zealand a bond issued by the New Zealand Society of Customs Agents on behalf of its members jointly is given in respect of licences granted to its members.

[17] Indian Regulations, reg. 3 (*a*), (*b*).

449 **Civil law countries**

In civil law countries, the customs agent is subject to control both for the protection of his clients and also of the customs authorities. Equally as elsewhere they will both clear and reforward shipments in respect of which they are instructed to make customs entries. Invariably they are subject to a form of licensing, and in most European countries are subject to a system of control similar to that found in common law countries which provides, *inter alia*, for an investigation of candidates prior to registration, with provision for their removal and disciplinary proceedings. Records must be kept as in the Commonwealth systems discussed below.

4. RIGHTS AND LIABILITIES OF THE CUSTOMS BROKER

(i) *General Provisions*

450 In the case of both Canada and India the regulations actually require adequate records and accounts to be kept by a broker of all financial transactions and customs entries made by him, which must be made available for inspection by authorised personnel.[18] No specific provision is made in the case of New Zealand or Australia, but such are recommended by the rules of the trade association concerned, and in any case are implicit in the high standards required to obtain a licence as a customs broker.[19] Where a client has failed to comply with any relevant legal provisions in respect of customs procedures, either by act or omission, the customs broker must inform his client of his noncompliance, and if he continues in his course of action, to inform the relevant customs authorities immediately.[20]

The customs broker must also use due diligence to ascertain that any information he imparts to his client with reference to customs business is accurate,[21] and not to withhold any information from the latter which appertains thereto.[22] The broker must also account to his client promptly for funds received either by way of refund from the customs authorities or where the client has paid the broker in excess of those charges properly payable in respect of customs business.[23] Conversely he must pay the customs authorities all sums received from his client when due in respect of any dues owing to the state.[24] However, these duties merely reiterate the agent's common law duties of good faith and due diligence and his corresponding duty to account for all moneys received and payable.

[18] Canadian Regulations, reg. 16. Indian Regulations, reg. 21.
[19] *i.e.* the *Customs Agents Handbook of the New Zealand Society of Customs Agents (Inc.)*, Wellington, 1956.
[20] Indian Regulations, reg. 16 (*d*). Canadian Regulations, reg. 19.
[21] Indian Regulations, reg. 16 (*e*).
[22] Indian Regulations, reg. 16 (*f*).
[23] Canadian Regulations, reg. 17 (*b*). Indian Regulations, reg. 16 (*g*).
[24] Canadian Regulations, reg. 18. Indian Regulations, reg. 16 (*g*).

(ii) *Liability in Respect of False Declarations*

451   A customs broker must if required by the customs authorities furnish an authorisation from any client on whose behalf he may be employed as a customs broker,[25] and a penalty may be imposed where a broker acts as such without authorisation.[26] The Australian and New Zealand statutes further provide that where a broker acts or assumes to act on behalf of a client in entering goods, he will himself be personally liable to the same penalties as if he were the principal himself.[27] Such a provision is not however intended to relieve the client of personal liability himself, but merely to place additional liability on the customs broker too. The Australian and New Zealand statutes also specifically provide that where a customs broker makes any declaration in the course of any customs procedures, it will be deemed to have been made by the client himself, who will be liable to the full penalties incurred under the regulations.[28] The New Zealand Act further provides that " for the purposes of this section the knowledge and intent of the agent shall be imputed to the principal in addition to his own," and that the section will apply whether the appointment of the customs agent is made in accordance with the statute or not.[29]

452   United Kingdom

As regards the United Kingdom, a customs declaration must be made in the form and manner as laid down by the regulations in force at any time, irrespective of who in fact is handling the clearance of a shipment. Where however a forwarder undertakes to effect clearance the customs authorities in practice will deal only with him on all questions relating to the entry. In such circumstances it would appear that the forwarder will be liable for the correctness of the details of entry and the payment of tax or duty. The forwarder will also be liable if he miscalculates the duty on a shipment of goods. However, Clause 9 of Standard Trading Conditions protects the forwarder by giving him a right of indemnity in respect of all claims, etc., which he may have been required to pay resulting from the inaccuracy of or omission to give correct descriptions and values.

(iii) *The Obligations undertaken by the Customs Broker to his Client*

453   One obvious problem is to decide whether the operation in question is, in fact, to clear goods through customs or whether it is merely a complementary operation which does not include actual clearance. Such a

---

[25] Indian Regulations, reg. 16 (*a*).   Australian Regulations, reg. 163 (*a*), and Customs Act, s. 181.

[26] Australian Regulations, reg. 163.

[27] Customs Act, s. 182 (Australia); Customs Act 1966, s. 235 (New Zealand).

[28] Customs Act, s. 183 (Australia); Customs Act 1966, s. 234 (1) (New Zealand).

[29] Customs Act 1966, s. 234 (2), (3) (New Zealand); furthermore " for the purposes of this section the agent of an agent shall be deemed also to be the agent of the principal." See also *The King* v. *Tarrant* (1912) 15 C.L.R. 172, where the action was under the Customs Act 1901 (Australia); *Dawson* v. *Jack* (1902) 28 V.L.R. 634; *The King* v. *Harris, Scarfe & Co. Ltd.* (1909) 8 C.L.R. 225.

problem however is not likely to arise where a system of licensed customs brokers is in operation, as the functions of the latter are clearly defined, and no doubt would arise if clearance of a shipment was required, as to whether it is in fact to be carried out by the agent in question. But in the United Kingdom, where no licensing system exists, there may well be uncertainty as to whether an agreement to effect clearance through customs has been undertaken, as the case of *Robert Shearer Ltd.* v. *Road Haulage Executive* [30] shows.

Here the question arose as to whether the defendant carriers, who were responsible for collecting a shipment of fruit from the docks, had actually agreed with the plaintiffs' London agent to clear it through customs on their behalf. Delay arose in delivery of the shipment through the defendants' inexperience in clearance, resulting in loss of market. The plaintiffs, who were Glasgow fruit brokers, sued the carriers for breach of contract in failing to obtain customs clearance so as to enable delivery to be effected to the buyer by a certain date.

The plaintiffs' London agent usually employed shipping agents to clear shipments for them, and either the plaintiffs or their agent could have made a similar arrangement in this case. The agent had never asked the defendant carriers to clear shipments before, but on this occasion he did ask them if they cleared shipments, to which he was given an answer in the affirmative. Accordingly, as the agent knew that it was not an uncommon practice for carriers to clear inwards shipments, he left it to the defendants.

In the ensuing action the court took the view that the defendants' confirmatory letter was consistent only with the plaintiffs' evidence, that the defendants had agreed to clear the goods through customs, and were therefore liable for any loss resulting from their delay in carrying out the plaintiffs' instructions, even though they had not understood the true import of what they had undertaken. The court rejected the argument that "clearing the goods" could merely refer to the physical taking away of the goods from the docks. [31]

Here a distinction must be drawn between an agreement to clear goods through customs and one merely to collect them from the docks. If only the latter responsibility is undertaken, a forwarder will not be liable for any loss resulting from delay in clearance, providing he effects collection when required to do so. However, if it is agreed that the agent will actually clear the shipment through customs as well, it is no defence for a carrier or other agent to plead that he is not qualified

---

[30] [1952] 1 Lloyd's Rep. 512.

[31] The vagueness of the courts is illustrated by the following dicta: " He told me in considerable detail what has to be done in order to get goods through the Customs and that what it is called is ' making a Customs entry.' A Customs entry really seems to be some kind of document, but he described what has to be done. A good deal has to be done apparently, but of course, anybody who knows how to do it can do it quite quickly," *ibid.* at p. 517, *per* Jones J. Such dicta as this one do not assist in clarifying clearance operations, which could be clearly established if a licensing system were operative.

to do so, and that only "bona fide shipping agents" are in a position to do so. Having once accepted the obligation to clear goods, any party engaged in transportation, whether as a carrier or as a forwarder, will be liable for any negligent act he commits in doing so.

454 Standard Trading Conditions

Standard Trading Conditions do not make any specific provision as to the duties of the forwarder in respect of inwards clearance and the payment of customs dues. However, the combination of Clause 10, whereby the client will be liable for all duties, taxes, etc., and Clause 13 (ii) and (iii) which relieve the forwarder of any liability for non-compliance with instructions given to him, unless he is guilty of wilful negligence or default in so doing, give the forwarder ample protection against any claims which may arise out of customs clearance operations.

455 Civil law countries

The problem faced in *Shearer's* case is specifically dealt with under the German A.D.S.P., which provides *inter alia* that where a forwarder is instructed to take delivery of an incoming shipment, he has a free hand in paying customs duties, but is not bound to do so.[32] In other words, unless there is a specific agreement to the contrary, such payment will be at the forwarder's discretion. Article 25 (*c*), A.D.S.P., further provides that where a forwarder is instructed to carry incoming goods, as opposed to merely taking delivery, while they are still in bond, or to deliver them carriage paid, he is to use his discretion in taking such steps as are necessary with the customs authorities to effect clearance and to pay the requisite dues.[33]

456   Article 6 of the Dutch Forwarding Conditions makes a similar provision to the effect that the dispatch of customs papers to a forwarder shall imply an authorisation to clear the goods in question. Consequently he is not obliged to obtain his principal's consent before clearing the shipment in question. This provision results from the fact that where a forwarder has registered with the customs authorities to enable him to act in relations with the customs in his own name,[34] he will obtain a *privilège* [35] in respect of duties paid to the customs on behalf of his principal, that is, he will obtain a first charge on all his movables and immovables for a period of one year after the date of payment, subject only to the priority of the state.

457   Under the civil law, as the customs broker is generally classified as being subject to a contract of commission, as a *commissionnaire en douane* he is therefore personally liable for customs duties to the

[32] Art. 26, A.D.S.P.
[33] *Cf.* Art. 13, A.D.S.P., which provides that " Failing sufficient or practical directions the forwarding agent, while acting in his principal's interests, is entitled to use his own discretion in choosing the kind, way or means of transport."
[34] In accordance with Art. 58, Dutch General Customs Act Jan. 26, 1961.
[35] See Chapter 14.

customs authorities. In France, for instance, as the authorities only recognise the customs broker[36] for the purpose of making customs entries, the latter is given a right of subrogation to the rights of the customs authorities to recover payments made on behalf of his clients. A person may or may not also be a commissionnaire de transport, dependent upon the scope of his operations. The *commissionnaire en douane* has a right of reimbursement in respect of customs dues and attendant expenses to the extent that he is not at fault in incurring them.[37]

458 C.M.R.

Finally, it should be noted that, in respect of the international carriage of goods by road, C.M.R. provides, in Article 11 (1), that the sender of goods must attach, *inter alia*, the customs documents to the consignment note, or else to place them at the carrier's disposal and to furnish him with all information he may require to effect customs clearance. The latter is under no duty to inquire into the accuracy of such documents, and Article 11 (2) specifically provides that the sender will be liable to the carrier, who is his agent,[38] for any damage or loss caused through any irregularity in them, or in information supplied, unless the carrier is negligent in respect of clearance operations. Accordingly, it seems that in effecting customs formalities the carrier will be able to obtain full redress from the sender in respect of any loss he may incur or for which he may be held responsible.

5. Payment and Reimbursement of Customs Dues

459 One of the main problems which has come before the courts has been the problem of reimbursement by the agent of customs dues and other charges which have been paid on behalf of a client by the agent clearing goods through customs for him, whether the agent is a forwarder, ship's agent or freight broker. Where an agent fails to request further instructions from his principal and this results in a higher tariff being payable, he may not be able to recover the excess amount paid. For instance, in *London Calais Shipping Co. Ltd.* v. *J. & B. Harding Ltd.*[39] the defendant forwarder shipped a consignment of paper on the plaintiff's ship under a consignment note which stated that, "pre-paid

---

[36] A decree of March 1, 1957, defines the commissionnaire en douane as " all persons professionally carrying out customs formalities for third parties relating to the detailed declaration of goods "—see Rodière, *op. cit.*, Section 1219.

[37] Code des douanes (Decr. Dec. 8, 1948) Art. 381. Art. 10, C.G. (France) restates this right. Comm.ca. Dec. 12, 1956, Bull transp., 1957.23 and on renvoi: Aix. March 17, 1958, Bull transp., 1958.259.

[38] See Art. 11 (3), C.M.R. N.B. Art. 23 (4), C.M.R., on repayment of dues by the carrier in the event of loss.

[39] (1924) 18 Ll.L.Rep. 272, *per* Bailhache J. *Cf. Commonwealth Portland Cement Co. Ltd.* v. *Weber, Lohmann & Co. Ltd.* [1905] A.C. 66. The Privy Council held that shipping agents had no duty of care to expedite a shipment through customs before a new duty was imposed, in the absence of an agreement to that effect. Nor is there any responsibility to note proposed alterations in customs duties unless there is a contractual obligation to do so. The duty of reasonable care in entering and clearing goods does not automatically include such a duty: *ibid.* at p. 70, *per* Lord Lindley.

domicile duty at the rate of 30f. per 100 kilos to be charged to us.''
The plaintiff's receiving agent at Calais in fact cleared the goods through
customs at a much higher rate of duty under a newly introduced
sliding scale of rates, without attempting to ask for further instructions
before doing so. The question therefore arose as to whether the plaintiff
could recover the increased rate of customs dues. Bailhache J. held
that as the receiving agent in Calais had been instructed to pay at a
rate of 30f., before paying any more he should have obtained further
instructions. The sending forwarder was therefore not liable for the
excess charges, which the plaintiffs would have to bear themselves.

460   Although no specific provision is made by Standard Trading
Conditions to cover the question of whether further instructions should
be requested by a forwarder or not, the German A.D.S.P., for instance,
specifically provides that where a forwarder is instructed to clear goods
through customs, such instructions are to be carefully carried out, and
if clearance proves to be impossible under the instructions given, the
forwarder must inform his principal of the fact immediately.[40] In other
words, A.D.S.P. makes the same provision as that reached by the
courts in the *London Calais* case.

461   Similarly, where an importer employs a forwarder to ship goods to
this country, unless the latter has in fact undertaken to be responsible
for the description and quality of the shipment, the former will be liable
to reimburse his agent in respect of customs dues and charges, which
the latter has paid on his behalf, whether, in fact, the goods fulfil
contract requirements or not.[41] Merely because an agent handles
customs documentation on behalf of his principal does not amount to
an undertaking to accept any responsibility for the description of such
goods as may arrive for reception and clearing. Furthermore, where
goods are detained by H.M. Customs until extraneous statutory charges
are paid, a forwarder will not be liable for failing to hand them over to
the importer, who has employed him to clear the shipment and to pay
customs dues in respect of them, as in such a situation he could not be
expected to pay the extraneous charges himself. Accordingly, where such
a charge was payable under the post-war Reparations Act, the defendant
forwarder was held not liable for breach of contract for not clearing
them.[42]

462   The converse situation occurs where, instead of an agent failing
to request further instructions from his principal, the principal himself
fails to give instructions to facilitate the clearance of a shipment. Such
a situation arose in *World Transport Agency Ltd.* v. *Royte* (*England*)
Ltd.[43] where customs entries had been made by a forwarder for a period

---

[40] Art. 25 (*d*), A.D.S.P.
[41] *Margolis* v. *Newson Bros. Ltd.* (1941) 71 Ll.L.Rep. 47.   *Cf.* Arts. 9 (3), 11 (1) and 16,
D.F.C.
[42] *Donner* v. *London & Hamburg Agency* (1923) 15 Ll.L.Rep. 63.
[43] [1957] 1 Lloyd's Rep. 381.

of years on behalf of a firm of potato importers. However, the latter had instructed the forwarders only to clear shipments on their specific instructions. Both parties were aware that the duties on this vegetable were to be increased on a certain date, immediately prior to which a shipment arrived at Liverpool for clearance and onward transit. Although the details of the shipment and a health certificate were sent to the forwarders, they were given no instructions to make a customs entry, and they were unable to contact the defendants through no fault of their own to obtain instructions to clear the goods or not. Eventually though, instructions were given to this effect the day after the increased duty took effect. In the ensuing action, the forwarders claimed reimbursement of the increased customs duty, while the defendants counterclaimed for negligence on the part of the plaintiffs in not making a customs entry prior to the increase in duty.

In discussing the relative duties of the parties, Jones J.[44] pointed out that the sole obligation on the shipper in such circumstances is to give the forwarder clear instructions in accordance with the normal trade practice. Accordingly where goods are sold afloat, clearance would be left to the purchasers or their agents, whereas if goods are to be received by the importers themselves at the port for onward transit, the forwarder would be required to clear them on their behalf. Having failed, however, to give such instructions the importers could not claim that the forwarder had been negligent in not carrying them out. The latter was therefore entitled to recover the duty paid on behalf of his principal.

463   The position therefore seems to be that where there is an impending change in import duties, a forwarder will be bound to inform his client of the alteration, or at least to attempt to do so, provided, however, that his client is not aware of the change, or the forwarder has no reason to believe that he is in possession of such knowledge. Otherwise, it seems that the reasonable course will be for him to clear the shipment in question, unless he has been specifically instructed to the contrary, in pursuance of his general duty to protect his client's interests. If a

---

[44] " All that [the defendants] had to do was to give the plaintiffs clear instructions in accordance with what I find to have been the practice between them to deal with such of these goods as he wanted them to deal with. If any of them had been sold afloat, then he would not have wanted the plaintiffs to deal with them because the purchasers or the purchasers' agents could deal with them and could present the entry to the Customs. Any others which the defendants were going to receive themselves in Liverpool and pass on to other people there, of course, they would want the plaintiffs to deal with. If the plaintiffs had been asked to do so they would, I am quite sure, have acted in the ordinary way. They would have made the Customs entry, they would have paid the duty, they would have received the document back from the Customs House, they would have received the documents from the ship, they would have attached the documents from the Customs House to the documents from the ship, they would have presented them all to the Customs Officer on the quay, the goods would have been released, and they would then have handed them to such purchasers from the defendants as had bought these particular goods. . . . It is perfectly true that agents have got to behave reasonably and properly and energetically. I see nothing to make me doubt that these plaintiffs did not always behave energetically in their agency ": *ibid.* at p. 386.

forwarder fails to clear a shipment without incurring the increased import duties he will be liable to his client for the excess duty paid if he has failed to act reasonably in the circumstances, which will be a question of fact in each case.

464   Where H.M. Customs refuse to clear a shipment until further information is obtained relating to the goods in question, the forwarder responsible for clearing the shipment and forwarding it to its destination will not be liable for any loss occurring prior to him obtaining actual possession of the goods. Accordingly where goods disappeared from a bonded warehouse into which they had been discharged from a ship, and delay in clearance resulted through the owner's tardiness in supplying further information as to value, followed by further delay by the forwarder in collecting the goods, the latter was held not liable when, on attempting to make collection, the goods were found to have disappeared.[45]

465   A situation that may affect a forwarder's duties in respect of customs clearing operations is the question of who is liable to pay customs dues, the buyer or the seller.[46] This will depend upon the terms of the contract, and in particular whether it is a c.i.f. contract or not. Under a c.i.f. contract, the seller is only responsible for the transit but may undertake payment of customs dues at the port of entry for the account of the buyer. Moreover, the mere fact that the buyer nominates the forwarder, which may merely be expressing his preference, would not normally affect this arrangement.[47]

However, under an " arrived " contract the buyer is usually directly responsible for customs dues. So, where the importation of goods destined for London is carried out by a forwarder nominated by the buyer, and the former notifies him of the arrival of the goods in the customs warehouse at the port of entry, and requests that clearance instructions should be given to him and customs duties paid, if the buyer fails to take any action, it will be no defence when sued for the price by the seller to plead that the seller is under a duty to tender documents.[48] Nor can the buyer plead that the seller is bound to deliver the goods to London, as such an agreement must be treated as subject to an implied term that the buyer will pay customs duties so as to enable the seller to effect delivery under the terms of the contract.[49]

---

[45] *Wessely* v. *Rosenberg, Loewe & Co. Ltd.* (1940) 67 Ll.L.Rep. 16.
[46] In the United States case of *T. D. Downing Co.* v. *Shawmut Corp.* (1923) 245 Mass. 106, 139 N.E. 525, the court held that a bank which financed an import shipment could not be held liable for advances made by a custom-house broker to release goods from customs, where a warehouseman permitted an importer, who had given a trust receipt in exchange for shipping documents, to remove part of the shipment without payment of customs dues.
[47] *Tiberghien Draperie S.A.* v. *Greenberg & Sons (Mantles) Ltd.* [1953] 2 Lloyd's Rep. 739 at p. 743, *per* Devlin J.
[48] *Ibid.*
[49] *Ibid.*

In such circumstances if a buyer is notified of the arrival of the goods in question in the customs warehouse and of the need to pay the customs dues to release them, he cannot complain if delivery cannot be effected in London through reason of his own default. It is no defence for him to plead that the seller's agent is not entitled to ask for the customs dues until the goods actually reach their destination. The mere fact that the forwarder has a choice of sending the goods by an alternative route, which would not have required the payment of duty until the shipment reached its destination, will not be relevant in the absence of specific instructions from the buyer, provided the forwarder chooses a reasonable route for getting the goods to their destination.[50]

466 Standard Trading Conditions

Owing to the fact that customs clearance is not the subject of specific regulation, and that clearance cannot be effected by power of attorney in this country, the only provision found in Standard Trading Conditions concerning clearance is that in Clause 10, which provides that the client is liable for all customs dues in connection with the goods, and for any payments made by the forwarder in connection therewith.[51] Although there has been no litigation to date concerning this particular section of Standard Trading Conditions, it seems that, in conjunction with the other limitations of liability therein, the forwarder would obtain ample protection against such claims as arose in *Shearer's* case, the *London Calais* case and the *World Transport Agency* case.[52] However it must be taken into consideration that, when acting as inwards clearance agents, forwarders do not always use Standard Trading Conditions, no special standard conditions being applicable to cover the former, so that forwarders tend to use various forms of contract many of which seem to offer inadequate cover. In any case the question of whether they will be binding in respect of such operations will of course depend upon whether the contents have been brought to the notice of the principal, which may often take place after the contract has been entered into, having regard to the trading pattern common at the moment.

6. CONCLUSIONS

467 The law and practice relating to customs clearance in the United

---

[50] " It is quite sufficient for me that what they chose was an ordinary, reasonable and commercial route; and, they having chosen that ordinary way, then I think the obligation that was put upon the buyers was to provide the customs duty at whatever point on that route it became necessary to pay the duty in order that the process of delivery might be continued," *per* Devlin J., *ibid.* at p. 744.

See also *C. A. Pisani & Co. Ltd.* v. *Brown, Jenkinson & Co. Ltd.* (1939) 64 Ll.L.Rep. 340, where a firm of shipping agents was requested to clear a shipment of marble slabs through customs and to land them. Here again the question arose as to whose agent they were, that of the second defendants, stevedores, or alternatively that of the importers to effect clearance and arrange delivery. See Chapter 3 generally.

[51] *Cf.* Arts. 4, 6, 11 (1), D.F.C.; Arts. 11, 14, N.F.C.; Arts. 5, 34, Y.F.C.; Art. 30, A.D.S.P.; Art. 12, C.G. (Switzerland). As to the question of refund of customs dues under C.M.R. and C.I.M. see § 248.

[52] *Supra.*

Kingdom is therefore in a totally unorganised state. The fact that there is no licensed system of brokers has meant that the courts have not been able to formulate any clear rules as to the rights and duties of a customs broker. The obligations of anyone in fact performing such operations on behalf of an importer will merely be those of an ordinary agent, or at the best those of a forwarder who has undertaken *inter alia* to clear a shipment of goods.

Although on the Continent the customs broker has generally been made the subject of a contract of commission, this in practice is of less importance than in respect of forwarding operations. The reason is that even in common law countries where no contract of commission exists, the customs broker is placed in virtually the same position by regulation, with the notable exception of the United Kingdom. Generally the broker will be personally liable to the authorities for all dues, etc., so that the question of whether privity is, or is not, created between the shipper and third parties is of less importance. However the existence of a contract of commission in relation to customs brokerage operations in civil law countries does offer a legal framework which can reflect more accurately the relationships created where such personal liability is imposed on the customs broker.

If therefore a system of licensed customs brokers together with a system of guaranteed credit in respect of customs dues is introduced into the United Kingdom the courts will find it necessary to develop the law in this field. It is unfortunate that in the past where such cases have come before the courts the judges concerned have not always appeared to understand the problems on which they are required to adjudicate. As Jones J. said, on the question of the nature of customs clearance,[53]

> " I found it very difficult at the time to discover what the process is, but I think I have in the end discovered what the process is. Mr. Butcher [a witness] agreed that it is a special business and certain people do it, but he himself did not know about it."

Such statements both by the Bench and those in the field of transportation do not inspire much confidence in the clarification of the legal position of those engaged in customs clearance operations unless some form of government regulation is introduced.

---

[53] *Robert Shearer Ltd.* v. *Road Haulage Executive* [1952] 1 Lloyd's Rep. 512 at p. 516.

CHAPTER 17

THE FORWARDER AND INSURANCE

1. INTRODUCTION

468 As an intermediary in arranging transportation, the forwarder is well placed to arrange insurance cover for goods in transit on behalf of his client, and in many cases he will combine both the functions of a forwarder and of an insurance agent. In the case of the very large forwarders, a separate insurance brokerage company may be formed as a convenient method of handling insurance business, which will deal with risks which may emanate from the parent forwarding company or from other sources. Medium-sized forwarders who cannot generate sufficient business to warrant a separate company may possess an insurance department, from which most of the brokerage companies run by the larger groups have developed as business expanded. Smaller forwarders generally have no insurance facilities at all and place their business through brokers or the local insurance company offices.

Although the larger shippers often arrange their own cover by means of a declaration policy covering their shipments generally, the forwarder will arrange cover for the shipper in many cases as it is often easier for a client to sign the necessary documents and leave the matter completely to the forwarder. There are certain advantages for a shipper to employ a forwarder to handle insurance risks on his behalf. First, while performing forwarding services, insurance can be dealt with automatically at the same time, saving both money and the chance of omission or incorrect cover. Secondly, the large volume of goods in transit business handled by the larger forwarders places them in a favourable position with insurance underwriters in respect of rates, difficult risks and the payment of claims. Furthermore, the forwarder will generally be in possession of the necessary documents himself to effect the contract of insurance on behalf of his principal.

469 Where a forwarding group possesses its own broking company, the relationship between the former's client and the latter is a normal relationship of principal and agent when obtaining insurance cover. Likewise in covering the forwarder's own liability to third parties, the broking company acts as the forwarder's agent in arranging the insurance. From the procedural viewpoint, in arranging normal marine insurance, the broking company will not usually deal with the client direct, but will act through the forwarding company. The client will not therefore have any contact with the broking company, and may not know of its existence. In the case of non-marine cover and open marine cover, the broker may deal direct with the client, as would any other insurance broker, who is not part of a forwarding group. The reason for this is that such business may not arise out of the forwarding side of the business.

2. DUTIES OF A FORWARDER IN RELATION TO INSURANCE

470   In undertaking to arrange for the insurance of goods in transit the forwarder acts as an agent on behalf of his principal, who may either be the consignor or consignee of the shipment in question. The duties of the forwarder in so doing can be divided into three categories. First, his obligations at common law in respect of insurance cover of goods in transit. Secondly, his obligations under Standard Trading Conditions. Thirdly, the duties of a forwarder where he is given special instructions to effect insurance cover. Each category will be considered in turn.

471   Common law

At common law in " the ordinary case of a forwarding agent dealing, in the ordinary course of his business, with commercial goods," there is no obligation on a forwarder either to insure goods on behalf of his client or to inquire whether the latter has effected cover for them whilst in transit or not.[1]

Accordingly in *W.L.R. Traders Ltd.* v. *B. & N. Shipping Agency Ltd.*[2] where a forwarder was employed to arrange the collection of an f.o.b. shipment of nylon stockings from a client's premises to be delivered to the docks for shipment, and which was not insured, the court rejected the seller's argument that the forwarder had a duty either to insure the goods or to inquire whether the seller had covered them, on the grounds that it is normal practice for a seller to cover them himself under an f.o.b. contract from his warehouse to the ship's rail.[2]

However, the forwarder also has a common law duty to exercise reasonable care and skill in undertaking the task of forwarding and this may involve obtaining instructions as to whether insurance cover should be obtained. Instructions may in fact not be given directly by a shipper, but by a sending forwarder, as in *Von Traubenberg* v. *Davies Turner & Co. Ltd.*[3] The facts were that the defendants were instructed, as receiving agents in the United Kingdom, to forward a suitcase on arrival by air from Germany to the plaintiff's home in Liverpool. This they did by railway from London, the case being irrecoverably lost. The case was consigned at "company's risk," that is, liability was limited in accordance with the Carriers Act to £25. Although the forwarders knew that the case contained valuable heirlooms, they failed to make a declaration under the Act and to pay a

---

[1] *W.L.R. Traders Ltd.* v. *B. & N. Shipping Agency Ltd.* [1955] 1 Lloyd's Rep. 554 at p. 558.

[2] *Ibid.*

[3] [1951] 2 Lloyd's Rep. 462 at p. 466, *per* Somervell L.J.

higher rate for the railway company to accept a greater liability than £25. Such a procedure would have been quite reasonable if the goods in question had been otherwise insured, which they were not. The court held that the forwarder had undertaken " to arrange the transfer of this consignment from Berlin to this country," and had a duty to exercise reasonable care and skill in doing so. This they failed to do by not getting instructions from the plaintiff as to the protection required for the transit.[4] Instead, "The defendants ... made up their own minds without getting any instructions from or giving any information to the plaintiff as to what she required, and ... it is at that point that they failed in their duty." To take such care in forwarding shipments is "the whole object of the employment of forwarding agents" and they were therefore liable for the loss in question.

472   The question therefore arises as to how these two cases are to be reconciled with each other, as *Von Traubenberg's* case was distinguished by the court in the *W.L.R. Traders* case. The basis of such a distinction is not very clear, but it can be justified on the grounds of the terms of the particular contract entered into, and perhaps on the grounds that *Von Traubenberg's* case was not a transaction involving commercial goods, unlike the *W.L.R. Traders* case, as it involved a client's personal possessions. The logical inference is therefore that a forwarder must exercise more care when dealing with non-professional clients than with those habitually engaged in commerce. Furthermore, in the *W.L.R. Traders* case the forwarding was in connection with a normal f.o.b. contract involving carriage from the seller's premises to the ship's rail, in respect of which it is customary for the seller to effect cover himself, whereas no such question of any established trade practice arose in *Von Traubenberg's* case. The general rule is therefore that expressed in the *W.L.R. Traders* case, and that laid down by the Court of Appeal in *Von Traubenberg's* case seemingly only applicable in limited circumstances.[5]

473 Open cover

In undertaking to effect insurance the forwarder does not undertake to effect an individual policy for each consignment, unless specifically instructed, but reserves the right to declare a consignment under an open cover or floating policy, which most forwarders invariably take out.[6]

The problem was discussed in *James Vale & Co.* v. *Van Oppen & Co. Ltd.*[7] Here the defendants were a firm of forwarders who were

---

[4] Being a receiving agent the forwarder would not act subject to S.T.C., otherwise s. 10 would offer adequate protection.

[5] See *Club Speciality (Overseas) Inc.* v. *United Marine* [1971] 1 Lloyd's Rep. 482.

[6] See §§ 483 *et seq.*

[7] (1921) 6 Ll.L.Rep. 167 at p. 168, a full report, but with errors. 37 T.L.R. 367, a short report.

"neither insurance brokers themselves nor ... carriers or insurers," but in connection with their business of forwarding "procure the insurance of goods which they undertake to forward."[8] The plaintiffs employed them to forward goods from Leeds to Barcelona, the shipment being covered under a floating policy, which the defendants had effected. On the loss of the shipment, the insurers refused to pay on the grounds that it had not been established that the loss was the result of any of the risks insured against. The cover actually obtained was subject to W.A. conditions only. The plaintiffs argued that they had instructed the forwarders to insure against all risks, although it appeared that this was extremely difficult on the London market, W.A. being then the normal cover under a marine policy.

The question therefore arose as to whether the forwarder was negligent in not effectively covering the shipper's goods but merely obtaining cover under its existing floating policy. The court held that the mistake did not constitute negligence, and the forwarder was therefore not liable, having effected the customary marine cover as accepted at that time on the market.

474 Forwarder's duty of care in effecting insurance cover

It seems therefore that where a forwarder is not actually acting as an insurance broker he will not be expected to use the skill and care expected from one. Where however he functions as both, he may be subject to a greater obligation, inasmuch as his obligations will not merely be those of a forwarder placing insurance on behalf of his principal as a service for his clients, but will be subject to the standard of care that is expected of a person holding himself out as a professional insurance broker.[9]

Where a forwarding group has its own broking company, a further consideration arises, as it will be necessary to decide first, where advice is given, whether it emanates from the broking company, or as in *Vale's* case from the forwarding company itself. Secondly, if it merely emanates from the latter, can it rely on the fact as in *Vale's* case, that it is not a professional insurance broker and therefore does not hold itself out to have knowledge of the insurance market to a professional degree, or will it be considered in breach of duty to its client and therefore prima facie negligent in not referring the matter to the broking company in its group, whose advice would be readily available? Such a question has not come before the courts for consideration as yet, but it seems that in such a case the standard of care expected of the forwarder should, if not actually that of an insurance broker himself, at least demand that reference should be made to its associate broking company, especially considering the artificiality of the divisions

---

[8] *Ibid.* at p. 168.
[9] *Cf. United Mills Agencies* v. *Harvey Bray, infra.*

between such legal corporate bodies in their relationships with each other in multiple corporate trading groups.

475   It is instructive to compare the duty of an insurance broker with that of a forwarder in a similar situation. For example, if a broker is instructed to effect an open marine cover at Lloyd's on behalf of its client, being instructed that a normal export cover is required, that is on "warehouse to warehouse" terms, without any mention being made of goods being sent to packers en route, such a provision not being a regular clause, there is no obligation on the broker to raise the matter with his client. In *United Mills Agencies* v. *Harvey Bray* [10] a shipment was burnt at the packers (Lep Transport) who regularly packed and then forwarded the goods to the port. The court rejected the plaintiff's argument that the broker was negligent in not covering the goods at the packers, not having been specifically instructed to do so, and considered that no duty lay upon him to do so merely because he had been informed that the goods in question were actually at the packers. In such circumstances he is " entitled to assume that the merchant has conducted his business prudently and has covered his goods . . . , while they were . . . at packers." [11]

Furthermore, McNair J. observed, that although it is the practice of insurance brokers to notify their client as soon as possible, when cover has been obtained, it is not part of their duty to do so, and no case law exists to this effect. Such a situation would put an intolerable burden on a broker, so that the mere fact that the latter delayed in sending the cover note to his client, and thus prevented him from checking the terms of the insurance, did not constitute negligence.[12] As to what extent a broker can rely on a merchant's " prudent " conduct of his business will depend upon the particular circumstances and upon the customary trade usages, and depending on this whether or not such omission will constitute negligence on the part of a broker or forwarder.

476 Standard Trading Conditions

The basic obligation of the forwarder will depend in practice upon the particular contract made with the shipper, which in the case of a British forwarder will usually be subject to Standard Trading Conditions. The relevant provision is laid down in Clause 12 as follows:

" No insurance will be effected except upon express instructions given in writing by the Customer and all insurances effected by the Company are subject to the usual exceptions and conditions of the

---

[10] [1951] 2 Lloyd's Rep. 631.
[11] *Ibid.* at p. 643, *per* McNair J. *Cf.* the position of a forwarder in respect of non-commercial shipments, or where the forwarder has failed in his overall duty as such, neither of which factors were applicable here.
[12] *Ibid.*

policies of the insurance company or underwriters taking the risk. The Company shall not be under any obligation to effect a separate insurance on each consignment but may declare it on any open or general policy. Should the insurers dispute their liability for any reason the insured shall have recourse against the insurers only and the Company shall not be under any responsibility or liability in relation thereto notwithstanding that the premium upon the policy may not be at the same rate as that charged by the Company or paid to the Company by its customer."

This clause is intended to overcome many of the problems discussed above. First, the forwarder will only effect insurance on the express written instructions of his client, irrespective of whether he has notice of the value or nature of the goods or not. Accordingly, where a forwarder failed to insure a valuable consignment of watches which he had undertaken to clear and forward from London Airport to his client's premises in London, as the contract was subject to Standard Trading Conditions he was not bound to insure it, having had no express instructions in writing to that effect. The goods were therefore at the owner's risk.[13] It therefore appears that if in *Von Traubenberg's* case the contract had been subject to Standard Trading Conditions the forwarder would have been fully protected. Similarly in the *W.L.R. Traders* case although the forwarder was exonerated in any case by law, unnecessary litigation would have been avoided in establishing the exact position if Clause 12 had been incorporated into the contract.

477   Secondly, the forwarder reserves the right to declare a consignment under any open cover or floating policy he may possess, unless instructed to the contrary, which merely reiterates the apparent position at common law.[14] Thirdly, irrespective of the method of insurance used, all insurances entered into by the forwarder will be subject to the usual terms of the insurer concerned. The exact meaning of this provision is not clear, but presumably it is intended to cover any special limitations which underwriters may from time to time impose, as in *Vale's* case above, subject again to any special instructions the forwarder may be given.[15]

478   Finally, Clause 12 provides that the forwarder does not accept any personal liability where an insurer disputes a claim, the client only having recourse against the latter.[16] This proviso is to take effect even though the premium charged to the client may be different (*i.e.* greater) to that charged by the insurer. This covers both the question

---

[13] *Colverd & Co. Ltd.* v. *Anglo-Overseas Transport Co. Ltd.* [1961] 2 Lloyd's Rep. 352 at pp. 357 *et seq.*
[14] *Supra.*
[15] See below.
[16] *Cf. J. H. Brown* v. *American Express Co.* at note 20, which was not subject to S.T.C.

of agency commission paid by the insurer to the forwarder, and also the related problem that a premium payable under a forwarder's floating policy may be substantially lower than that rated for a particular consignment when treated as an individual risk, the latter rate being charged by the forwarder to his client, and the difference between the two rates being retained by the forwarder by way of profit. In practice therefore Clause 12 has furnished the forwarder with comprehensive protection as regards the insurance of goods in transit. Furthermore even if he fails to perform any written instructions which his client may give him, Clause 13 (ii) protects the forwarder against all liability for "non-compliance or mis-compliance" unless caused by his wilful negligence or that of his servants.[17]

479   Special instructions

At common law however where an agent is given special instructions by his client as to insurance he is bound to comply with them exactly. If he is unable to do so, he has a duty to inform his principal promptly of the fact, and if he fails to do so, he will be personally liable for any loss resulting. For instance, in a case before the Mayor's Court,[18] forwarders were engaged to ship cloth to Amsterdam, with instructions to insure against all risks. This they did, but through late delivery the shipment was refused by the consignees, instructions being given to return it, and again to insure against all risks on the return journey. In fact the defendants took out a policy which excluded liability for pilfering as the underwriters would not cover it, and which unfortunately occurred. The court held the forwarders liable for the loss.

If, however, the forwarder fulfils his obligation and effects the requisite insurance cover in accordance with his principal's instructions, he will not be liable to the latter merely because the underwriters refuse to pay on the particular claim because they are not satisfied with the evidence of the loss. Accordingly, in *Jones* v. *European & General Express Company Ltd.*[19] where forwarders were employed to forward merchandise and to insure it against loss by pilferage, which they declared under an open policy, the latter were held not liable for non-payment by the insurer on these grounds. The court stated that they had not "guaranteed that the underwriters would pay or would make no dispute. They undertook to place the plaintiff's risk with the underwriters at that time and they did so, and there is no ground for

---

[17] It should be noted, however, that where a forwarder whether in the capacity of a Lloyd's broker in which case he accepts personal liability for the premium, or else on account, has paid or is obliged to pay insurance premiums to an underwriter, he will not necessarily be able to recover them from the consignors even if accustomed to receiving shipping instructions from them, if it was known that the latter were merely acting as agents on behalf of a third party and not as principals in relation to the forwarder. *J. S. Holt & Moseley (London) Ltd.* v. *Sir Charles Cunningham & Partners* (1949) 83 Ll.L.Rep. 141.

[18] *Tubbs, Hiscocks & Co. Ltd.* v. *Ancre Transport Co.*, Lloyd's List, July 23, 1921. *Cf. Mabillon & Co.* v. *L.E.P. Transport Ltd.* at note 23 below.

[19] (1920) 4 Ll.L.Rep. 127.

complaint against them because the underwriters took what the plaintiff thinks is an unjustifiable view."[20]

480   Where however a forwarder fails to fulfil his broader duty of care in respect of the whole forwarding operation of which the arranging of insurance is but one aspect, the rule in *Jones's* case does not prevent a client from recovering independently from a forwarder, as insurance cover for any risk is merely a collateral protection, intended to give a guaranteed indemnity in respect of any loss, rather than to obviate the right of action against the party in breach.

It therefore appears that where a forwarder undertakes responsibility for arranging transit insurance of a shipment which he has also undertaken to forward, his duty, although still that of an agent, will be enhanced by his obligation to arrange the safest method of transportation available, together with his obviously greater knowledge of the risks involved.[21] An insurance agent as such can only act upon the instructions of his principal, the insured, but in the case of a forwarder, the obligation to arrange insurance cover is but one aspect of a larger transaction, and cannot be considered in isolation from the whole.

3. INADEQUACY OF COVER

481 The purpose of insurance cover for goods in transit is normally to reimburse the shipper against any physical loss or damage to his interest. If the duty of effecting such cover is undertaken by a forwarder, his prime duty will be to ensure that the cover obtained is both adequate and effective, and he will be liable if he fails to ensure that this is so.

For example, in effecting insurance for a shipper forwarders obtained a policy which stipulated that only goods to the value of £2,000 were to be shipped in one bottom. A shipment in excess of that amount was in fact so shipped, instead of being allocated to several

---

[20] *Ibid.* at p. 127, *per* Rowlatt J.   *Cf. J. H. Brown* v. *American Express Co. Lloyd's List*, June 10, 1921, where the defendants who were held to be forwarders and not common carriers, had agreed to forward goods to Poland which never arrived even after a 15 months' delay owing to wartime conditions. They had effected insurance on the parcel at Lloyd's on behalf of the plaintiff who had signed the defendants' trading conditions, which stated, *inter alia*, that any insurances effected were subject to all conditions and exceptions applicable at Lloyd's. The question therefore arose as to whether the forwarders were liable for the value of the sum insured, as the underwriter refused to meet the claim on the grounds that no definite proof of loss had been offered. The court held that as the insured could not get satisfaction from the insurer, even though the insurance had been effected by the defendants as the agent of the shipper, the forwarders were liable to the plaintiff for the amount in question. Although the ratio of this case is not clear as few reasons appear in the judgment, the decision can be explained on the grounds that as the forwarder was obviously aware of the disturbed state of the country of destination, he should have taken this into consideration when obtaining insurance cover, so that an acceptable proof of loss could have been arranged particularly as the client was not engaged in commercial shipment of the goods in question.

[21] *Cf. Anglo-African Merchants Ltd.* v. *Bayley* [1969] 1 Lloyd's Rep. 268 (insurance broker).

ships so as not to exceed the limit. In such a case, if the insurer refused to pay the whole loss, which was in excess of £2,000, then the forwarders could be liable for the balance of the sum, as it was their duty to ensure that the method of shipment was within the terms of the insurance cover obtained. The fact that they had acted merely as agents in obtaining insurance cover and had informed their principal that the goods were insured under one cover, would not relieve them of their duty as forwarders.[22] Similarly, where a forwarder undertakes to pack and store goods and to arrange insurance cover for them whilst held in warehouse pending shipment, he will be liable if he stores them in a manner not covered by the policy.[23]

The forwarder must also ensure that when a policy is taken out under-insurance does not occur, that is, that the sum insured fairly represents the value of the goods in question. However, forwarders generally arrange the maximum cover possible unless specifically instructed to the contrary.[24]

482   Where a client instructs a forwarder to check whether a valid insurance policy is in existence or not in respect of a through shipment, which the former is transhipping, he will be liable for negligent performance of his duty if he fails to do so. In *Gomer* v. *Pitt & Scott*,[25] such a situation occurred, the forwarders being required to ascertain whether the policy in question which was lodged with a bank merely covered a shipment as far as London, or also for the further leg of the voyage to Lisbon, so as to enable the plaintiff consignee to insure the latter if no cover existed. Accordingly the plaintiff instructed the forwarders to "call at the bank and see the policy." This they failed to do, merely contenting themselves with a bank clerk's ambiguous note confirming that the bank held the policy, but without mentioning the voyage covered. The Court of Appeal considered that the failure to obtain a more explicit assurance from the bank constituted negligence on the part of the forwarders, and that the latter were guilty of a further breach of duty in not insisting on inspecting the policy, and if this was refused,

---

[22] *Guignan Frères* v. *Cox* (1920) 5 Ll.L.Rep. 49, *per* Bailhache J.
[23] *Firmin & Collins Ltd.* v. *Allied Shippers Ltd.* [1967] 1 Lloyd's Rep. 633, 639.
[24] But where a forwarder was instructed to obtain " insurance in full," and in fact only obtained 75 per cent. cover owing to a condition ruling at that time that underwriters would only underwrite that amount, it was held that the forwarder had performed his duty adequately, and was not liable in respect of the uninsured balance, even though he had not brought this limitation to the notice of his client. *Mabillon & Co.* v. *L.E.P. Transport Ltd.*, *World's Carriers*, June 15, 1921, Westminster County Court, quoting *Jones* v. *European & General Express Co. Ltd.*, *supra*. As to baggage, etc., policies see *King* v. *Travellers' Insurance Association Ltd.* (1931) 41 Ll.L.Rep. 13. Similarly, an underwriter may include a warranty in a policy that one of a nominated list of specialist packers should be employed to pack valuable articles. If a forwarder fails to do so, and damage results to the goods, resulting in non-payment of the claim, the forwarder will be liable himself for the loss if he has effected insurance himself or is aware of the terms of the policy—the question was briefly discussed in *International Art Depositories* v. *Wingate & Johnson Ltd.*, *Lloyd's List*, April 27, 1928, *per* Roche J.
[25] (1922) 12 Ll.L.Rep. 115.

for failing to inform their principal of the fact and the statement made by the bank, which they failed to do.

4. METHODS OF EFFECTING INSURANCE BY A FORWARDER FOR HIS CLIENT

483 The responsibilities of a forwarder in effecting insurance on behalf of his client have already been discussed in the previous Section. It is now necessary to consider the methods by which insurance can be effected to cover the various interests in a consignment whilst it is in transit, or else being packed or warehoused. This is normally achieved by a forwarder negotiating with an underwriter one or more contracts whereby the latter undertakes to cover all shipments handled by the forwarder against various risks, conditions and voyages. This will be for a limited period of time or for a specified amount. The interest to be covered is that of the client and not that of the forwarder. The latter's interest will normally be covered by a separate policy.

484 Floating policies

The form of policy used is known as a floating policy.[26] Under such a policy, the forwarder avoids the necessity of negotiating on behalf of his client an individual policy to cover each shipment. Under this blanket policy, which is effected in the name of the forwarder, the latter may be authorised to issue a certificate of insurance in respect of each shipment which incorporates the principal terms and conditions of the master policy. The forwarder is supplied with special forms for the purpose. The procedure is that the latter prepares a quadruplicate set of certificates, one being returned to the underwriter, one retained by the forwarder for the record and the other copies normally passed on to the assured. As such policies are on a declaration basis, the copy to the insurer fulfils this function.[27]

485 Open cover

An alternative method is for an open cover to be effected. This is similar in effect to a floating policy, but although it is a contract between the forwarder and the underwriter to cover all shipments for a certain period

---

[26] In *Jones* v. *European and General Express Co. Ltd.* (1920) 4 Ll.L.Rep. 127, Rowlatt J. discussed the duty of a forwarder when effecting cover under an open policy which appears to be a " floating policy." See Marine Insurance Act 1906, s. 29.

[27] The distinction should be noted between the operative effect of a declaration under an existing " open " policy and an application for cover in respect of a fresh risk, as in the latter case there must be both an application for cover and an acceptance of the risk by the underwriter before a valid contract of insurance arises, which is not automatic unlike in the case of a declaration under an open policy. Furthermore there is no duty on the part of the underwriter to act promptly on an application for cover, as he is under no obligation to accept the risk: *French American* v. *Fireman's Fund* [1942] A.M.C. 28.

of time, normally twelve months, it is not a valid contract of insurance. Stamped policies must therefore be issued for all consignments in respect of which a declaration has been made under the open cover. Certificates may be declared or issued under an open cover in exactly the same way as under a floating policy.[28]

486 Certificate of insurance

The use of the floating policy in conjunction with a certificate of insurance to cover a specific risk can create problems in ascertaining the exact cover obtained. In *Macleod Ross & Co. Ltd.* v. *Compagnie d'Assurances Générales l'Helvétia*,[29] Danzas, a French firm of forwarders, took out a *police d'abonnement* or open cover with the defendants, Swiss insurers, against all risks in respect of goods shipped by the forwarders' clients, on a declaration basis. The plaintiffs purchased goods from S., a client of Danzas, in respect of which the latter made a declaration and the defendants issued a certificate of insurance in Switzerland to S. who sent it to the plaintiffs. The goods in question were damaged.

In the action which ensued when the insurers refused to meet the claim, the question arose as to whether the plaintiffs were bound by Article 31 of the General Conditions of the open cover which stated that "underwriters . . . can only be sued before Tribunals of Commerce of the place where the contract was entered into," *i.e.* Switzerland. Certain special conditions in respect of war risks were included in the certificate, which were not in the open cover, and conversely certain extracts from the General Conditions of the latter were printed on the back of the certificate, Article 31 did not appear. The question therefore arose as to whether the certificate was a new self-contained contract, and Article 31 having been deliberately omitted did not apply, or was it to be incorporated into the certificate as a term of the insurance contract.

487   The Court of Appeal considered that there were in fact two contracts between the insurers and the forwarders. The first, in which the defendants were principals with "rights and obligations under this contract," was

> " 1. The *police d'abonnement*—or " open cover " whereby the insurance company agreed to insure all goods of which the forwarding agents took charge, provided that their customers had asked them to effect insurance of them. In order that the goods

---

[28] It should be noted that a certificate of insurance or broker's cover are not acceptable under a c.i.f. contract unless a trade usage to the contrary exists. See *Harper & Co. Ltd.* v. *R. D. MacKechnie & Co.* (1925) 22 Ll.L.Rep. 514, *per* Roche J., Arnould, *Marine Insurance*, para. 195. Consequently a forwarder may be in breach of his duty to his principal in arranging cover under an open policy by a certificate, when the terms of the shipment require an actual policy.
[29] [1952] 1 Lloyd's Rep. 12.

should be covered the forwarding agents, on taking charge of them, had to enter details in a book and send corresponding declarations to the insurance company.

2. The *avenant d'assurance* or " certificate of insurance," whereby the insurance company implemented the contract contained in the open cover. Each of these certificates was . . . a new contract in respect of the goods covered by it."[30]

In other words although it was implied that in certain circumstances the open cover should be referred to in order to ascertain the complete terms of the insurance, in the circumstances the certificate was a complete insurance contract in itself, and Article 31 merely a collateral procedural condition by which the plaintiffs were not bound. Furthermore, although an open cover is a contract entered into by a forwarder as a principal, the court considered that, at least in the form used by the defendants, a second contract, that of the certificate of insurance, was entered into by the forwarders as agents for the shippers as well as for themselves. It should be noted that when the certificate is issued by an insurer in such a case, the certificate is made out to the order of the insured, that is the forwarder. The certificate usually provides that the indemnity is payable to the holder, which renders it freely assignable, this being effected by indorsement, initially by the forwarder to the shipper and thence onwards by him to any subsequent transferee to whom the shipping documents are transferred.

488 Payment of claims

Where under a floating policy insurance is effected in respect of a particular shipment by a forwarder, a cover note or certificate of insurance may be issued by the forwarder or the broker and indorsed to the client. In such circumstances the client will normally employ the same broker to collect any claim on his behalf. It will be no defence for the broker to plead that payment has been made to the forwarder because the policy is in his name, when the latter goes into liquidation before having paid his client. As Bailhache J. observed " Of course they were in possession of the policy, because it was a policy not only on these goods, but on many other consignments, and was an open policy on [the policy holder]. I see no reason why . . . the defendants should have paid [the policy holder]." [31] The broker will be bound to pay the holder of the certificate and not the forwarder who holds the policy, or else he will have failed to account to his principal in respect of the claim, and will therefore still remain liable for the amount.[32]

---

[30] *Ibid.* at p. 16, *per* Denning L.J.
[31] *Wolf & Korkhaus* v. *Tyser & Co.* (1921) 8 Ll.L.Rep. 340 at p. 341.
[32] However, if the forwarder is owed the premium for the insurance on which the claim has arisen, he may have in respect thereof a particular lien on the certificate and a right of set-off against the proceeds of such claim: *Mildred* v. *Maspons* (1883) 8 App.Cas. 874.

5. PROVISIONS IN OTHER COUNTRIES

489 U.S.A.

It is not possible to discuss more than a few countries whose provisions are particularly relevant to the United Kingdom forwarding trade. Moreover certain countries such as Australia and New Zealand have no regular form of contractual provision, so that no generalisations are possible. In the United States, the New York Foreign Freight Forwarders and Brokers Association Inc. has recently published a revised version of the Association's " Terms and Conditions," of which Article 7 makes similar provision to Clause 12 of Standard Trading Conditions.

490 The Federal Maritime Commission is empowered by statutory provision to regulate ocean freight forwarders in relation to insurance matters. By section 44 (c) of the Shipping Act, the Commission is authorised to require that a forwarder furnish a " bond or other security " to " insure financial responsibility." The forwarder is also required to set forth in his invoice to a shipper the charge for each accessorial service performed, including the placing of insurance.[34] A uniform schedule of fees for " arranging insurance " must be filed with the Commission. The Interstate Commerce Act and the Civil Aeronautics Board also make provision for the regulation of freight forwarders engaged in interstate and air forwarding. The Interstate Commerce Commission is empowered by section 403 (c) and (d) of the Interstate Commerce Act to prescribe reasonable rules and regulations in relation to surety bonds, policies of insurance and self-insurance in respect of the forwarder's various activities.[35] The Civil Aeronautics Board's Economic Regulations require that no freight forwarder is to engage in air transportation unless he first files a suitable insurance policy, surety bond or evidence of self-insurance covering damage or loss to cargo and also with respect to public liability, etc.[36]

491 Continental countries—France

In European countries subject to the civil law, similar provisions are also found restricting the forwarder's liability when effecting insurance on behalf of a client.[37] In France Conditions Générales are the principal form of standard contract in use, although here, as in the United Kingdom, the question is one that has relied upon case law

---

[34] Rule 510.23 (j), General Order 4.
[35] See § 38.
[36] S. 296.51, C.A.B. Econ. Regulations.
[37] Where a forwarder is in effect operating as a carrier for the purposes of C.M.R. in respect of a contract of international carriage, although no specific mention is made of insurance, it seems that as the parties will be bound by the terms of the consignment note, there will be no obligation to insure unless instructions are included in the note to this effect: see Art. 6 (2) (e), C.M.R.

for an authoritative statement of the law. If there is a specific stipulation to insure against certain risks, as at English common law, the forwarder will be liable for any loss if he fails to do so.[38] Conversely, where the contract provides that the forwarder is only to insure when formally instructed by his client, he will not be liable if he does not do so, although if he does so of his own volition he cannot recover the amount of the premium from his client.[39] Where the contract is silent upon the question of insurance, that is, where it is not effected subject to Conditions Générales, it seems that again there will be no obligation on a forwarder to insure.[40] Provision is also made in Conditions Générales that if a client does not place his insurance through the forwarder, he undertakes that it is to be a stipulation in the policy that the insurers will not exercise any right of recourse against the forwarder in excess of that permitted under the Conditions, which otherwise they might do to reimburse themselves against any claim paid, under their right of subrogation.[41]

492 Scandinavia

Under the Northern Forwarding Conditions, which compass the four Scandinavian countries, provision is made under Article 8 that, as under British Standard Trading Conditions, the forwarder will only insure on receipt of written instructions to that effect. It does, however, go further in providing that prior general instructions in writing to effect insurance on shipments will be sufficient authorisation, that is where a regular trading relationship has been established, but the mere fact that a forwarder has insured shipments in the past for a particular person does not imply any obligation either to insure subsequent shipments or even to inquire whether insurance is to be effected or not.[42] Furthermore, the mere fact that a statement of value is included in forwarding instructions does not imply an order to insure. If the forwarder has received instructions to insure a certain shipment, without the risks to be covered being specified, an ordinary transport insurance, or in the case of storage, an ordinary fire insurance will be sufficient. This means that the category of policy customary in such circumstances in the country in question should be obtained.[43]

---

[38] Civ. Nov. 6, 1929, Rev.gen.ass.terr., 1930, p. 306.
[39] Art. 5, C.G. (France) provides that insurance against risks of transit will only be effected on the written instructions of the client. Douai, Jan. 2, 1930, Gaz. Pal., 1930.1.512. *Cf.* Arts. 29–30, C.G. (Italy).
[40] Trib. Cce. Seine, Nov. 27, 1941, Gaz. Pal., 1942.I.213. Rodière, *Droit des transports*, Section 1342, suggests that either the nature of the goods or special circumstances may give a forwarder implied authority to insure against certain risks.
[41] Art. 5, C.G. (France); Art. 44, C.G. (Belgium). *Cf. Coupar Transport (London) Ltd.* v. *Smith's (Acton) Ltd.* [1959] 1 Lloyd's Rep. 369 at p. 375.
[42] Art. 8, N.F.C. *Cf.* Arts. 35, 49, 50, Y.F.C.
[43] Art. 8, N.F.C. The ordinary transport policy must be free of particular average except stranding in the case of sea transport, and against traffic accidents in the case of rail or road transport. *Cf.* Art. 35, Y.F.C.

493   In a judgment of February 29, 1916, of the Cour Commerciale et
Maritime de Copenhagen,[44] a forwarder was held responsible for not
insuring a shipment of soap which had been lost at sea. As the consignor had already asked that two earlier shipments should be insured
unless shipped by a route with the minimum of war risks, the forwarder
could not ship by a more risky route without first asking the consignor
if he wished to insure against war risks. On appeal to the Danish
Supreme Court though, in its judgment of April 27, 1917, the court
reversed the decision at first instance, holding that under the Conditions
insurances are not effected by forwarders except under express
instructions in writing,[45] the latter therefore being protected.

However, in a more recent decision the Danish courts have rendered
the position concerning the validity of such a provision in relation to
insurance more obscure. The facts were that a Danish forwarder acted
on behalf of a Swedish company for certain shipments of a Danish
supplier to Switzerland, having effected insurance against war risks on
the instructions of his principal. After the conditions of insurance were
modified, the forwarder gave insufficient information to his principal
so that the cover for seven wagons, which were lost, was invalid. By
a judgment of March 7, 1951, the Danish Supreme Court [46] held
that the forwarder was liable for the loss, having failed " gravement "
in his obligations, the exceptions clause (Article 8) of the Conditions
not being applicable. A minority in the court supported the effectiveness of such a limitation, though.

494 Germany

In Germany the forwarder has a more definite protection under
A.D.S.P., which virtually carry the weight and authority of delegated
legislation, and which therefore apply almost universally. Articles
35–38 deal with the insurance of goods by forwarders. A provision
similar to that above is included, whereby insurance is only to be
effected upon written instructions, together with the value of the goods
and the specific risks to be covered. It should be noted though that if
full instructions are not given to the forwarder or are impracticable,
the latter has a discretion as to the cover to be obtained.[47] Such a
discretion is not found in the forwarding conditions of other countries,
where the most he is permitted to do is to take out an " ordinary "
policy, but this proviso would seem to offer a much wider discretion.[48]

---

[44] *Jacob Furstenberg* v. *Adams Express Co.*
[45] Now included in Art. 8, N.F.C. The Scandinavian cases discussed in this section
have been extracted from unpublished Unidroit materials.
[46] Reversing the decision of the Commercial and Maritime Court of Copenhagen of
December 18, 1948. *Cf.* the *Suisse Atlantique* case and the other English decisions
relating to fundamental breach discussed at §§ 158 *et seq.*
[47] Art. 35 (*a*), A.D.S.P., A.Ö.S.P.
[48] *Cf.* Art. 43, C.G. (Belgium), which provides that insurance will only be effected on the
specific instructions in writing which must be repeated in writing for each shipment.
Furthermore a mere indication of the value does not constitute a formal instruction.
Cf. Art. 35, Y.F.C.

In effecting an insurance policy, the forwarder does not take upon himself any of the obligations of the insured, although he is bound to take such steps as may be necessary to preserve any claims which may occur under the policy, such as giving notice to the company, etc.[49] Furthermore, the principal is only entitled to the amount received by the forwarder from an insurer under the terms of the policy— he will not be liable for any excess which is not covered by it.

However, these provisions are supplemented by Articles 39–41 whereby the forwarder is bound to take out a SVS policy covering forwarding risks other than insurance of the goods, and a RVS policy, covering cartage risks, unless expressly forbidden to do so in writing by his client. This will be effected at the client's expense, though, and will be subject to the terms and conditions of the SVS and RVS policies which are published as annexed documents to A.D.S.P. conditions. Providing the forwarder does effect such cover, he is relieved of liability for any loss which is covered by the policies although if he has failed to effect cover subject to the terms of the SVS and RVS policies with the nominated insurers,[50] he cannot rely upon the provisions of A.D.S.P. in any dispute with his client.[51]

495 Holland

The Dutch Forwarding Conditions, like the British Standard Trading Conditions, do not carry any official standing, and again precedents have conflicted as to the circumstances in which they will operate. Similar provisions to those in the Northern Forwarding Conditions are found in respect of insurance with a further proviso that the forwarder accepts no responsibility either as to choice of insurer or his ability to pay, though presumably this would not protect him if he was grossly negligent in choosing an underwriter of dubious standing.[52] A similar provision is to be found in the Swiss Conditions

---

[49] Art. 35 (c), A.D.S.P., A.Ö.S.P.

[50] Or other insurers granting policies under terms similar to SVS and RVS—according to a recent decision of the Bundesgerichtshof.

[51] Art. 41, A.D.S.P. The scheme known as SVS provides for the compensation of torts by a fund subscribed by compulsory premiums paid by the forwarder's client, the forwarder invoicing him for the premium together with his other charges. It is a low charge on an *ad valorem* basis. The Austrians adopted a similar system after 1945. In Sweden the German system is in use, but is not followed by all forwarders, although it has been approved by the Chambers of Commerce. In Finland participation is voluntary, although once a shipment has been insured by a client he must also insure all further shipments. In Belgium is found the other principal forwarder's liability scheme called AREX. This pool scheme is used by about one-third of Belgian forwarders. It is operated by affixing Pool-Arex stamps to invoices, of which the premiums are paid by the client. The scheme differs from SVS inasmuch as it is a mutual scheme worked through an insurance pool, which in fact functions as a re-insurance company, which undertakes the administration and re-insurance with normal insurance companies. Many forwarders offer this insurance through individual policies though.

[52] Art. 5 (3), D.F.C.

Générales.[53] Special provisions are also included in all three concerning the assignment of the forwarder's rights under an insurance policy to his client.[54]

496   It can therefore be seen that although certain conditions concerning the effecting of insurance by a forwarder for his client are common to most European countries, each does have minor variants, which like the principal conditions may either have quasi-statutory authority, such as in the case of Germany, or else have achieved recognition by the relevant courts. Otherwise, whether such provisions will bind a client or not will depend upon whether the Standard Trading Conditions in question are either treated by the law as being of general commercial knowledge, and therefore universally binding or else incorporated by specific agreement between the parties into the contract, in which case they will bind the parties as would any other terms voluntarily agreed upon.

497 Unidroit

It is interesting to note however that the recent " Draft Convention on the contract of agency for forwarding agents relating to the international carriage of goods " drawn up by Unidroit, does not make any provision relating to the obligations of a forwarder in respect of insurance, so that even if this is adopted and eventually becomes of binding force, reliance will still have to be placed upon the individual national trading conditions in this respect.

498 F.I.A.T.A. documents

The situation will be similar where a contract is entered into subject to the F.I.A.T.A. sponsored Forwarders Certificate of Receipt (F.C.R.), or the Forwarders Certificate of Transport (F.C.T.). Although the latter specifies that insurance will only be effected on the express written instructions of a client, it really only reiterates the standard clause found in virtually all national trading conditions so that it does not effect any material change in current contractual conditions. F.C.R. does not mention the point, but as both F.C.R. and F.C.T. also expressly incorporate the national standard trading conditions of the country in question into any contract entered into subject to them, the position seems to be exactly the same as if the initial forwarding contract had been entered into under standard trading conditions, as regards the question of insurance.[55]

6. CONCLUSIONS

499 The duties of a forwarder in effecting insurance cover on behalf of his

---

[53] Art. 8 (3), C.G. (Switzerland).
[54] Art. 5 (2), D.F.C. See Art. 9, N.F.C.; Art. 8 (3), C.G. (Switzerland).
[55] For further discussion, see Chapter 13.

client will vary dependent upon certain criteria. First, if the forwarder is also operating as an insurance broker he may be subject to the same degree of professional care as would be expected of a broker. In other words, a thorough knowledge of insurance underwriting procedures would be required of him. However, in certain circumstances a broker may not be required to inquire whether his client has obtained insurance cover or not, whereas in his capacity of a forwarder such an inquiry may be an integral part of his duty as such, particularly where the client is not a merchant.[56]

The duties of a forwarder in relation to insurance will be those appertaining at common law, either in effecting the actual cover itself, or else under the general duty of care expected of a forwarder in performing his forwarding operations. Where a client has instructed a forwarder to effect cover, the latter's duty will generally be limited to carrying out his principal's instructions on the matter, and compliance therewith will normally exonerate him from further liability, although the forwarder will be bound to inform his principal of any discrepancies as to the cover obtained, unless this is a matter of common knowledge among the merchant community.[57] Here again, the forwarder's duty to a non-mercantile client will presumably be more onerous.[58]

500 In practice, many of these problems will not arise where the contract is subject to Standard Trading Conditions as Clause 12 only renders the forwarder liable to effect insurance cover where instructions in writing are given, thus relieving him of any obligation to use any discretion on the matter.[59] As yet no dispute has arisen where a forwarder has volunteered erroneous advice on the question of insurance of goods in transit, but as Clause 12 does not cover the point presumably the common law duty of reasonable care would apply, irrespective of whether the forwarder also operated as an insurance broker or not.

As regards the method of effecting cover, as it is common practice for a forwarder to effect cover for his client, through his own floating policy, rather than through a separate policy, Clause 12, Standard Trading Conditions, specifically gives the forwarder complete discretion on this point. As can be seen from *Macleod's* case, difficulties can arise where the certificate issued by a forwarder to a client is not *ad idem* with the principal policy, but this is an administrative matter rather than one of law.

501 Finally, the provisions in the forwarding conditions of other countries are very similar to those in Standard Trading Conditions. This similarity is more marked than in other provisions owing to the

---

[56] *Cf. United Mills Agencies* v. *Harvey Bray, supra*, with *Von Traubenberg* v. *Davies, Turner & Co. Ltd.* and *W.L.R. Traders Ltd.* v. *B. & N. Shipping Agency Ltd., supra*
[57] *Mabillon & Co.* v. *L.E.P. Transport Ltd., supra*, note 24.
[58] See § 472.
[59] See § 476.

essentially international character of insurance underwriting and the greater uniformity that exists in this field of commercial relationships, particularly where marine insurance is concerned. In the question of insurance there does not seem to be any marked differences between the common law and civil law countries, in contrast to the position where questions of the forwarder's status arises. This is presumably because of the strong influence that this country has had upon the insurance world generally.

APPENDIX

THE INSTITUTE OF FREIGHT FORWARDERS LTD.
STANDARD TRADING CONDITIONS*

1970 EDITION

600   1. All and any business undertaken by............................
(*name and style of Company*) (hereinafter called " the Company ") is transacted subject to the conditions hereinafter set out each of which shall be deemed to be incorporated in and to be a condition of any agreement between the Company and its Customers. The Company is not a common carrier and only deals with goods subject to these conditions. No agent or employee of the Company has the Company's authority to alter or vary these conditions.

2. Customers entering into transactions of any kind with the Company expressly warrant that they are either the owners or the authorised agents of the owners of any goods to which the transaction relates and further warrant that they are authorised to accept and are accepting these conditions not only for themselves but also as agents for and on behalf of all other persons who are or may thereafter become interested in the goods.

3. Any instructions given to the Company may in the absolute discretion of the Company be complied with by the Company itself by its own servants performing part or all of the relevant services or by the Company employing or instructing or entrusting the goods to others on such conditions as such others may stipulate to perform part or all of the services.

4. Subject to express instructions in writing given by the Customer, the Company reserves to itself absolute discretion as to the means, route and procedure to be followed in the handling, storage and transportation of goods. Further, if in the opinion of the Company it is at any stage necessary or desirable in the Customer's interests to depart from those instructions, the Company shall be at liberty to do so.

5. Pending forwarding or delivery, goods may be warehoused or otherwise held at any place or places at the sole discretion of the Company and the cost thereof shall be for the account of the Customer.

6. Except where the Company is instructed in writing to pack the goods the Customer warrants that all goods have been properly and sufficiently packed and/or prepared.

7. The Company is entitled to retain and be paid all brokerages, commission, allowances and other remuneration customarily retained by or paid to Shipping and Forwarding Agents (or Freight Forwarders) and Insurance Brokers.

8. Quotations are given on the basis of immediate acceptance and subject to the right of withdrawal or revision. If any changes occur in the rates of freight, insurance premiums or other charges applicable to the goods, quotations and charges shall be subject to revision accordingly with or without notice.

9. The Customer shall be deemed to be bound by and to warrant the accuracy of all descriptions, values and other particulars furnished to the

* Reproduced by kind permission of the Institute of Freight Forwarders Ltd.

[297]

Company for Customs, Consular and other purposes and he undertakes to indemnify the Company against all losses, damages, expenses and fines arising from any inaccuracy or omission, even if such inaccuracy or omission is not due to any negligence.

10. The Customer shall be liable for any duties, taxes, imposts, levies, deposits or outlays of any kind levied by the authorities at any port or place for or in connection with the goods and for any payments, fines, expenses, loss or damage incurred or sustained by the Company in connection therewith.

11. When goods are accepted or dealt with upon instructions to collect freight, duties, charges or other expenses from the consignee or any other person the Customer shall remain responsible for the same if they are not paid by such consignee or other person.

12. No insurance will be effected except upon express instructions given in writing by the Customer and all insurances effected by the Company are subject to the usual exceptions and conditions of the policies of the insurance company or underwriters taking the risk. The Company shall not be under any obligation to effect a separate insurance on each consignment but may declare it on any open or general policy. Should the insurers dispute their liability for any reason the insured shall have recourse against the insurers only and the Company shall not be under any responsibility or liability in relation thereto notwithstanding that the premium upon the policy may not be at the same rate as that charged by the Company or paid to the Company by its Customer.

601   13. (i) The Company shall only be responsible for the goods whilst they are in its actual custody and under its actual control and the Company shall not be liable for loss of or damage to goods or failure to deliver the goods unless it is proved that such loss or damage or failure to deliver the goods occurred whilst the goods were in the actual custody of the Company and under its actual control and that such loss or damage or failure to deliver the goods was due to the wilful neglect or default of the Company or its own servants.

(ii) The Company shall only be liable for any non-compliance or mis-compliance with the instructions given to it if it is proved that the same was caused by the wilful neglect or default of the Company or its own servants.

(iii) Save as aforesaid the Company shall be under no liability in connection with the goods or instructions given to it.

(iv) Further and without prejudice to the generality of the preceding sub-condition, the Company shall not in any event be under any liability for any delay or consequential loss or loss of market however caused nor for any loss, damage or expense arising from or in any way connected with the marks, weights, numbers, brands, contents, quality or description of any goods however caused.

14. In no case shall any liability of the Company howsoever arising and notwithstanding that the circumstances or cause of loss or damage may be unexplained exceed the value of the goods or a sum at the rate of £100 per ton of 20 cwt on the gross weight of the goods, whichever shall be the less.

15. In any event the Company shall be discharged from all liability—

(a) for loss from a package or an unpacked consignment or for damage, deviation or misdelivery (however caused), unless notice be received in writing within *seven* days after the end of the transit where the transit ends in the British Isles or within *fourteen* days after the end of the transit where the transit ends at any place outside the British Isles;

(b) for loss or non-delivery of the whole of a consignment or any separate package forming part of the consignment (however caused), unless notice be received in writing within *twenty-eight* days of the date when the goods should have been delivered.

16. (a) The Company shall not be obliged to make any declaration for the purpose of any statute or contract as to the nature or value of any goods or as to any special interest in delivery, unless required by law or expressly instructed by the Customer in writing.

(b) Where there is a choice of rates according to the extent or degree of the liability assumed by carriers, warehousemen or others, goods will be forwarded, dealt with etc. at Customer's risk or other minimum charges, and no declaration of value (where optional) will be made, unless express instructions in writing to the contrary have previously been given by the Customer.

17. Instructions to collect payment on delivery (C.O.D.) in cash or otherwise are accepted by the Company upon the condition that the Company in the matter of such collection will be liable for the exercise of reasonable diligence and care only.

18. Perishable goods which are not taken up immediately upon arrival, or which are insufficiently addressed or marked or otherwise not readily identifiable, may be sold or otherwise disposed of without any notice to the Customer and payment or tender of the net proceeds of any sale after deduction of charges shall be equivalent to delivery. All charges and expenses arising in connection with the sale or disposal of the goods shall be paid by the Customer.

602 19. The Company shall be entitled to sell or dispose of all non-perishable goods which in the opinion of the Company cannot be delivered either because they are insufficiently or incorrectly addressed or because they are not collected or accepted by the Consignee or for any other reason, upon giving 21 days' notice in writing to the Customer. All charges and expenses arising in connection with the storage and sale or disposal of the goods shall be paid by the Customer.

20. Except under special arrangements previously made in writing the Company will not accept or deal with any noxious, dangerous, hazardous or inflammable or explosive goods or any goods likely to cause damage. Should any Customer nevertheless deliver any such goods to the Company or cause the Company to handle or deal with any such goods otherwise than under special arrangements previously made in writing, he shall be liable for all loss or damage caused by or to or in connection with the goods however arising and shall indemnify the Company against all penalties, claims, damages, costs and expenses arising in connection therewith and the goods may be destroyed or otherwise dealt with at the sole discretion of the Company or any other person in whose custody they may be at the relevant time. If such goods are accepted under arrangements previously made in writing they may nevertheless be so destroyed or otherwise dealt with if they become dangerous to other goods or property. The expression " goods likely to cause damage " includes goods likely to harbour or encourage vermin or other pests.

21. Except under special arrangements previously made in writing the Company will not accept or deal with bullion, coins, precious stones, jewellery, valuables, antiques, pictures, livestock or plants. Should any Customer nevertheless deliver any such goods to the Company or cause the Company to

handle or deal with any such goods otherwise than under special arrangements previously made in writing the Company shall be under no liability whatsoever for or in connection with the goods however caused.

22. Without prejudice to Condition 2 the Company shall have the right to enforce any liability of the Customer under these Conditions or to recover any sums to be paid by the Customer under these Conditions not only against or from the Customer but also if it thinks fit against or from the sender and/or consignee and/or owner of the goods.

23. All goods (and documents relating to goods) shall be subject to a particular and general lien and right of detention for monies due either in respect of such goods or for any particular or general balance or other monies due from the Customer or the sender, consignee or owner to the Company. If any monies due to the Company are not paid within one calendar month after notice has been given to the person from whom the monies are due that such goods are being detained, they may be sold by auction or otherwise at the sole discretion of the Company and at the expense of such person, and the proceeds applied in or towards satisfaction of such indebtedness.

24. In addition to and without prejudice to the foregoing Conditions the Customer undertakes that he shall in any event indemnify the Company against all liabilities suffered or incurred by the Company arising directly or indirectly from or in connection with the Customer's instructions or their implementation or the goods, and in particular the Customer shall indemnify the Company in respect of any liability it may be under to any servant, agent or sub-contractor, or any haulier, carrier, warehouseman, or other person whatsoever at any time involved with the goods arising out of any claim made directly or indirectly against any such party by the Customer or by any sender, consignee or owner of the goods or by any person interested in the goods or by any other person whatsoever.

25. All agreements between the Company and its customers shall be governed by English Law and be within the exclusive jurisdiction of the English Courts.

ROAD HAULAGE ASSOCIATION LIMITED
CONDITIONS OF CARRIAGE
PUBLISHED JANUARY 1961*

603   1. In these conditions of carriage (hereinafter called " these conditions ")

    (*a*) " Contractor " means

        and (unless the context forbids) includes the Contractor's servants and agents and any person or persons carrying goods under a sub-contract with the Contractor;

    (*b*) " Consignment " means goods (whether contained in one or more parcel or package) sent or consigned at any one time by one consignor from one address to one address, or, in the case of goods despatched in bulk, goods which are sent or consigned at one time from one address by one consignor to one address; and where the consignor is not the owner of the goods he shall be deemed to be the owner's agent;

    (*c*) " Dangerous goods " means goods which are specified in the special classification of dangerous goods issued by the Railway Clearing House or which, although not specified therein, are not accepted by the British Transport Commission for conveyance on the ground of their dangerous or hazardous nature.

*Reproduced by kind permission of the Road Haulage Association Ltd.

2. The Contractor is not a common carrier and will accept goods for carriage only on these conditions.

3. No agent of or person employed by the Contractor has any authority to alter or vary in any way these conditions unless he is expressly authorised to do so by the Contractor.

4. Where for any reason the goods cannot be delivered or where goods are held by the Contractor " To wait order " or " To be kept till called for " and such order is not given or such goods are not removed within a reasonable time, the Contractor shall be under no liability for loss or damage and will, in the case of perishable goods forthwith and in the case of other goods 14 days after giving to the consignor or the consignee notice (by post or otherwise including public notice where the names and addresses of the consignor and the consignee are not known) of his intention to do so, sell the same and may deduct out of the proceeds of sale all proper charges in respect of the carriage and warehousing of the goods and any other expenses incurred by the Contractor in relation thereto.

5. The Contractor shall not in any case be liable for:—

(a) Loss of a particular market (whether held daily or at intervals); or

(b) Indirect or consequential damages; or

(c) Loss or damage arising from:—

(i) Insufficient or improper packing or addressing; or

(ii) The perishable, hazardous, fragile or brittle nature or the mechanical derangement of the goods; or

(iii) Riots, civil commotion, strikes, lockouts, stoppages or restraint of labour from whatever cause, whether partial or general; or

(iv) Failure by the consignee to take delivery within a reasonable time.

6. Every consignment of merchandise shall be addressed in such manner and accompanied by such documents as the Contractor may require but no receipt given by the Contractor in respect of a consignment shall be evidence of the condition or of the correctness of the declared nature, quantity or weight of the consignment at the time when it is received by the Contractor.

604 7. In the absence of a special contract between the Contractor and the consignor or consignee the liability of the Contractor in respect of loss of or damage to goods shall in no circumstances exceed the value of the goods or where neither the consignor nor the consignee is the owner thereof then the liability of such consignor or consignee to the owner (whichever is the less) and shall in any case be limited as follows:—

(a) Where the consignment exceeds ¼ hundredweight to the sum of £40 per gross hundredweight and *pro rata* for any part of a hundredweight of the goods so lost or damaged; and

(b) Where the consignment does not exceed ¼ hundredweight to the sum of £10 for the whole or part of such consignment so lost or damaged: Provided that the Contractor shall in every event have the protection of the Carriers Act 1830.

8. The Contractor shall not be liable for delay or detention of goods or for any loss, damage or deterioration arising therefrom except upon proof that the delay, detention, loss, damage or deterioration was due solely to the wilful negligence of the Contractor or the Contractor's servants.

9. If the Contractor agrees to accept dangerous goods for carriage such goods must be accompanied by a full declaration of their nature and contents and be properly and safely packed in accordance with any statutory regulations for the time being in force for transport by road. The consignor shall

indemnify the Contractor against all loss, damage or injury however caused arising out of the carriage of any dangerous goods.

10. Where goods are consigned to places beyond the limits of the Contractor's usual delivery radius the responsibility of the Contractor shall cease when such goods are held available by the Contractor at his depot or elsewhere for collection by or delivery to another contractor, but the Contractor may nevertheless contract as agent for the consignor or consignee for the further carriage of such goods. All goods are carried subject to the conditions of other carriers (if any) through whose hands they may pass and the consignor shall be deemed to have knowledge of and to have agreed to such conditions. Provided that the Contractor's liability shall be limited but shall not be extended thereby.

11. The Contractor's charges for carriage shall be payable by the consignor without prejudice to the Contractor's rights against the consignee or any other person.

12. The Contractor shall in no circumstances whatsoever be liable:—

> (a) For non-delivery (however arising) of a consignment or any part thereof unless he is advised of the non-delivery at the forwarding or delivery depot within 28 days and receives the detailed claim for the value of the goods within 42 days after receipt of the consignment by the contractor to whom the same was handed by the consignor;

> (b) For loss (however arising) from a parcel or package or from an unpacked consignment or for damage unless he is advised thereof at the forwarding or delivery depot within 3 days and he receives the detailed claim for the value of the goods within 7 days after the termination of the carriage of the consignment or the part of the consignment in respect of which the claim arises:

Provided that every notice given to the Contractor under this clause shall be in writing and otherwise than upon any of the Contractor's documents.

605   13. A claim or counterclaim shall not be made the reason for deferring or withholding payment of moneys payable or liabilities incurred to the Contractor.

14. The place of collection and delivery shall be the usual place at the collection or delivery address at which goods are loaded and unloaded into and from vehicles (provided that there is safe and adequate access and adequate loading and unloading facilities) and the consignor or consignee shall at his own risk and cost provide or procure the provision of any plant or power or labour (additional to the Contractor's servants) required for loading or unloading and shall be liable for any damage, loss or personal injury (including injury to the Contractor's servants) occasioned by any defect in any such plant or power or by the negligence of any such labour. The Contractor shall not be liable in respect of damage to goods arising from a defect in any vehicle, container or equipment not provided by him. Where there is no adequate access notice of arrival of the goods at the Contractor's premises or depot will be despatched by post to the address of the consignee and delivery will be deemed to be complete at the expiration of one clear day after the despatch of such notice.

15. The Contractor shall have a special lien on all goods for charges on such goods and shall also have a general lien against the owner of any goods for any moneys on account due from such owner to the Contractor. If any lien is not satisfied within a reasonable time the Contractor may at his absolute discretion sell the goods concerned and apply the proceeds in or towards discharge of the lien and the expenses of sale.

16. The Contractor shall not when collecting or delivering goods at the premises of the consignor or consignee be liable for damage to private road-ways, mains, pipes, manholes, weighbridges, bridges or approaches to such premises caused by the weight of the vehicle and load (if any) or the nature of the goods carried.

17. These conditions shall apply by whatever route the goods are carried.

18. The Contractor shall not be liable for failure to collect " paid on " charges in any case where either before or after delivery the person from whom such charges are to be collected fails to pay after a reasonable demand has been made for payment thereof.

19. The consignor shall be liable for the cost of unreasonable detention of vehicles, container and sheets before, during and after transit, but the Contractor's right against any other person shall remain unaffected.

20. The Consignor or other the customer of the Contractor shall save harmless and keep the Contractor indemnified from and against all claims costs and demands by whomsoever made or preferred in excess of the legal liability of the Contractor under the terms of these Conditions.

ROAD HAULAGE ASSOCIATION LIMITED
CONDITIONS OF CARRIAGE

REVISED APRIL 1967*

606 (hereinafter referred to as " the Carrier ") accepts goods for carriage subject to the Conditions (hereinafter referred to as " these conditions ") set out below. No agent or employee of the Carrier is permitted to alter or vary these conditions in any way unless he is expressly authorised to do so.

1. Definitions
In these Conditions the following expressions shall have the meanings hereby respectively assigned to them, that is to say:—

" *Trader* " shall mean the customer who contracts for the services of the Carrier.

" *Consignment* " shall mean goods in bulk or contained in one parcel or package, as the case may be, or any number of separate parcels or packages sent at one time in one load by or for the Trader from one address to one address.

" *Dangerous goods* " shall mean
(a) goods which are specified in the special classification of danger-ous goods issued by the British Railways Board or which, al-though not specified therein, are not acceptable to the British Railways Board for conveyance on the ground of their dangerous or hazardous nature; or
(b) goods which though not included in (a) above are of a kindred nature.

" *Contract* " shall mean the contract of carriage between the Trader and the Carrier.

" *Sub-contracting parties* " includes all persons (other than the Carrier and the Trader) referred to in clause 3 (3).

" *Carrier* " save in the expression Carrier/Contractor includes sub-contracting parties in clauses 4 (2), 5 (2) and (3), and 11 (proviso).

" *Carrier/Contractor* " means the Carrier and any other carrier within clause 3 (2).

*Reproduced by kind permission of the Road Haulage Association Ltd.

[303]

2. Carrier is not a Common Carrier

The Carrier is not a common carrier and will accept goods for carriage only on these conditions.

3. Parties and Sub-Contracting

(1) Where the Trader is not the owner of some or all of the goods in any consignment he shall be deemed for all purposes to be the agent of the owner or owners.

(2) The Carrier may employ the services of any other carrier for the purpose of fulfilling the Contract. Any such other carrier shall have the like power to sub-contract on like terms.

(3) The Carrier enters into the Contract for and on behalf of himself and his servants, agents and sub-contractors and his sub-contractors' servants, agents and sub-contractors; all of whom shall be entitled to the benefit of the Contract and shall be under no liability whatsoever to the Trader or anyone claiming through him in respect of the goods in addition to or separately from that of the Carrier under the Contract.

(4) The Trader shall save harmless and keep the Carrier indemnified against all claims or demands whatsoever by whomsoever made in excess of the liability of the Carrier under these conditions.

4. Dangerous Goods

(1) If the Carrier agrees to accept dangerous goods for carriage such goods must be accompanied by a full declaration of their nature and contents and be properly and safely packed in accordance with any statutory regulations for the time being in force for transport by road.

(2) The Trader shall indemnify the Carrier against all loss, damage or injury however caused arising out of the carriage of any dangerous goods, whether declared as such or not.

5. Loading and Unloading

(1) When collection or delivery takes place at the Trader's premises the Carrier/Contractor shall not be under any obligation to provide any plant, power, or labour which, in addition to the Carrier/Contractor's carmen, is required for loading or unloading at such premises.

(2) Any assistance given by the Carrier beyond the usual place of collection or delivery shall be at the sole risk of the Trader, who will save harmless and keep the Carrier indemnified against any claim or demand which could not have been made if such assistance had not been given.

(3) Goods requiring special appliances for unloading from the vehicle are accepted for carriage only on condition that the sender had duly ascertained from the consignee that such appliances are available at destination. Where the Carrier/Contractor is, without prior arrangement in writing with the Trader, called upon to load or unload such goods the Carrier shall be under no liability whatsoever to the Trader for any damage however caused, whether or not by the negligence of the Carrier, and the Trader shall save harmless and keep the Carrier indemnified against any claim or demand which could not have been made if such assistance had not been given.

607 6. Consignment Notes

The Carrier/Contractor shall, if so required, sign a document prepared by the sender acknowledging the receipt of the consignment; but no such document shall be evidence of the condition or of the correctness of the declared nature, quantity or weight of the consignment at the time it is received by the Carrier/Contractor.

7. Transit

(1) Transit shall commence when the consignment is handed to the

Carrier/Contractor whether at the point of collection or at the Carrier/ Contractor's premises.

(2) Transit shall (unless otherwise previously determined) end when the consignment is tendered at the usual place of delivery at the consignee's address within the customary cartage hours of the district.
Provided:

- (a) that if no safe and adequate access or no adequate unloading facilities there exist then transit shall be deemed to end at the expiry of one clear day after notice in writing (or by telephone if so previously agreed in writing) of the arrival of the consignment at the Carrier/ Contractor's premises has been sent to the consignee; and
- (b) that when for any other reason whatsoever a consignment cannot be delivered or when a consignment is held by the Carrier/Contractor " to await order " or " to be kept till called for " or upon any like instructions and such instructions are not given, or the consignment is not called for and removed, within a reasonable time, then transit shall be deemed to end.

8. Undelivered or Unclaimed Goods

Where the Carrier/Contractor is unable for whatever reason to deliver a consignment to the consignee, or as he may order or where by virtue of the proviso to clause 7 (2) hereof transit is deemed to be at an end the Carrier/ Contractor may sell the goods and payment or tender of the proceeds after deductions of all proper charges and expenses in relation thereto and all outstanding charges in relation to the carriage and storage of the goods shall (without prejudice to any claim or right which the Trader may have against the Carrier otherwise arising under these conditions) discharge the Carrier/ Contractor from all liability in respect of such goods, their carriage and storage.
Provided that:

- (a) the Carrier/Contractor shall do what is reasonable to obtain the value of the consignment; and
- (b) the power of sale shall not be exercised where the name and address of the sender or of the consignee is known unless the Carrier/Contractor shall have done what is reasonable in the circumstances to give notice to the sender, or if the name and address of the sender is not known, to the consignee that the goods will be sold unless within the time specified in such notice, being a reasonable time in the circumstances from the giving of such notice, the goods are taken away or instructions are given for their disposal.

9. Carrier's Charges

(1) The Carrier's charges for carriage shall be payable by the Trader without prejudice to the Carrier's rights against the consignee or any other person. Provided that when goods are consigned " carriage forward " the Trader shall not be required to pay such charges unless the consignee fails to pay after a reasonable demand has been made by the Carrier/Contractor for payment thereof.

(2) Except where the quotation states otherwise all quotations based on a tonnage rate shall apply to the gross weight, unless the goods exceed 80 cubic feet in measurement per ton weight, in which case the tonnage rate shall be computed upon and apply to each measurement of 80 cubic feet or any part thereof.

(3) A claim or counterclaim shall not be made the reason for deferring or withholding payment of monies payable, or liabilities incurred, to the Carrier.

10. Time Limit for Claims

The Carrier shall not be liable:

(1) (*a*) for loss from a package or from an unpacked consignment: or

(*b*) for damage, deviation, misdelivery, delay or detention;

unless he is advised thereof in writing otherwise than upon a consignment note or delivery document within three days and the claim be made in writing within seven days after the termination of transit;

(2) for loss or non-delivery of the whole of the consignment or of any separate package forming part of the consignment;

unless he is advised of the loss or non-delivery in writing (other than upon a consignment note or delivery document) within twenty-eight days and the claim be made in writing within forty-two days after the commencement of transit.

608 ### 11. Liability for Loss and Damage

Subject to these Conditions the Carrier shall be liable for any loss, or misdelivery of or damage to goods occasioned during transit unless the Carrier shall prove that such loss, misdelivery or damage has arisen from:

(*a*) Act of God;

(*b*) any consequence of war, invasion, act of foreign enemy, hostilities (whether war be declared or not), civil war, rebellion, insurrection, military or usurped power or confiscation, requisition, destruction of, or damage to property by or under the order of any government or public or local authority;

(*c*) seizure under legal process;

(*d*) act or omission of the Trader or owner of the goods or of the servants or agents of either;

(*e*) inherent liability to wastage in bulk or weight, latent defect or inherent defect, vice or natural deterioration of the goods;

(*f*) insufficient or improper packing;

(*g*) insufficient or improper labelling or addressing;

(*h*) riots, civil commotion, lockouts, general or partial stoppage or restraint of labour from whatever cause;

(*j*) consignee not taking or accepting delivery within a reasonable time;

Provided that the Carrier shall not incur liability of any kind in respect of a consignment where there has been fraud on the part of the Trader or the owner of the goods or the servants or agents of either in respect of that consignment.

12. Limitation of Liability

Subject to these Conditions the liability of the Carrier in respect of any one consignment shall in any case be limited:

(1) where the loss or damage however sustained is in respect of the whole of the consignment to a sum at the rate of £800 per ton on either the gross weight of the consignment as computed for the purpose of charges under clause 9 hereof or where no such computation had been made, the actual gross weight;

(2) where loss or damage however sustained is in respect of part of a consignment to the proportion of the sum ascertained in accordance with (1) of this condition which the actual value of that part of the consignment bears to the actual value of the whole of the consignment.

Provided that:

(*a*) nothing in this clause shall limit the Carrier's liability below the sum of £10 in respect of any one consignment;

(*b*) the Carrier shall not in any case be liable for indirect or consequential damages or for loss of a particular market whether held daily or at intervals;

(c) the Carrier shall be entitled to require proof of the value of the whole of the consignment.

13. General Lien

The Carrier shall have a general lien against the owner of any goods for any moneys whatsoever due from such owner to the Carrier. If any lien is not satisfied within a reasonable time the Carrier may at his absolute discretion sell the goods as agents for the owner and apply the proceeds towards the moneys due and the expenses of the sale, and shall upon accounting to the Trader for the balance remaining, if any, be discharged from all liability whatsoever in respect of the goods.

14. Unreasonable Detention

The Trader shall be liable for the cost of unreasonable detention of vehicles, containers and sheets but the Carrier/Contractor's rights against any other person shall remain unaffected.

15. Computation of Time

In the computation of time where the period provided by these conditions is seven days or less, the following days shall not be included:—

In England and Wales: Sunday, Good Friday, Christmas Day or a Bank Holiday.
In Scotland: Sunday, 1st and 2nd January, Spring Holiday or Autumn Holiday.

ROAD HAULAGE ASSOCIATION LIMITED
CONDITIONS OF SUB-CONTRACTING
REVISED APRIL 1967*

609

(hereinafter referred to as " the Carrier ") sub-contracts for the carriage of goods subject to the Conditions (hereinafter referred to as " these conditions ") set out below. No agent or employee of the Carrier is permitted to alter or vary these Conditions in any way unless expressly authorised to do so.

1. Definitions

Expressions in these Conditions shall bear the same meanings as the like expressions in the current Conditions of Carriage of Road Haulage Association Limited (copies of which may be obtained on request).

" Sub-contractor " means the haulier with whom the Carrier enters into this sub-contract.

2. Future Contracts

These Conditions shall apply to all future sub-contracts between the Carrier and the Sub-contractor, unless otherwise agreed in writing.

3. Benefit of Contract

(1) The Carrier warrants that the contract has been entered into upon the terms of the current Conditions of Carriage of Road Haulage Association Limited.

(2) The Carrier will do all such things as may be reasonable to secure to the Sub-contractor the benefit of the contract and will in particular, but without prejudice to the generality of the foregoing, lend his name to the Sub-contractor so far as may be necessary in the bringing or defending of any action or other proceeding to obtain such benefit.

Provided that where the Carrier so lends his name to the Sub-contractor the Sub-contractor shall bear all the costs of doing so and shall indemnify the Carrier against all costs or other liabilities whatsoever incurred thereby.

*Reproduced by kind permission of the Road Haulage Association Ltd.

(3) In so far as the Carrier entered into the contract for and on behalf of the Sub-contractor the Sub-contractor adopts or ratifies the action of the Carrier for and on behalf of himself, his servants or agents and sub-contractors.

4. Further Sub-Contracting

The Sub-contractor may perform the sub-contract by sub-contracting in whole or in part but shall remain liable to the Carrier as if he had himself performed the contract.

5. Performance of Sub-Contract

The Sub-contractor shall

(1) collect and deliver the goods to be carried within a reasonable time and within normal working hours;

(2) inform the Carrier by telephone or telegram of any unusual delay;

(3) in the event of loss, damage or misdelivery, immediately such loss damage or misdelivery is discovered, inform the Carrier and as soon as practicable thereafter supply a full report of the cause and circumstances together with any further information which the Carrier may reasonably require;

(4) if any loss is or is suspected to be due to the theft or pilferage, in addition to action under (3), immediately inform the Police and take all reasonable steps to identify apprehend and convict the guilty person and to trace and recover the goods;

(5) where goods are consigned " carriage forward," unless otherwise directed by the Carrier, collect the charges due before parting with the goods and account daily for all moneys received.

610 6. Failure in Course of Performance

If a vehicle breaks down or for any other reason the Sub-contractor fails or is unable to collect the goods or complete delivery within a reasonable time the Carrier may recover the goods and carry them to their destination and the Sub-contractor shall pay the Carrier's charges therefor.

7. Receipts, Invoices and Statements

(1) All receipt notes shall be the property of the Carrier and must be returned duly signed to the office from which the order for the work was issued within seven days of the delivery date together with the Sub-contractor's invoice for the carriage.

(2) Statements of account for work done during a month must be rendered to the Carrier in the first week of the succeeding month and shall identify the work done, the corresponding invoice, and the office from which the order for the work was issued.

(3) The Carrier shall be under no liability to the Sub-contractor for any work in respect of which a duly signed receipt note has not been returned.

8. Sub-Contractor's Liability

Subject to the terms of the contract and to clause 3 hereof the Sub-contractor will indemnify the Carrier against any liability under the contract arising:

(1) after the collection of the goods by the Sub-contractor and before transit ends or is deemed to end; and

(2) out of any failure by the Sub-contractor to collect the goods within a reasonable time.

9. Insurance

The Sub-contractor shall take out in his own name policies of insurance acceptable to the Carrier against his liabilities under these Conditions and shall produce such policies and the receipts for the current premiums thereon to the Carrier on demand. In the event of the Sub-contractor failing so to insure, or failing to pay the premium, the Carrier shall be at liberty to do so himself and the Carrier may, at his sole option,

(1) recover the full cost from the Sub-contractor on demand; or

(2) deduct the full cost from any moneys due or thereafter becoming due to the Sub-contractor from the Carrier; or

(3) pay the Sub-contractor's invoices at a reasonable discount to allow for the cost of the Carrier effecting such insurance or of carrying the risk of the Sub-contractor's default himself.

BRITISH ROAD SERVICES LTD.
CONDITIONS OF CARRIAGE*

[These Conditions are common to Freightliners Ltd., and also to British Railways Board and National Carriers Ltd. with the addition of the provisions in square brackets.]

611 Definitions

1. " The Carriers " means British Road Services Ltd. and includes unless the context otherwise requires their sub-contractors, agents and servants.

" Trader " means any person sending or receiving goods by the Carriers' services and includes unless the context otherwise requires his servants and agents.

" sender " and " consignee " include unless the context otherwise requires their respective servants and agents.

" consignment " means goods accepted by the Carriers at one time from one sender at one address for carriage to one consignee at one address.

" sub-contractor " means any carrier engaged by the Carriers to carry goods on their behalf.

" [private siding " means a railway or siding not belonging to the Board or their sub-contractor.]

" dangerous goods " means goods included in the list of dangerous goods published by the British Railways Board or goods which present a comparable hazard.

Parties and sub-contracting

2. (1) The Carriers may engage sub-contractors to perform the contract of carriage or any part thereof on their behalf.

(2) The Carriers enter into the contract of carriage for themselves and on behalf of their sub-contractors, agents and servants all of whom shall have the benefit of the contract and shall be under no liability to the Trader in respect of the goods greater than or in addition to that of the Carriers under the contract.

Addressing, labelling and consignment note

3. (1) Every consignment of goods shall be addressed and labelled in accordance with the Carriers' requirements and except when otherwise agreed be accompanied by a consignment note containing such particulars as the Carriers may reasonably require.

(2) The Carriers shall if so required sign a document prepared by the sender acknowledging receipt of the consignment but no such document shall be evidence of the condition or of the correctness of the declared nature, quantity and weight of the consignment at the time it is received by the Carriers.

Warranties

4. (1) In the absence of written notice to the contrary given to the Carriers at the time of delivery to them, all goods are warranted by the sender to be fit to be carried or stored.

*Reproduced by kind permission of the National Freight Corporation.

(2) The sender also warrants that if the goods are not his own unencumbered property he has the authority of all persons owning or interested in the goods to enter into the contract, and contracts on their behalf.

Liability for loss, misdelivery, damage or delay

5. Subject to these conditions the Carriers shall be liable for:—

[A. Where goods are accepted by the Board for carriage at Board's risk subject to these conditions the Board shall be liable for:—]

    (1) loss or misdelivery of or damage to the goods occurring during transit as defined by these conditions unless the Carriers shall prove that such loss, misdelivery or damage has arisen from:—

        (a) Act of God;

        (b) any consequence of war, invasion, act of foreign enemy, hostilities (whether war be declared or not), civil war, rebellion, insurrection, military or usurped power or confiscation, requisition, destruction of or damage to property by or under the order of any government or public or local authority;

        (c) seizure under legal process;

        (d) act or omission of the Trader;

        (e) inherent liability to wastage in bulk or weight, latent defect or inherent defect, vice or natural deterioration of the goods;

        (f) insufficient or improper packing;

        (g) insufficient or improper labelling or addressing;

        (h) riot, civil commotion, strikes, lockouts, stoppage or restraint of labour from whatever cause;

        (j) consignee not taking or accepting delivery within a reasonable time.

Provided that:—

        (i) where loss, misdelivery or damage arises and the Carriers have failed to prove that they used all reasonable foresight and care in the carriage of the goods the Carriers shall not be relieved from liability for such loss, misdelivery or damage;

        (ii) the Carriers shall not incur liability of any kind in respect of goods where there has been fraud on the part of the Trader;

        (iii) when goods are consigned as damageable goods not properly protected by packing the Carriers shall not be liable for loss or misdelivery of or damage to the goods under this condition except upon proof by the Trader:—

            (a) that the same was caused by the wilful misconduct of the Carriers or,

            (b) that it would have been suffered if the goods had been properly protected by packing.

    (2) loss proved by the Trader to have been caused by delay in the carriage of the goods unless the Carriers prove that such delay has arisen without negligence on the part of the Carriers.

[B. Where goods are accepted by the Board for carriage at Owner's risk, the Board shall not be liable for any loss or misdelivery of or damage or delay to the goods except upon proof by the Trader that the same was caused by the wilful misconduct of the Board. Provided that the Board's liability for non-delivery of a consignment or of any separate package forming part of a consignment (not being attributable to fire or to an accident to a train or vehicle) shall be determined as if the goods had been accepted for carriage at Board's risk.]

612 **Limit of liability**

6. (1) Subject to these conditions, the liability of the Carriers in respect of any one consignment shall in any case be limited:—

    (a) where the monetary loss however sustained is in respect of the whole of the consignment to a sum calculated at the rate of £800 per ton on the gross weight of the consignment;

(b) where the monetary loss however sustained is in respect of part of a consignment to the proportion of the sum ascertained in accordance with (a) of this condition which the value of that part of the consignment bears to the value of the whole of the consignment.

Provided that:—

(i) nothing in this condition shall limit the Carriers' liability below the sum of £10 in respect of any one consignment, and

(ii) the Carriers shall be entitled to require proof of the value of the whole consignment.

(2) The Carriers shall not in any case be liable for indirect or consequential damages or for loss of a particular market whether held daily or at intervals.

Time limit for claims

7. The Carriers shall not in any event be liable:—

(a) (i) for loss from a package or from an unpacked consignment, or

(ii) for damage, misdelivery or delay

unless they are advised thereof in writing (otherwise than upon any of the Carriers' documents) within three clear days and the claim is made in writing within seven clear days of the end of the transit of the consignment, or the part of the consignment in respect of which the claim arises;

(b) for non-delivery of the whole of the consignment [or of any entire wagon load] or of any separate package forming part of the consignment unless they are advised of the non-delivery in writing (otherwise than upon any of the Carriers' documents) within twenty-eight days and the claim be made in writing within forty-two days after transit began.

Provided that if in any particular case the Trader proves that:—

(i) it was not reasonably possible for the Trader to advise the Carriers in writing within the aforesaid times; and

(ii) such advice or claim was given or made within a reasonable time the Carriers shall not have the benefit of this condition.

Charges

8. (1) The Carriers' charges for carriage and services incidental thereto shall be payable by the sender without prejudice to the Carriers' rights against the consignee or any other person. Provided that where the Carriers have accepted goods " Carriage Forward " the sender shall only pay such charges if the consignee fails to pay on demand.

(2) A claim or counter-claim shall not be made the reason for deferring or withholding payment of moneys payable to the Carriers.

(3) The Trader shall pay the Carriers charges for the detention of the Carriers' wagons and other vehicles, containers, coverings and other equipment, or the use or occupation of any siding or other accommodation, whether before or after transit, or whilst transit is suspended, where such detention, use or occupation is at his request or for his convenience.

Undelivered or unclaimed goods

9. Where goods are held by the Carriers after transit or whilst transit is suspended:—

(a) the Carriers may sell the goods and payment or tender of the proceeds of such sale after deducting the expenses of the sale and all other charges due in respect of the goods shall (without prejudice to any outstanding claim which the Trader may have against the Carriers) discharge the Carriers from all liability in respect of the goods. Provided that:—

    (i) the goods shall not be sold unless the Carriers have done what is reasonable in the circumstances to notify the sender or the consignee that the goods will be sold unless within a reasonable time of the giving of the notice the goods are removed or instructions are given for their disposal;

   (ii) the Carriers shall do what is reasonable to obtain the value of the goods.

  (b) In respect of dangerous goods, at the Trader's sole risk and expense, the Carriers may, if they are satisfied it is reasonable to do so, destroy the goods, return them to the sender (who shall receive them at once) or otherwise dispose of them.

613   Transit

10. (1) Transit begins when the goods are handed to or collected by the Carriers for carriage.

(2) Transit shall be suspended:—

    (a) when goods are held by the Carriers at some place other than the destination at the request or for the convenience of the Trader or because the Trader refuses or is unable to take delivery at the destination; or

    (b) when the goods are detained for customs purposes;

and shall be resumed when the Carriers resume the carriage of the goods.

(3) Transit shall (unless otherwise previously determined) end:—

    (a) in the case of goods to be delivered by the Carriers, when they are tendered at the usual place of delivery within the customary cartage hours of the delivery district, or at such other times or places as may be agreed between the Carriers and the Trader;

    (b) in the case of goods not to be delivered by the Carriers or to be retained by the Carriers awaiting order, at the expiration of one clear day after notice of arrival has been given either orally or in writing to the consignee or, where the address of the consignee is not known, to the sender or, where the addresses of both sender and consignee are not known, or in the case of goods to be kept till called for, at the expiration of one clear day after the arrival of the goods at the place to which they are consigned;

   [(c) in the case of goods consigned to a private siding, when they are delivered at that siding, or at the place where the Trader has agreed with the Board to take delivery of goods consigned to the siding. Provided that if the Board through no fault of theirs are unable to deliver goods at such siding or place, transit shall end at the expiration of one clear day after notice has been given, either orally or in writing, to the consignee that the Board are ready and willing to deliver.]

Warehousing

11. (1) After termination or during suspension of transit as defined in Condition 10 hereof, unless otherwise agreed in writing the Carriers will hold goods other than dangerous goods as warehousemen subject to their usual charges and Conditions for Warehousing and to the condition that the Carriers will not be liable for any loss of or damage to:—

    (a) goods not properly protected by packing except upon proof that such loss or damage arose from the wilful misconduct of the Carriers or would have been suffered if the goods had been properly protected by packing;

[312]

(b) goods which have arrived at the destination or depot and for which the Carriers give notice that they have no suitable accommodation, by whomsoever and howsoever such loss or damage may be caused and whether or not occasioned by the neglect or default of the Carriers.

Provided that this condition shall not relieve the Carriers from any liability the Carriers might otherwise incur under these conditions in the unloading of the goods.

(2) The Carriers' liability for any loss of or damage to goods held by them as warehousemen pursuant to this condition shall in any case be subject to the limits and exclusions in Condition 6.

(3) Dangerous goods held by the Carriers after termination or during suspension of transit will be subject to:—

(a) the condition that the Carriers will not be liable for any loss of or damage to the goods except upon proof by the Trader that such loss or damage arose from wilful misconduct of the Carriers;

(b) the provisions of Condition 19 (2) (e) hereof.

Means of transport

12. (1) Goods accepted by the Carriers for carriage may be carried by such means of transport and by such route as the Carriers think fit and these conditions shall apply by whatever means or route the goods are carried.

[(2) Goods carried wholly or partly by water shall in respect of the carriage by water be carried subject to the applicable Conditions of Carriage by Water of the water carrier who carries the goods such conditions to be read as though reference therein to the water carrier (if not the Board) were reference to the Board.

In the absence of proof to the contrary where goods are carried partly by land and partly by water, any loss, damage or delay shall be deemed to have occurred whilst the goods are being carried by land.]

614 Loading and unloading

13. (1) On collection or delivery at a Trader's premises the Carriers shall be under no obligation to provide any plant, power or labour (other than assistance by the Carriers' carmen) for loading or unloading.

(2) The Carriers' servants have no authority to give assistance other than in loading and unloading at the usual place of collection or delivery and the Carriers shall not be liable for any loss or damage however caused by any such other assistance being given.

(3) Goods requiring special appliances for unloading from a road vehicle are accepted for carriage only on condition that the sender has duly ascertained from the consignee that such appliances are available at destination. Where the Carriers are, without prior arrangement in writing with the Trader, called upon to load or unload goods for which special appliances are required the Carriers shall be under no liability whatsoever to the Trader for any damage howsoever caused, whether or not by the negligence of the Carriers, and the Trader shall be responsible for and indemnify the Carriers against any damage or liability which the Carriers may suffer or incur.

Computation of time

14. In the computation of time where the period provided by these conditions is seven days or less, Saturdays, Sundays and public holidays shall not be included.

Lien

15. Goods delivered to the Carriers will be received and held by them subject:—

(a) to a lien for moneys due to them for the carriage of and other proper charges or expenses upon or in connection with such goods, and

[313]

    (b) to a general lien for any moneys or charges due to them from the owners of such goods for any services rendered or accommodation provided in relation to the carriage or custody of goods,

and in case any lien is not satisfied within a reasonable time from the date upon which the Carriers first gave notice of the exercise of their lien to the owners of the goods, the goods may be sold and the proceeds of sale applied in or towards the satisfaction of every such lien and all proper charges and expenses in relation thereto, and the Carriers shall account to the owners of the goods for any surplus.

The general lien conferred by this Condition shall not prejudice an unpaid vendor's right of stoppage in transitu.

Other published regulations

16. Goods are carried subject also to any other published byelaws and regulations relating to the carriage of goods by the Carriers for the time being in force and in the event of conflict between such byelaws and regulations and these conditions the said byelaws and regulations shall prevail.

Advice by post

17. Service of a notice sent by post shall be deemed to have been made at the time when the notice would have been delivered in the ordinary course of post.

Goods consigned in bond

18. In respect of dutiable goods consigned in bond the Trader will indemnify the Carriers against claims made upon them by the Commissioners of Customs and Excise whether or not transit has been ended or suspended.

Dangerous goods

19. (1) Where the Carriers accept dangerous goods (in this condition called " the goods ") for carriage the goods will be carried subject to all the foregoing conditions and subject also to the special conditions specified and referred to in this condition and in the event of conflict between the said special conditions and the foregoing the special conditions shall prevail.

    (2) The special conditions relating to the carriage of the goods are:—

    (a) previous arrangements shall be made with the Carriers for the conveyance of the goods;

    (b) at the time of tendering the goods for carriage the sender shall supply to the Carriers a declaration in writing stating the nature of the goods;

    (c) the goods shall be packed in accordance with any statutory regulations in force applicable to the carriage of the goods and unless otherwise agreed in writing with the regulations for the packing, labelling and loading of dangerous goods published by the British Railways Board;

    (d) any additional conditions set out or referred to on the consignment note which, in the event of any inconsistency with these conditions, shall prevail;

    (e) the Trader will be responsible for and indemnify the Carriers [(and the London Transport Board where goods are carried over their lines)] against loss or damage and claims made upon them for which they may be or become liable in respect of injury to persons or damage to property arising from non-compliance with any of the provisions of this condition unless the Trader proves that the loss damage or injury is due to the wilful misconduct of the Carriers.

    (3) The Carriers shall not be liable for loss of, or damage or delay to the goods unless the Trader proves that such loss damage or delay was not caused wholly or partly by failure on his part to comply with any of the special conditions in paragraph (2) hereof.   OCTOBER 1, 1969

CONVENTION ON THE CONTRACT FOR THE INTERNATIONAL CARRIAGE OF GOODS BY ROAD

CHAPTER I

SCOPE OF APPLICATION

Article 1

615   1. This Convention shall apply to every contract for the carriage of goods by road in vehicles for reward, when the place of taking over of the goods and the place designated for delivery, as specified in the contract, are situated in two different countries, of which at least one is a Contracting country, irrespective of the place of residence and the nationality of the parties.

2. For the purposes of this Convention, " vehicles " means motor vehicles, articulated vehicles, trailers and semi-trailers as defined in article 4* of the Convention on Road Traffic dated 19th September 1949.

3. This Convention shall apply also where carriage coming within its scope is carried out by States or by governmental institutions or organizations.

4. This Convention shall not apply:
    (*a*) to carriage performed under the terms of any international postal convention;
    (*b*) to funeral consignments;
    (*c*) to furniture removal.

5. The Contracting Parties agree not to vary any of the provisions of this Convention by special agreements between two or more of them, except to make it inapplicable to their frontier traffic or to authorise the use in transport operations entirely confined to their territory of consignment notes representing a title to the goods.

Article 2

1. Where the vehicle containing the goods is carried over part of the journey by sea, rail, inland waterways or air, and, except where the provisions of article 14 are applicable, the goods are not unloaded from the vehicle, this Convention shall nevertheless apply to the whole of the carriage. Provided that to the extent that it is proved that any loss, damage or delay in delivery of the goods which occurs during the carriage by the other means of transport was not caused by an act or omission of the carrier by road, but by some event which could only have occurred in the course of and by reason of the carriage by that other means of transport, the liability of the carrier by road shall be determined not by this Convention but in the manner in which the liability of the carrier by the other means of transport would have been determined if a

---

* The definitions set out in this article are, so far as material, as follows:—
    " Motor vehicle " means any self-propelled vehicle normally used for the transport of persons or goods upon a road, other than vehicles running on rails or **conn**ected to electric conductors.
    " Articulated vehicle " means any motor vehicle with a trailer having no front axle and so attached that part of the trailer is superimposed upon the motor vehicle and a substantial part of the weight of the trailer and of its load is borne by the motor vehicle. Such a trailer shall be called a " semi-trailer ".
    " Trailer " means any vehicle designed to be drawn by a motor vehicle.

contract for the carriage of the goods alone had been made by the sender with the carrier by the other means of transport in accordance with the conditions prescribed by law for the carriage of goods by that means of transport. If, however, there are no such prescribed conditions, the liability of the carrier by road shall be determined by this Convention.

2. If the carrier by road is also himself the carrier by the other means of transport, his liability shall also be determined in accordance with the provisions of paragraph 1 of this article, but as if, in his capacities as carrier by road and as carrier by the other means of transport, he were two separate persons.

CHAPTER II

PERSONS FOR WHOM THE CARRIER IS RESPONSIBLE

Article 3

616   For the purposes of this Convention the carrier shall be responsible for the acts and omissions of his agents and servants and of any other person of whose services he makes use for the performance of the carriage, when such agents, servants or other persons are acting within the scope of their employment, as if such acts or omissions were his own.

CHAPTER III

CONCLUSION AND PERFORMANCE OF THE CONTRACT OF CARRIAGE

Article 4

617   The contract of carriage shall be confirmed by the making out of a consignment note. The absence, irregularity or loss of the consignment note shall not affect the existence or the validity of the contract of carriage which shall remain subject to the provisions of this Convention.

Article 5

1. The consignment note shall be made out in three original copies signed by the sender and by the carrier. These signatures may be printed or replaced by the stamps of the sender and the carrier if the law of the country in which the consignment note has been made out so permits. The first copy shall be handed to the sender, the second shall accompany the goods and the third shall be retained by the carrier.

2. When the goods which are to be carried have to be loaded in different vehicles, or are of different kinds or are divided into different lots, the sender or the carrier shall have the right to require a separate consignment note to be made out for each vehicle used, or for each kind or lot of goods.

Article 6

1. The consignment note shall contain the following particulars:
   (a)   the date of the consignment note and the place at which it is made out;
   (b)   the name and address of the sender;
   (c)   the name and address of the carrier;

(*d*) the place and the date of taking over of the goods and the place designated for delivery;

(*e*) the name and address of the consignee;

(*f*) the description in common use of the nature of the goods and the method of packing, and, in the case of dangerous goods, their generally recognised description;

(*g*) the number of packages and their special marks and numbers;

(*h*) the gross weight of the goods or their quantity otherwise expressed;

(*i*) charges relating to the carriage (carriage charges, supplementary charges, customs duties and other charges incurred from the making of the contract to the time of delivery);

(*j*) the requisite instructions for Customs and other formalities;

(*k*) a statement that the carriage is subject, notwithstanding any clause to the contrary, to the provisions of this Convention.

2. Where applicable, the consignment note shall also contain the following particulars:

(*a*) a statement that transhipment is not allowed;

(*b*) the charges which the sender undertakes to pay;

(*c*) the amount of " cash on delivery " charges;

(*d*) a declaration of the value of the goods and the amount representing special interest in delivery;

(*e*) the sender's instructions to the carrier regarding insurance of the goods;

(*f*) the agreed time-limit within which the carriage is to be carried out;

(*g*) a list of the documents handed to the carrier.

3. The parties may enter in the consignment note any other particulars which they may deem useful.

Article 7

618 1. The sender shall be responsible for all expenses, loss and damage sustained by the carrier by reason of the inaccuracy or inadequacy of:

(*a*) the particulars specified in article 6, paragraph 1, (*b*), (*d*), (*e*), (*f*), (*g*), (*h*) and (*j*);

(*b*) the particulars specified in article 6, paragraph 2;

(*c*) any other particulars or instructions given by him to enable the consignment note to be made out or for the purpose of their being entered therein.

2. If, at the request of the sender, the carrier enters in the consignment note the particulars referred to in paragraph 1 of this article, he shall be deemed, unless the contrary is proved, to have done so on behalf of the sender.

3. If the consignment note does not contain the statement specified in article 6, paragraph 1 (*k*), the carrier shall be liable for all expenses, loss and damage sustained through such omission by the person entitled to dispose of the goods.

Article 8

1. On taking over the goods, the carrier shall check;

(*a*) the accuracy of the statements in the consignment note as to the number of packages and their marks and numbers, and

(*b*) the apparent condition of the goods and their packaging.

2. Where the carrier has no reasonable means of checking the accuracy of the statements referred to in paragraph 1 (*a*) of this article, he shall enter his reservations in the consignment note together with the grounds on which

they are based. He shall likewise specify the grounds for any reservations which he makes with regard to the apparent condition of the goods and their packaging. Such reservations shall not bind the sender unless he has expressly agreed to be bound by them in the consignment note.

3. The sender shall be entitled to require the carrier to check the gross weight of the goods or their quantity otherwise expressed. He may also require the contents of the packages to be checked. The carrier shall be entitled to claim the cost of such checking. The result of the checks shall be entered in the consignment note.

Article 9

1. The consignment note shall be prima facie evidence of the making of the contract of carriage, the conditions of the contract and the receipt of the goods by the carrier.

2. If the consignment note contains no specific reservations by the carrier, it shall be presumed, unless the contrary is proved, that the goods and their packaging appeared to be in good condition when the carrier took them over and that the number of packages, their marks and numbers corresponded with the statements in the consignment note.

Article 10

The sender shall be liable to the carrier for damage to persons, equipment or other goods, and for any expenses due to defective packing of the goods, unless the defect was apparent or known to the carrier at the time when he took over the goods and he made no reservations concerning it.

Article 11

619   1. For the purposes of the Customs or other formalities which have to be completed before delivery of the goods, the sender shall attach the necessary documents to the consignment note or place them at the disposal of the carrier and shall furnish him with all the information which he requires.

2. The carrier shall not be under any duty to enquire into either the accuracy or the adequacy of such documents and information. The sender shall be liable to the carrier for any damage caused by the absence, inadequacy or irregularity of such documents and information, except in the case of some wrongful act or neglect on the part of the carrier.

3. The liability of the carrier for the consequences arising from the loss or incorrect use of the documents specified in and accompanying the consignment note or deposited with the carrier shall be that of an agent, provided that the compensation payable by the carrier shall not exceed that payable in the event of loss of the goods.

Article 12

1. The sender has the right to dispose of the goods, in particular by asking the carrier to stop the goods in transit, to change the place at which delivery is to take place or to deliver the goods to a consignee other than the consignee indicated in the consignment note.

2. This right shall cease to exist when the second copy of the consignment note is handed to the consignee or when the consignee exercises his right under article 13, paragraph 1; from that time onwards the carrier shall obey the orders of the consignee.

3. The consignee shall, however, have the right of disposal from the time when the consignment note is drawn up, if the sender makes an entry to that effect in the consignment note.

4. If in exercising his right of disposal the consignee has ordered the delivery of the goods to another person, that other person shall not be entitled to name other consignees.

5. The exercise of the right of disposal shall be subject to the following conditions:

(*a*) that the sender or, in the case referred to in paragraph 3 of this article, the consignee who wishes to exercise the right produces the first copy of the consignment note on which the new instructions to the carrier have been entered and indemnifies the carrier against all expenses, loss and damage involved in carrying out such instructions;

(*b*) that the carrying out of such instructions is possible at the time when the instructions reach the person who is to carry them out and does not either interfere with the normal working of the carrier's undertaking or prejudice the senders or consignees of other consignments;

(*c*) that the instructions do not result in a division of the consignment.

6. When, by reason of the provisions of paragraph 5 (*b*) of this article, the carrier cannot carry out the instructions which he receives, he shall immediately notify the person who gave him such instructions.

7. A carrier who has not carried out the instructions given under the conditions provided for in this article, or who has carried them out without requiring the first copy of the consignment note to be produced, shall be liable to the person entitled to make a claim for any loss or damage caused thereby.

Article 13

1. After arrival of the goods at the place designated for delivery, the consignee shall be entitled to require the carrier to deliver to him, against a receipt, the second copy of the consignment note and the goods. If the loss of the goods is established or if the goods have not arrived after the expiry of the period provided for in article 19, the consignee shall be entitled to enforce in his own name against the carrier any rights arising from the contract of carriage.

2. The consignee who avails himself of the rights granted to him under paragraph 1 of this article shall pay the charges shown to be due on the consignment note, but in the event of dispute on this matter the carrier shall not be required to deliver the goods unless security has been furnished by the consignee.

Article 14

620 1. If for any reason it is or becomes impossible to carry out the contract in accordance with the terms laid down in the consignment note before the goods reach the place designated for delivery, the carrier shall ask for instructions from the person entitled to dispose of the goods in accordance with the provisions of article 12.

2. Nevertheless, if circumstances are such as to allow the carriage to be carried out under conditions differing from those laid down in the consignment note and if the carrier has been unable to obtain instructions in reasonable time from the person entitled to dispose of the goods in accordance with the provisions of article 12, he shall take such steps as seem to him to be in the best interests of the person entitled to dispose of the goods.

Article 15

1. Where circumstances prevent delivery of the goods after their arrival at the place designated for delivery, the carrier shall ask the sender for his instructions. If the consignee refuses the goods the sender shall be entitled to

dispose of them without being obliged to produce the first copy of the consignment note.

2. Even if he has refused the goods, the consignee may nevertheless require delivery so long as the carrier has not received instructions to the contrary from the sender.

3. When circumstances preventing delivery of the goods arise after the consignee, in exercise of his rights under article 12, paragraph 3, has given an order for the goods to be delivered to another person, paragraphs 1 and 2 of this article shall apply as if the consignee were the sender and that other person were the consignee.

Article 16

1. The carrier shall be entitled to recover the cost of his request for instructions and any expenses entailed in carrying out such instructions, unless such expenses were caused by the wrongful act or neglect of the carrier.

2. In the cases referred to in article 14, paragraph 1, and in article 15, the carrier may immediately unload the goods for account of the person entitled to dispose of them and thereupon the carriage shall be deemed to be at an end. The carrier shall then hold the goods on behalf of the person so entitled. He may however entrust them to a third party, and in that case he shall not be under any liability except for the exercise of reasonable care in the choice of such third party. The charges due under the consignment note and all other expenses shall remain chargeable against the goods.

3. The carrier may sell the goods, without awaiting instructions from the person entitled to dispose of them, if the goods are perishable or their condition warrants such a course, or when the storage expenses would be out of proportion to the value of the goods. He may also proceed to the sale of the goods in other cases if after the expiry of a reasonable period he has not received from the person entitled to dispose of the goods instructions to the contrary which he may reasonably be required to carry out.

4. If the goods have been sold pursuant to this article, the proceeds of sale, after deduction of the expenses chargeable against the goods, shall be placed at the disposal of the person entitled to dispose of the goods. If these charges exceed the proceeds of sale, the carrier shall be entitled to the difference.

5. The procedure in the case of sale shall be determined by the law or custom of the place where the goods are situated.

Chapter IV

Liability of the Carrier

Article 17

621   1. The carrier shall be liable for the total or partial loss of the goods and for damage thereto occurring between the time when he takes over the goods and the time of delivery, as well as for any delay in delivery.

2. The carrier shall however be relieved of liability if the loss, damage or delay was caused by the wrongful act or neglect of the claimant, by the instructions of the claimant given otherwise than as the result of a wrongful act or neglect on the part of the carrier, by inherent vice of the goods or through circumstances which the carrier could not avoid and the consequences of which he was unable to prevent.

3. The carrier shall not be relieved of liability by reason of the defective condition of the vehicle used by him in order to perform the carriage, or by reason of the wrongful act or neglect of the person from whom he may have hired the vehicle or of the agents or servants of the latter.

4. Subject to article 18, paragraphs 2 to 5, the carrier shall be relieved of liability when the loss or damage arises from the special risks inherent in one or more of the following circumstances:

(*a*) Use of open unsheeted vehicles, when their use has been expressly agreed and specified in the consignment note;

(*b*) the lack of, or defective condition of packing in the case of goods which, by their nature, are liable to wastage or to be damaged when not packed or when not properly packed;

(*c*) handling, loading, stowage or unloading of the goods by the sender, the consignee or persons acting on behalf of the sender or the consignee;

(*d*) the nature of certain kinds of goods which particularly exposes them to total or partial loss or to damage, especially through breakage, rust, decay, desiccation, leakage, normal wastage, or the action of moth or vermin;

(*e*) insufficiency or inadequacy of marks or numbers on the packages;

(*f*) the carriage of livestock.

5. Where under this article the carrier is not under any liability in respect of some of the factors causing the loss, damage or delay, he shall only be liable to the extent that those factors for which he is liable under this article have contributed to the loss, damage or delay.

Article 18

1. The burden of proving that loss, damage or delay was due to one of the causes specified in article 17, paragraph 2, shall rest upon the carrier.

2. When the carrier establishes that in the circumstances of the case, the loss or damage could be attributed to one or more of the special risks referred to in article 17, paragraph 4, it shall be presumed that it was so caused. The claimant shall however be entitled to prove that the loss or damage was not, in fact, attributable either wholly or partly to one of these risks.

3. This presumption shall not apply in the circumstances set out in article 17, paragraph 4 (*a*), if there has been an abnormal shortage, or a loss of any package.

4. If the carriage is performed in vehicles specially equipped to protect the goods from the effects of heat, cold, variations in temperature or the humidity of the air, the carrier shall not be entitled to claim the benefit of article 17, paragraph 4 (*d*), unless he proves that all steps incumbent on him in the circumstances with respect to the choice, maintenance and use of such equipment were taken and that he complied with any special instructions issued to him.

5. The carrier shall not be entitled to claim the benefit of article 17 paragraph 4 (*f*), unless he proves that all steps normally incumbent on him in the circumstances were taken and that he complied with any special instructions issued to him.

Article 19

622   Delay in delivery shall be said to occur when the goods have not been delivered within the agreed time-limit or when, failing an agreed time-limit, the actual duration of the carriage having regard to the circumstances of the

case, and in particular, in the case of partial loads, the time required for making up a complete load in the normal way, exceeds the time it would be reasonable to allow a diligent carrier.

Article 20

1. The fact that goods have not been delivered within thirty days following the expiry of the agreed time-limit, or, if there is no agreed time-limit, within sixty days from the time when the carrier took over the goods, shall be conclusive evidence of the loss of the goods, and the person entitled to make a claim may thereupon treat them as lost.

2. The person so entitled may, on receipt of compensation for the missing goods, request in writing that he shall be notified immediately should the goods be recovered in the course of the year following the payment of compensation. He shall be given a written acknowledgment of such request.

3. Within the thirty days following receipt of such notification, the person entitled as aforesaid may require the goods to be delivered to him against payment of the charges shown to be due on the consignment note and also against refund of the compensation he received less any charges included therein but without prejudice to any claims to compensation for delay in delivery under article 23 and, where applicable, article 26.

4. In the absence of the request mentioned in paragraph 2 or of any instructions given within the period of thirty days specified in paragraph 3, or if the goods are not recovered until more than one year after the payment of compensation, the carrier shall be entitled to deal with them in accordance with the law of the place where the goods are situated.

Article 21

Should the goods have been delivered to the consignee without collection of the " cash on delivery " charge which should have been collected by the carrier under the terms of the contract of carriage, the carrier shall be liable to the sender for compensation not exceeding the amount of such charge without prejudice to his right of action against the consignee.

Article 22

1. When the sender hands goods of a dangerous nature to the carrier, he shall inform the carrier of the exact nature of the danger and indicate, if necessary, the precautions to be taken. If this information has not been entered in the consignment note, the burden of proving, by some other means, that the carrier knew the exact nature of the danger constituted by the carriage of the said goods shall rest upon the sender or the consignee.

2. Goods of a dangerous nature which, in the circumstances referred to in paragraph 1 of this article, the carrier did not know were dangerous, may, at any time or place, be unloaded, destroyed or rendered harmless by the carrier without compensation; further, the sender shall be liable for all expenses, loss or damage arising out of their handing over for carriage or of their carriage.

Article 23

1. When, under the provisions of this Convention, a carrier is liable for compensation in respect of total or partial loss of goods, such compensation shall be calculated by reference to the value of the goods at the place and time at which they were accepted for carriage.

2. The value of the goods shall be fixed according to the commodity exchange price or, if there is no such price, according to the current market

price or, if there is no commodity exchange price or current market price, by reference to the normal value of goods of the same kind and quality.

3. Compensation shall not, however, exceed 25 francs per kilogram of gross weight short. " Franc " means the gold franc weighing 10/31 of a gramme and being of millesimal fineness 900.

4. In addition, the carriage charges, Customs duties and other charges incurred in respect of the carriage of the goods shall be refunded in full in case of total loss and in proportion to the loss sustained in case of partial loss, but no further damages shall be payable.

5. In the case of delay, if the claimant proves that damage has resulted therefrom the carrier shall pay compensation for such damage not exceeding the carriage charges.

6. Higher compensation may only be claimed where the value of the goods or a special interest in delivery has been declared in accordance with articles 24 and 26.

Article 24

623   The sender may, against payment of a surcharge to be agreed upon, declare in the consignment note a value for the goods exceeding the limit laid down in article 23, paragraph 3, and in that case the amount of the declared value shall be substituted for that limit.

Article 25

1. In case of damage, the carrier shall be liable for the amount by which the goods have diminished in value, calculated by reference to the value of the goods fixed in accordance with article 23, paragraphs 1, 2 and 4.

2. The compensation may not, however, exceed:
   (a) if the whole consignment has been damaged the amount payable in the case of total loss;
   (b) if part only of the consignment has been damaged, the amount payable in the case of loss of the part affected.

Article 26

1. The sender may, against payment of a surcharge to be agreed upon, fix the amount of a special interest in delivery in the case of loss or damage or of the agreed time-limit being exceeded, by entering such amount in the consignment note.

2. If a declaration of a special interest in delivery has been made, compensation for the additional loss or damage proved may be claimed, up to the total amount of the interest declared, independently of the compensation provided for in articles 23, 24 and 25.

Article 27

1. The claimant shall be entitled to claim interest on compensation payable. Such interest, calculated at five per centum per annum, shall accrue from the date on which the claim was sent in writing to the carrier or, if no such claim has been made, from the date on which legal proceedings were instituted.

2. When the amounts on which the calculation of the compensation is based are not expressed in the currency of the country in which payment is claimed, conversion shall be at the rate of exchange applicable on the day and at the place of payment of compensation.

Article 28

1. In cases where, under the law applicable, loss, damage or delay arising out of carriage under this Convention gives rise to an extra-contractual claim, the carrier may avail himself of the provisions of this Convention which exclude his liability or which fix or limit the compensation due.

2. In cases where the extra-contractual liability for loss, damage or delay of one of the persons for whom the carrier is responsible under the terms of article 3 is in issue, such person may also avail himself of the provisions of this Convention which exclude the liability of the carrier or which fix or limit the compensation due.

Article 29

1. The carrier shall not be entitled to avail himself of the provisions of this chapter which exclude or limit his liability or which shift the burden of proof if the damage was caused by his wilful misconduct or by such default on his part as, in accordance with the law of the court or tribunal seised of the case, is considered as equivalent to wilful misconduct.

2. The same provision shall apply if the wilful misconduct or default is committed by the agents or servants of the carrier or by any other persons of whose services he makes use for the performance of the carriage, when such agents, servants or other persons are acting within the scope of their employment. Furthermore, in such a case such agents, servants or other persons shall not be entitled to avail themselves, with regard to their personal liability, of the provisions of this chapter referred to in paragraph 1.

CHAPTER V

CLAIMS AND ACTIONS

Article 30

624 1. If the consignee takes delivery of the goods without duly checking their condition with the carrier or without sending him reservations giving a general indication of the loss or damage, not later than the time of delivery in the case of apparent loss or damage and within seven days of delivery, Sundays and public holidays excepted, in the case of loss or damage which is not apparent, the fact of his taking delivery shall be *prima facie* evidence that he has received the goods in the condition described in the consignment note. In the case of loss or damage which is not apparent the reservations referred to shall be made in writing.

2. When the condition of the goods has been duly checked by the consignee and the carrier, evidence contradicting the result of this checking shall only be admissible in the case of loss or damage which is not apparent and provided that the consignee has duly sent reservations in writing to the carrier within seven days, Sundays and public holidays excepted, from the date of checking.

3. No compensation shall be payable for delay in delivery unless a reservation has been sent in writing to the carrier, within twenty-one days from the time that the goods were placed at the disposal of the consignee.

4. In calculating the time-limits provided for in this Article the date of delivery, or the date of checking, or the date when the goods were placed at the disposal of the consignee, as the case may be, shall not be included.

5. The carrier and the consignee shall give each other every reasonable facility for making the requisite investigations and checks.

Article 31

1. In legal proceedings arising out of carriage under this Convention, the plaintiff may bring an action in any court or tribunal of a contracting country designated by agreement between the parties and, in addition, in the courts or tribunals of a country within whose territory

    (*a*) the defendant is ordinarily resident, or has his principal place of business, or the branch or agency through which the contract of carriage was made, or

    (*b*) the place where the goods were taken over by the carrier or the place designated for delivery is situated,

and in no other courts or tribunals.

2. Where in respect of a claim referred to in paragraph 1 of this article an action is pending before a court or tribunal competent under that paragraph, or where in respect of such a claim a judgment has been entered by such a court or tribunal no new action shall be started between the same parties on the same grounds unless the judgment of the court or tribunal before which the first action was brought is not enforceable in the country in which the fresh proceedings are brought.

3. When a judgment entered by a court or tribunal of a contracting country in any such action as is referred to in paragraph 1 of this article has become enforceable in that country, it shall also become enforceable in each of the other contracting States, as soon as the formalities required in the country concerned have been complied with. The formalities shall not permit the merits of the case to be re-opened.

4. The provisions of paragraph 3 of this article shall apply to judgments after trial, judgments by default and settlements confirmed by an order of the court, but shall not apply to interim judgments or to awards of damages, in addition to costs against a plaintiff who wholly or partly fails in his action.

5. Security for costs shall not be required in proceedings arising out of carriage under this Convention from nationals of contracting countries resident or having their place of business in one of those countries.

Article 32

625   1. The period of limitation for an action arising out of carriage under this Convention shall be one year. Nevertheless, in the case of wilful misconduct, or such default as in accordance with the law of the court or tribunal seised of the case, is considered as equivalent to wilful misconduct, the period of limitation shall be three years. The period of limitation shall begin to run:

    (*a*) in the case of partial loss, damage or delay in delivery, from the date of delivery;

    (*b*) in the case of total loss, from the thirtieth day after the expiry of the agreed time-limit or where there is no agreed time-limit from the sixtieth day from the date on which the goods were taken over by the carrier;

    (*c*) in all other cases, on the expiry of a period of three months after the making of the contract of carriage.

The day on which the period of limitation begins to run shall not be included in the period.

2. A written claim shall suspend the period of limitation until such date as the carrier rejects the claim by notification in writing and returns the documents attached thereto. If a part of the claim is admitted the period of limitation shall start to run again only in respect of that part of the claim still in dispute. The burden of proof of the receipt of the claim, or of the reply and of the return of the documents, shall rest with the party relying upon these

facts. The running of the period of limitation shall not be suspended by further claims having the same object.

3. Subject to the provisions of paragraph 2 above, the extension of the period of limitation shall be governed by the law of the court or tribunal seised of the case. That law shall also govern the fresh accrual of rights of action.

4. A right of action which has become barred by lapse of time may not be exercised by way of counter-claim or set-off.

Article 33

The contract of carriage may contain a clause conferring competence on an arbitration tribunal if the clause conferring competence on the tribunal provides that the tribunal shall apply this Convention.

Chapter VI

Provisions Relating to Carriage Performed by Successive Carriers

Article 34

If carriage governed by a single contract is performed by successive road carriers, each of them shall be responsible for the performance of the whole operation, the second carrier and each succeeding carrier becoming a party to the contract of carriage, under the terms of the consignment note, by reason of his acceptance of the goods and the consignment note.

Article 35

1. A carrier accepting the goods from a previous carrier shall give the latter a dated and signed receipt. He shall enter his name and address on the second copy of the consignment note. Where applicable, he shall enter on the second copy of the consignment note and on the receipt reservations of the kind provided for in article 8, paragraph 2.

2. The provisions of article 9 shall apply to the relations between successive carriers.

Article 36

Except in the case of a counter-claim or a set-off raised in an action concerning a claim based on the same contract of carriage, legal proceedings in respect of liability for loss, damage or delay may only be brought against the first carrier, the last carrier or the carrier who was performing that portion of the carriage during which the event causing the loss, damage or delay occurred; an action may be brought at the same time against several of these carriers.

Article 37

A carrier who has paid compensation in compliance with the provisions of this Convention, shall be entitled to recover such compensation, together with interest thereon and all costs and expenses incurred by reason of the claim, from the other carriers who have taken part in the carriage, subject to the following provisions:

    (a) the carrier responsible for the loss or damage shall be solely liable for the compensation whether paid by himself or by another carrier;

(b) when the loss or damage has been caused by the action of two or more carriers, each of them shall pay an amount proportionate to his share of liability; should it be impossible to apportion the liability, each carrier shall be liable in proportion to the share of the payment for the carriage which is due to him;

(c) if it cannot be ascertained to which carriers liability is attributable for the loss or damage, the amount of the compensation shall be apportioned between all the carriers as laid down in (b) above.

Article 38

If one of the carriers is insolvent, the share of the compensation due from him and unpaid by him shall be divided among the other carriers in proportion to the share of the payment for the carriage due to them.

Article 39

1. No carrier against whom a claim is made under articles 37 and 38 shall be entitled to dispute the validity of the payment made by the carrier making the claim if the amount of the compensation was determined by judicial authority after the first mentioned carrier had been given due notice of the proceedings and afforded an opportunity of entering an appearance.

2. A carrier wishing to take proceedings to enforce his right of recovery may make his claim before the competent court or tribunal of the country in which one of the carriers concerned is ordinarily resident, or has his principal place of business or the branch or agency through which the contract of carriage was made. All the carriers concerned may be made defendants in the same action.

3. The provisions of article 31, paragraphs 3 and 4, shall apply to judgments entered in the proceedings referred to in articles 37 and 38.

4. The provisions of article 32 shall apply to claims between carriers. The period of limitation shall, however, begin to run either on the date of the final judicial decision fixing the amount of compensation payable under the provisions of this Convention, or, if there is no such judicial decision, from the actual date of payment.

Article 40

Carriers shall be free to agree among themselves on provisions other than those laid down in articles 37 and 38.

Chapter VII

Nullity of Stipulations Contrary to the Convention

Article 41

627   1. Subject to the provisions of Article 40, any stipulation which would directly or indirectly derogate from the provisions of this Convention shall be null and void. The nullity of such a stipulation shall not involve the nullity of the other provisions of the contract.

2. In particular, a benefit of insurance in favour of the carrier or any other similar clause, or any clause shifting the burden of proof shall be null and void.

[Chapter VIII of the Convention is not reproduced. This deals with the coming into force of the Convention, the settlement of disputes between the High Contracting Parties and related matters.]

PROTOCOL OF SIGNATURE

1. This Convention shall not apply to traffic between the United Kingdom of Great Britain and Northern Ireland and the Republic of Ireland.

NEW YORK FOREIGN FREIGHT FORWARDERS AND BROKERS ASSOCIATION INC. TERMS AND CONDITIONS OF SERVICE

628   All shipments to or from the Customer, which term shall include the exporter, importer, sender, receiver, owner, consignor, consignee, transferor or transferee of the shipments, will be handled by —— (hereinafter called the " Company ") on the following terms and conditions:

Services by third parties

1. Unless the Company carries, stores or otherwise physically handles the shipment, and the loss, damage, expense or delay occurs during such activity, the Company assumes no liability as a carrier and is not to be held responsible for any loss, damage, expense or delay to the goods to be forwarded or imported except as provided in paragraph 10 and subject to the limitations of paragraph 8 below, but undertakes only to use reasonable care in the selection of carriers, truckmen, lightermen, forwarders, customhouse brokers, agents, warehousemen and others to whom it may entrust the goods for transportation, cartage, handling and/or delivery and/or storage or otherwise. When the Company carries, stores or otherwise physically handles the shipment, it does so subject to the limitation of liability set forth in paragraph 8 below unless a separate bill of lading, air waybill or other contract of carriage is issued by the Company, in which event the terms thereof shall govern.

Liability limitations of third parties

2. The Company is authorized to select and engage carriers, truckmen, lightermen, forwarders, customhouse brokers, agents, warehousemen and others, as required, to transport, store, deal with and deliver the goods, all of whom shall be considered as the agents of the Customer, and the goods may be entrusted to such agencies subject to all conditions as to limitation of liability for loss, damage, expense or delay and to all rules, regulations, requirements and conditions, whether printed, written or stamped, appearing in bills of lading, receipts or tariffs issued by such carriers, truckmen, lightermen, forwarders, customhouse brokers, agents, warehousemen and others. The Company shall under no circumstances be liable for any loss, damage, expense or delay to the goods for any reason whatsoever when said goods are in custody, possession or control of third parties selected by the Company to forward, enter and clear, transport or render other services with respect to such goods.

Choosing routes or agents

3. Unless express instructions in writing are received from the Customer, the Company has complete freedom in choosing the means, route and procedure to be followed in the handling, transportation and delivery of the goods. Advice by the Company to the Customer that a particular person or firm has been selected to render services with respect to the goods shall not be construed to mean that the Company warrants or represents that such person or firm will render such services.

Quotations not binding

4. Quotations as to fees, rates of duty, freight charges, insurance premiums or other charges given by the Company to the Customer are for informational

purposes only and are subject to change without notice and shall not under any circumstances be binding upon the Company unless the Company in writing specifically undertakes the handling or transportation of the shipment at a specific rate.

Duty to furnish information

5. (a) On an import at a reasonable time prior to entering of the goods for U.S. Customs, the Customer shall furnish to the Company invoices in proper form and other documents necessary or useful in the preparation of the U.S. Customs entry and, also, such further information as may be sufficient to establish the dutiable value, the classification and admissibility pursuant to U.S. law or regulation. If the Customer fails in a timely manner to furnish such information or documents in whole or in part, as may be required to complete U.S. Customs entry, or if the information or documents furnished is inaccurate or incomplete, the Company shall be obligated only to use its best judgment in connection with the shipment. Where a bond is required by U.S. Customs to be given for the production of any document or the performance of any act, the Customer shall be deemed bound by the terms of the bond notwithstanding the fact that the bond has been executed by the Company as principal, it being understood that the Company entered into such undertaking at the instance and on behalf of the Customer, and the Customer shall indemnify and hold the Company harmless for the consequences of any breach of the terms of the bond. (b) On an export at a reasonable time prior to the exportation of the shipment the Customer shall furnish to the Company the commercial invoice in proper form and number, a proper consular declaration, weights, measures, values and other information in the language of and as may be required by the laws and regulations of the U.S. and the country of destination of the goods. (c) On an export or import the Company shall not in any way be responsible or liable for increased duty, penalty, fine or expense unless caused by the negligence or other fault of the Company, in which event its liability to the Customer shall be governed by the provisions of paragraph 8. The Customer shall be bound by and warrant the accuracy of all invoices, documents and information furnished to the Company by the Customer or its agent for export, entry or other purposes and the Customer agrees to indemnify and hold harmless the Company against any increased duty, penalty, fine or expense, including attorneys fees, resulting from any inaccuracy or omission or any failure to make timely presentation, even if not due to any negligence of the Customer.

Declaring higher valuation

6. Inasmuch as truckers, carriers, warehousemen and others to whom the goods are entrusted usually limit their liability for loss or damage unless a higher value is declared and a charge based on such higher value is agreed to by said truckers, etc., the Company must receive specific written instructions from the Customer to pay such higher charge based on valuation and the trucker, etc., must accept such higher declared value; otherwise the valuation placed by the Customer on the goods shall be considered solely for export or customs purposes and the goods will be delivered to the truckers, etc., subject to the limitation of liability set forth herein in paragraph 8 with respect to any claim against the Company and subject to the provisions of paragraph 2 above.

Insurance

7. The Company will make reasonable efforts to effect marine, fire, theft

[329]

and other insurance upon the goods only after specific written instructions have been received by the Company in sufficient time prior to shipment from point of origin, and the Customer at the same time states specifically the kind and amount of insurance to be placed. The Company does not undertake or warrant that such insurance can or will be placed. Unless the Customer has its own open marine policy and instructs the Company to effect insurance under such policy, insurance is to be effected with one or more insurance companies or other underwriters to be selected by the Company. Any insurance placed shall be governed by the certificate or policy issued and will only be effective when accepted by such insurance companies or other underwriters. Should an insurer dispute its liability for any reason, the insured shall have recourse against the insurer only and the Company shall not be under any responsibility or liability in relation thereto, notwithstanding that the premium upon the policy may not be at the same rates as that charged or paid to the Company by the Customer, or that the shipment was insured under a policy in the name of the Company. Insurance premiums and the charge of the Company for arranging the same shall be at the Customer's expense. If for any reason the goods are held in warehouse, or elsewhere, the same will not be covered by any insurance, unless the Company receives written instructions from the Customer. Unless specifically agreed in writing, the Company assumes no responsibility to effect insurance on any export or import shipment which it does not handle.

Limitation of $50 per shipment

8. The Customer agrees that the Company shall in no event be liable for any loss, damage, expense or delay to the goods resulting from the negligence or other fault of the Company for any amount in excess of $50·00 per shipment (or the invoice value, if less) and any partial loss or damage for which the Company may be liable shall be adjusted pro rata on the basis of such valuation. The Customer has the option of paying a special compensation to increase the liability of the Company in excess of $50 per shipment in case of any loss, damage, expense or delay from causes which would make the Company liable, but such option can be exercised only by specific written agreement made with the Company prior to shipment, which agreement shall indicate the limit of the Company's liability and the special compensation for the added liability by it to be assumed.

Presenting claims

9. In no event shall the Company be liable for any act, omission or default by it in connection with an exportation or importation, unless a claim therefor shall be presented to it at its office within one hundred eighty (180) days from date of exportation or importation of the goods in a written statement to which sworn proof of claim shall be attached. No suit to recover for any claim or demand hereunder shall in any event be maintained against the Company unless instituted within six (6) months after presentation of the said claim, as above provided. No agent or employee of the Company shall have authority to alter or waive any of the provisions of this clause.

Liability of company

10. It is agreed that any claim or demand for loss, damage, expense or delay shall be only against the carriers, truckmen, lightermen, forwarders, customhouse brokers, agents, warehousemen or others in whose actual custody or control the goods may be at the time of such loss, damage expense or delay, and that the Company shall not be liable or responsible for any claim or demand from any cause whatsoever, unless in each case the goods

were in the actual custody or control of the Company and the damages alleged to have been suffered be proven to be caused by the negligence or other fault of the Company, its officers or employees, in which event the limitation of liability set forth in paragraph 8 herein shall apply. The Company shall not in any circumstances be liable for damages arising from loss of profit.

629 Advancing Money

11. The Company shall not be obliged to incur any expense, guarantee payment or advance any money in connection with the importing, forwarding, transporting, insuring, storing or coopering of the goods, unless the same is previously provided to the Company by the Customer on demand. The Company shall be under no obligation to advance freight charges, customs duties or taxes on any shipment, nor shall any advance by the Company be construed as a waiver of the provisions hereof.

Indemnification for freight, duties

12. In the event that a carrier, other person or any governmental agency makes a claim or institutes legal action against the Company for ocean or other freight, duties, fines, penalties, liquidated damages or other money due arising from a shipment of goods of the Customer, the Customer agrees to indemnify and hold harmless the Company for any amount the Company may be required to pay such carrier, other person or governmental agency together with reasonable expenses, including attorney fees, incurred by the Company in connection with defending such claim or legal action and obtaining reimbursement from the Customer. The confiscation or detention of the goods by any governmental authority shall not affect or diminish the liability of the Customer to the Company to pay all charges or other money due promptly on demand.

Sale of perishable goods

13. Perishable goods or live animals to be exported or which are cleared through customs concerning which no instructions for disposition are furnished by the Customer may be sold or otherwise disposed of without any notice to the Customer, owner or consignee of the goods, and payment or tender of the net proceeds of any sale after deduction of charges shall be equivalent to delivery. In the event that any shipment is refused or remains unclaimed at destination or any transshipping point in the course of transit or is returned for any reason, the Customer shall nevertheless pay the Company for all charges and expenses in connection therewith. Nothing herein contained shall obligate the Company to forward or enter or clear the goods or arrange for their disposal.

C.O.D. shipments

14. Goods received with Customer's or other person's instructions to " Collect on Delivery " (C.O.D.) by drafts or otherwise, or to collect on any specified terms by time drafts or otherwise, are accepted by the Company only upon the express understanding that it will exercise reasonable care in the selection of a bank, correspondent, carrier or agent to whom it will send such item for collection, and the Company will not be responsible for any act, omission, default, suspension, insolvency or want of care, negligence, or fault of such bank, correspondent, carrier or agent, nor for any delay in remittance lost in exchange, or loss during transmission, or while in the course of collection.

General Lien on any property

15. The Company shall have a general lien on any and all property (and documents relating thereto) of the Customer, in its possession, custody or control or en route, for all claims for charges, expenses or advances incurred by the Company in connection with any shipments of the Customer and such claim remains unsatisfied for thirty (30) days after demand for its payment is made, the Company may sell at public auction or private sale, upon ten (10) days written notice, registered mail (R.R.R.), to the Customer, the goods, wares and/or merchandise, or so much thereof as may be necessary to satisfy such lien, and apply the net proceeds of such sale to the payment of the amount due to the Company. Any surplus from such sale shall be transmitted to the Customer, and the Customer shall be liable for any deficiency in the sale.

Compensation of company

16. The compensation of the Company for its services shall be included with and is in addition to the rates and charges of all carriers and other agencies selected by the Company to transport and deal with the goods and such compensation shall be exclusive of any brokerage, commissions, dividends or other revenue received by the Company from carriers, insurers and others in connection with the shipment. In any referral for collection or action against the Customer for monies due to the Company, upon recovery by the Company, the Customer shall pay the expenses of collection and/or litigation, including a reasonable attorney fee.

Picking up shipments or samples

17. The Company shall not itself be obligated to pick up a shipment from a carrier or a sample from U.S. Customs. Should the Company render such a service for and on behalf of the Customer, the Company shall not be responsible for loss or damage to the shipment unless it is in the actual custody and control of the Company or its employee and the loss or damage is caused by the negligence or other fault of the Company or its employee, in which event the limitation of liability set forth in paragraph 8 herein shall apply.

No responsibility for governmental requirements

18. It is the responsibility of the Customer to know and comply with the marking requirements of U.S. Customs, the regulations of the U.S. Food and Drug Administration and all other requirements of law or official regulations. The Company shall not be responsible for action taken or fines or penalties assessed by any governmental agency against the shipment because of the failure of the Customer to comply with the law or the requirements or regulations of any governmental agency or with a notification issued to the Customer by any such agency.

Loss, damage or expense due to delay

19. Unless the services to be performed by the Company on behalf of the Customer are unduly delayed by reason of the negligence or other fault of the Company, the Company shall not be responsible for any loss, damage or expense incurred by the Customer because of such delay. In the event the Company is at fault, as aforesaid, its liability is limited in accordance with the provisions of paragraph 8 above.

Construction of terms and venue

20. The foregoing terms and conditions shall be construed according to the laws of the State of —— . Unless otherwise consented to in writing by the Company, no legal proceeding against the Company may be instituted by the Customer, its assigns, or subrogee except in the City of —— .

[332]

Approved by:

National Customs Brokers & Forwarders Assoc. of America, Inc. — New York Foreign Freight Forwarders & Brokers Assoc., Inc. — Customs Brokers & Forwarders Assoc. of Miami, Inc. — San Francisco Customs Brokers Assoc. — Customs Brokers Assoc. of Chicago, Inc. — Boston Customs Brokers & International Forwarders Assoc. — Customhouse Brokers & International Freight Forwarders Assoc. of Washington State — Los Angeles Customs & Freight Brokers Assoc., Inc. — Customs Brokers Assoc., Northern U.S. Border — Baltimore Customhouse Brokers & Forwarders Assoc. — Philadelphia Freight Brokers, Forwarders & Customs Brokers Assoc. — New Orleans Assoc. of Customs Brokers, Inc. — Detroit Customhouse Brokers & Foreign Freight Forwarders Assoc. — Columbia River Customs Brokers & Foreign Freight Forwarders Assoc. — Independent Freight Forwarders & Brokers Assoc. of Savannah, Inc. — Assoc. of Forwarding Agents & Foreign Freight Brokers of Mobile — Customs Brokers & Freight Forwarders Assoc. of Charleston, S.C. Inc. — Export-Import Assoc. of Virginia.

July 1970.

DUTCH FORWARDING CONDITIONS

GENERAL CONDITIONS OF THE
FEDERATION OF DUTCH FORWARDING AGENTS' ORGANISATIONS

deposited at the Registry of the District Courts at Amsterdam, Arnhem, Breda and Rotterdam on March 15, 1956.

Applicability

Article 1

630 1. The present general conditions shall apply to all the forwarding agent's operations and activities, including those which are not specifically part of his forwarding work.

2. The latter operations and activities, such as those of shipbrokers, stevedores, carriers, insurers, warehousing and superintending firms, etc., shall also be governed by the conditions customary in the particular trade or by conditions stipulated to be applicable. In the event of any conflict between such conditions and the present conditions, it shall be for the forwarding agent to decide which provisions he claims the benefit of.

3. The forwarding agent may at any time declare applicable the conditions stipulated by third parties with whom he has made contracts for the purpose of carrying out the order given to him.

4. The forwarding agent may have his orders and/or the work connected therewith carried out by third parties or the servants of third parties. In so far as such third parties or their servants bear statutory liability towards the forwarding agent's principal, it is stipulated on their behalf that in doing the work for which the forwarding agent employs them they shall be regarded as solely in the employ of the forwarding agent. All the provisions (inter alia) regarding non-liability and limitation of liability and also regarding indemnification of the forwarding agent as described herein shall apply to such persons.

5. Instructions for delivery C.O.D., against banker's draft, etc., shall be deemed to be forwarding work.

Contracts

Article 2

631 1. All quotations made by the forwarding agent shall be without any obligation on his part.

[333]

2. All prices quoted and agreed shall be based on the rates, wages, social insurances and/or other provisions, freight and exchange rates applying at the time of quotation or contract.

3. Upon any change in any one or more of these factors the quoted or agreed prices shall likewise be altered, automatically in accordance therewith and retroactively to the time such change occurred.

Article 3

1. In the event of loading and/or unloading time being inadequate—regardless of the cause thereof—all costs resulting therefrom, such as demurrage, etc., shall be borne by the principal, even when the forwarding agent has accepted the bill of lading and/or charter party from which the additional costs arise without protestation.

2. Expenses of an exceptional nature and higher wages arising whenever carriers by virtue of any provision in the shipping documents load or unload goods in the event, at night, on Saturday afternoon or on Sundays or public holidays, shall not be included in the agreed prices, unless specifically stipulated. Any such costs shall therefore be refunded by the principal to the forwarding agent.

3. For work of a special nature, unusual jobs or work requiring a special amount of time or effort, an additional reasonable amount may at all times be charged.

Article 4

Unless the contrary be stipulated, contract prices shall not include (inter alia): postage, teleprinter, telegram and telephone charges, stamps, import duties and excise, statistical duties, consular and attestation fees, customs formalities, cost of preparing shipping documents and bankers' guarantees, the cost of weighing, measuring, tallying, taring, sampling and repairing, cranage, additional costs of handling heavy objects, insurance premiums, all extra costs such as warehousing charges and quayside charges for consignments missing a connection, and also demurrage for detention or delay of vessels, trucks or other transport, hire of tarpaulins, overtime pay, the cost of working in the evening, at night, on Saturday afternoon, Sunday and public holidays and cost of providing watchmen.

Article 5

1. Insurance of any kind shall be arranged only upon specific instructions in writing at the principal's expense and risk. The risks to be covered shall be clearly stated. A mere statement of the value is not enough.

2. If the forwarding agent has arranged an insurance in his own name he shall be bound—if so requested—only to transfer his claims against the insurer to his principal.

3. The forwarding agent shall not be responsible as regards the choice of the insurer and his ability to pay.

4. When the forwarding agent uses derricks and any other such equipment for carrying out his orders he shall be entitled to arrange an insurance at his principal's expense to cover the forwarding agent's risks arising through the use of such equipment.

Article 6

Despatch of customs papers to the forwarding agent shall imply an authority to clear the goods.

Performance of the Contract

Article 7

632   If the principal has not given any specific instructions with his order, the mode and route of transport shall be at the forwarding agent's option and he may at all times accept the documents customarily used by the firms with which he contracts for the purpose of carrying out his orders.

Article 8

1. The principal shall ensure that the documents required for receipt and for despatch, and also the instructions, are in the forwarding agent's possession in proper time.

2. The principal shall be liable for all consequences arising from inaccurate, obscure and inadequate documents and/or instructions, and through the same not being furnished or not furnished in time.

3. In the absence of documents, the forwarding agent shall not be obliged to receive against a guarantee. Should the forwarding agent furnish a guarantee, he shall be indemnified by his principal for all the consequences thereof.

Article 9

1. All operations such as superintending, sampling, taring, tallying, weighing, measuring, etc., and receiving goods under judicial survey, shall take place only on the principal's specific instructions and upon reimbursement of the costs thereof.

2. Nevertheless the forwarding agent shall be entitled, but not obliged, on his own authority and at his principal's expense and risk to take all action which he considers necessary in the principal's interest.

3. The forwarding agent shall not act as an expert. He shall in no way be liable for any notification of the state, nature or quality of the goods; nor shall he be under any obligation to see that samples are identical with the lot.

Article 10

The addition of the word " approximately " shall allow the principal the freedom to supply $2\frac{1}{2}$ per cent. more or less.

Liability

Article 11

1. All operations and activities shall be at the principal's expense and risk.

2. The principal shall be liable for all damage caused to the forwarding agent by the principal, the persons working under him and the goods entrusted by him to the forwarding agent.

3. The principal shall indemnify the forwarding agent against third party claims in respect of damage as described in paragraph 2 hereof.

4. The forwarding agent shall be liable to his principal in respect of damage only if the latter proves that the damage has been caused by the forwarding agent wilfully or by fault on his part tantamount to a wilful act.

5. If, while the order and/or any work connected therewith is being carried out, any damage occurs for which the forwarding agent bears no liability the forwarding agent shall—if requested so to do—waive in his principal's favour his claims under contract against third parties engaged by him for the purpose of carrying out such order and/or such work.

6. Even in the event of taking over transport, the forwarding agent shall be liable under the present conditions and not as carrier.

Article 12

The following shall (inter alia) be regarded as *force majeure*:

    a. war, threat of war, official action, quarantine, civil disturbance, sabotage, strike, lock-out, interference with communications, lack of transport, labour and/or storage accommodation;

b. storm, fog, lightning, flood, high and low tide, frost, freezing, ice;
c. fire, explosions, water used against fires, smoke, burglary, theft, loss, subsidence, collapse, water, seepage, damp odour, stench, worms and rodents, damage through rats, mice, insects and other creatures;
d. the natural properties of goods, changes in quality, spontaneous deterioration, self-generated heat, combustion, explosion, drying, mould, yeasts, leaks, rot and mildew, rust and sweating;
e. breakage of glass, wickered bottles and flasks, cast-iron and other brittle articles, inadequate packing;
f. all other things which the forwarding agent could not reasonably prevent.

Article 13

1. In the event of *force majeure*, the contract shall remain in force; the forwarding agent's obligations shall, however, be suspended for so long as the *force majeure* lasts.

2. All additional costs caused by *force majeure*, such as carriage and storage charges, warehouse or yard rentals, demurrage for vessels or trucks, insurance, delivery from warehouses, bonded or otherwise, etc., shall be borne by the principal.

Article 14

1. The mere statement by the principal of a time for delivery shall not be binding upon the forwarding agent.

2. Arrival times are not guaranteed by the forwarding agent.

Article 15

1. The forwarding agent shall not be liable on account of errors in particulars of freights, duties and expenses notified to him by third persons.

2. Nor shall the forwarding agent be liable should freights, costs of duties be wrongly charged. Demands and back demands arising on this account shall be charged to the principal.

3. If the carriers refuse to sign for number of pieces or items, weight, etc., the forwarding agent shall not be liable for the consequences thereof.

Payment

Article 16

634 1. The principal shall pay to the forwarding agent in cash the freights, duties, remuneration, etc., upon arrival or despatch of goods which are being received or forwarded respectively. The risk of exchange fluctuations shall be borne by the principal.

2. If the principal does not pay the amount due immediately upon notification thereof, the forwarding agent shall be entitled to charge interest at the rate of 4 per cent. per annum over the bank rate of De Nederlandsche Bank N.V.

3. The principal shall by reason of the forwarding contract and upon demand by the forwarding agent furnish security for any amount in which the principal is or may be indebted to the forwarding agent.

4. The forwarding agent shall not be obliged out of his own resources to furnish security for the payment of freight, duties and/or other costs should the same be demanded. All the consequences of non-compliance or of failure to comply forthwith with a demand to furnish security shall be borne by the principal.

If the forwarding agent has furnished security out of his own resources, he may demand payment of the amount for which security has been furnished from the principal forthwith.

5. Unless otherwise provided, Articles 1844 to 1848 inclusive of the Civil Code shall apply conformably.

Article 17

The principal shall not be entitled to apply any set-off in respect of sums charged by the forwarding agent to the principal under any contract existing between them.

Article 18

1. Notwithstanding the provisions of Article 1435 of the Civil Code, cash payments shall be deemed in the first place to have been made on account of non-preferential debts, regardless of whether any other instructions have been given at the time of payment.

2. If legal proceedings or other means are resorted to in the event of failure to pay by due date, the amount of the indebtedness shall be increased by 10 per cent. for clerical expenses, while the legal and other costs shall be borne by the principal up to the amount paid by or due from the forwarding agent.

Article 19

1. The forwarding agent shall be entitled to retain goods, documents and moneys at the principal's and/or owner's expense and risk until the sums due to him have been paid or, if the goods are forwarded on, to collect the sum due on subsequent delivery or draw a bill therefor with the shipping documents annexed.

2. All goods, documents and moneys which the forwarding agent for whatsoever reason or purpose has or may have in his possession shall serve as security for all sums which are or may be due to him from the principal or owner.

3. Failing payment of the amount due the security shall be sold as provided by statute or—if agreed upon—by private sale.

Final Provisions
Article 20

635   No legal or arbitration proceedings shall be taken against third parties by the forwarding agent unless he states his readiness to take the same at the principal's request and expense.

Article 21

All claims against the forwarding agent shall be barred by the mere expiration of six months since the claim originated and shall be extinguished by the mere expiration of one year since the claim originated.

Article 22

The place for settlement and adjustment of damage shall be that where the forwarding agent's business is situated.

Disputes
Article 23

636   1. All disputes which may arise between the forwarding agent and the other party shall be decided by three arbitrators to the exclusion of the ordinary courts of law, and their decision shall be final.

A dispute shall exist whenever any of the parties declares this to be so.

2. One arbitrator shall be appointed by the Chairman of the group affiliated to the Federation of Dutch Forwarding Agents' Organisations within whose jurisdiction the forwarding agent's business is situated; the second one shall be appointed by the Dean of the Order of Advocates of the district in which the aforesaid group is established; the third shall be appointed by mutual arrangement by both the arbitrators so appointed. Only persons of Dutch nationality may be appointed arbitrators.

3. The Chairman of the forwarding agent's group shall appoint as such an expert on forwarding questions; the Dean of the Order of Advocates shall be asked to appoint a member of the legal profession; the third arbitrator shall preferably be an expert on the trade or industry in which the forwarding agent's opposite party is engaged.

4. The party desirous of having the dispute determined shall inform the Secretariat of the Federation of Dutch Forwarding Agents' Organisations hereof by registered letter, giving a brief description of the dispute and of his claim and at the same time sending twenty-five guilders in payment of the Federation's administrative work.

5. After receipt of the above-mentioned registered letter the Secretariat of the Federation shall as quickly as possible send a copy thereof to the other party, to the Chairman of the forwarding agents' group, to the Dean of the Order of Advocates, with a request to each of the latter to appoint an arbitrator and to notify the Secretariat of the name and address of the person appointed. Upon receipt of such notification the Secretariat shall as soon as possible notify the persons concerned of their appointment at the same time sending them a copy of the application for arbitration and a copy of these general conditions and requesting them to appoint a third arbitrator and notify the Secretariat of the person so appointed. Upon receipt hereof the Secretariat shall forthwith notify the third arbitrator of his appointment, at the same time sending him a copy of the application for arbitration and a copy of these general conditions. The Secretariat shall also notify both parties what persons have been appointed arbitrators.

6. If all three arbitrators have not been appointed within thirty days of the application for arbitration having been lodged all of them shall be appointed by the District Court within whose jurisdiction the forwarding agent's business is situated upon the application of whichever party shall first make the same.

7. The person appointed by the Dean shall act as Chairman of the arbitration board. If the arbitrators are appointed by the Court, the arbitrators shall themselves decide who is to function as chairman.

The arbitrators shall make their award equitably as good men and true. They shall prescribe the order of the proceedings, subject to the parties being given facilities for putting forward their cases in writing and elucidating the same orally.

8. The arbitrators shall continue in office until the final award. They shall deposit their award at the Registry of the District Court within whose jurisdiction the forwarding agent's business is situated, while a copy thereof shall be sent to each of the parties and to the Secretariat of the Federation.

The arbitrators may require the Plaintiff or both parties to deposit a sum beforehand in respect of the arbitration costs; during the proceedings they may require an additional amount to be deposited. In their award the arbitrators shall order which of the two parties shall bear the costs of arbitration or what proportion thereof each shall bear. They shall include the arbitrators' fees and disbursements, the twenty-five guilders paid with the application and the costs incurred by the parties in so far as the arbitrators deem the same to be reasonably necessary.

The sums due to the arbitrators shall as far as possible be taken from the amounts deposited.

Article 24

These general conditions may be cited as the " Dutch Forwarding Conditions." In case the English translation differs from the Dutch text the latter will prevail.

Amsterdam,
Weesperzijde 150.

Rotterdam,
Pieter de Hoochweg 110

NORDISKT SPEDITÖRFÖRBUND

(Federation of Forwarding Agents' Associations in Denmark, Finland, Norway and Sweden)

GENERAL RULES

Adopted at the Ordinary General Meeting on July 1, 1919, and last revised in the year 1959

637 These rules, which shall apply to all commissions executed by the Forwarding Agents who are members of the Association of Northern Forwarding Agents (Nordiskt Speditörförbund), have been agreed after discussion between the Association on the one hand and the following organizations on the other.

Denmark:
Grosserer-Societetets Komité
Industrirådet
Landbrugsrådet
Provinshandelskammeret
Butikshandelens Fællesraad

Norway:
Befraktningsutvalget
Norges Grossistförbund
Norges Handelsstands Förbund
Norges Industriförbund
Norges Kooperative Landsforening

Sweden:
Näringslivets Trafikdelegation
Handelskamrarnas Nämnd
Kooperativa Förbundet
Sveriges Grossistförbund
Sveriges Hantverks- och
    Småindustriorganisation
Sveriges Industriförbund
Sveriges Köpmannaförbund
Sveriges Lantbruksförbund

Finland:
Centralhandelskammaren
Finlands Grossistförbund
Finlands Industriförbund
Finska Träförädlingsindustriernas
    Centralförbund

Definition § 1

The task of the Forwarding Agent is to attend against remuneration for the account of clients but in his own name, to the transportation of goods and everything connected therewith, to undertake the clearance of goods through the customs, the trans-shipment, storage and insurance of goods and all steps connected therewith.

§ 2

It is incumbent upon the Forwarding Agent carefully to protect the interests of his Clients; and nothing in the following rules is to be taken to imply any departure from the above-mentioned general obligations of the Forwarding Agent towards his Clients.

Quotations   § 3

All quotations submitted shall be based on goods of normal weight, volume and condition. The Forwarding Agent's fee included in a quotation covers measures normally taken in the execution of the forwarding order.

Any outlays and special expenses included in a quotation shall be based on the charges, tariffs and rates of exchange current at the time when the quotation is submitted.

Execution of Forwarding Order   § 4

In the absence of instructions to the contrary, the Forwarding Agent has the right to choose any customary routes or means of transportation.

§ 5

The Forwarding Agent may send communications and documents by ordinary mail. Where this may be done without difficulty, however, securities and negotiable documents may be sent by registered mail.

§ 6

Should the Forwarding Agent in executing a forwarding order find it necessary, whether during transportation, trans-shipment, storage or otherwise, to take action without first obtaining instructions, he shall do so on behalf of and at the risk of his Client.

Should there arise a risk of loss in the value of goods in the charge of the Forwarding Agent and should the owner or person who has the right of disposition over the goods not be available or upon request fail to arrange for the removal of the goods as early as possible, the Forwarding Agent is entitled to take any necessary steps with respect to the goods and if necessary to sell the goods by Public Auction or, if this is not expedient, to sell the goods in some other suitable way.

The Forwarding Agent may, according to circumstances, without notice sell or destroy for the account of the Owner perishable goods which are liable to destruction or deterioration in value.

Should the packing be found to be damaged, the Forwarding Agent may, without specially informing the Owner, have the damage repaired at the Owner's expense.

§ 7

When clearing goods through the Customs, the Forwarding Agent is not bound to have the goods examined more thoroughly than is required by the Customs Officer concerned.

Insurance   § 8

638   The Forwarding Agent shall not insure goods against any risk whatever unless he has either received written instructions to do so in the particular case or has previously received general instructions in writing to that effect. The fact that a Forwarding Agent has on previous occasions insured consignments from a certain Client or to a certain Consignee does not involve an obligation to insure subsequent consignments or to inquire whether insurance should be effected. A statement of value in forwarding instructions does not imply an order to insure.

If the Forwarding Agent has received instructions to insure certain transports or consignments without specification of the risks to be covered, the Forwarding Agent is only bound to take out an ordinary Transport Insurance (in the case of sea transport free of particular average except in case of stranding, and in the case of rail or road transport against traffic accidents) or, in the event of storage, an ordinary (fire) insurance.

§ 9

If goods insured by the Forwarding Agent by order of his Client are lost or damaged, the Client can only claim in respect of the insurance that the Agent's rights against the insurance company shall be transferred to him.

Fees, Remuneration, etc.   § 10

Even when goods have been dispatched against payment of freight upon arrival, the Client is bound to pay to the Forwarding Agent upon request all outstanding freights and charges on the goods, money advanced and other sums due to him, if the consignment is lost in transit, appreciably delayed or not redeemed within eight days of arrival.

§ 11

The Forwarding Agent is entitled to receive an advance payment covering estimated outlays for freights, Custom dues, etc. If no advance payment has been received by him, he may charge a commission on his outlays. After the invoice has been made out, the Agent is entitled to interest as from the date payment is due.

§ 12

The Forwarding Agent is entitled to charge separate fees for collecting Cash on Delivery payments, checking transmission of payment through banks, clearing, obtaining acceptance of Bills of Exchange, issuing Delivery Orders, and similar work.

He is also entitled to separate fees for work outside what is normally involved in the carrying out of a forwarding order, e.g. negotiations with authorities, banks and insurance companies, preparation of consular documents and Certificates of Origin, presentation of claims on carriers and insurance companies in case of damage, and similar services.

§ 13

A statement of sums collected on behalf of the Client shall be rendered without unreasonable delay; and in doing this, if he has not been able to make up his final account at the time the statement is made out, the Forwarding Agent is entitled to deduct an amount corresponding to the estimated sum due to him from the Client. If the Forwarding Agent has observed these rules, he is not responsible for losses on exchange. Profits on exchange are credited to the Client.

§ 14

The Forwarding Agent is not responsible for Customs dues, freights or the like which have been debited incorrectly. Should he receive supplementary invoices or bills for such items, his Client and/or the Consignee shall be liable to pay the amounts in question on demand.

§ 15

If a forwarding order is withdrawn, the Forwarding Agent is entitled to payment for work performed and disbursements made.

Lien, etc. § 16

639   The Forwarding Agent shall have a lien on goods in his charge for all costs
relating to such goods, including forwarding fees and storage charges as well
as for all other claims against the Client for work arising from executed
forwarding orders.

Should the goods be lost or destroyed, the Forwarding Agent has the
same right as above in respect of compensation paid by Insurance Companies,
carriers or others.

Failing payment for claims due to him, the Forwarding Agent is entitled
to sell by Public Auction, or, if this is not expedient, in some other suitable
way, so much of the goods as is required to cover his total claims and the
costs of the sale. He shall as far as possible give notice in due time to the
Owner and to holders of liens on the goods of the time and place of such
sale.

Responsibility § 17

The Forwarding Agent is responsible for damage caused by his failure to
observe due care in the execution of a forwarding order.

He shall not be responsible for damage occasioned by an error or mistake
on the part of the carrier, trans-shipper or distributing agent, or other third
party, unless he has failed to exercise due care in selecting such person. The
same applies when the Forwarding Agent is instructed to collect money.

Where the Forwarding Agent notices that damage or loss has occurred, he
shall be responsible for taking any necessary steps to secure the Client's claim
for compensation against the person who has caused such damage or loss or
who is answerable for it.

§ 18

When forwarding goods, the Forwarding Agent is not responsible as a
carrier unless he himself executes the transportation.

§ 19

The Forwarding Agent is not responsible for the number of packages until
he has taken charge of the goods and has had an opportunity to check the
number. Nor shall he be responsible for weight, measurement, quality, contents
or value unless he has expressly undertaken such responsibility.

If goods are stored in port on the quay, or in a public warehouse or shed,
the Forwarding Agent is not responsible for the number of packages, or for
loss or depreciation of or damage to the goods, unless he has received written
instructions from the Client to check the number of packages and have the
goods watched.

The Client is himself responsible in respect of any remarks made on Shipping Notes, Bills of Lading, or Way-Bills as to the conditions of the goods,
packing, etc.

In the absence of written instructions to the contrary, the Forwarding
Agent shall not be responsible for private tarpaulins.

§ 20

The liability of the Forwarding Agent towards his Client is limited to
20.000 kr. (in Finland 1.000.000 Fmk) for each incident.

The Forwarding Agent is not responsible for money, securities or valuables except when specially agreed.

The term " incident " means all damage suffered by the Client which has
arisen on one and the same occasion.

§ 21

The Forwarding Agent is not responsible for misunderstandings or errors due to the failure of the Client to give written instructions in due time to the Agent's office.

§ 22

The Forwarding Agent is not responsible for the consequences of any delay, non-delivery, or distortion of messages dispatched by him by post, telegram or any other suitable means.

§ 23

After the Consignee has received the delivery documents, he is responsible for any risk and expenses in respect of the goods. Should loss of or damage to the goods occur subsequently, the Forwarding Agent shall be held responsible for this only where it is shown that such loss or damage was occasioned by him or by someone for whom he is answerable.

§ 24

The Forwarding Agent is not responsible for damage or loss resulting from war or acts of war, substantial changes in an already existing state of war, mobilization, insurrection or disturbances, strikes, lockouts, acts of God, disruptions of traffic, a shortage of waggons, loading space in ships, berths, storage space on quays or in warehouses or other force majeure or events beyond the Forwarding Agent's control.

Nor shall he be responsible for damage to goods arising through no fault of his own from frost, heat, or other atmospheric influences, leakage, faulty gas, water or electric conduits, or caused by rats, mice, moths or the like.

Nor is the Forwarding Agent responsible for the natural deterioration of the goods.

Storage § 25

640   In addition to what is otherwise laid down in these General Rules, the following shall apply to the storage of goods:

1. When goods have been stored the Owner is to be notified thereof. The Forwarding Agent shall, at the request of the Client, issue either a Certificate of Receipt or a Warehouse Certificate.

The Certificate of Receipt is evidence of the quantity of goods received, but not of the amount of the goods remaining after receipt for the account of the party concerned.

The Forwarding Agent shall have a lien on the goods stored, in the manner laid down in § 16 above.

2. Objections to the choice of warehouse or to the storage of the goods shall be made immediately. If the Forwarding Agent has exercised due care in selecting the warehouse premises and in storing the goods, and the Owner of the goods does not avail himself of his right to inspect the premises and the storing, the Owner shall not be entitled to lodge a claim on account of deficiencies in these respects.

3. If goods are stored in the open air in accordance with customary practice or with the consent of the Owner, the Forwarding Agent shall not be liable for any damage to the goods due to this manner of storing.

4. Provided that he has exercised due care in selecting the warehouse premises, the Forwarding Agent shall not be responsible for goods stored in a Free-Port warehouse, Customs House or other public warehouse, or on private premises not belonging to him.

5. If samples are taken from goods stored, or if the Owner takes any other steps with regard to the goods, the Owner, together with the Forwarding Agent, shall again check the number, weight and condition of the goods. In the event of his omission to do this, the Forwarding Agent is relieved of responsibility for any damage or loss discovered subsequently, unless it is shown that such damage or loss was occasioned by the Forwarding Agent or by someone for whom he is answerable.

6. If it is found that by their nature the goods are likely to damage other goods on the premises, the Owner shall be liable to remove his goods. If damage has already occurred, the Owner of the goods shall be held responsible for this, provided that such damage has been occasioned by his error or negligence. Should the damage be caused by properties in the goods that could not reasonably have been foreseen by the Forwarding Agent, liability for compensation will lie with the Owner.

7. Should the Forwarding Agent have to evacuate the warehouse premises unexpectedly and through no fault of his own, the Client or the person for whose account the goods are received and stored shall at his own expense have the goods removed or if the goods are moved to other storage premises, pay the costs of removal and any increase of the rent due to the removal.

8. Warehouse rent is payable in advance, and is calculated for the current calendar month as from the day when the goods are placed in store and for every subsequent month or part thereof as for a whole month. The Owner or the person for whose account the goods are received and stored is responsible for all charges arising in connection with the storage.

9. In the absence of other arrangement, the Forwarding Agent may at any time terminate the storage agreement on fourteen days' notice.

10. When goods are stored, the Client shall immediately inform the Forwarding Agent of the address to which all communications relating to the goods are to be sent and from which instructions are to be obtained. The Forwarding Agent shall immediately be notified if this address is changed.

Claims   § 26
Any person who wishes to claim damages, or otherwise lodge complaints, shall give written notice thereof to the Forwarding Agent without undue delay.

Legal Proceedings   § 27
Any legal action against the Forwarding Agent shall be instituted in the Court of his own country, and shall be settled in accordance with the law of that country.

CONDITIONS GENERALES DE LA FEDERATION FRANCAISE DES COMMISSIONNAIRES ET AUXILIAIRES DE TRANSPORT, COMMISSIONNAIRES EN DOUANE, TRANSITAIRES, AGENTS MARITIMES ET AERIENS

Article 1

Tout engagement, expédition ou opération quelconque, sauf convention particulière entre les parties, vaut acceptation pour la clientèle des conditions ci-après.

Les membres affiliés à la Fédération, quelle que soit la qualité juridique ou la fonction au titre de laquelle ils interviennent, sont désignés dans les Conditions Générales ci-après par le terme: " Transitaire."

Article 2

641 COTATIONS.—Les cotations étant basées sur les tarifs, règlements et conventions en vigueur dans les Administrations et/ou les Services et Entreprises de transport et de manutention utilisés, peuvent être changées et même suspendues, sans préavis, notamment en cas de:

Modification de ces règlements et conventions.

Modification du cours des devises étrangères.

Interruption du trafic sur les parcours prévus.

Force majeure ou toutes circonstances imprévues.

Les prix cotés ne sont valables que si l'expédition a lieu selon les instructions d'acheminement qui devront être demandées au préalable.

Sauf stipulations contraires, les cotations ne comprennent ni les droits, redevances et impôts perçus par les Administrations fiscales ou douanières (tels que droits d'entrée, timbres, taxes, etc.), ni le bâchage, ni les frais de stationnement et de réparations ou tous autres frais accessoires, à moins que ces frais ne soient expressément spécifiés dans l'offre.

Les cotations sauf précisions contraires, ne s'appliquent qu'à des colis de nature, de poids et dimensions considérés comme normaux par les transporteurs.

Article 3

INSTRUCTIONS.—Les instructions complètes doivent être remises pour chaque envoi; les instructions d'ordre général et permanent ne sont pas admises.

La vérification des déclarations et renseignements fournis par les clients n'est pas obligatoire.

Les marchandises inflammables, dangereuses, infectes ou toxiques doivent faire l'objet d'une déclaration expresse. La non observation de cette prescription par l'expéditeur engagerait son entière responsabilité.

Il appartient à l'expéditeur d'une marchandise contre remboursement de préciser si l'encaissement auprés du destinataire doit être exigé en espèces (dans la limite légale) ou en chèque certifié. A défaut de cette précision, la responsabilité du destinataire seule peut être recherchée pour remise d'un chèque bancaire ou postal non provisionné.

Le montant des remboursements n'est payable qu'après encaissement auprès des destinataires.

Les clients conservent seuls la responsabilité de toutes les conséquences provenant de déclarations ou documents erronés, incomplets ou fournis tardivement.

[345]

Article 4

Ne peut, en aucun cas, être considéré comme laissé à l'initiative du " Transitaire," le soin d'effectuer des formalités ou opérations particulières, hors le transport proprement dit.

Notamment pour les expéditions à l'étranger, toutes formalités consulaires ou autres, ne sont remplies que sur la demande expresse du client et sans responsabilité au cas où ne seraient pas remis les éléments pour les établir, comme au cas où ceux-ci seraient erronés.

Article 5

ASSURANCE.—Aucune assurance n'est contractée sans ordre écrit et répété pour chaque expédition. La couverture en est faite soit par police spéciale, soit par la police flottante du " Transitaire" et sous exclusion de toute responsabilité personnelle, la police étant souscrite auprès de Compagnies notoirement solvables au moment de la couverture. Les conditions de la police sont réputées connues et agréés par les expéditeurs et destinataires.

Les clients désireux d'assurer des risques spéciaux sont tenus d'indiquer, selon la nature de marchandises, les risques à couvrir (tels que casse, coulage, déformation, rouille, oxydation, ainsi que vol et disparition, séjour, etc.). A défaut de cette précision l'assurance sera seulement couverte contre les risques ordinaires de transport.

N'agissant en l'espèce que comme mandataire, le " Transitaire" n'accepte aucune solidarité avec les Assureurs.

Aucune réclamation ne sera admise sans la production d'un certificat régulier de constat d'avarie ou de perte délivré par l'Agent des Assureurs indiqué (à son défaut, par les Autorités compétentes) et sans la justification des actes nécessaires à la conservation des recours. L'indemnité d'assurance ne sera payée qu'autant que celle-ci aura été encaissée des Compagnies d'assurances par le " Transitaire."

Le client qui couvre lui-même les risques du transport doit préciser à ses assureurs qu'ils ne pourront prétendre exercer leurs recours contre le " Transitaire" que dans les limites précisées à l'article 8.

Article 6

En l'absence d'instructions spéciales du donneur d'ordre, le " Transitaire" emploie toutes voies et moyens à sa convenance pour l'acheminement des marchandises qui lui sont confiées, ainsi que tous intermédiaires, commissionnaires et/ou transporteurs divers, qui sont par avance réputés agréés par le client.

Les dates de départ ou d'arrivée sont données aux clients à titre indicatif.

Article 7

642 Les marchandises en cours de transit, soit à l'exportation, soit à l'importation, celles en prolongation de séjour à destination ou celles en retour ne sont ni garanties, ni couvertes contre les risques de mouille, de vol, d'incendie, d'avaries ou autres, sauf en cas d'assurance spécialement prescrite à cet effet et dans la limite des stipulations des polices d'assurances.

Les opérations de bâchage et de gardiennage n'entraînent aucune responsabilité du " Transitaire " et notamment en cas de mouille, vol et incendie.

En cas de refus des marchandises par le destinataire comme en cas de défaillance du destinataire pour quelque cause que ce soit, les obligations à l'égard du " Transitaire " resteront à la charge du donneur d'ordre.

En cas de retards, pertes, avaries ou autres dommages, subis par la marchandise, aucun recours ne pourra être exercé contre le " Transitaire," si les constatations régulières, les réserves légales au transporteur et en général tous les actes nécessaires à la conservation des recours n'ont pas été faits par le destinataire ou le réceptionnaire dans les formes et délais légaux.

Article 8

La responsabilité du " Transitaire " est pour toutes opérations de transports, strictement limitée à celle encourue par les transporteurs utilisés et mandataires et/ou organismes et enterprises substitués pour l'execution de l'opération confiée.

La responsabilité du Transitaire ne pourra davantage être retenue, lorsque le transporteur pourra dégager la sienne propre dans le cas où des manquants ou des avaries seraient constatés à la suite de transbordement de marchandises direct ou non d'un moyen de transport sur tout autre moyen qu'il soit terrestre, maritime, fluvial ou aérien.

La responsabilité propre du " Transitaire " lorsqu'elle est pour une cause quelconque, engagée dans l'exécution des opérations qui lui sont confiées est limitée à 50 F par kg avec maximum de 1000 F par colis, quels qu'en soient le poids, le volume ou la dimension et à 0,10 F par kg pour les marchandises expediées en vrac.

Les cotations sont établies compte tenu de ces limitations de responsabilité.

Lorsque l'expéditeur confie des marchandises dont la valeur dépasse les limites indiquées ci-dessus, il lui appartient de donner des ordres pour leur assurance ou d'assumer les risques du transport pour cette valeur excédentaire.

En aucun cas, d'ailleurs, l'indemnité à allouer ne peut excéder, dans les limites ci-dessus, la valeur réelle justifiée de la marchandise.

Article 9

MODALITÉS DE PAIEMENT.—Les factures sont en totalité payables au comptant.

Les frais de transport exposés, ainsi que ceux engagés pour la conservation et la protection de la marchandise, sont dus dans tous les cas.

Lorsque exceptionnellement des délais de paiement auront été consentis par l'émission de traite ou autre moyen, tout paiement partiel sera imputé en premier lieu sur la partie non privilégiée des créances. Le non paiement à une seule échéance emportera sans aucune formalité déchéance du terme, le solde devenant immédiatement exigible.

L'acceptation dans des conditions dérogatoires au principe du paiement comptant n'emporte aucune novation, le " Transitaire " conservant la totalité de ses droits et prérogatives.

Article 10

SURETES.—Le " Transitaire " a sur toutes les marchandises et valeurs qui lui sont confiées droit de rétention et de préférence en garantie de toutes ses créances même nées à propos d'opérations antérieures ou étrangères aux marchandises et valeurs retenues.

Conformément à l'article 381 du Code des Douanes, le " Transitaire " agissant en tant que Commissionnaire en Douane est subrogé dans le privilège de l'Administration des Douanes.

Quelles que soient les modalités de facturation ou de paiement (incorporation dans un forfait, inscription en compte, tirage d'effets de commerce, etc.) les droits et privilèges du Transitaire Commissionnaire de Transport et/ou Commissionnaire en Douane conservent leur plein et entier effet, aucune fusion ni novation ne pouvant êntre opposées.

Article 11

Les conditions générales, ci-dessus, peuvent être complétées par des Conditions particulières et clauses attributives de juridiction.

CONDITIONS GENERALES
DES EXPEDITEURS DE BELGIQUE
1969

CONDITIONS GENERALES

I. GENERALITES

A. *Champ d'application*

643 Art. 1. Les présentes Conditions Générales annulent et remplacent toutes les précédentes. Elles ont été dûment approuvées par les Unions Professionnelles d'Expéditeurs affiliées à la Fédération des Expéditeurs de Belgique et elles régissent toutes les affaires traitées par les membres de celles-ci.

Sauf dérogation conventionnelle expresse, elles sont d'application nonobstant tous usages ou dispositions légales de droit supplétif, qui y seraient contraires.

Art. 2. Vu la publicité qui leur a été donnée et leur notoriété, les présentes conditions générales, qui sont conformes aux usages du commerce belge d'expédition seront tenues pour acceptées par les parties. Elles seront considérées comme us et coutumes établis et d'application même sans qu'il y soit référé explicitement dans une convention.

En cas de doute, une seule référence à ces conditions ou la communication de celles-ci suffit pour les rendre applicables à tous les ordres subséquents donnés par un commettant à un expéditeur.

Art. 3. Ces conditions régissent tous les ordres, cotations et offres, les missions et les conventions tacites ou explicites, en un mot toutes les relations professionnelles des expéditeurs avec leurs clients, tant commerçants et industriels que particuliers.

Elles sont applicables à toutes les opérations, sans exception, qui ont trait à l'expédition de marchandises, et qui sont confiées aux firmes d'expédition visées à l'art. 4, quelle que soit la qualité juridique en laquelle elles exécutent ces opérations. Les rémunérations, tarifs, offres et cotations sont basées sur leur application.

B. *Définition de l'expéditeur*

Art. 4. Par expéditeur ou commissionnaire-expéditeur on entend, dans les présentes conditions, le commerçant qui fait sa profession d'organiser et de faire exécuter ou d'exécuter partiellement par ses propres moyens l'expédition de marchandises et les diverses opérations y relatives, pour compte de tiers mais en nom propre.

Seront considérés comme expéditeurs et/ou firmes d'expédition, pour l'application des présentes conditions générales, les personnes physiques et/ou morales membres d'une des unions professionnelles affiliées à la Fédération des Expéditeurs de Belgique. Tous les membres veilleront à ce que leur affiliation soit mentionnée sur leur papier à firme.

Art. 5. Comme opérations se rattachant à la mission de l'expéditeur sont considérés e.a.:

la réception et la délivrance de marchandises;
les livraisons C.I.F., F.O.B., F.A.S. et F.O.R.;
le pesage, le jaugeage, l'échantillonnage et le contrôle;
l'entreposage et le magasinage;
l'agréation de marchandises;

l'assurance;

la procuration du transport de marchandises par tous les moyens, tant sur le plan international qu'intercommunal et local;

l'accomplissement des formalités économiques et douanières;

l'emballage et la manipulation des marchandises;

le groupage de plusieurs envois;

l'affrètement d'allèges ou de navires de mer;

l'engagement et le paiement de fret;

l'encaissement de remboursements;

les démarches et l'accomplissement des différentes formalités relatives à l'expédition de marchandises;

la rédaction et la signature de tous documents relatifs à l'expédition;

l'entreprise à forfait d'expéditions de marchandises d'un point à un autre du globe.

La mission de l'expéditeur comprend généralement plusieurs de ces opérations, groupées dans un contrat global.

Pour un contrat déterminé, elle peut ne comprendre que deux ou même une seule de ces opérations sans que, pour autant, le commissionnaire perde son caractère d'expéditeur au sens des présentes conditions générales.

C. *Droits et devoirs*

Art. 6. La cession des droits du commettant à un tiers ainsi que les recours contre l'expédituer au nom et pour compte d'un tiers, ne peuvent se faire que pour autant que sur base des présentes conditions générales il y ait des droits contre l'expéditeur et que celui-ci soit personnellement obligé.

Art. 7. Les opérations relatives aux expéditions se font pour compte et aux risques des commettants. L'expéditeur accordera à l'exécution des missions qui lui sont confiées, les soins appropriés dans la mesure de ses moyens au mieux des intérêts de son commettant.

Toutefois, ce dernier ne pourra exiger de l'expéditeur que l'accomplissement des opérations dont il l'a chargé explicitement d'une manière non équivoque et à titre onéreux.

Art. 8. A moins que l'expéditeur n'en ait été préalablement avisé par écrit, les envois ne peuvent contenir des marchandises dangereuses, périssables, inflammables, explosives ou pouvant occasionner des dommages à des personnes, des animaux et des biens. Si telles marchandises sont remises à l'expéditeur sans mention spéciale préalable quant à leur nature, le commettant, même si aucune faute ne lui est imputable, répond de tous les dommages qui peuvent en résulter.

L'expéditeur peut, pour autant que les circonstances le justifient, de sa seule autorité, faire vendre, éloigner ou détruire de telles marchandises.

Dans cette éventualité, il doit cependant en aviser son commettant au plus tôt.

Art. 9. Toute cotation ou prix forfaitaire se fait, et tout contrat d'expédition est conclu et exécuté sur base des conditions et des règlements, lettres de voiture, connaissements, polices d'assurance, certificats et d'autres documents émanant des administrations publiques, des chemins de fer, directions de ports et de bassins, armements, compagnies maritimes et aériennes, entrepreneurs de transports, nations, banques, sous-traitants et assureurs, intervenant dans l'exécution du transport.

Lorsque ces stipulations ou règlements sont invoqués contre l'expéditeur, ils vaudront également à l'égard de son commettant et des tiers ayants-droit éventuels.

II. OFFRES ET COTATIONS

A. *Delai de validité*

644   Art. 10. Sauf stipulation contraire prévue explicitement, une offre ou cotation n'est valable que durant un délai de 8 jours. Elle n'engagera l'expéditeur que lorsque celui-ci sera en possession de l'acceptation du commettant endéans ce délai.

B. *Modifications de prix*

Art. 11. Toutes offres et conventions de prix, même forfaitaires, ne valent, sauf stipulation contraire, que pour expédition ou acheminement immédiat, et sont basées sur les tarifs, salaires, cours et frets en vigueur.

Si entretemps un ou plusieurs de ces facteurs ont subi des modifications, les offres ou conventions de prix y seront adaptées de plein droit et ce avec effet rétroactif, le cas échéant.

C. *Suspensions et annulations*

Art. 12. En cas de force majeure ou d'autres événements prévus à l'art. 35, toutes les conventions, cotations, tarifs, prix forfaitaires et de transport, même s'ils ont déjà été acceptés, seront suspendus pour la durée de ces événements, sans avis préalable et sans qu'une indemnité quelconque puisse être réclamée à l'expéditeur pour la non-exécution de son offre ou convention.

Tant l'expéditeur que le commettant seront autorisés dans ce cas à annuler leur offre ou convention.

D. *Frais speciaux*

Art. 13. En cas de force majeure ou d'autres événements cités à l'art. 35, et les difficultés qui en résultent, les frais spéciaux exposés par l'expéditeur pour l'exécution de sa mission et/ou pour la conservation des marchandises, sont à charge du commettant aussi bien dans le cas de suspension que dans celui d'annulation.

Art. 14. Sauf stipulation contraire, les cotations ou prix forfaitaires ne comprennent que le port, le fret, l'accomplissement des formalités douanières. les frais de réception ou d'embarquement.

Seront portés en compte séparément: la commission sur débours, le port de lettres, les frais de télégrammes, de télex et de téléphone, les droits fiscaux, les redevances douanières, les frais consulaires et de légalisation, de pesage, d'échantillonnage, de comptage, de réparation, de grue, les frais spéciaux pour manipulation de colis lourds et ceux résultant de surestaries ou de travail de nuit, du dimanche ou de jours fériés légaux, les primes d'assurance, les frais d'emmagasinage de marchandises qui ont manqué une correspondance, les frais de veille, de bâchage, de stationnement et tous autres frais accessoires.

Opérations F.O.B.

Art. 15. Les opérations F.O.B. se font suivant les règlements et usages locaux des ports. Pour les marchandises arrivant par navire ou allège le commettant est tenu d'accorder à l'expéditeur un délai de starie suffisant pour assurer les opérations de transbordement ou de réception. Si ce délai est insuffisant, les frais qui en résulteront (surestaries, etc.) seront à charge du commettant.

Sauf stipulation contraire, les prix convenus ne comprennent pas les

frais supplémentaires résultant d'un chargement, transbordement ou déchargement des marchandises pendant la nuit, dimanche ou jour férié légal en vertu
de clauses figurant aux connaissements ou chartes-parties.

Les dits frais spéciaux sont à charge du commettant.

III. MISSIONS ET INSTRUCTIONS

A. *Ordres écrits en temps utile*

645   Art. 16. Les ordres accompagnés des documents nécessaires et mention-
nant toutes les données requises, doivent être en possession de l'expéditeur en
temps utile, par écrit, signés et répétés pour chaque envoi. S'il sont donnés
verbalement, ou par téléphone, ils ne feront foi que s'ils ont été confirmés,
au moment même où ils ont été donnés, par écrit et sans modification, par
les personnes habilitées à cette fin.

B. *Données requises*

Art. 17. Les instructions transmises à l'expéditeur comprendront les
marques, numéros, nombre, espèce, contenu des colis, poids, dimensions,
valeur, numéro de la rubrique du tarif des douanes ainsi que tous renseignements indispensables pour le paiement des droits et taxes.

Les licenses nécessaires, factures, listes de colisage et, le cas échéant, les
certificats d'origine et sanitaires, les déclarations consulaires rédigées éventuellement en la langue du pays de destination et tous autres documents seront
remis en temps voulu à l'expéditeur.

Les colis dont le poids dépasse 500 kg. doivent être signalés séparément
et porter l'indication de leur poids.

En outre, les adresses de l'envoyeur et du destinataire, le lieu de livraison
des marchandises, le mode de paiement des frais de transport et toutes autres
instructions d'expédition doivent être fournis avec précision et exactitude.

Des modifications éventuelles aux instructions ne pourront être invoquées
à l'égard de l'expéditeur que pour autant qu'elles aient été données par écrit
et qu'elles soient arrivées chez l'expéditeur en temps utile.

C. *Instructions spéciales*

Art. 18. Si une déclaration d'intérêt à la livraison doit être faite, le commettant doit le signaler explicitement dans ses instructions. Si la destination
réelle de la marchandise ne doit pas être connue de l'envoyeur, si l'origine
réelle ne doit pas être connue du destinataire, celui qui dispose de la marchandise doit donner des instructions en conséquence. Les frais supplémentaires en
résultant sont à sa charge.

D. *Responsabilité en matière d'instructions*

Art. 19. Celui qui donne les ordres répond vis-à-vis de l'expéditeur de
toutes suites, amendes, dommages, retard, rappel de droits etc. pouvant
résulter d'une omission, inexactitude, imprécision, traduction fautive, interprétation différente dans l'énoncé des données nécessaires, de l'absence ou de
la remise tardive des instructions, des connaissements, papiers de douane,
autorisations, licences etc.

Art. 20. L'expéditeur n'est pas tenu de vérifier l'exactitude des instructions
et des indications y contenues, notamment celles concernant le poids et le
contenu.

Ces indications sont acceptées comme telles de bonne foi, pour servir
uniquement à établir les documents nécessaires et le coût de la prestation,
Elles ne peuvent en aucun cas être invoquées contre l'expéditeur comme
preuve d'un manquant ou d'une avarie, puisque l'expéditeur ne doit pas

procéder lui-même au pesage, à l'inventaire ou au contrôle des marchandises sans instructions explicites à cet effet. Un reçu délivré par l'expéditeur n'étant basé que sur les données fournies par les documents qui lui ont été remis, ne garantit pas l'espèce, le contenu, la valeur, le poids ou l'emballage des marchandises.

E. *Vérification des documents*

Art. 21. A la réception de documents (tels que lettres de voiture, connaissements, factures consulaires, licences, certificats d'origine, polices d'assurance) lui envoyés par l'expéditeur, le commettant s'engage à les examiner attentivement et à lui signaler immédiatement les discordances ou erreurs éventuelles, afin que l'expéditeur puisse faire établir les rectifications nécessaires.

L'omission de ce faire par le commettant, dégagera l'expéditeur de toute responsabilité.

IV. EXECUTION DE LA MISSION

A. *Choix des moyens et des itinéraires*

646   Art. 22. A défaut d'instructions précises, suffisantes et exécutables, ou de conventions spéciales, l'expéditeur aura le libre choix de l'itinéraire, du mode d'acheminement, du moyen de transport et des tarifs à appliquer.

B. *Opérations sans instructions*

Art. 23. Si dans des circonstances données, l'expéditeur juge de l'intérêt de son commettant, d'agir sans attendre des instructions, il y est autorisé aux risques et pour compte de son commettant.

Lorsqu'au lieu de transbordement ou à destination, l'expéditeur représente simultanément l'envoyeur et le destinataire, il défendra de son mieux les intérêts des deux parties à leurs risques et pour leur compte. Il leur en fera rapport dans le plus bref délai.

C. *Lettre de garantie*

Art. 24. L'expéditeur n'est pas obligé de réceptionner contre garantie faute de documents ou de fournir une garantie pour éviter des clauses restrictives dans les connaissements.

Lorsqu'il le fait, il est en droit d'exiger, à son tour, une garantie suffisante et dans l'attente de celle-ci de retenir les marchandises ou les documents, tandis qu'il devra être dédommagé de tous les frais spéciaux qui pourraient en résulter.

D. *Avarie grosse*

Art. 25. En cas d'avarie grosse l'expéditeur est en droit de réclamer immédiatement à son commettant ou au propriétaire de la marchandise, la somme qui pourrait être exigée par le capitaine, à titre de garantie et comme contribution provisoire dans le règlement de l'avarie grosse.

Il peut exiger que son commettant ou le propriétaire de la marchandise signe le compromis d'avarie grosse ou il peut le signer lui-même en leur nom, avec les réserves d'usage. Dans ce dernier cas, l'expéditeur peut réclamer des espèces ou une garantie de banque à fournir par le commettant ou le propriétaire de la marchandise, pour la contribution définitive qui sera due après rédaction de la dispache.

E. *Avarie particulière*

Art. 26. En cas d'avaries et/ou manquants apparents l'expéditeur procèdera à leur constatation pour compte de qui il appartiendra.

Il est autorisé également à procéder en lieu et place de son commettant, mais aux frais de ce dernier, à l'accomplissement des formalités et démarches que la situation exige.

F. *Groupage*

Art. 27. Sauf stipulation contraire, l'expéditeur peut toujours expédier en groupage, les marchandises qui lui seront confiées. Il n'y est cependant pas obligé. Des délais de livraison ne seront jamais garantis.

G. *Formalités douanières et économiques*

Art. 28. Lorsque l'expéditeur devra remplir des formalités douanières, il le fera sur base des données qui lui auront été fournies par son commettant. Il n'est pas obligé de procéder à un inventaire préalable.

Les concessions éventuelles à des exigences formulées par la douane ne pourront lui être reprochées. Pour toutes les amendes, demandes supplémentaires, suppléments et cautionnements basés sur les règlements douaniers et économiques, le commettant ou le propriétaire des marchandises devra toujours garantir immédiatement l'expéditeur et lui fournir les sommes nécessaires en espèces.

La vérification des marchandises ne se fait que pour les besoins de la douane et n'est pas faite plus en détail que celle-ci ne l'exige. Elle n'entraîne pour l'expéditeur aucune reconnaissance préjudiciable ou responsabilité, quant au poids, valeur, espèce ou conditionnement des marchandises, emballages ou contenu des colis. Si l'expéditeur s'est porté caution pour l'apurement d'un document, il est en droit de porter en compte une rémunération appropriée jusqu'au moment où sa caution sera automatiquement dégagée par la douane.

H. *Envois refusés ou qui ne peuvent être remis*

Art. 29. Sauf instructions contraires, l'expéditeur pourra faire revenir toutes marchandises refusées par le destinataire ou qui, pour une raison quelconque, ne peuvent être délivrées.

Il emmagasinera ces marchandises à leur retour aux risques et pour compte de son commettant.

I. *Missions purement administratives*

Art. 30. Chaque fois que l'intervention de l'expéditeur se limitera à la partie administrative de l'opération, telle que: appel des marchandises, remise de reçu, rédaction éventuelle de connaissements, accomplissement de formalités consulaires ou douanières et économiques, les marchandises voyageront, séjourneront sur quai, seront livrées ou réceptionnées aux seuls risques et périls des différents commettants et/ou ayants-droit.

L'expéditeur ne se chargera de la vérification, de la garde et des soins aux marchandises que lorsque des instructions lui auront été données à cet effet et qu'une rémunération adéquate lui sera octroyée.

Pour les marchandises réexpédiées sans rompre charge ou transbordement, c.à.d. poursuivant leur route par les wagons ou autres véhicules par lesquels elles sont arrivées, et pour lesquelles l'expéditeur à dû donner réglementairement décharge au transporteur précédent, il n'assume aucune responsabilité pour manquant, perte ou avarie et son intervention n'implique aucune vérification interne ou externe du chargement, même si des formalités ou vérifications douanières ont été accomplies avec son concours.

J. *Emmagasinage*

Art. 31. L'emmagasinage des marchandises peut avoir lieu soit en vertu d'instructions formelles du commettant, soit dans l'attente d'instructions, soit à la suite d'une interruption du transport, sans toutefois que, dans ces deux derniers cas, l'expéditeur soit tenu de prendre des mesures d'emmagasinage ou de garde des marchandises.

Il se fait au choix de l'expéditeur dans ses propres magasins ou dans ceux de tiers (publics ou privés).

Sauf stipulations contraires convenues et répétées expressément pour chaque envoi, l'emmagasinage de marchandises est régi par les présentes conditions générales.

Les limitations de responsabilité prévues dans les différents articles des présentes conditions générales seront également applicables au cas d'emmagasinage dans les propres magasins de l'expéditeur.

Celui-ci peut se prévaloir des privilèges et des dispositions protectrices accordés par la loi aux dépositaires sans que la limitation de sa responsabilité s'en trouve affectée.

L'expéditeur qui aura déposé les marchandises dans les magasins appropriés d'un tiers dépositaire aura pour seule obligation de réserver les recours éventuels de son commettant contre ce tiers.

Il est renvoyé en outre aux dispositions de l'art. 32. Sauf stipulation contraire, écrite et répétée pour chaque envoi, l'expéditeur n'est pas tenu de faire veiller les marchandises où qu'elles se trouvent, même en plein air, ni de les assurer.

Néanmoins s'il a pris de telles mesures, il sera autorisé à en porter les frais en compte à charge de son commettant.

Pour un entreposage autre que celui qui est accessoire au transport ou qui s'effectue à l'étranger, l'expéditeur sera tenu d'indiquer à son commettant le magasin dans lequel il aura entreposé les marchandises. Celui-ci ayant toute liberté d'inspecter la marchandise et le magasin, formulera sans tarder ses observations éventuelles.

S'il n'use pas de son droit d'inspection, le commettant ne pourra introduire des réclamations contre lui pour faute ou négligence relative à l'emmagasinage ou au local.

Si, au moment de la réception de la marchandise ou pendent l'emmagasinage, il est constaté que l'emballarge est endommagé, l'expéditeur peut immédiatement procéder aux réparations nécessaires aux frais du commettant.

Le propriétaire de la marchandise répond des dégâts occasionnés éventuellement par celle-ci à d'autres marchandises entreposées dans le même local. Si l'expéditeur est forcé, pour des raisons imprévisibles au moment de l'emmagasinage, d'evacuer son magasin, les propriétaires des marchandises pourront en assurer le transfert eux-mêmes. Ils supporteront en tout cas les frais occasionés par le transfert et le magasinage supplémentaire éventuel dans le nouveau local:

Les taux de magasinage se calculent par mois de calendrier et tout mois commencé est dû en entier.

La cession par le commettant à des tiers de marchandises entreposées n'aura d'effet vis-à-vis de l'expéditeur que lorsque celui-ci aura marqué son accord et pour autant que cette cession ne compromette pas le recouvrement de la créance de l'expéditeur vis-à-vis de son commettant.

Le dépositaire pourra à tout moment mettre fin au contrat d'emmagasinage en donnant un dédit de quinze jours.

Lorsqu'après sommation de l'expéditeur le commettant n'enlève pas ses marchandises ou lorsque le montant de la créance de l'expéditeur risque de n'être plus couvert par la valeur de la marchandise, il a le droit de la faire vendre et de retenir le montant de sa créance du produit de la vente, conformément à l'art. 56.

K. *Fin du contrat d'expédition*

Art. 32. Le contrat d'expédition prend fin par l'obtention de la décharge.

L'expéditeur obtient décharge par la remise des marchandises à l'ayantdroit dans le conditionnement apparent où il les a réceptionnées ou à la personne désignée par celui-ci, au chemin de fer ou à la compagnie d'aviation, au transporteur maritime ou routier.

Pour les marchandises à remettre à domicile par l'expéditeur, la mission de même que la responsabilité de celui-ci prennent fin par la présentation des marchandises sur le véhicule devant le domicile du destinataire ou devant un lieu de déchargement normal que celui-ci aura indiqué préalablement.

Le destinataire devra s'occuper sans retard du déchargement à ses frais, risques et périls.

Le fait qu'occasionnellement l'expéditeur décharge la marchandise chez le commettant ne peut en aucun cas être considéré comme un précédent.

Les colis d'un poids supérieur à 100 kg. ne seront déchargés par l'expéditeur que moyennant rémunération spéciale.

Il est entendu qu'une intervention quelconque du personnel, au service de l'expéditeur dans ces opérations, même régulièrement rétribuée, n'entraîne aucune responsabilité ni de la part de ce personnel, ni de celle de l'expéditeur.

La mise en cave, le port aux étages ou arrière-bâtiments ne sont effectués que moyennant convention avec l'expéditeur et rétribution spéciale.

V.   RESPONSABILITÉ DE L'EXPÉDITEUR

A. *Généralités*

647   Art. 33. Dans le trafic international des marchandises il y a lieu de distinguer:

1. les opérations d'expédition spécifiques et les opérations accessoires y relatives telles que pesage, comptage, contrôle, camionnage local, transbordement, marquage, emballage, etc., opérations que l'expéditeur accomplit luimême, ou à l'intervention de sous-traitants, auxiliaires ou intermédiaires, et

2. le transport par mer, air, route et fer, l'assurance, les opérations de financement et de paiement, etc. Pour les opérations reprises au 2, l'expéditeur agit uniquement pour compte de son commettant. Il contracte avec des tiers qui ne sont pas ses auxiliaires pour l'exécution d'un contrat de transport. Même si l'expéditeur a fixé un prix forfaitaire, il ne sera jamais responsable comme transporteur, assureur ou banquier, sa mission sera toujours celle d'un expéditeur.

L'expéditeur contracte une obligation de moyen et non pas une obligation de résultat.

Il ne répond que des erreurs ou omissions commises par lui-même ou par ses préposés dans les limites, strictement entendues, de la mission définie à l'alinéa précédent.

Cette responsabilité est cependant limitée à 20 Frs. par kg. pour les produits manufacturés emballés avec un maximum de 2.000 Frs. par colis et à 3

Frs. par kg. pour les marchandises expédiées en vrac avec un maximum de 30.000 Frs. par envoi, sans que l'indemnité à allouer puisse excéder la valeur réelle justifiée de la marchandise. Indépendamment des stipulations en matière de responsabilité de l'expéditeur prévues en d'autres articles des présentes conditions générales, celle-ci est encore limitée ou exclue en vertu des stipulations suivantes.

Même si l'expéditeur, ainsi qu'il est prévu à l'art. 5, n'a qu'une mission restreinte à exécuter ou s'il agit en une autre qualité juridique p.ex. comme transporteur ou commissionnaire de transport, sa responsabilité personnelle ne pourra jamais excéder les limites posées dans le présent article. Le commettant peut cependant, en dehors des possibilités d'assurance offertes à l'art. 42, convenir expressément avec l'expéditeur d'une responsabilité spéciale, moyennant une commission adéquate.

B. *Sous-entrepreneurs et tiers participant ou intéressés aux opérations d'expédition*

Art. 34. Lorsque pour l'exécution de sa mission un expéditeur fait appel à des entrepreneurs de transports de toutes espèces, à des compagnies d'assurances, à des sous-expéditeurs, dépositaires, banques ou à d'autres entreprises intervenant dans l'expédition de marchandises, il ne répond que du soin apporté à son choix et de la remise des instructions nécessaires et exactes. Si au cours de l'expédition un sinistre se produit, auquel l'expéditeur est étranger, il est simplement tenu de céder à son commettant ses droits contre les tiers en cause.

Il pourra également, à la demande mais pour compte et aux risques de son commettant, faire valoir lui même ses droits à l'égard des dits tiers.

Lorsque l'expéditeur confie tout ou partie des opérations dont il s'est chargé, à un ou à plusieurs intermédiaires et/ou sous-traitants, sa responsabilité personnelle n'excèdera jamais celle des intermédiaires et/ou sous-traitants intervenant dans l'exécution et sera, en tout cas, limitée aux sommes qu'il pourra lui-même récupérer chez ces intermédiaires et/ou sous-traitants.

En dehors de cas limitativement prévus par les alinéas précédents, l'expéditeur ne répond d'aucune perte ni d'aucune avarie, quelle qu'en soit la cause et à quelque moment qu'elle se soit produite au cours des opérations généralement quelconques dont il s'est chargé pour compte de son commettant.

C. *Force majeure et événements assimilés*

Art. 35. L'expéditeur ne supporte aucune responsabilité pour toutes les conséquences tant directes qu'indirectes de cas fortuits, de force majeure, ou faits du prince, qui empêchent ou entravent l'exécution de sa mission.

Sont notamment considérés comme tels: guerre, émeute, révolution, grève, lock-out, interruption des trafics pour quelque cause que ce soit, manque de wagons, de place dans les navires, sur les quais, hangars ou entrepôts, pannes de moyens de transport, entraves au trafic par suite de verglas, neige, inondation, ou en raison de phénomènes imprévisibles de la nature. Est expressément assimilé au cas de force majeure tout vol commis par des tiers au cours du transport ainsi que le vol qualifié, lorsque les marchandises se trouvaient sous la garde personnelle de l'expéditeur.

Lorsque les susdits événements se sont produits, il y a présomption que les sinistres éventuels doivent y être attribués.

D. *Vice propre et emballage défectueux*

Art. 36. De plein droit l'expéditeur est exonéré de toute responsabilité quant aux pertes, manquants, avaries et détériorations causés aux colis insuffisamment emballés ou emballés dans des emballages de réemploi, ou dans des emballages s'altérant par le temps, par les manipulations ou par les produits y emballés.

Sauf convention spéciale à ce sujet avec son commettant, l'expéditeur est autorisé dans ces cas à permettre aux entreprises de transports de formuler, dans les documents de transport, des réserves quant au conditionnement ou à l'emballage des marchandises.

Tout emballage renfermant des marchandises périssables, dangereuses, fragiles ou craignant l'humidité, le gel ou la chaleur, doit porter en vue sur chacune de ses faces une mention indiquant les dangers aux-quels sont exposées ces marchandises. Cette mention figurera dans la langue du pays de provenance et dans celle du pays de destination.

E. *Délais de livraison*

Art. 37. Les délais de livraison ne sont garantis que s'il y a eu convention spéciale écrite à ce sujet. Dans ce cas, la responsabilité éventuelle de l'expéditeur ne peut dépasser celle des entreprises de transport utilisées, dont il a exigé les mêmes délais. En aucun cas l'expéditeur ne peut être rendu responsable des conséquences de renseignements erronés fournis par des entreprises de transport ou leurs agents concernant les dates ou délais de chargement, de déchargement ou de livraison.

F. *Ordres d'encaissement*

Art. 38. L'expéditeur n'est pas responsable de la bonne fin des ordres d'encaissement qui lui sont confiés, à moins qu'il ne soit prouvé que l'inexécution de sa mission est due à négligence. Le décompte des remboursements ne se fera qu'après leur encaissement total et définitif, sous déduction d'une rémunération appropriée.

Si le destinataire refuse de payer les frais éventuels d'encaissement, ceux-ci seront à charge du commettant.

G. *Renseignements—conseils—paiements*

Art. 39. L'expéditeur qui procure des renseignements au sujet des réglementations d'expédition, d'importation, d'exportation, de transit etc., les donne à simple titre indicatif, sans aucun engagement, ni responsabilité. Pour des erreurs dans les informations au sujet des taux de fret, droits, taxes, frais et tarifs fournis par des tiers à l'expèditeur, celui-ci n'assume aucune responsabilité. Il en est de même pour le cas où des frets, droits ou frais inexacts auraient été perçus. De tels recours ainsi que ceux relatifs à des suppléments de fret, droits ou frais calculés sur une base erronée, sont à la charge du commettant, qui devra dédommager l'expéditeur à sa première demande.

H. *Marchandises dangereuses, périssables et pondereuses*

Art. 40. De plein droit l'expéditeur est exonéré de toute responsabilité et de tous risques de manipulation ou de transport pour les marchandises dangereuses, périssables ou fragiles ainsi que pour les marchandises de dimensions et/ou poids anormaux et pour celles exigeant l'emploi d'engins de levage, d'outillage ou d'emplacements spéciaux.

Il est de plein droit autorisé à donner aux transporteurs ou manutentionnaires intermédiaires les exonérations ou garanties correspondant aux risques précités, sans pour cela devoir faire des réserves au moment de l'acceptation de sa mission.

I. *Dépôt en magasin—sur quai ou en plein air*

Art. 41. Sauf instruction spéciale et explicite de la part du commettant de faire veiller les marchandises, l'expéditeur n'est pas responsable des avaries ou pertes survenues durant leur séjour en des lieux de déchargement, de chargement ou de dépôt, ni pendant le transport, le chargement ou le déchargement, à la suite d'incendie, d'effraction, de vol, de coulage, de sudation, de perte de poids, de grandes eaux et inondations, de vermine, de rongeurs, d'actions de tiers ou pour quelque cause que ce soit. L'expéditeur n'assume aucune responsabilité pour les marchandises qui séjournent à quai ou en plein air.

J. *Assurance—risques d'expédition* (*Police AREX*)

Art. 42. L'expéditeur met à la disposition de son commettant la police AREX, lui permettant de couvrir chaque envoi dépendant d'un transport international, contre les risques afférents à sa mission. Il est expressément recommandé à la clientèle de se couvrir de cette manière contre les suites des limitations de responsabilité stipulées dans les présentes conditions.

Les frais de cette assurance sont dûs par le commettant.

Un modèle de pareilles conditions d'assurance contre les risques d'expédition est reproduit en annexe aux présentes conditions.

VI. Assurances

A. *Ordre d'assurer*

648 Art. 43. Dans la mesure du possible, l'ordre d'assurer les risques afférents au transport et à l'emmagasinage de marchandises devra toujours être confié à l'expéditeur.

L'expéditeur n'assure ces risques que sur ordre formel, écrit et répété pour chaque envoi.

La simple mention de valeur ne constitue pas un ordre formel.

B. *Présomption d'assurance—exclusion de recours*

Art. 44. Si aucun ordre d'assurer n'a été donné à l'expéditeur, celui-ci est autorisé à supposer que tous les risques afférents à l'expédition, le transport et l'entreposage des marchandises ont été assurés par une des parties intéressées à ces opérations et ce en considération des clauses d'exonération de responsabilité prévues au Chapitre V ci-dessus. L'expéditeur n'assume par conséquent aucune responsabilité du chef de pertes ou d'avaries pouvant faire l'objet d'une telle assurance.

Aucune indemnité ne pourra donc lui être réclamée de ce chef, ni directement ni par voie de recours des assureurs éventuels.

Si l'ordre d'assurer n'a pas été confié à l'expéditeur, le commettant s'engage à obtenir que dans les conditions d'assurance soit stipulé qu'aucun droit de recours ne sera exercé par les assureurs vis-à-vis de l'expéditeur.

C. *Conditions d'assurance—risques spéciaux—vol sur quai*

Art. 45. Sauf stipulation contraire, les assurances sont contractées aux clauses d'une police locale usuelle, aux conditions usuelles pour le genre de marchandises expédiées et pour les valeurs à indiquer par le commettant, auprès de compagnies à indiquer notoirement solvables au moment de la couverture.

Les risques spéciaux tels que guerre, mines, émeutes, casse, coulage, déformation, rouille, oxydation, vol et disparition, séjour, etc. ne sont couverts que sur indication spéciale du commettant.

Les risques spéciaux signalés dans le présent article n'y figurent qu'à titre de simple indication, sans que leur énumération ait un caractère limitatif. Chaque fois qu'à l'occasion du transport de marchandises, une interruption, un séjour ou un transbordement est prévu, le commettant est tenu de faire assurer spécialement tous les risques y afférents ou de les faire comprendre dans les conditions de l'assurance générale avec exclusion du recours contre l'expéditeur.

D. *Forfait*

Art. 46. Sauf convention contraire explicite ou mention contraire dans la facture, les montants portés en compte par l'expéditeur pour assurance doivent être considérés comme des forfaits.

En aucun cas, l'expéditeur ne peut être considéré comme co-assureur.

E. *Devoirs et responsabilité*

Art. 47. En cas d'avarie à des marchandises assurées à l'intervention de l'expéditeur, celui-ci satisfait à ses obligations en subrogeant son commettant dans ses droits vis-à-vis de l'assureur. Le commettant n'aura pas d'autre recours contre l'expéditeur que celui que ce dernier pourra exercer contre les assureurs. Il n'existe aucune solidarité entre l'expéditeur et les assureurs. L'expéditeur n'assume aucune responsabilité quant à la liquidation des réclamations présentées aux assureurs ni quant à leur solvabilité. Lorsque l'expéditeur est chargé d'exercer le recours contre les assureurs, tous frais généralement quelconques, y compris éventuellement les honoraires d'avocat, sont à charge du commettant. En outre, l'expéditeur aura droit à une rétribution équitable pour son intervention personnelle.

VII. REMUNÉRATIONS ET CONDITIONS DE PAIEMENT

A. *Généralités*

649   Art. 48. Sauf convention contraire, l'expéditeur est toujours autorisé à porter des montants forfaitaires en compte pour ses débours, frais, soins et interventions. Cette manière de facturer n'altère d'aucune façon le caractère de commission de la convention, mais exonère l'expéditeur de toute obligation de reddition de compte au sujet de ses frais et débours.

A défaut de tarifs convenues d'avance, seul le montant global porté en compte pourra être sujet a discussion, à la condition que le commettant prouve que cette somme n'est pas en rapport avec les prestations fournies.

Le commettant s'engage à vérifier immédiatement les factures qui lui seront adressées et renonce explicitement à toute réclamation au sujet des frais ou prix portés en compte, si cette réclamation n'est pas introduite auprès de l'expéditeur endéans les huit jours suivant la réception de la facture, note de frais, etc. . . .

Dans le cas où le commettant à donné ordre d'encaisser la note de frais d'expédition auprès d'un tiers, il garantit cependant son paiement vis-à-vis de l'expéditeur.

B. *Frais spéciaux et avance de fonds*

Art. 49. En plus des frais encourus, l'expéditeur est autorisé à exiger une rémunération raisonable pour toute intervention de sa part, y compris la transmission ou la rédaction de documents, l'encaissement de remboursements, l'introduction d'une réclamation, l'établissement d'un contrat, l'échantillonnage, le marquage, la constitution du dossier-assurance, l'intervention en avarie commune etc,

En cas de retrait d'un ordre, alors que l'expéditeur avait déjà pris des dispositions pour son exécution, il est autorisé à réclamer des frais et indemnités.

L'expéditeur n'est jamais tenu de faire l'avance des fonds pour port, fret, droits de douane, taxe de transmission ou autres frais.

Il réclamera à son choix, soit une avance appropriée, soit une commission pour avance de fonds, lorsqu'il consent à effectuer celle-ci.

La commission est due depuis le jour des débours.

C. *Factures—modalités de paiement*

Art. 50. Les factures de l'expéditeur sont payables immédiatement et au comptant sans escompte et les paiements ne peuvent en aucun cas être subordonnés à des circonstances particulières ou à la bonne exécution des opérations portées en compte ou autres. Les réclamations éventuelles relatives à nos factures doivent se faire endéans les huit jours.

Sauf double facturation ou erreur dans la personne du débiteur, des discussions au sujet d'une facture ne peuvent jamais exonérer le débiteur du paiement et elles ne donnent éventuellement lieu à remboursement qu'après paiement préalable.

Sauf stipulation contraire, le lieu de règlement et de paiement de la facture est celui où l'expéditeur est établi.

La remise de traites ou la délégation de créance n'emporte pas novation.

D. *Intérêts*

Art. 51. L'envoi de la facture tient lieu de sommation d'en payer le montant. En conséquence, en cas de retard dans le règlement de la facture, l'expéditeur pourra réclamer les intérêts légaux depuis la date de la facture, sans qu'il soit tenu d'adresser une nouvelle sommation à son commettant.

E. *Cours de change*

Art. 52. Le risque de changement des cours de change est à charge du commettant.

Les cotations et les prix fixés en francs belges sont basés sur la valeur donnée au franc par l'Arrêté Royal du 31 mars 1955 et/ou les arrêtés subséquents et seront sujets à un réajustement proportionnel, si la valeur légale du franc était modifiée.

Les cotations et les prix établis en une monnaie autre que le franc belge sont basés sur la valeur de cette monnaie au moment de la conclusion du contrat et sont sujets à réajustement, si cette monnaie subit sur le marché officiel des changes à la bourse de Bruxelles une modification de valeur.

L'expéditeur pourra à tout moment et sur simple avis convertir en francs belges et compenser entre eux les soldes des différents comptes en devises étrangères qu'il a ouverts à son commettant.

F. *Clause pénale*

Art. 53. Lorsque dans le délai de quinze jours à dater de l'envoi d'une mise en demeure par lettre recommandée à la poste, le débiteur n'a présenté, également par lettre recommandée, aucun moyen de défense raisonable et admissible, le montant de la dette sera majoré de plein droit et sans nouvelle mise en demeure de 20 % avec minimum de 1.500 F et maximum de 50.000 F à titre de dommages-intérêts forfaitaires et irréductibles.

G. *Frais de procès*

Art. 54. Les rétributions prévues aux articles 51 et 53 sont cumulées et ne comprennent pas les frais de justice.

VIII. PRIVILEGE ET DROIT DE GAGE

A. *Privilège*

650   Art. 55. Les différentes créances de l'expéditeur à charge de son commettant, même lorsqu'elles sont relatives à des expéditions différentes et à des marchandises qui ne sont plus en sa possession, constituent une créance unique et indivisible à concurrence de laquelle l'expéditeur peut exercer tous les recours, droits et privilèges qui lui sont reconnus par la loi et par les présentes conditions.

B. *Droit de gage*

Art. 56. En plus de ce qui est dit à l'art. 55, les parties conviennent explicitement par la présente que tous les biens, documents ou espèces, qui depuis la date du premier ordre entrent fictivement ou réellement en possession de l'expéditeur, serviront de gage pour le paiement de ses créances envers son commettant ou envers le propriétiare des marchandises. Ce gage est régi par les règles du gage commercial.

C. *Droit de rétention*

Art. 57. En vue garantir l'exercice de ses droits et privilèges, l'expéditeur jouit, pour les revendications qu'il peut faire valoir vis-à-vis d'une des parties intéressées au transport ou à l'emmagasinage, à la suite d'opérations antérieures ou en cours, du droit de rétention sur toutes les marchandises, qui lui ont été remises pour expédition, camionnage, réception, dédouanement ou entreposage, ainsi que sur celles qui lui sont adressées pour être remises à ses commettants. En plus, il est autorisé, en vue de suavegarder l'exercice de ses privilèges et de son droit de gage, à refuser la remise d'un certificat de dépôt.

IX. PRESCRIPTION ET DÉCHÉANCE DE DROIT

A. *Prescription*

651   Art. 58. Le commettant qui entend exercer un recours juridictionnel contre l'expéditeur doit, sous peine de déchéance, intenter son action dans un délai de six mois. Ce délai prend cours dès la fin de la mission ou, en cas de désaccord à de sujet, à partir de la date d'envoi de la facture finale. Si le motif de la contestation n'est connu que plus tard, l'action devra en tous cas être introduite sous peine de déchéance endéans les six mois suivant la délivrance des marchandises.

Ce délai réduit de prescription constitue une clause essentielle de la convention conclue entre le commettant et l'expéditeur, de telle manière que si le commettant n'a pas agi dans le délai fixé, l'expéditeur se trouvera définitivement dégagé de toute responsabilité.

B. *Déchéance de droit*

Art. 59. En dehors de la déchéance prévue à l'art. 58, aucune plainte n'est recevable, si, à la réception des marchandises, le destinataire n'a pas fait des réserves en due forme vis-à-vis du dernier transporteur, s'il n'a pas fait procéder à une constatation contradictoire par une personne habilitée à cette fin, et s'il n'a pas immédiatement formulé ses réserves vis-à-vis de l'expéditeur.

X. COMPÉTENCE ET PROCÉDURE

A. *Tribunal compétent*

652   Art. 60. A défaut de clause compromissoire ou de compromis, toutes actions judiciaires découlant d'un différend entre l'expéditeur et son commettant, même par voie de garantie et même en cas de pluralité de défendeurs

[361]

devront être portées devant le tribunal de commerce du lieu où l'expéditeur a son principal établissement. Toutefois l'expéditeur seul est toujours autorisé à porter le litige devant le tribunal compétent ratione loci.

B. *Droit international privé*

Art. 61. Toutes les relations juridiques entre expéditeur et commettant ou ayant-droit seront, avec application des présentes conditions, régies par les règles de droit belge.

STANDARD CONDITIONS (1970) GOVERNING F.I.A.T.A. COMBINED TRANSPORT BILLS OF LADING

653 Definitions

" Merchant " means and includes the Shipper, the Consignor, the Consignee, the Holder of this Bill of Lading, the Receiver and the Owner of the Goods.

" The Freight Forwarder " means the issuer of this Bill of Lading as named on the face of it.

The headings set forth below are for easy reference only.

CONDITIONS

1. Applicability

Notwithstanding the heading " Combined Transport Bill of Lading," the provisions set out and referred to in this document shall also apply if the transport as described on the face of the Bill of Lading is performed by one mode of transport only.

2. Issuance of the " Combined Transport Bill of Lading "

2.1 By the issuance of this " Combined Transport Bill of Lading," the freight Forwarder:
  (a) undertakes to perform or to procure the performance of the entire transport from the place at which the goods are taken in charge to the place designated for delivery in this Bill of Lading.
  (b) assumes liability as set out in these Conditions.

2.2 For the purposes and subject to the provisions of this Bill of Lading, the Freight Forwarder shall be responsible for the acts and omissions of any person of whose services he makes use for the performance of the contract evidenced by this Bill of Lading.

3. Negotiability and title to the goods

3.1 This Bill of Lading shall be deemed to be negotiable, unless marked " non-negotiable."

3.2 By accepting this Bill of Lading the Merchant and his transferees agree with the Freight Forwarder that unless it is marked "non-negotiable" it shall constitute title to the goods and the holder by endorsement of this Bill of Lading shall be entitled to receive or to transfer the goods herein mentioned.

3.3 This Bill of Lading shall be prima facie evidence of the receipt by the Freight Forwarder of the goods as herein described in respect of the particulars inserted on the face of the Bill of Lading. However, proof to the contrary shall not be admissible when this Bill of Lading has been negotiated or transferred for valuable consideration to a third party acting in good faith.

4. Dangerous goods and indemnity

4.1 When the Consignor hands to the Freight Forwarder goods which are of a dangerous nature, he shall inform the Freight Forwarder of the exact nature of the danger and indicate, if necessary, the precautions to be taken.

4.2 Goods of a dangerous nature which the Freight Forwarder did not know were dangerous may, at any time or place, be unloaded, destroyed or rendered harmless, without compensation; further, the Consignor shall be liable for all expenses, loss or damage arising out of their handing over for carriage or of their carriage.

5. Description of goods and Merchant's packing

5.1 The Consignor shall be deemed to have guaranteed to the Freight Forwarder the accuracy, at the time the goods were taken in charge by the Freight Forwarder, of the description of the goods, marks, number, quantity and weight as furnished by him, and the Consignor shall indemnify the Freight Forwarder against all loss, damage and expenses arising or resulting from inaccuracies in or inadequacy of such particulars. The right of the Freight Forwarder to such indemnity shall in no way limit his responsibility and liability under this Bill of Lading to any person other than the Consignor.

5.2 Without prejudice to Clause 6 (A) (2) (d), the Merchant shall be liable for any loss, damage or injury caused by faulty or insufficient packing of goods or by faulty loading or packing within containers and trailers and on flats when such loading or packing has been performed by the Merchant or on behalf of the Merchant, or by the defect or unsuitability of the containers, trailers or flats, when supplied by the Merchant, and shall indemnify the Freight Forwarder against any additional expenses so caused.

6. Extent of liability

A. (1) The Freight Forwarder shall be liable for loss or damage to the goods occurring between the time when he received the goods into his charge and the time of delivery.

(2) The Freight Forwarder shall, however, be relieved of liability for any loss or damage if such loss or damage arose or resulted from:

(a) the wrongful act or neglect of the Consignor or the Consignee;

(b) compliance with the instructions of the person entitled to give them;

(c) the lack of, or defective condition of packing in the case of goods which, by their nature, are liable to wastage or to be damaged when not packed or when not properly packed;

(d) handling, loading, stowage or unloading of the goods by the Consignor, the Consignee or any person acting on behalf of the Consignor or the Consignee;

(e) inherent vice of the goods;

(f) insufficiency or inadequacy of marks or numbers on the goods, coverings, or unit loads;

(g) strikes or lockouts or stoppage or restraint of labour from whatever cause whether partial or general;

(h) any other cause or event which the Freight Forwarder could not avoid and the consequences whereof he could not prevent by the exercise of reasonable diligence.

(3) Where under paragraph 2 the Freight Forwarder is not under any liability in respect of some of the factors causing the loss or damage, he shall only be liable to the extent that those factors for which he is liable under this Clause have contributed to the loss or damage.

(4) The burden of proving that the loss or damage was due to one or more of the causes, or events, specified in (a), (b) and (h) of paragraph 2 shall rest upon the Freight Forwarder.

When the Freight Forwarder establishes that in the circumstances of the case, the loss or damage could be attributed to one or more of the causes, or events, specified in (c) to (g) of paragraph 2, it shall be presumed that it was so caused. The Claimant shall, however, be entitled to prove that the loss or damage was not, in fact, caused either wholly or partly by one or more of these causes or events.

B. Notwithstanding anything provided for in other clauses of these Conditions, if it can be proved where the loss or damage occurred, the Freight Forwarder and the Merchant shall, as to the liability of the Freight Forwarder, be entitled to require such liability to be determined by the provisions contained in any international convention or national law, which provisions

(i) cannot be departed from by private contract, to the detriment of the claimant, and

(ii) would have applied if the Merchant had made a separate and direct contract with the Freight Forwarder in respect of the particular stage of transport where the loss or damage occurred and received as evidence thereof any particular document which must be issued if such international convention or national law shall apply.

7. Paramount clause

The Hague Rules contained in the International Convention for the unification of certain rules relating to Bills of Lading, dated Brussels 25th August, 1924, as enacted in the Country of Shipment, shall apply to all carriage of goods by sea or by inland waterways and such provisions shall apply to all goods whether carried on deck or under deck.

8. Limitation amount

8.1 When the Freight Forwarder is liable for compensation in respect of loss or of damage to the goods, such compensation shall be calculated by reference to the value of such goods at the place and time they are delivered to the Consignee in accordance with the contract or should have been so delivered.

8.2 The value of the goods shall be fixed according to the commodity exchange price, or, if there be no such price, according to the current market price or, if there be no commodity exchange price or current market price, by reference to the normal value of goods of the same kind and quality.

8.3 Compensation shall not, however, exceed 30 Francs (" Franc " meaning a unit consisting of 65,5 mgs of gold of millesimal fineness 900) per ilo of gross weight of the goods lost or damaged.

9. Delay, consequential loss, etc.

Arrival times are not guaranteed by the Freight Forwarder. If the Freight Forwarder is held liable in respect of delay, consequential loss or damage other than loss of or damage to the goods, the liability of the Freight Forwarder shall be limited to the double freight for the transport covered by this Bill of Lading, or the value of the goods as determined in Clause 8, whichever is the less.

654 ### 10. Defences

10.1 The defences and limits of liability provided for in these Conditions shall apply in any action against the Freight Forwarder for loss or damage to the goods whether the action be founded in contract or in tort.

10.2 The Freight Forwarder shall not be entitled to the benefit of the limitation of liability provided for in paragraph 3 of Clause 8 if it is proved that the loss or damage resulted from an act or omission of the Freight Forwarder done with intent to cause damage or recklessly and with knowledge that damage would probably result.

11. Liability of servants and sub-contractors

11.1 If an action for loss of or damage to the goods is brought against a person referred to in paragraph 2 of Clause 2, such person shall be entitled to avail himself of the defences and limits of liability which the Freight Forwarder is entitled to invoke under these Conditions.

11.2 However, if it is proved that the loss or damage resulted from an act or omission of this person, done with intent to cause damage or recklessly and with knowledge that damage would probably result, such person shall not be entitled to benefit of limitation of liability provided for in paragraph 3 of Clause 8.

11.3 Subject to the provisions of paragraph 2 of Clause 10 and of paragraph 2 of this Clause, the aggregate of the amounts recoverable from the Freight Forwarder and the person referred to in paragraph 2 of Clause 2 shall in no case exceed the limits provided for in these Conditions.

12. Method and route of transportation

The Freight Forwarder reserves to himself a reasonable liberty as to the means, route and procedure to be followed in the handling, storage and transportation of goods.

13. Delivery

If delivery of the goods or any part thereof is not taken by the Merchant at the time and place when and where the Freight Forwarder is entitled to call upon the Merchant to take delivery thereof, the Freight Forwarder shall be entitled to store the goods or the part thereof at the sole risk of the Merchant, whereupon the liability of the Freight Forwarder in respect of the goods or that part thereof stored as aforesaid (as the case may be) shall wholly cease and the cost of such storage (if paid by or payable by the Freight Forwarder or any agent or sub-contractor of the Freight Forwarder) shall forthwith upon demand be paid by the Merchant to the Freight Forwarder.

14. Freight and charges

14.1 Freight to be paid in cash without discount and, whether prepayable or payable at destination, to be considered as earned on receipt of the goods and not to be returned or relinquished in any event.

14.2 Freight and all other amounts mentioned in this Bill of Lading are to be paid in the currency named in the Bill of Lading or, at the Freight Forwarder's option in the currency of the country of dispatch or destination at the highest rate of exchange for bankers sight bills current for prepayable freight on the day of dispatch and for freight payable at destination on the day when the Merchant is notified of arrival of the goods there or on the date of withdrawal of the delivery order, whichever rate is the higher, or at the option of the Freight Forwarder on the date of the Bill of Lading.

14.3 All dues, taxes and charges or other expenses in connection with the goods shall be paid by the Merchant.

14.4 The Merchant shall reimburse the Freight Forwarder in proportion to the amount of freight for any costs for deviation or delay or any other increase of costs of whatever nature caused by war, warlike operations, epidemics, strikes, government directions or force majeure.

14.5 The Merchant warrants the correctness of the declaration of contents, insurance, weight, measurements or value of the goods but the Freight Forwarder reserves the right to have the contents inspected and the weight, measurements or value verified. If on such inspection it is found the declaration is not correct it is agreed that a sum equal either to five times the difference between the correct figure and the freight charged, or to double the correct freight less the freight charged, whichever sum is the smaller, shall be payable as liquidated damage to the Freight Forwarder for his inspection costs and losses of freight on other goods notwithstanding any other sum having been stated on the Bill of Lading as freight payable.

15. Lien

The Freight Forwarder shall have a lien on the goods for any amount due under this Bill of Lading including storage fees and for the cost of recovering same, and may enforce such lien in any reasonable manner which he may think fit.

16. General Average

The Merchant shall indemnify the Freight Forwarder in respect of any claims of a General Average nature which may be made on him and shall provide such security as may be required by the Freight Forwarder in this connection.

17. Notice

Unless notice of loss of or damage to the goods and the general nature of it be given in writing to the Freight Forwarder or the persons referred to in Clause 2, paragraph 2 above, at the place of delivery before or at the time of the removal of the goods into the custody of the person entitled to delivery thereof under this Bill of Lading, or if the loss or damage be not apparent, within six consecutive days thereafter, such removal shall be prima facie evidence of the delivery by the Freight Forwarder of the goods as described in this Bill of Lading.

18. Time bar

The Freight Forwarder shall be discharged of all liability under the rules of these Conditions unless suit is brought within nine months after delivery of the goods. In the case of total loss of the goods, the period shall begin to run two months after the goods have been taken in charge by the Freight Forwarder.

19. Jurisdiction

Actions against the Freight Forwarder may only be instituted in the country where the Freight Forwarder has his principal place of business and shall be decided according to the law of such country.

INDEX